W9-DJG-465

A BEHAVIOURAL ANALYSIS OF JOINT-COST ALLOCATION AND TRANSFER PRICING

By
Arthur L. Thomas
Harmon Whittington Professor
Rice University

1977

Arthur Andersen & Co. Lecture Series

Library of Congress No.
79-92264

ISBN 0-87563-179-7

© Copyright 1980
Stipes Publishing Company

To Mary, who made this book possible.

CONTENTS

PART TWO: TRANSFER PRICING

APPENDIXES

vii

Figures

FOREWORD

The work of Professor Arthur Thomas on the allocation problem in accounting is well known to all thinking accountants. He has ploughed a deep furrow through the conventional wisdom of accounting, and it is my view that his ideas are destined to have a profound impact upon financial reporting in the future.

It was for this reason that I invited him to come to Lancaster in the spring of 1977 to deliver the Arthur Andersen Lectures. He characteristically decided not to give us a mere re-hash of things he had said before. Instead he thrust his ideas out of the area of financial accounting, where they had been developed, and into that of management accounting.

His research has continued since he left Lancaster, and the fruits of it are contained in this volume.

I hope that what Professor Thomas has to say will be widely read, and that it will cause practitioners to reflect deeply enough so that ultimately they will be moved to adapt—and thereby to survive.

Edward Stamp
Director of ICRA.

xiii

ACKNOWLEDGMENTS

This book is an expanded version of the Fourth Arthur Andersen Visiting Lectures, presented at the International Centre for Research in Accounting of The University of Lancaster during May 1977. It is also the first installment of a study of managements' uses of allocation in evaluation, control and pricing. Years ago, Carl Allen got me started on this project by remarking, seemingly casually, that most managerial-accounting allocations were transfer prices. They're joint-cost allocations, too, of course. And the similarity of the two, especially evident for allocations of the costs of service departments, is an important, if little noticed, feature of our intellectual landscape.

For the peace and leisure to think through this book's several topics, I am indebted to the purchasers of my elementary accounting textbook, royalties from which financed a 4½-year leave of absence from teaching. Beyond this, I'm deeply grateful to The International Centre for Research in Accounting and Arthur Andersen & Company for this book's main external financial support, to The Clarkson, Gordon Foundation for a 1976 research grant supporting preliminary investigations, and to The Peat, Marwick, Mitchell Foundation for a 1978 summer support grant under which I wrote the final draft. I'm also grateful to Susan Thomas for typing successive drafts and to Rashad Abdel-khalik, Joe Basu, Phil Bell, Jake Birnberg, John Butterworth, Ed Caplan, Bob Crandall, Clive Emmanuel, Tom Hedges, Yuji Ijiri, Dan Jensen, Nancy Johnson, Joe Louderback, Alex Milburn, Shane Moriarity, David Ottley, Mary Thomas, Murray Wells, Steve Zeff, an anonymous referee for *The Accounting Review,* the staffs of McMaster University's Mills Memorial Library and Rice University's Fondren Library, and discussants at The University of Illinois, The University of Lancaster, The University of Pittsburgh and Southern Methodist University for assistance at various stages of writing, and owe a special debt to Eddie Stamp for commissioning this book. I would like to thank Ms Margaret Howard and Ms J. Conway for conducting empirical research in support of my conclusions; but, alas, that's no longer feasible.

Durham and Dundalk, Ontario
Houston, Texas
September 1973 - September 1978

xv

CHAPTER ONE

INTRODUCTION

No science matures until it has developed at least one workable theory that may be used to make sense of existing knowledge and at the same time points to areas that require further exploration. Someone has to make such an attempt and I am interested and willing to try.

The task of creating the foundations for a theory is difficult, and it becomes even more formidable when one desires to create a scaffolding upon which to hang and interrelate as much of the existing literature as possible without doing violence to the basic results of each individual study. —[Argyris, 1957, p. x]

Farewell, my love: I'm off to the Hundred Years' War. —H.A. Wichelns

This book, though self-contained, extends two earlier studies, [Thomas, 1969; 1974], which discussed financial accounting's notional, one-to-many allocations. In particular, it concerns two closely related types of allocations that are ubiquitous in companies' *internal* (managerial) accounting, and the various possible impacts of such allocations on the behaviours of these companies' decision makers.

An *allocation* is any partitioning of a whole into parts, any division of a subject among objects. Examples of allocation include splitting a bottle of whiskey among one's guests, and assigning the cost of a machine or a particular lot of inventory to different batches of product. (At the extreme, an allocation might be entirely to *one* object: one guest might drink all the whiskey while the rest drank beer, or accountants might assign the entire cost of the inventory lot to one product batch.) Some allocations are real-world distributions of resources—the whiskey is an instance. Others, such as the allocation of inventory and machine costs, are *notional:* they occur only in our minds or on our records. When a company divides an inventory lot between products manufactured in different departments there usually are two distinct allocations: the physical *resource distribution* of external objects possessing mass, extension and other tangible properties to different, spacially separated, external locations,[1] and an assignment of numbers to different storage loci in a recording system. My previous studies

[1] I'm well aware of taking a debatable philosophical position here. It's called *naïve realism.* In economic affairs, which are what this book is about, even philosophers are naïve realists; ask any Dean of Humanities.

1

were concerned only with the latter, notional, kinds of allocations. So is this book, unless stated otherwise.

Figure 1-1

Three Kinds of Allocations

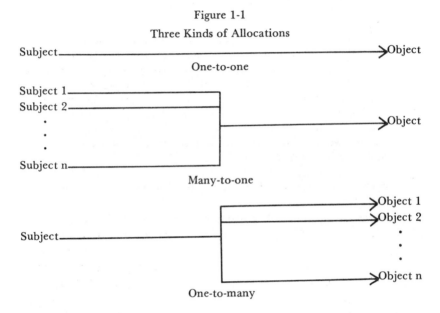

Figure 1-1 shows three different kinds of notional allocations. *One-to-one* allocations assign a single subject to a single object, as when accountants charge the entire cost of an inventory lot to a particular batch of product. *Many-to-one* allocations are merely aggregations of one-to-one allocations having the same object, as when accountants charge the entire costs of several lots of inventory to a single batch of product, or perform other kinds of *tracing*.[2] My 1969 and 1974 studies argued that these first two kinds of notional allocations are often objective and legitimate, and that they offer relatively few theoretical problems. Accordingly, these studies disregarded one-to-one and many-to-one allocations; this book will do the same.

In contrast, *one-to-many* allocations assign a single subject to two or more objects. Classic examples are the charging of a machine's cost (less estimated scrap value) to the costs of the different products that it produces, and joint-cost allocations generally. Transfer pricing also offers many instances of one-to-many allocation. The simplest occurs when a manufacturing division produces

---

[2]For a good, early discussion of such tracing (which the author calls *physical identification*) see [Vatter, 1945, pp. 167-68].

an intermediate good which it transfers to a distribution division, which sells it, and the company's total profit on the external sale ends up divided, one-to-two, between the two divisions.[3]

In what follows, whenever I use the word "allocation" without qualifying it, I mean "one-to-many allocation."

One-to-many allocations are afflicted with exceptionally severe theoretical difficulties.[4] Much of [Thomas, 1969; 1974] is spent surveying these. Within a range of ambiguity that exceeds whatever dollar magnitudes are involved, *any* one-to-many allocation method is just as defensible (or indefensible) theoretically as any other. Because of this, all allocations within this range are *incorrigible*, a technical term signifying that they can neither be refuted nor verified.[5]

Their incorrigibility renders one-to-many allocations arbitrary to a degree so extreme that we're unaccustomed to it in our ordinary intellectual lives. For it transpires that what's involved here isn't just an unfortunate weakness in theory, but theory's complete breakdown—Chaos and Old Night. Proof of this is far too complex to recapitulate here.[6] But Ijiri [1975, p. 184] draws a fine parallel from the Zen Koans: Trying to defend a one-to-many allocation is like clapping one's hands, then trying to defend how much of the sound is attributable to each hand.

As we'll soon see, accountants and economists widely recognize that joint-cost allocations are arbitrary (though not always that they are arbitrary to the degree claimed here). But extension of this conclusion to all allocations of the same, one-to-many form (such as those involved in financial accounting and transfer pricing) remains controversial. Fortunately, resolution of this controversy isn't essential to this book. The next subsection indicates why.

---

[3]This is discussed in detail in Chapters Eight and Nine. Please keep in mind that no profit to one division and all profit to the other is as much an allocation as is 50/50.

[4]There is one exception. Many companies make expedient use of one-to-many allocations to charge traceable overheads to products. Detailed tracing is possible, but would cost more than the resulting information is worth. Such use of one-to-many allocations is legitimate. But it is also the top of a slippery slope that leads to taking other one-to-many allocations for granted.

[5]Allocations falling *without* this range can be refuted, and therefore may be dismissed.

[6][Thomas, 1979] is a quick summary. A reader of an earlier draft commented:
   Actually, you don't have to have much of a "proof" to show that any allocation is arbitrary . . . . An optimum allocation can be defined only with respect to a given objective function, but there is no reason why that particular objective function should be used and nothing else. This is because the choice of a utility function (which determines the objective function) is entirely left to the individual and not to the scientists—Nobody is forced to like apples, thank god!
I agree, but this argument does not reveal how *radical* the arbitrariness is.

For brevity, the rest of this book will call all responsibility centres *divisions*.[7] I'll call top management or headquarters the *central office*, in part to emphasize that although this book is written in terms of profit-seeking, private-sector companies, its analysis is also applicable to socialist (and other planned) economies.

Internal Use of One-to-Many Allocations

We begin with an observation that, to the surprise of practitioner friends, is itself controversial among academics: Companies not only *make* one-to-many joint-cost and transfer-price allocations, but sometimes use them in making internal decisions. Of course, often they're not supposed to. For instance, with one exception (which we shall consider in Chapter Three), there is broad, mainstream academic agreement that joint-cost allocations, at least, are useless for planning and evaluation purposes,[8] and theoretical consensus that they are wholly arbitrary and needless.[9] [10]

---

[7]Though in practice, of course, they could be anything from departments to affiliated companies.

[8]For examples, see [Vatter, 1945, p. 171], [American Accounting Association, 1952, pp. 187-88], [National Association of Accountants, 1957b, p. 2 and *passim*], [Baumol et al., 1962, pp. 358-60], [Wiles, 1963, pp. 109-171], [Alchian and Allen, 1967, pp. 240-241], [Caplan, 1971, p. 59], [Dearden, 1973, pp. 168-69, 172], [Ferrara, 1977, pp. 41•21-22], [Horngren, 1977, pp. 549, 553] and [Shillinglaw, 1977a, p. 39•8; 1977b, pp. 379-80].

[9]For examples, see [Vatter, 1945, pp. 168, 172], [American Accounting Association, 1952, pp. 187-88], [Edwards, 1952b, pp. 313-15], [Lawson, 1957, pp. 431-32], [National Association of Accountants, 1957b, pp. 1,2,4,28, 30], [Wiles, 1963, pp. 109-17], [Stigler, 1966, p. 165], [Alchian and Allen, 1967, p. 240], [Dearden, 1973, pp. 167-68], [Jensen, 1974, p. 465] and [Ferrara, 1976, p. 16; 1977, p. 41 • 22]. [Kreps, 1930, p. 426] supplies a classic instance (though compare [Feller, 1977]):

> An example of the manner in which various firms utilizing the same process will choose different bases of allocating joint costs (all of them perfectly arbitrary) came to the writer's attention. . .in the course of a recent inspection of electrolytic caustic soda and chlorine plants. The joint costs of the process up to the point of the split-off of the chlorine from the caustic were found to be distributed between the bundle of products derived from the caustic and that derived from the chlorine in several different ratios: 50-50, 40-60; 60-40, 39.008-35.46 (atomic weights of sodium hydroxide and chlorine), and 56.73 to 43.27. The pseudomathematical precision of the last ratio had its origin in a criterion no more scientific than that of distributing the joint costs so that both the caustic and the chlorine would earn an equal book profit. The plant in question had formerly used a 50-50 basis, which resulted in the chlorine department showing a loss. The absentee bankers who controlled the enterprise gave orders to discharge the chlorine foreman, but the superintendent at the works managed to retain an efficient subordinate by establishing the new ratio.

[Butler, 1971] is an attempt at an allocation-free way of dealing with joint products.

[10]Some, such as Manes and Smith [1965, p. 31], would distinguish between situations where outputs are partly variable and ones where they are fixed. But as Clark

Of course, companies use joint-cost and transfer-price allocations for taxation,[11] financial accounting (e.g., inventory valuation)[12] and various regulatory[13] purposes. But, outside of pricing (where their use is notorious[14]), do they use them for internal decision making? The National Association of Accountants [1957b, pp. 36-53] urge that companies not use *joint costs* this way, and the empirical portions of this NAA study could lead one to conclude that, by and large, companies don't.[15]

Yet, there is evidence (not as substantial as one would like, but evidence nonetheless) that this conclusion would be mistaken—that internal decision makers use results of both joint-cost and transfer-price allocations as inputs to their decisions:

1. Any belief that companies do not use one-to-many allocations for internal decision-making purposes necessarily implies that they can base all of their internal decisions on allocation-*free*[16] data. What evidence is there for *that?* The allocation-free decision models recommended in the literature are mostly globally optimizing ones[17] that assume solution of various practical problems that often seem impossible to solve in the real world.[18] Perhaps inter-

[1923, pp. 99-100] pointed out, the partly variable proportions have a fixed component: though certain cost elements may be separable, *some* jointness is irreducible—and it's to this irreducible jointness that this book's arguments refer. See [Kreps, 1930, pp. 448-49] on this point (but compare [pp. 457-58]). This is why I also disregard Bierman's [1963, p. 59] distinction between joint and indirect costs.

Of course, where output proportions are *wholly* variable, there's no one-to-many joint-cost problem to worry about.

[11]See, for instance, [Shulman, 1966].

[12]For another example, [Financial Accounting Standards Board, 1974, pp. 7, 12, 29-35, 93-95; 1976, pp. 6, 13, 35-37] discuss financial accounting's joint cost allocations with particular reference to segment reporting. The former has good introductory bibliographies.

[13]See, for instance, [Cost Accounting Standards Board, 1975b, pp. 198-215, 247-56; 1976a; 1976b, e.g., pp. 21-21A, 131-34, 165-66]. See [Cost Accounting Standards Board, 1978a] for background.

[14]See, for instance, [Littlechild, 1970b, p. 326].

[15]Clearly, *some* companies that carry out internal, one-to-many allocations don't use them in making seemingly related decisions. [Menge, 1961] presents a case from the automotive industry in which profit centres decided what, and how much, to buy from other profit centres, *then* decided on the price. Yet it's implicit throughout this case that the central office used these transfer prices (which allocated global profits one-to-many) in evaluating the divisions, and in consequent decisions—see, for instance, [p. 231].

[16]I use *allocation-free* as shorthand for *free of one-to-many allocations.*

[17]For an example of such an allocation-free decision model for joint processes (one generalizable to any number of products), see [Henderson and Quandt, 1958, pp. 67-72].

[18]To paraphrase a reader of an earlier draft:

First, it is often impossible to nail down the structure of an appropriate allocation-free decision method. We are like the blind touching an elephant. Only

nal decision makers use suboptimal allocation-free methods instead. But what follows suggests that they don't restrict themselves to these.

2. As Shubik [1964, p. 209] implies (and as is evident from their common, one-to-many form), all cost-accounting allocations of fixed costs are joint-cost allocations, not just those explicitly labelled as such.[19] In fact, in multiple-product companies all products will be joint in this sense, if only because they share certain central-office inputs.[20]

Now, as Hughes and Scheiner [1977, p.3] remark, casual observation alone shows that many companies do, in fact, allocate fixed costs for internal purposes.[21] The roots of this full costing lie in what Demski and Feltham [1976, pp. 4-5] call an "historical communication" approach to managerial accounting, which they see as dominating its literature until about 1960, and being still widely used and advocated. They comment:

> Implicitly, this approach is based on the concept of absolute truth; there is a unique cost of producing an automobile, a barrel of oil, a space mission, an MBA, or a research product. By implication, the major problem facing the accountant is one of selecting a measurement procedure that identifies (or at least approximates) the true cost.

the god knows what a project's ultimate profitability will be, but we, humans, must evaluate its performance based on year-by-year data. It might be *conceptually* possible to imagine an allocation-free decision approach (involving millions of variables) for, say, General Motors, but it would be impossible to implement it because no one could tell whether the model thus developed was a global one or merely part of a yet larger model.

Second, even were it possible to nail down the model's structure, there would be enormous problems estimating its parameters, and the costs of implementation would be apt to be prohibitive. Third, even were we to estimate these parameters, the model's complexity might prevent deriving an optimal solution. Fourth, even were this problem solvable, some parameters may change by the time the optimal decision is derived.

The sad thing about allocation is that practical considerations of cognitive limits on rationality, cost, solvability and timeliness leave us unable to deal with global optimality.

[19] See [Edwards, 1952b, pp. 310-11]. Taggart [1977, pp. 43·4-5] sees this as particularly true of distribution costs.

[20] As [Pfouts, 1961, p. 657] observes:

> It is only in the case in which there is excess capacity in all fixed factors that ...it can be claimed in any meaningful sense that the multiproduct firm is simply a collection of single-product firms.

See [National Association of Accountants, 1957b, p. 1], [Wiles, 1963, pp. 108-09], [Wright, 1966], [Horngren, 1972, p. 570] and [Dopuch, Birnberg and Demski, 1974, p. 561].

[21] To cite one empirical study of this, [Baumes, 1963, p. 3] found that 53% of the 158 companies studied allocated all "central expenses" of maintaining a corporate entity

In context, it's obvious that this "true" cost is a full one. Indeed, the very continued existence of a direct-costing/contributions-accounting literature directed at *practitioners* leads one to presume that some practitioners continue to use full costs, and thus joint costs, in internal decision making.

3. Again, as Hirschleifer [1956, p. 182] noted, whenever divisions are technologically dependent,[22] transfer price problems are essentially joint-cost problems. Later we'll see that a more general claim may be made: Transfer pricing involves joint-cost allocation whenever the transferor "sells" the intermediate product to two or more transferees, or whenever it uses the same facilities to produce transfer and other goods. This latter becomes especially evident when one reads the literature on service departments whose costs are allocated to production departments—one can equally well perceive such allocations to be either transfer-price or joint-cost ones.

Now, as readers are invited to verify, studies of real-world transfer pricing reveal conflict between division managers *over* transfer prices to be commonplace. Why should it be so unless central offices base evaluations of products, divisions or their managers (and related central-office decisions) at least in part *upon* such one-to-many allocated data?[23] In fact, if divisions are profit centres, any division manager who is concerned to maximize short-run book profits *must* base decisions upon such data.

4. There is some empirical evidence to support a conclusion that decision makers often base decisions upon one-to-many allocations. It's especially strong for transfer prices.[24]

and a central office to divisions, while an additional 36% made partial allocations. Doubtless, much of this represented traceable costs: "charges for specific services rendered." But clearly some were joint—see, for instance, [pp. 9, 83].

In turn [p. 30], half of 81 companies studied reallocated central expenses to product lines or to products. But see note 33, below.

[22]That's to say, whenever one division's production affects another division's costs.

[23]See [Shubik, 1964, pp. 209-10]. I hypothesize that the difference between my conclusions and the National Association of Accountants' [1957b] ones on use of joint costs in internal decision making rests in part on my having seen joint-cost allocation in a wider range of phenomena than they did. For instance, it's striking how little their [1957a and b] studies of transfer pricing and joint-cost allocation recognize the extent to which both studies address the same phenomena.

[24]Perhaps the best evidence is supplied by Reece and Cool's [1978] survey of 1976 *Fortune* "1000" companies. First, their Exhibit VI [p. 36] reveals widespread use of internal, one-to-many cost allocations (for instance, only about 3% of reporting companies used direct costing instead of full, absorption costing). Second, most of these companies evaluated their divisions in terms of their returns on investment or residual incomes [p. 30], both of which will be affected by one-to-many allocations. It immedi-

5. Further evidence is supplied by the cautionary homework problems in our textbooks that are designed to train students *not* to base decisions on joint-cost and other one-to-many allocations,[25] the field research conducted for [Financial Accounting Standards Board, 1974, pp. 31, 93-95], the wishes, frequently mentioned in the literature, of managers for information about divisional and product profitabilities (as contrasted with their contributions), and the ways that articles directed by practitioners to practitioners often display ingenuous faith in the economic meaningfulness of joint-cost allocations.[26]

Overall, it seems fair to conclude that there is satisfactory evidence that decision makers base internal decisions on transfer-price allocations, and at least plausible evidence that, [National Association of Accountants, 1957b] to the contrary, some do the same with joint-cost allocations.[27] If so, there's no reason to expect that managerial accountants and decision makers will suddenly get religion and eschew one-to-many allocations.

Perverse Allocations

Thus, a question arises which, at the least, is fascinating intellectually, and which may have considerable practical import: Assuming that managerial accountants will allocate and internal decision makers will base decisions upon the results, are there any ways in which one could select one or more allocation methods as being preferable to others? As a parallel, it's now notorious that no one

---

ately follows that most of these companies used one-to-many allocations in at least some of their internal decision making.

See also [National Association of Accountants, 1957a], [Baumes, 1963], [Livesey, 1967], [McCulloch, 1967], [Mautz and Skousen, 1968], [Rook, 1971], [Centre for Business Research, 1972], [Emmanuel, 1977c] and [Milburn, 1977].

[25]Another form of preaching that would be pointless were there no practitioner sinners.

[26]For a fairly recent example of this, chosen by happenstance, see [Brack, 1975, p. 48], which introduces its discussion of how to allocate joint costs of a personnel department as follows:

> In this article, we will show how the various costs can be allocated to individual departments in direct proportion to the number and type of employees carried by the department. In that way, top management will know its true costs of doing business; it will be able to trace every dollar of expense incurred to the responsible party.

[27]A side comment to any readers who may remain unconvinced about joint-cost allocations: My analyses of them in Chapters Two through Six provide much of the conceptual foundation for later chapters' analyses of transfer pricing. Since the evidence that some internal decision makers base decisions on transfer prices does seem solid, such readers are asked to bear with the joint-cost discussion and, at least, read Chapter Six.

should smoke. Yet people do, and are apt to continue to do so for some time. It is entirely legitimate, indeed laudible, research to examine properties of different kinds of cigarettes to learn which types are preferable on different health dimensions.

Similarly, I shall explore the properties of different allocation approaches under various circumstances and for different decisions.[28] Here are some of the results that we shall encounter, results that are significant whether or not one believes that managers should be educated out of basing decisions on one-to-many allocations. For brevity, let's presuppose a company that has an overall objective of maximizing its immediate, short-run profits, and whose division managers desire to maximize their immediate, short-run *book* profits. Then:

1. Many joint-cost allocation approaches tempt division managers to make globally dysfunctional decisions whether to make or buy products, or whether to continue or discontinue products (tempt them to do things that would reduce overall immediate, short-run profits). Two approaches don't.

2. In one way or another, all joint-cost allocation methods risk violating division managers' senses of what is fair, encouraging unproductive conflict among managers (and related gaming), or doing other things that can lead division managers to make globally dysfunctional decisions (such as to work less hard, or less imaginatively, than they have been). But different allocation methods do this in different ways, and some do so in more ways than do others.

3. Most joint-cost allocation methods tend to confuse the central office's evaluations of divisions, products and division managers by violating a key tenet of responsibility accounting: That the figures used in such evaluations should reflect only the division's, product's or manager's efforts and accomplishments (as distinct from those of others). One method doesn't create these confusions, though it's perverse on various other dimensions. And the *ways* that remaining methods violate this tenet vary.

4. Relatedly, in different circumstances, and with respect to different decisions, all joint-cost allocation methods can reward divisional behavior that's dysfunctional or useless in fulfilling compa-

---

[28] By now it should be evident why resolution of controversies over the severity of one-to-many allocations' arbitrariness isn't crucial to this book. My goal is not to persuade readers to cease making such allocations (though I hope that, by the end of this book, those who needed convincing will have been encouraged to do so whenever that's possible). Instead, it is to identify the operating properties of different allocation methods. These, as one might expect, reflect that arbitrariness.

ny goals, or can penalize behavior that advances these goals. But, again, the extent of these perversities varies considerably from method to method, as do the circumstances and decisions under which they occur.

5. Similarly, different *transfer-pricing* approaches offer different information economies and temptations to gaming, and have different ways of confusing central managements' evaluations of divisions, their products and their managers.

6. Lacking what, for brevity, may be described as perfect external markets for intermediate products, a review of the literature will indicate that no transfer-pricing approach can reliably guide division managers to make globally optimal decisions on outputs of transfer goods without effectively destroying divisional autonomy. This incongruity threatens the very motivational devices via which most such transfer-pricing systems purport to work.

Behaviour-Congruence

> Progress in any profession is associated with the ability to predict and control, and this is true also of industrial management. One of the major tasks of management is to organize human effort in the service of the economic objectives of the enterprise. Every managerial decision has behavioral consequences. Successful management depends—not alone, but significantly—upon the ability to predict and control human behavior. —[McGregor, 1960, pp. 3-4]

> For however sophisticated the procedures of management accounting may be, and they are continually getting more sophisticated, their fundamental rationale always remains behavioural in nature. The accountant contributes to the success of an enterprise primarily by the way in which he influences the behaviour of other people and, at least in theory, his procedures should be designed to stimulate managers and employees to behave in a manner which is likely to contribute to the effectiveness of the enterprise as a whole. —[Hopwood, 1976, p. xiv]

Later chapters will expand greatly on points made in the previous subsection. The thing to recognize at this introductory stage is that all joint-cost and transfer-price approaches generate dysfunctional decisions, confuse decision makers or are otherwise perverse. *But they offend in different ways.* And, given a particular set of central-office wants, there are identifiable circumstances in which some internal allocation methods are demonstrably *not* perverse, in the sense that they reliably avoid generating decisions or confusions that hinder satisfaction of these wants.

I shall use Dyckman's [1975, p. 40] term, *behaviour-congru-ent*,[29] to refer to such (comparatively) benign one-to-many, internal allocations. This term is, of course, a generalization of the concept of *goal*-congruence, familiar from the writings of Anthony [e.g., 1970, pp. 313-14] and others.[30] *Behaviour*-congruence's main advantages over the latter lie in its making no implicit assumption that the company's goals are explicit (or even *known*),[31] in its allowing for the possibility, which Dyckman [1975, p. 39] hypothesizes, that organizations *avoid* setting goals by instead selecting "objective" performance measures, and in its recognizing that the central office is often more concerned with subordinates' actions than with their ideology [Dyckman, 1975, pp. 40-41]. Instead, an allocation method will be behaviour-congruent if it reliably encourages actors to act in ways that are consistent with

---

[29]Cited approvingly by [Horngren, 1977, p. 163]. This book uses the term *behavioural* in the unrestrictive sense that accountants have given to it during the last decade. Despite that much of this book explores economic theories of organization, I use *behavioural* in this book's title to emphasize that my primary concern is with how actors *react* to economic data. That (both for brevity and in harmony with the literature we'll review) these reactions are often those of the economic man/woman trying to maximize his/her profits doesn't alter that such reactions are behaviour. A North American button and bumper-sticker slogan of the late 1960s was: Dirty Old Men Need Love, Too. Economic men behave, too.

[30]For a good, recent exposition, see [Ferrara, 1976, p. 13]. Contrast [Parker, 1976], whose arguments aren't germane to what follows. Parker is concerned to show that a company's internal organization can be designed so that employees won't behave dysfunctionally with respect to global goals, whereas this book describes ways of avoiding such perversities by design of the company's internal *accounting*.

[31]As mentioned earlier, for brevity much of this book assumes that central offices and divisions are rather naïve profit maximizers; here we *can* speak of "goals". But this *is* a simplification. See [Simon, 1964] for the more diverse goals of real-life companies, and the problems of specifying what these are. In a context that will be of considerable importance to Chapter Four, Arrow [1964b, p. 398] observes:

> An organization is a group of individuals seeking to achieve some common goals, or, in different language, to maximize an objective function. Each member has objectives of his own, in general not coincident with those of the organization. Each member also has some range of decisions to make within limits set partly by the environment external to the organization and partly by the decisions of other members. Finally, some but not all observations about the workings of the organization and about the external world are communicated from one member to another.

I would add only that usually much of this is forever opaque to the external analyst. Related points are raised by [Williamson, 1963, pp. 237-44, 251-52], [Parker, 1976] (with its complex, decentralized goals) and by various works discussed in Chapter Ten and its Appendix J (on mathematical programming approaches). They also emerge in my discussion (later in this chapter and in Chapters Five and Six) of élan impacts of allocations.

See [Simon, 1964, pp. 21-22] for one sense, at least, in which the simplification of assuming a single goal of profit maximization is apt to be legitimate.

whatever it is that the central office can be discovered to want (in a context of specific decisions to be made and particular surrounding circumstances).[32] [33]

Despite this deliberate avoidance of assumptions about goals in the conceptual underpinnings of this book's analysis, a simplifying assumption that central offices and division managers are immediate, short-run profit maximizers allows us to put all this in perspective. In both planned economies and private-sector companies, superordinates notoriously devote much effort to controlling subordinates—central offices try to get division managers to behave in ways that seem right to central offices. Much of the literature of managerial accounting concerns purported ways of attaining such behaviour-congruence.[34] Many of these methods are allocation-

[32] Notions related to behaviour-congruence are common in the literature, often taking the negative form of the following (by an economist):

> Indeed, *any* allocation of common cost to one product is irrational if it affects the amount of the product produced, for the firm should produce the product if its price is at least equal to its minimum marginal cost.—[Stigler, 1966, p. 165]

Here, the decisions involved concern product output quantities and, ordinarily, further processing past joint processes' split-off points. Other examples, chosen only for being ready to hand, are [Bodnar and Lusk, 1977, pp. 857, 859-60, 864-65] and:

> . . .an appropriate transfer price would be one which results in the division manager making the same decision that corporate management would make in viewing the overall benefit to the firm. —[Larson, 1971, p. 20n]

Readers will notice that behaviour-congruence is a more limited concept than Chambers' [1966, p. 164] and Lee's [1972b, p. 29] *neutrality*. This book also disregards discussion at the level of abstraction of, say:

> Optimal systems are not derived, nor is the existence issue addressed. Instead, I focus on a statement of the optimization problem. The more mundane questions of existence of and search for an optimum can only be addressed within a context far too specific for what is required for a general statement of the class of problems. —[Demski, 1972, p. 243]

for their lack of specific, mundane allocation proposals (see [pp. 243-44, 254-55] generally).

Of course, efforts to make allocations behaviour-congruent are only one aspect of a more general phenomenon: Most performance indicators have, at least potentially, perverse side effects that must be minimized. Allocations are only one element of the internal statistics that central offices use to evaluate divisions and their managers, products, sales territories, etc.—classic articles here include [Ridgeway, 1956] and [Nove, 1958].

[33] An allocation method is also behaviour-congruent (in a somewhat degenerate way) if decision makers simply disregard it. For, if so, it cannot have any perverse effects beyond, perhaps, requiring a useless expenditure of accounting resources). We'll see mathematical-programming examples of this later. The phenomenon is probably a common one; for instance, [Baumes, 1963, p. 82] finds companies ignoring central corporate expense allocations when making profit sharing or bonus computations—see also [p. 83].

Another (degenerate) way to render an allocation behaviour-congruent is to correct by supplementary action any problems that it creates. We'll see a few examples of this too, later. But both this and ignoring allocations lack theoretical interest, and will be only a minor theme in this book.

[34] See [Arrow, 1964a] for an excellent, brief summary of the problems of control with which this book's analysis is concerned.

free (an example would be a direct order to a division manager to produce a given quantity of an intermediate product then transfer it to another division).[35] However, other methods of control, including mathematically elaborate ones prominent in the economics and management-science literatures, involve incorrigible allocations.

This book studies a major subset of these: in particular, joint-cost and transfer-price allocations used in attempts to achieve divisional behaviour-congruence via direct or indirect manipulation of divisions' book profits.[36] The intended mechanism of control is easily described: Division managers are assumed to desire certain rewards that the central office has to bestow (esteem, increased prerequisites, bonuses, promotion, etc.). Division managers are led to understand that receipt of such rewards will be positively correlated with the book profits of their divisions. If joint-cost or transfer-price allocations are behaviour-congruent, they will make divisional book profits increase when division managers do what the central office wants and decrease otherwise.[37] Division managers are then left to maximize their own self-interests (somewhat narrowly construed) by satisfying the central office.

Of course there are apt to be various side decisions branching from this rather idealized process: the central office will evaluate product, division and division-manager performances, then base decisions upon these evaluations; in turn, as we'll soon see, division managers may base various personal decisions (not all of them intended by the central office) on these allocations. The particular allocation method that the company uses will be behaviour-congruent with respect to some of these central-office and divisional decisions but, as we'll also see, cannot be with respect to all possible decisions.

The Purposes of This Book

Readers familiar enough with psychology or organizational behaviour to be made queasy by the foregoing will please notice that I do not claim that this approach to control necessarily *works*. In-

---

[35]For analyses of various situations in which decisions about *joint* products should be made allocation-free, see [Bierman and Dyckman, 1971, pp. 168-72] and [Dopuch, Birnberg and Demski, 1974, pp. 564-70].

[36][Gordon, 1964, pp. 4-5] discusses the general phenomenon, of which this is an aspect: control of subordinates via pseudo income statements.

[37]Or, as we'll see, in some cases move from zero to a negative amount otherwise.

stead, one main purpose of this book is to explore a set of reasons why it often backfires. Also, such readers are asked to note that I just wrote "a set of reasons." There are other reasons, too, but *this book is a limited inquiry.*

Another purpose is to essay something that's never been done before: a survey of all operating properties of all significant approaches to joint-cost and transfer-price allocation that have been mentioned in the accounting, economics and management-science literatures through this book's cut-off dates.[38] If successful, this survey will:

1. Allow practitioners and researchers to compare these approaches on different dimensions of behaviour-congruence,

2. In consequence, give some of these approaches decent burial,[39]

3. Persuade any readers who now feel fairly comfortable with one or more joint-cost or transfer-price approaches that their confidence may be misplaced, and innoculate them against such appeals for expanded internal allocating as [Anthony, 1975],

4. Explain the more mathematical of these joint-cost and transfer-price approaches in language comprehensible to lay readers,

5. Ease the consciences of any readers who may be feeling guilty about not comprehending the details of, or not trying to implement, the more prestigious such approaches,

6. Relatedly, slay some intellectual chimaeras that have already waxed fat on researchers into transfer pricing, and

---

[38]I say *dates* because my literature cut-off is a bit ragged. The References list all pertinent-seeming accounting works brought to my attention through October 1977 as well as a fairly wide selection of non-accounting works with a June 1977 cutoff. To these I've added a few items explicitly recommended by readers of earlier drafts, or that were sent to me in manuscript form.

The References disregard many technical studies of mathematical programming, welfare economics and game theory that are adequately cited in the works listed. Nonetheless, they impound a much broader group of articles and journals than those that [Boer, et al., 1976] covers in its management-accounting literature abstracts. It would be a great service to accounting researchers were another AAA committee to extend this 1976 compendium by a thoroughgoing survey of articles that bear upon managerial accounting but have appeared in economics, management-science, behavioural-science and other non-accounting journals—and also survey related books.

[39]Just as any healthy ecological system needs decomposers, so managerial accounting needs researchers who will play sexton beetle to dead theories. Otherwise, our intellectual landscape will end up as littered with unproductive rubbish as *financial* accounting's is today. An analogy is the melancholy state of Australia's pastures—see [Waterhouse, 1974].

7. Provide a methodology that may help slay new chimaeras (new approaches to one-to-many allocations) as they emerge from the egg.[40]

As mentioned earlier (footnote 18) and discussed in Chapter Twelve, *some* internal, one-to-many allocating may be unavoidable. If so, I hope to persuade readers that, at least, companies should:

1. Recognize that these allocations are highly arbitrary and prone to perverse, unintended side effects,

2. Be constantly aware of their behavioural dimensions (rather than becoming fixated on number crunching), and

3. Keep them just as simple as possible.

From time to time I shall suggest ways in which the last might be accomplished. If my analyses are convincing, I'd also hope that textbook writers will ultimately opt for simplicity, too.[41] Finally, from time to time I'll make suggestions for additional research, a few of which suggestions might lead to feasible dissertations.

A Few Caveats

I shall end this section with some points that readers who are following the analysis closely should keep in mind while reading the rest of this book:

1. The notion of behaviour-congruence makes no assumption that there is some globally optimal, allocation-free decision method with which allocation is to be compared.[42] If such a method exists, the problems outlined in footnote 18 may make its use entirely impractical. And one may not even exist. Perhaps the complexity of the decision situation exceeds the capacities of existing

---

[40] In the late 19th century, Anthony Trollope got into trouble with critics and readers by openly admitting that he wrote his novels to make money. Nowadays, in our sober discipline one runs equal risks by admitting to writing books out of curiosity—because of intellectual itches that badly need scratching. Naturally, therefore, I do not include such a motive among this book's purposes.

[41] After spending four years away from teaching, I was recently startled upon returning to academia by the complexities of the allocations that we routinely expect our students to master. If this book's conclusions are correct, much of this complexity is needless, and can be justified only as a rite of passage, a way of hazing the young.

Such hazing *can* be defended. But surely it could take more productive forms. Why not instead require students to learn Latin? Or, if their university has disbanded its Classics department, why not make them learn how to program in assembly language?

[42] Such an assumption was a weakness of [Thomas, 1974]'s related concept of *sterilization*.

intellectual technology.[43] Or there may be a multitude of conflicting global goals, with no way to set weights. Or such global goals, their proper hierarchical rankings, or even who should decide them may be ill understood. (Here, many allocation-free decision methods might be possible, of which none are demonstrably superior to the others—perhaps because all methods have perverse properties, and these can't be ranked.)

All that behaviour-congruence with respect to particular central-management need(s), decision(s) and circumstances implies is that an allocation method escapes certain specifically identified perversities. Later, we shall see approximately 40 such perversities for joint-cost allocation methods, and various additional transfer-price perversities.

2. Behaviour-congruence (in the sense that I use the term) is meaningless outside very narrow contexts of particular wants, decisions and circumstances. One shouldn't try to discuss it in the abstract, but only *in* these contexts. In particular, I shall make no attempts to find allocation methods that are "true" or that measure companies' objective characteristics. (I've argued elsewhere that such notions are simply inapplicable to incorrigible allocations.) Instead, the spirit of my discussion will be that of Anthony's [1957, p. 231] example of how to think about allocating a university's duplicating costs:

> ...to the extent that cost constructions are involved in this problem, the decision as to what type of cost should be used is arrived at, not by trying to find the true, objective cost of duplicating—if there is such a thing—but rather by using cost constructions that are calculated to motivate the department head to act as the administration wishes him to act.

3. The six general examples of allocation perversities given a while back include decisions that many would regard as incommensurable. For example, a central management's evaluation of a product is quite a different thing from the personal decisions that a division manager might make because an allocation method outraged his or her sense of equity. Yet all six potentially affect satisfaction of the central office's wants, and it is these effects with which this book is concerned. Thus, the notion of behaviour-con-

---

[43] Similarly, we shall see that in realistically complex situations, for the central office to make what it perceives to be optimal *resource* (as contrasted to notional) allocations to divisions, information economies or information overload may force it to use decomposed mathematical-programming procedures that generate allocated transfer prices as shadow prices. If so, it's meaningless to ask transfer prices to, say, lead divisions to make the same decisions as would the central office under a globally optimal, allocation-free procedure: no such procedure exists.

gruence serves something of the same function for our managerial-accounting purposes as the numéraire does in allowing financial accountants to report on various incommensurable assets and liabilities simultaneously.[44]

Examples of Behaviour-Congruence

It remains to give a few more examples of behaviour-congruence. I'll begin with a trivial one, merely to illustrate the concept. In it, I deliberately have the decision maker follow a foolish decision rule—for one purpose of making allocation methods behaviour-congruent is to ensure that the central office's wants are satisfied even when decision makers are misguided.

First, then, a variation on Vatter's [1974, p. 198] man who, concerned to reduce the cost per mile of operating his car, hires a boy to spend several hours each Saturday driving it around the block. A man, who walks at three miles per hour and lives in a suburb forty miles from his job, decides each weekday whether to walk or drive to work. He bases his decision on whether or not his car will depreciate that day: if it will, he intends to drive, not wishing to waste the depreciation.

His wife, who plays the role of central office and who sets family accounting policy, wants him gainfully employed. To be so, he must drive (walking takes too long). One way to *get* him to drive is for her to specify use of straight-line depreciation (which will generate a positive daily depreciation charge). Please note, though, that there's nothing unique about the straight-line method here: *any* depreciation method that gives a positive daily charge would also be behaviour-congruent. In Chapter Six we'll see many examples of decisions for which more than one allocation method is behaviour-congruent.

For a more significant example, division managers who are evaluated according to their returns on investment (rates of return on capital employed) or residual incomes are sometimes reluctant to propose globally advantageous, long-lived, capital-budgeting products, even when these projects' internal rates of return exceed their divisions' target rates. For under accelerated, or even straight-line, depreciation such projects are apt to yield low book returns during their initial years, thereby harming the managers' perceived performances. To be sure, later returns will be correspondingly

---

[44]Though behaviour-congruence does not even lead to ordinal, much less a numéraire's cardinal, rankings.

high, but by then the managers affected are likely to have been promoted (or fired) and therefore won't benefit.

It can be proved that the implicit-rate ("economic") method of depreciation is uniquely behaviour-congruent with respect to such project-proposing decisions under plausible circumstances. For, assuming that expectations were correct, it ensures that each period a project's book rate of return will exactly equal its long-run average rate of return. Since, as the situation is framed, that return will be satisfactory to division managers, they'll find it personally advantageous to propose the projects.[45]

Such behaviour-congruent allocations are a common feature of managerial accounting.[46] Other instances of them may be found in responsibility accounting, absorption costing, central-office decisions based on divisional, regional or product profitabilities, allocations of costs of service departments to production departments and, as we'll see, other forms of transfer-price and joint-cost allocations.

Multiple Congruence

If an allocation method is behaviour-congruent with respect to two or more decisions and sets of circumstances, we may speak of *multiple congruence*. Unfortunately, multiple congruence is by no means guaranteed: like freedom from sin among incorrigible mortals, universal behaviour-congruence with respect to all decisions, circumstances and central-office goals is unattainable by incorrigible allocation methods. In one event an allocation method may guide decision makers to do what the central office wants, yet in other situations it may generate perverse behaviour.[47]

To begin with a simple example, an oligopolist uses implicit-rate depreciation internally, to encourage division managers to make project-proposing decisions that will maximize global profits. The

---

[45] For a more detailed discussion of this, see [Thomas, 1974, pp. 40-42]. Readers are warned that this example makes certain implicit simplifications that are discussed by McIntyre [1977]; relax these, and behaviour-congruence may fail.

[46] We've already seen another instance in Kreps' (footnote 9 above) anecdote of the allocation method that saved the foreman's job. [Shubik, 1964, pp. 212-13] provides a nice, simple example of allocation methods that are behaviour-congruent and perverse with respect to decisions on whether to liquidate divisions.

[47] This could be argued on strictly *a priori* grounds. Lack of complete knowledge of alternatives, their consequences, and the values to be associated with these consequences renders fully rational decision making impossible—see [Simon, 1957, pp. 80-84, 99, 189-90]. Therefore, behaviour-congruence will be possible only in terms of bounded rationality, and must (except by sheer luck) occur with respect to only a few of the myriad possible decisions and circumstances that an allocation may involve.

central office wishes to revise the company's price schedule. Circumstances are such that it should base any pricing decisions on analyses of such things as demand and probable reactions of competitors. Instead, though, it follows the traditional rule of setting prices equal to products' full costs plus an "equitable" percentage markup. There's no reason to expect that implicit-rate depreciation will be behaviour-congruent here (lead to setting profit-maximizing prices) despite its being behaviour-congruent for project-proposing decisions.

Elan Effects and Elan-Congruence

The mention of equity introduces a dimension of behaviour-congruence that will be quite important later in this book. By now it should be apparent that behaviour-congruence often involves the central office's deciding what divisions should do, then rigging allocations so that they will do it, in effect pre-empting their decisions (though often maintaining a façade of divisional autonomy).

Now, division managers base various *personal* decisions on their perceptions of how fair the company's accounting system is, how genuine it renders any autonomy supposedly granted to them, whether the central office seems to be trying to manipulate their behaviour, and the like. Doubtless some division managers are thick-skinned here. But with others, such perceptions and decisions (which can be profoundly influenced by the company's choice of allocation methods) affect matters significant to satisfaction of central-office wants: the seriousness with which these division managers take the company's internal accounting data, their trust in the equitability of its system of internal evaluation and control (or, alternatively, their alienation), how much time they waste in unproductive efforts to improve their divisions' book profits rather than global profits, the degree of conflict between divisions,[48] and, it's widely believed, the amount and quality of division-manager contributions—their creativity and general élan.[49]

For lack of better terms, let's call these *élan effects* and, when they are negative, speak of *alienation*. For the nonce, I've deliber-

---

[48] A major concern of [Watson and Baumler, 1975, e.g., pp. 471-72].

[49] Once again, all this is merely a particular instance of a more general phenomenon: central-office decisions of *any* kind generating unintentional personal behaviour. The situation is common in mythology. For instance, Frigg, wife of Odin, persuaded all living and nonliving things save the mistletoe never to harm Balder. This inspired the other gods to disport themselves by throwing everything imaginable at Balder, under cover of which Loki had blind Hölder cast the sprig of mistetoe that slew Balder.

ately avoided specifying the exact natures of these élan effects, the altered decisions and the mechanics of their impacts on overall profitability. Certainly, allocations can have positive consequences in these areas.[50] But economists and accountants either assume or can demonstrate that *some* significant dysfunctional consequences will ensue from division managers deeming allocations to be unfair, experiencing diminished autonomy, or feeling manipulated— for instance, as we shall see, this is a prime concern of much recent literature on transfer pricing.[51] (Appendix G explores the behavioural-science literature on this matter in some detail.) In turn, I shall call allocation methods that are behaviour-congruent with respect to élan effects *élan-congruent*. In summary, *élan decisions* will be shorthand for *decisions based on motivational factors other than (book) profits*—that's to say, based on motivational factors other than those upon which economists base their traditional models. In turn, *élan-congruent* will signify behaviour-congruent with respect to *division managers' élan decisions.*[52]

Congruence Properties

For brevity, I'll speak of behaviour-congruence with respect to a specific decision, goals and circumstances as a *congruence property* (and usually won't describe the circumstances if they're commonplace). Chapter Five discusses a wide variety of congruence properties for joint-cost allocations. For the present, readers are just asked to note that different congruence properties assume different decision loci. For instance, division managers make élan decisions and central offices make decisions based on evaluations of division managers' performances. Some decisions are ambiguous in this regard: for instance, either the central office or division managers might make make-or-buy decisions, depending on the degree

---

[50] Such, for example, as stabilization and dissonance-reduction in the face of conflicting interests and uncertainty.

[51] The essence of this problem is that central offices, by decentralization and its associated systems of evaluation and control, try to encourage division managers to behave as entrepreneurs are traditionally supposed to behave in free markets. Alienation stems from the central office's substituting what is all too often a visible ham-hand for the invisible hand. Thus do some of our most prominent corporate exponents of free enterprise imitate socialist states.

[52] [Bodnar and Lusk, 1977] is a good general discussion of some of the things that central offices must take into consideration when designing allocation methods to be élan-congruent. (I'm concerned, though, that under their particular approach division managers may spend much of their time confused as to just what the central office wants them to do, and that this confusion will delay and dilute the élan-congruence of the allocation methods that the authors recommend.)

of autonomy allowed division managers. In such ambiguous cases, I merely assume that the decision makers, whoever they are, base their decisions upon the related allocated data.

One advantage of becoming aware of congruence properties is that should we encounter an unfamiliar allocation method and discover that its properties seem identical to those of a familiar approach, we're alerted to the possibility that the former may be a variant of the latter. For instance, even readers whose mathematical sophistication is negligible should be able to detect (from reading either of their first two pages) that, as Appendix A demonstrates, the allocation proposals in both Kaplan and Thompson [1971] and its sequel, Kaplan and Welam [1974], are a variant of the NRV approach.

Methodology and Structure of This Book

As its title indicates, this book's methodology will be analytical (not empirical, but also not deductive). This book will survey an enormous body of literature and related accounting practices. It will try to understand what motivates that literature and those practices, then seek to discover whether motives, recommendations and practices can be made to be consistent. A remark by Ijiri [1975, p. 28], though made in another context, is highly pertinent to this:

> This type of inductive reasoning to derive goals implicit in the behavior of an existing system is not intended to be pro-establishment or to promote the maintenance of the status quo. The purpose of such an exercise is to highlight where changes are most needed and where they are feasible. Changes suggested as a result of such a study have a much better chance of being actually implemented. Goal assumptions in normative models or goals advocated in policy discussions are often stated purely on the basis of one's conviction and preference, rather than on the basis of inductive study of the existing system. This may perhaps be the most crucial reason why so many normative models or policy proposals are not implemented in the real world.

Despite this book's being an analytical one and despite its often dealing with topics that are mathematically complex, it is deliberately written at the level of mathematical sophistication of an intelligent layperson. (This will become especially evident in my discussions of mathematical-programming approaches to transfer pricing, and of Shapley allocations.) For I'm convinced, and hope to convince readers, that a failure of literature on the former to express its reasoning in ordinary, lay English has contributed to allowing its authors to avoid facing up to fundamental questions, and encouraged them to frolic off on long, largely sterile, tangents. On the other hand, practical-minded readers may well be troubled by this book's use of algebra and mathematical notation, and its abstraction from day-by-day operating concerns. To them, I can only quote McGregor's [1960, p. 7] defense of theory:

> It is possible to have more or less adequate theoretical assumptions; it is not possible to reach a managerial decision or take a managerial action uninfluenced by assumptions, whether adequate or not. The insistence on being practical really means, "Let's accept *my* theoretical assumptions without argument or test."[53]

The Structure of This Book

The remainder of this book is divided into two parts, the first concerned with joint-cost allocations, the second with transfer prices. Chapters Two through Four describe eight joint-cost allocation methods and their main variants. Chapter Five surveys all joint-cost congruence properties that I've been able to detect in the literature. This provides the framework for Chapter Six's systematic comparisons of how the properties of the several methods differ.

Chapter Seven introduces Part Two by trying to identify the main purposes purportedly served by transfer pricing. Chapter Eight considers the simplest, two-division transfer-price situations, paying particular attention to Hirshleifer's work. Chapter Nine extends this discussion to more complicated situations described by Hirshleifer, and to Gould's and Naert's extensions of his analyses. I shall conclude that, in the absence of effectively perfect markets for intermediate products, all three authors' approaches are destructive of divisional autonomies in ways that risk defeating the very mechanisms by which they're supposed to operate.

I make a similar criticism of most of the mathematical-programming approaches that are Chapter Ten's subject. If this critique is correct, it leads to a conclusion that this literature has far less practical import than many now suppose. Chapter Eleven surveys all remaining transfer-price proposals that I've been able to uncover, while Chapter Twelve summarizes Part Two, considers alternatives to transfer-price allocation, and makes a few practical suggestions.

Throughout this book I'm concerned, on the micro level, with what The American Accounting Association's Committee on So-

---

[53] See also [p. 8].

cial Consequences of Accounting Information [1977, p. 4], operating at the *macro* level, called "the potential social and economic consequences of accounting policies." Two comments of theirs may suffice to end this introduction:

> In a nutshell...the accounting-consequences argument may be viewed as claiming that *changes in accounting descriptions induce behavioral changes which can have broad and extensive consequences.* [p. 18] [54]

* * *

> Clearly, this subject has become *the* central contemporary issue in accounting. [p. 4]

---

[54] Preliminary draft.

CHAPTER TWO

THE NRV, SV, MORIARITY, LOUDERBACK, JIM AND JIL APPROACHES

Joint cost allocation is a perpetual problem in product costing and divisional performance measurement and control. It continues to plague the accountant due to management's desire for full product costing for pricing purposes and internal and external requirements for performance monitoring on a divisional or product basis. Joint cost allocation is pervasive in a manufacturing firm; the most common example is fixed factory overhead, normally allocated on the basis of an activity level such as direct labor hours. However, joint cost allocation also exists in retail establishments, in the form of administrative and marketing costs. — [Hamlen, Hamlen and Tschirhart, 1977, p. 616].

Ideas have their seasons. Long dismissed as an intellectually sterile topic, theoretical interest in joint-cost allocation has recently revived in response to Moriarity's [1975] proposals and loosely related analyses rooted in the game-theoretic work of L. S. Shapley [1953].[1]
This is hardly surprising. As Chapter One indicated, although academics rejected joint-cost allocations on grounds that businessmen should be educated out of making them, the businessmen have stubbornly persisted in allocating (and regulators have persisted in requiring that they continue). Sooner or later, theorists were bound to confront the issue: Given that companies *will* allocate, how best should they do so?

Joint Costs and Joint Products Narrowly Defined

At this stage perhaps it would be as well to adopt a definition of joint products. Professor Jacob Viner, an authority on cost problems, suggests that joint products are "commodities which are sufficiently distinguishable from each other to have different markets and to com-

---

[1]Notable recent managerial accounting works are [Moriarity, 1976; 1976], [Louderback, 1976], [Hamlen, Hamlen and Tschirhart, 1977], [Hughes and Scheiner, 1977] and [Jensen, 1977]. On the financial-accounting level, see [Callen, 1978].
  For basic literature on Shapley allocations, see also [Luce and Raiffa, 1957, esp. pp. 192-96, 245-52], [Shubik, 1962 or 1964], [Mossin, 1968], [Shapley and Shubik, 1969a], [Loehman and Whinston, 1971; 1974; 1976] and [Littlechild and Owen, 1973]. For extensions, see [Scarf, 1967], [Shapley and Shubik, 1969b], [Shapley, 1971], [Maschler, Peleg and Shapley, 1972], [Littlechild, 1975], [Sorenson, Tschirhart and Whinston, 1976], [Butterworth, Hayes and Matsumura, 1977] and [Roth and Verrecchia, 1977].

mand different prices even under competitive conditions, but which are partly or wholly the outcome of a common process of production."— [Edwards, 1952b, p. 311]

Viner's is an especially clear version of the most common conception of *joint products*. In turn, joint *costs* are those of the joint processes that yield these products. The next five chapters will usually conform to the literature that we must review by adopting Viner's definition. But readers are reminded that his joint costs are merely particular instances of a much more general phenomenon (under which overhead allocating and transfer pricing may also be regarded as joint-cost allocation). Readers are invited to verify that the analytical techniques developed in this book are also applicable to joint-cost allocations when more broadly defined, and lead to similar conclusions.[2]

The next three chapters survey all theoretically significant approaches to joint-cost allocation (in Viner's narrow sense) that I've been able to find in the literature,[3] including a few variations on these approaches. These are the approximated relative sales values, or net realizable value *(NRV)*, method, the sales value *(SV)* approach, Moriarity's and Louderback's proposals, two improved versions of these *(JIM* and *JIL)*, the marginal approach (in Chapter Three) and the "Democratic" approach and two other interpretations of the Shapley approach (in Chapter Four). To be sure, in practice one encounters additional techniques, such as allocation of joint costs to goods in proportion to their relative weights or volumes. But these are notoriously arbitrary and without theoretical pretensions;[4] we may largely ignore them.

Simplifications and Notation

As just mentioned, I shall usually conform my analysis to the assumptions made by the literature that it reviews. For I'm trying

---

[2] For general background on joint-cost allocations, and how their significance and ubiquity are perceived by accountants, see [Vatter, 1945, pp. 164–73], [Avery, 1951], [National Association of Accountants, 1957b], [Baumes, 1963] and [Mautz and Skousen, 1968]. For economists' perspectives, see [Clark, 1923, pp. 98–103], [Kreps, 1930, pp. 416–26, 450–61], [Lewis, 1946, pp. 233–34], [Walters, 1960, pp. 419–20] and [Pfouts, 1961]. Kreps' article contains a bibliography of earlier works.

[3] Excepting one or two approaches to allocating costs of service departments that could equally well be classified as transfer pricing (with which I'll deal in Part Two) and an approach suggested by Horngren, mentioned in note 18, below.

[4] [Feller, 1977] discusses attempts (not convincing to its author, either) to give a theoretical rationale to units-of-output allocation of joint costs in the petroleum industry. See also Chapter One's footnote 9.

to prove the limitations of this literature, and the only fair way do so is to meet it on its own terms and show that, even when one does so, it still experiences grave difficulties.[5]

Accordingly, unless indicated otherwise I'll make the customary assumptions that companies seek to maximize their immediate, short-run,[6] overall profits,[7] that division managers do the same at the book-profit level, that joint products are produced in fixed proportions (constant product mix),[8] that joint products are technologically independent[9] and have independent demands,[10] that joint products have zero split-off values,[11] that there is no external market in which one can buy joint products that haven't been processed further, that demands are known with certainty, that marginal cost and revenue curves are horizontal (there being some implicit, overriding capacity constraint)[12] but that there are no other capacity constraints (i.e., no need to rank products),[13] that production functions are proportional (e.g., that when all inputs are doubled all outputs are also doubled) and that costs of information are nominal and may be disregarded.[14]

---

[5] In this connection, readers who are following things closely are warned that use of Viner's narrow definition of *joint products*, though dictated by the bulk of the literature, understates the significance of approaches (like the Moriarity, Louderback, JIM, JIL and Shapley ones) that aren't as restricted. However, they are again invited to verify that my analysis and conclusions can be extended to the broader arenas.

[6] Cf. [Solomons, 1977, p. 44 • 12].

[7] See [Paik, 1975, pp. 78-79] for other possible global goals, and for a brief survey of the empirical evidence that *some* such additional goals do affect companies' behaviours. Additional goals, not mentioned by Paik, include corporate survival and increase in the organization's size and growth (with their consequent magnification of its prestige and power)—see [Simon, 1957, pp. 117-19].

[8] The distinction, sometimes to be found in the literature, between joint and common costs assumes otherwise. But, as mentioned in Chapter One, this book assumes that common costs have been analyzed into their separate and purely joint components—what [Thomas, 1974, p. 19] called their separate and interaction effects. See [Baumol, et al., 1962, p. 359].

[9] Beyond the joint process itself, of course.

[10] For a discussion of the consequences of assuming that joint products are either complementary or competitive, see [Wiles, 1963].

[11] That's to say, that they aren't saleable at split-off from the joint process, but can be discarded at zero cost.

[12] This last assumption isn't innocuous—see [Walters, 1960] and [Jensen, 1974], which I discuss in Chapter Three.

[13] I'll reserve discussion of mathematical-programming approaches to joint-cost allocation (which, of course, relax this assumption) for Part Two.

[14] This, of course, bypasses issues central to [Demski and Feltham, 1976]. More precisely, my assumption is that when there's sufficient information to make use of a joint-cost allocation method feasible its costs are nominal. This assumption loads the dice slightly in favour of the Moriarity, Louderback, JIM, JIL, marginal and Shapley ap-

I'll make several other simplifying assumptions that aren't as ubiquitous. I'll suppose that each product of a joint process is the separate responsibility of a division, and that each division is responsible for only one such product. Since allocations of joint costs are equally allocations of profits, I'll often perceive them from the latter vantage point. I'll join Moriarity [1975; 1976] and Louderback [1976], who implicitly assume that if companies can choose between processing joint products internally or buying them externally it just happens that outsiders sell these products in batches exactly the same size as those that the joint process yields. Finally, in part consequent upon disregarding costs of information, I shall ignore the conventional distinction between joint products and by-products.[15]

Notation

Some notation will be convenient. In what follows, to avoid both (a) "compounding" effects of allocating what are already allocations of joint costs and (b) the sorts of ambiguities discussed in [Lawson, 1956, pp. 441-42], all joint, separate and (for that matter) external costs (J, f_i, and x_i) are assumed to be out-of-pocket, traceable ones. In particular, none of their components are allocations of fixed costs.

h,i,k = Products of a joint process, i being the general case

j_i = The amount of joint cost allocated to a batch of product i

f_i = The total separate cost of a completed batch of product i— its *further-processing* cost, encompassing all costs incurred on it after split-off

$t_i = j_i + f_i$ = The total book cost of a completed batch of product i

x_i = The cost of the least expensive way of buying a batch of completed product i separately and externally

proaches, something that readers who are following the analysis closely might want to keep in mind.

I will *not* disregard costs of information in Part Two, though its analysis will still be at a less sophisticated level than Demski's and Feltham's.

[15]As additional reasons for doing so, (a) none of this book's conclusions are pertinent when costs aren't material, (b) costs of by-products rarely are material and (c) when they *are*, with one exception (discussed in Chapter Three) there's nothing distinctive about by-products within the analytical framework that I shall develop. As Ferrara [1977, p. 41·21] comments:

> Joint products of lesser value are called by-products, whereas those of greater value retain the title joint product (sometimes prime or coproduct). Thus, the only real difference between by-products and joint products is in relative values.

See also [Dearden, 1973, p. 173]. Indeed, the distinction seems purely one of practical expediency, not of theory.

y_i = The cost of the least expensive way of acquiring a batch of completed product i separately, whether internally or externally

p_i = The total selling price of a batch of product i

$n_i = p_i - f_i$ = The total net realizable value of a batch of product i given further processing past the split-off point

b_i = The book profit on a batch of product i, either $p_i - t_i$ or $p_i - x_i$

$\min|p_i,x_i|$ = The lesser of p_i and x_i

J,F,T,X,Y,P,N,B,MIN = Related summations; for instance, $MIN = \sum_j \min|p_i,x_i|$.

I'll routinely alter other authors' notations to fit this scheme (without further notice), and shall introduce additional notation later, as needed.

Six Easy Joint-Cost Allocation Approaches

This section describes six mathematically simple joint-cost allocation methods.[16]

The NRV Approach

The NRV approach seems to be one of the two most popular in accounting textbooks.[17] As its name suggests, it allocates joint

---

[16]For origins of the NRV and SV approaches (discussed in this chapter) and the marginal approach (discussed in the next) in the 19th Century economic theory, see [Kreps, 1930, pp. 420-21, 450-53].

[17]Under our assumptions that all products have zero split-off values, and that there is no external market in which one can buy joint products that haven't been processed further, this is true even of [Horngren, 1977, p. 552]:

> ...the best approach to assigning joint costs is the relative sales values at the *split-off point*. If these values are not explicitly available because there is no market for [the joint products] at the split-off point or because the products cannot be purchased from outsiders, the *next best* alternative—for product-costing purposes only—is to take the ultimate relative sales values at the point of sale and work backward to *approximate* (computed) relative sales values at the split-off point.

[Dopuch, Birnberg and Demski, 1974, pp. 574-75] makes similar observations.

To the best of my knowledge, these are the only authors besides myself [1974, pp. 168-73] who have seriously considered relaxing these assumptions. Although consequences of such relaxation deserve investigation, I have two reasons for not doing so here:

1. As the quotation suggests, Horngren refuses on principle to consider use of joint-cost allocations in internal decision making. The three other authors hold parallel views. Therefore, this proposed relaxation isn't directed toward the sorts of things analyzed in this book.

2. Once one admits exit or entry values at split-off, calculations of characteristic functions under Chapter Four's Shapley approach become quite complicated.

I hope to tackle these complications in a later monograph (if someone doesn't beat me

costs and book profits to products in proportion to their net realizable values:[18]

$$j_i = J \cdot n_i \div N$$
$$t_i = j_i + f_i$$
$$b_i = p_i - t_i = B \cdot n_i \div N.$$

The SV Approach

Devine [1950a, pp. 118-19] and some subsequent authors[19] have proposed a different rule: Each joint product's gross margin should be the same percentage of its selling price as that of any other joint product. To accomplish this, one allocates *book profits* in proportion to selling prices, with the following consequences:

$$b_i = p_i \cdot (P - T) \div P = B \cdot p_i \div P$$
$$t_i = T \cdot p_i \div P$$
$$j_i = t_i - f_i$$

I shall designate this the *sales value,* or *SV,* approach.

Both the NRV and SV approaches should be distinguished from another sales-value approach, which allocates *joint costs* in proportion to selling prices:

$$j_i = J \cdot p_i \div P$$

Except as a rare, limiting case of the NRV approach (when further-processing costs are negligible),[20] this method is generally agreed to lack theoretical merit. I shall disregard it hereafter.[21]

to solution of what looks to be a most engrossing puzzle). Meanwhile, though, any research project must eventually be brought to publication, even if less complete than one would desire. And I can only plead, with Hayek [1960, pp. vii-viii], that:

> On a subject as comprehensive as that of this book, the task of making it as good as one is capable of is never completed while one's faculties last....Respect for the reader certainly demands that one present a tolerably finished product. But I doubt whether this means that one ought to wait until one cannot hope to improve it further. At least where the problems are of the kind on which many others are actively working, it would even appear to be an overestimate of one's own importance if one delayed publication until one was certain that one could not improve anything. If a man has, as I hope I have, pushed analysis a step forward, further efforts by him are likely to be subject to rapidly decreasing returns. Others will probably be better qualified to lay the next row of bricks of the edifice to which I am trying to contribute.

[18] [Horngren, 1977, pp. 553, 562] suggests a variation on the NRV method under which one uses the net realizable value minus a normal profit margin rather than the net realizable value *per se.* I will not discuss this alternative in what follows, instead leaving it to readers of Chapter Six to verify that, on balance, this variant's operating properties seem inferior to those of the NRV approach *per se.*

[19] E.g., Lorig [1955, pp. 634n, 635] and Ferrara [1977, pp. 41·25-26].

[20] See [Wiles, 1963, p. 108] for its rarity.

[21] Similarly, I'll disregard approaches, whereby by-product revenues are subtracted from total costs to obtain book costs of main products, as mere expedient variants on the NRV and SV approaches—see footnote 15.

Moriarity's Approach[22]

Moriarity [1975; 1976] points out that usually it's possible to obtain joint products in ways alternative to one's joint process if one is willing to pay enough—and that companies manufacture such products jointly in order to obtain cost savings over these alternatives. His approach allocates these savings to products in proportion to the alternative costs escaped, with the following consequences:

$$t_i = T \cdot y_i \div Y$$
$$j_i = t_i - f_i$$
$$b_i = p_i - t_i$$

Louderback's Approach

Louderback [1976] suggested modifying Moriarity's approach by comparing external costs of acquiring joint products with their further-processing costs.[23] For all products such that $x_i > f_i$:

$$j_i = J \cdot (x_i - f_i) \div (X' - F')$$
$$t_i = j_i + f_i$$
$$b_i = p_i - t_i$$
$$= n_i - j_i$$

---

[22]For motivation of, and further details on, the next four approaches, see [Johnson and Thomas, 1979].

[23]For brevity, our discussion will assume that the least expensive alternative way of acquiring joint products *in*ternally is to manufacture a batch of them and discard all but the one in question. This may sound a bit strange, but it merely boils down to assuming that the company's actual joint production process is efficient in minimizing cost.

More problematically, I shall also assume that if the company doesn't acquire goods jointly it must acquire them altogether separately. This assumption is necessitated by a fundamental limitation of the Moriarity and Louderback approaches, neither of which can cope with more complicated circumstances. Let's presuppose a joint process that costs J and generates m products, 1, 2,..., m, with respective, separate further-processing costs of $f_1, f_2, ..., f_m$. The company can also acquire these products externally: x_1 is the cost of so acquiring product 1 separately, x_{12} the cost of acquiring a batch of products 1 and 2 externally, etc. J and all f and x terms are positive (indeed, it could be that some x terms are unbounded, to reflect the impossibility of buying that sort of batch outside). All refer to the quantities of what would be produced internally as a single batch of joint product. Finally, I'll arbitrarily number products for convenience of exposition.

Let's now suppose that, with one exception, $x_1 > J + f_1, x_2 > J + f_2, ... x_{12} > J + f_1 + f_2, ..., x_{12...m} > J + f_1 + f_2 + ... + f_m$. The exception is that $x_{12...k} < J + f_1 + f_2 + ... f_k$, but $x_{12...k} > g(J, f_i)$, where $g(J, f_i)$ successively assumes all the values $J + f_1, J + f_1 + f_2, ..., J + f_1 + f_2 + ... + f_{k-1}, J + f_2 + ... + f_k, J + f_1 + f_3 + ... + f_k$, etc. $(k \leqslant m, 1 \leqslant i \leqslant k)$. Under these, and all parallel, circumstances each of the j_i's is undefined for Moriarity's and Louderback's approaches. Indeed, all that either of their systems can handle is situations where either (a) products bought externally must be purchased separately from all other products or (b) it's to the company's profit advantage to buy a batch of products, 1, 2,...,k, and throw away all but one product.

where X' and F' are the sums of such x_i and f_i.[24] But for all other products ($x_i \leq f_i$):

$$j_i = 0$$
$$t_i = f_i$$
$$b_i = p_i - f_i = n_i.[25]$$

The JIM and JIL Approaches

Especially attentive readers may have noticed that the foregoing left an issue unresolved. Moriarity's analysis doesn't tell us what to do when $J + F < Y$ yet $f_i \geq y_i$, as with Figure 2-1's product V. Nor does either author tell us what to do when $f_i \geq p_i$, as with product U (for the simple reason that neither author's analysis considered revenues). One possibility would be to treat all such products as dummies—i.e., assign zero joint costs to them, as the Louderback approach does for products, like V, whose $f_i > x_i$. Another would be to treat them like products R and W, whose $f_i < \min|p_i, x_i|$. What should we do?

Because all joint-cost allocations are radically arbitrary—incorrigible—there is no theoretically "right" answer to this question except in terms of the two possibilities' comparative congruence properties. For efficiency of exposition, I shall conduct this comparison by making what seems to be the natural assumption (lacking specific guidance from the authors) that these approaches do *not* treat products whose $f_i \geq \min|p_i, x_i|$ as dummies except where their authors so stipulate (as Louderback did when $f_i \geq x_i$). Then, I'll contrast these with versions of the Moriarity and Louderback approaches, introduced by [Johnson and Thomas, 1979], that do assign zero joint costs to all such products. Finally, Chapter Six

---

[24] E.g., $X' = \sum_{i|x_i > f_i} x_i$

[25] One may make a two-way classification of these first four approaches. Let's call a joint-cost method that calculates book profits (b_i) from selling prices (p_i) a *gross* method, and one that calculates them from selling prices less further-processing costs ($p_i - f_i = n_i$) a *net* method. It's evident from their formulas that the SV and Moriarity approaches are gross ones, while the NRV and Louderback approaches are net. Again, both the Moriarity and Louderback approaches are based on alternative costs, whereas the NRV and SV approaches aren't. This gives us:

	Alternative Cost	
	No	Yes
Net	NRV	Louderback
Gross	SV	Moriarity

will show that the latter versions usually have better congruence properties than the former.[26]

I shall denote the first of these alternative versions the *Johnson's Improved Moriarity (JIM)* approach. Under it, for all products such that $f_i < \min|p_i, x_i|$:

$$t_i = (J + F') \cdot z_i \div Z'$$
$$j_i = t_i - f_i$$
$$b_i = p_i - t_{i'}$$

where $z_i = \min|(J + f_i), p_i, x_i|$ and F' and Z' are the sums of such products' respective f_i's and z_i's. For all other products $(f_i \geqslant \min|p_i, x_i|)$:

$$j_i = 0$$
$$t_i = f_i$$
$$b_i = p_i - f_i.$$

Under the second, or *Johnson's Improved Louderback (JIL)*, approach, for all products such that $f_i < \min|p_i, x_i|$:

$$j_i = J \cdot (\min|p_i, x_i| - f_i) \div (MIN' - F')$$
$$t_i = j_i + f_i$$
$$b_i = p_i - t_i.$$

For all other products $(f_i \geqslant \min|p_i, x_i|)$:

$$j_i = 0$$
$$t_i = f_i$$
$$b_i = p_i - f_i.$$

Initially, the algorithms for the JIM and JIL approaches may seem complex. But a little practice reveals this impression to be illusory. And, in any event, both methods are easy to program.

Comparison of These Approaches

We may use a simple example to compare these six approaches. Figure 2-1 depicts a situation in which a joint process that costs £9 per batch yields four products, R, U, V and W, that respectively sell for £21, £10, £18 and £13 per batch (p_i). Their respective further-processing costs are £7, £12, £15 and £5 (f_i), resulting in respective batch net realizable values of £14, £(2), £3 and £8 (n_i).

---

[26] though not always: in Chapter Six we'll see a couple of dimensions on which the Moriarity and Louderback approaches are superior to their modifications.

Figure 2-1

A Simple Case of Joint Production

J	n_i	f_i	p_i		x_i	y_i	$\min\|p_i,x_i\|$
	14	7	21	R	18	16	18
	(2)	12	10	U	13	13	10
9	3	15	18	V	11	11	11
	8	5	13	W	22	14	13
Totals	23	39	62			54	
	N	F	P			Y	

For purposes of later analysis, I stipulate that Figure 2-1's £9 joint cost must be incurred to produce any of one, two, three or four joint products, but can be entirely escaped by shutdown.

As in footnote 23, Figure 2-1 also assumes that further processing is the least expensive internal way to acquire batches of any of these products. The company could buy batches of products R, U, V and W separately and externally for £18, £13, £11 and £22 (x_i), these being the lowest-cost external alternatives. But, if the company were not to engage in its actual, four-product joint process the least expensive external or internal alternative ways in which it could acquire these products separately (the y_i's) would be to buy products U and V externally, but acquire product R by making a batch of joint products, discarding the U's, V's and W's, then processing the R's further at a total cost of £9 + £7 = £16 per batch (which is less than the R's external cost of £18). Similarly, under the assumptions of Moriarity's approach, y_w = £9 + £5 = £14 < £22 = x_w.[27]

[27]I deliberately designed this example to reflect a paradoxical aspect of Moriarity's approach. Clearly, the *least* expensive way for the company to acquire products R and W would be to manufacture a single batch of all four products, discard only U and V, then process R and W further, for a total cost of J + f_R + f_W = £9 + £7 + £5 = £21 < £30 = y_R + y_W. But, as we saw in footnote 23, above, Moriarity's approach doesn't contemplate this. If the company doesn't engage in the full, four-product joint process it must acquire all products separately (otherwise, synergy renders their individual joint costs indeterminate).

I'm not too troubled by this paradox: *all* joint-cost allocation approaches are inherently and drastically arbitrary. The paradoxical nature of Moriarity's y_i's can't make his approach significantly worse conceptually than it (or any other such approach) already is. If one's cow is dead it matters not that it's also cross-eyed. In evaluating joint-cost allocation techniques we can only say, Hang Theory, and instead compare their operating (congruence) properties. This we do in Chapter Six.

Readers will notice that the company isn't making as profitable decisions as it might. It could raise its total per-batch profits from the present $N - J = £23 - £9 = £14$ to $£20$ by manufacturing products R and W, buying product V and discontinuing product U.[28] However, we aren't concerned with what it *might* do, but with allocating in response to what it actually does: manufacture of all four products. For, later, we'll want to see how good each of the main joint-cost allocation methods is at guiding decision makers to do what the central office wants when (either in fact or in contemplation) they've behaved perversely. (Chapter Six expands this point slightly.)

Figure 2-2

Joint Costs, Total Costs and Book Profits
Under Six Different Joint-Cost Allocation Methods

Joint-Cost Allocation	NRV	SV	Moriarity	Louderback	JIM	JIL
R	5.48	9.26	7.22	3.41	4.59	5.21
U	(0.78)	(4.26)	(0.44)	0.31	0.00	0.00
V	1.17	(1.06)	(5.22)	0.00	0.00	0.00
W	3.13	5.06	7.44	5.28	4.41	3.79
Total	9.00	9.00	9.00	9.00	9.00	9.00
Total Cost						
R	12.48	16.26	14.22	10.41	11.59	12.21
U	11.22	7.74	11.56	12.31	12.00	12.00
V	16.17	13.94	9.78	15.00	15.00	15.00
W	8.13	10.06	12.44	10.28	9.41	8.79
Total	48.00	48.00	48.00	48.00	48.00	48.00
Book Profit						
R	8.52	4.74	6.78	10.59	9.41	8.79
U	(1.22)	2.26	(1.56)	(2.31)	(2.00)	(2.00)
V	1.83	4.06	8.22	3.00	3.00	3.00
W	4.87	2.94	0.56	2.72	3.59	4.21
Total	14.00	14.00	14.00	14.00	14.00	14.00

[28]$(p_R + p_W - f_R - f_W - J) + (p_V - x_V) = (21 + 13 - 7 - 5 - 9) + (18 - 11) = \underline{20}.$

Figure 2-2 shows the resulting joint-cost allocations (j_i), book costs (t_i) and book profits (b_i) under each approach. Here are a few representative calculations:[29]

<u>NRV.</u> $j_R = J \cdot n_R \div N = 9 \cdot 14 \div 23 \cong \underline{5.48.}$

<u>SV.</u> $t_R = T \cdot p_R \div P = 48 \cdot 21 \div 62 \cong \underline{16.26.}$

<u>Moriarity.</u> $t_R = T \cdot y_i \div Y = 48 \cdot 16 \div 54 \cong \underline{14.22.}$

<u>Louderback.</u> Since $f_V > x_V$, $j_V = 0$. $X' = x_R + x_U + x_W = 18 + 13 + 22 = 53$; $F' = f_R + f_U + f_W = 7 + 12 + 5 = 24$. $j_R = J \cdot (x_R - f_R) \div (X' - F') = 9 \cdot (18 - 7) \div (53 - 24) \cong \underline{3.41.}$

<u>JIM and JIL.</u> Since $f_U > \min |p_U, x_U|$, $j_U = \underline{0}$; since $f_V > \min |p_V, x_V|$, $j_V = \underline{0}$.

<u>JIM.</u> $z_R = \min |(J + f_R), p_R, x_R| = \min |(9 + 7), 21, 18| = 16$. $z_W = \min |(J + f_W), p_W, x_W| = \min |(9 + 5), 13, 22| = 13$. $z' = 16 + 13 = 29$. $F' = f_R + f_W = 7 + 5 = 12$. $t_R = (J + F') \cdot z_R \div Z' = (9 + 12) \cdot 16 \div 29 \cong \underline{11.59.}$

<u>JIL.</u> $\min |p_R, x_R| = \min |21, 18| = 18$; $\min |p_W, x_W| = \min |13, 22| = 13$. $MIN' = 18 + 13 = 31$. $F' = f_R + f_W = 7 + 5 = 12$. $j_R = J \cdot (\min |p_R, x_R| - f_R) \div (MIN' - F') = 9 \cdot (18 - 7) \div (31 - 12) \cong \underline{5.21.}$

It's evident that one's choice of allocation method can make a considerable difference in book costs and book profits. Yet, under plausible assumptions about market imperfections, this example is a conservative one.

---

[29]To expand on the points made in the last paragraph, it's evident from reading [Moriarity, 1975; 1976] and [Louderback, 1976] that both authors might contend that their approaches immediately signal the central office that the company should produce only products R and W internally. But a procedure's being designed to help decision makers make correct decisions doesn't guarantee that alarm bells will ring if decision makers err—and Chapter Six will demonstrate that, under both approaches, sometimes they *don't* ring.

This book is concerned with the properties that allocation methods possess *whether or not decision makers behave wisely*. And Figure 2-2 should be interpreted as showing what the Moriarity and Louderback approaches would report if the central office disregarded warning signals and went ahead to produce products U and V anyway.

CHAPTER THREE

THE MARGINAL APPROACH

For its thoroughness, clarity and the way that it illuminates other works, [Jensen, 1974] is the best single accounting-oriented discussion of the marginal (or marginal-cost) approach to joint-cost allocation.[1] However, for brevity and to avoid needless demands on both the author's and readers' mathematical facilities, I'll pattern my exposition upon that in [Bierman and Dyckman, 1971], using the following additional notation:

i,k = Two goods generated by a single joint process
TR_i = The total revenue from good i
MR_i = The marginal revenue from good i
MC_i = The marginal cost of good i
MC_{ik}= The combined marginal cost of goods i and k
AC_i = The average cost of good i
AC_{ik}= The combined average cost of goods i and k
q_i = The quantity of good i
q_{ik} = The quantity of good i or good k, indifferently, when these two goods are produced in equal amounts.

together with parallel expressions for good k.

What follows considers only two-product joint processes; readers interested in more complex situations (perhaps for verifying conclusions reached in Chapter Six) should consult Appendix B. Figure 3-1 depicts a joint process that costs £16 per batch of one unit of product i and one unit of product k (which it always produces in pairs). Their respective further-processing costs are £9 and £5.

Figure 3-1

A Two-Product Joint Process

	J	f_i	p_i
		9	?	i
16				
		5	?	k

---

[1]In correspondence, Jensen warns of a minor error (that doesn't affect the rest of his analysis) in Figure 3[p. 474]. The marginal approach is efficiently summarized by

36

Until now, we've been able to assume that marginal cost and revenue curves are horizontal (with an implicit, overriding capacity constraint). However, should we continue to do so the marginal approach would merely reduce to the NRV approach.[2] Accordingly, although I'll continue to assume horizontal marginal costs (so that marginal and average cost curves remain conveniently identical), we must allow periodic demands for both products to decline as their prices increase. As is customary, I'll again assume that the company seeks to maximize its immediate, short-run, overall profits, and will use linear demand functions,[3] as follows:

$$q_i = 40 - p_i \qquad q_k = 28 - 2p_k$$

From these, we may obtain:

$$p_i = 40 - q_i \qquad p_k = 14 - \tfrac{1}{2}q_k$$
$$TR_i = 40q_i - q_i{}^2 \qquad TR_k = 14q_k - \tfrac{1}{2}q_k{}^2$$

Therefore, by differentiating TR_i and TR_k, then adding the results:

$$MR_i = 40 - 2q_i$$
$$MR_k = 14 - q_k$$
$$\overline{MR_{ik} = 54 - 3q_{ik}}$$

We also know from Figure 3-1 that:

$$f_i = 9 \qquad J = j_{ik} = 16$$
$$f_k = 5 \qquad F = f_{ik} = 9 + 5 = 14$$
$$MC_{ik} = AC_{ik} = T = J + S = 16 + 14 = 30.$$

Under the marginal approach to joint-cost allocation, our first task is to determine optimal outputs (i.e., to calculate how many batches of pairs of products i and k the company should make in

---

[Wiles, 1963, pp. 114-15] and the note to [Weil, 1968b, pp. 1342-43]; see also the three numbered paragraphs on [p. 1343] and their note. For background to this procedure's literature, see [Colberg, 1941] and [Pfouts, 1961]; for elementary background, see [Harris and Chapin, 1973]. For the literature itself, see[Walters, 1960], [Manes and Smith, 1965], [Weil, 1968b], [Littlechild, 1970b, pp. 326, 329-31], [Hartley, 1971], [Jensen, 1974] and [Bierman and Dyckman, 1971, pp. 168-72, 176-77]. (The last repeats material in [Bierman, 1963, pp. 66-67; 1967, pp. 734-36]). For an approach with similar goals, again see[Harris and Chapin, 1973].

[2] [Bierman and Dyckman, 1971, p. 177].

[3] Readers adept in the calculus may verify that conclusions reached in what follows (and in Chapter Six) remain true for more complex production and demand functions.

order to maximize its immediate, short-run, overall profits). As a trial at calculating these, we first set MC_{ik} equal to MR_{ik} :[4]

$$MC_{ik} = 30 = 54 - 3q_{ik} = MR_{ik}$$
$$3q_{ik} = 24$$
$$q_{ik} = 8.$$

Next, we test whether at $q_i = q_k = 8$ each individual product's marginal revenue exceeds its further-processing cost per batch:

$$MR_i = 40 - 2 \cdot 8 = 24 > 9 = f_i$$
$$MR_k = 14 - 8 = 6 > 5 = f_k.$$

Here, each does and there's no need for further iterations. Accordingly, we divide *total* costs per batch ($J + S = T$) in proportion to batch marginal revenues:

$$t_i = T \cdot MR_i \div MR_{ik} = 30 \cdot 24 \div 30 = \underline{24}$$
$$t_k = T \cdot MR_k \div MR_{ik} = 30 \cdot 6 \div 30 = \underline{6};$$

therefore, the joint-cost allocation per batch is:

$$j_i = 24 - f_i = 24 - 9 = \underline{15}$$
$$j_k = 6 - f_k = 6 - 5 = \underline{1}.$$

Similarly, we may calculate book profits per batch, as follows:

$$p_i = 40 - q_i = 40 - 8 = 32$$
$$p_k = 14 - \tfrac{1}{2}q_k = 14 - 4 = 10;$$

therefore:

$$b_i = 32 - t_i = 32 - 24 = \underline{8}$$
$$b_k = 10 - t_k = 10 - 6 = \underline{4}.$$

Of course, all of these amounts should be multiplied by the calculated output (of 8 batches).

More Complex Situations

Next, let's consider what should be done if a product fails the test of its marginal revenue's exceeding its further-processing cost

---

[4] In the event that q_{ik} is either zero or negative, this indicates that there are no output levels at which the joint process is profitable. For instance, at $J = 110$, $f_i = f_k = 60$, $q_i = 300\text{-}3p_i$ and $q_k = 200\text{-}2p_k$, q_{ik} is a negative 18; readers may verify that, whatever the periodic output, this process cannot be profitable.

at the first iteration's tentative output solution. Such failure is easily arranged here by switching these costs so that $f_i = 5$, $f_k = 9$, and we have the situation depicted in Figure 3-2.

Figure 3-2

Same as Figure 3-1, Except That
Further-Processing Costs
Have Been Switched

J	f_i'	p_i	
	5	?	i
16			
	9	?	k

Readers may verify that MR_{ik} and MC_{ik} remain respectively $54 - 3q_{ik}$ and 30, so that q_{ik} still equals 8. At $q_i = q_k = 8$, $MR_i = 24 > 5 = f_i'$, but $MR_k = 6 < 9 = f_k'$. This last implies that the company should sell less than 8 units of product k. To calculate the output of k that will maximize the company's immediate, short-run, overall profits, we must now equate MR_k with k's further-processing cost:

$$MR_k = 14 - q_k = 9 = f_k'$$
$$q_k = \underline{5}.$$

But, having disregarded the joint cost in so calculating q_k, we must take (all of) it into consideration when calculating q_i:

$$MC_i' = J + f_i' = 16 + 5 = \underline{21}.$$

Setting MC_i equal to MR_i, we now have:

$$MR_i = 40 - 2q_i = 21 = MC_i$$
$$q_i = \underline{9.5.}$$

In other words, since we set $MC_k = f_k' = MR_k = 9$, the marginal approach necessarily (by elimination) allocates the entire joint cost to the product (i) that *didn't* fail the first iteration's test of its marginal revenue's exceeding its further-processing cost at q_{ik}. Thus:

$$j_i = J = \underline{16}$$
$$j_k = \underline{0}.$$

Implications

Given the foregoing, we can specify the marginal approach's main merit (reserving discussion of its other properties for Chapter Six): It allows us to relax assumptions (of constant marginal costs and revenues, and of all-or-nothing further-processing decisions) that are implicit in other approaches. Given our assumptions about central-office wants, whenever marginal costs or revenues vary with output and a company's immediate, short-run, overall profits will be maximized by discarding some (but not all) of at least one joint product at split-off, for an allocation method to be behaviour-congruent with respect to further-processing decisions based on products' book profitabilities it must assign zero joint costs to any product that should be partly (or wholly) discarded—and, in consequence, must assign all of the joint cost to the remaining product(s). The marginal approach does just that.

However, as should be evident from the analysis in Appendix B, whenever two or more products should be entirely further-processed and marketed, the marginal approach's allocations to products that *aren't* discarded possess no special merit. [Manes and Smith, 1965, pp 32-33] explicitly recognizes this for situations where no products are discarded. In effect, so do [Bierman, 1963, p. 67; 1967, p. 736] and [Bierman and Dyckman, 1971, p. 177], by default of saying anything more in favour of this approach than that it's "reasonable."[5]

Since marginal revenues pertain only to the final units sold of each product,[6] there's no reason (beyond the intellectual and, perhaps, status appeals of using a concept enormously useful in other disciplines and arenas of analysis) why marginal revenues *should* dictate joint-cost allocations for all prior units.[7] Anomalies of having them do so become even greater whenever (relaxing what's assumed in the works reviewed in this chapter) marginal costs increase or decline, oligopolistic demand curves are kinked, or when

---

[5]This isn't to deny the possible advantages of a company's making joint-product output decisions via a computationally efficient mathematical-programming approach, such as the linear-programming one advanced by [Hartley, 1971]. Opportunity-cost allocations of joint costs that are similar to marginal ones are by-products of such systems. But, once again, analyzed closely their only virtue here is the congruence property identified in the previous paragraph. Therefore, this book disregards them.

For further background on such mathematical-programming approaches, see [Feltham, 1970, esp. pp. 22-23].

[6]A point explicitly acknowledged by [Bierman, 1967, pp. 736-37].

[7]More generally, the marginal approach's attributions of the qualities of one member of a group (the final, marginal unit) to all other members involves the fallacy of composition—see [Fischer, 1970, p. 219] and [Thomas, 1974, pp. 19-20, 36-40].

one recognizes that, as [Lewis, 1946, pp. 231-33] among others points out, there's no such thing as *the* marginal cost of a product, but only a collection of costs that vary both dynamically and with one's time horizon.

Weil's and Walters' Analyses[8]

Similar observations apply to assertions by Weil [1968b] and Walters [1960]. Let's begin with Weil, and return to our first example, in which MR_i = 24 and MR_k = 6 at the first iteration's q_{ik}. Using different figures (and an imagined situation in which cattle are transformed into beef and hides without any further-processing costs), Weil asked: Suppose that an outside supplier offered to provide either product i or product k to the company. What's the maximum that the company should be willing to pay for either? Traditional analysis gives the obvious answer: No more than their £24 and £6 marginal revenues. From this, Weil would conclude that £24 and £6 are proper allocations of the *costs* of the two products—from which, as we've seen, it would immediately follow that £15 and £1 are proper allocations of the joint cost.

> Cost allocation as dictated by the maximum alternative prices leads to rational decision-making. If nothing else, these costs reveal what outside suppliers can be paid and how an inventory can be valued. If the cattle buyer asks "what is the cost of beef (or hides) alone?" for whatever reason, there is a basis for a justifiable and persuasive answer. —[p. 1343]

The reply is simple. The company *should* base its decisions on the products' marginal revenues, and that's exactly how Weil *has* it make these decisions. But if, for whatever reasons, decision makers base these decisions on allocated book costs, they will make them in ways a profit-maximizing central office would want *if the joint-cost allocation method reliably results in the book costs always equalling the marginal revenues.* As long as outputs are optimal,[9] this always will be possible; and, for this congruence property, the marginal approach is unique.

But please note that (a) this *is* just another instance of behaviour-congruence and (b) "surrounding circumstances" here are somewhat limiting: Companies are more likely to be tracking changing optima than to be occupying one, and whenever a com-

---

[8] The rest of this chapter is addressed to readers who are following this book's argument closely. Others may wish to skip to the beginning of Chapter Four.

[9] In the sense, the reader is reminded, of maximizing immediate, short-run, global profits.

pany misses optimal outputs by a significant margin the congruence breaks down. (For any possible implications in Weil's article that the marginal approach generates optimal price-output decisions in any other way, see [Jensen, 1974, pp. 465, 470, 474-76].)

Walters [1960] proposed basing allocations of joint costs upon products' marginal *expected* costs. These all derive from the following fundamental rule: When the entire output of one or more joint products is sold, whilst only part of the output of one or more other joint products is sold (the rest being discarded at zero cost and revenue), assign the entire joint cost to the former group of products. The purpose of this rule is to find prices and outputs that will maximize the company's expected profits.

These, of course, are identical with the rule and purpose under the marginal approach, and Walters' proposals are simply a sophisticated, probabilistic version of this approach. (It takes a close reading of his entire article to bring this out, but his middle paragraph on [p. 420] and the paragraphs overlapping [pp. 422-23, 426-27] offer initial insight.) It's in this sense, and this only, that we should interpret such claims as, "In the case of fixed proportions, the allocation of joint cost is both rational and necessary in order to find profit-maximizing price and output."[p. 429].[10]

Summary

Wiles [1963, p. 115] dismissed the marginal approach as an "academic exercise". Chapter Six will demonstrate that that goes too far. But it *is* true that, aside from the congruence properties noted there, the marginal approach is an instance of something that I've discussed at length elsewhere: extension of marginal analysis into regions where it's not germane.[11]

---

[10] Similar conclusions pertain to [Smith, 1962], another proposal to allocate joint costs in terms of expectations. [Manes and Smith, 1965, p. 32] provides insight into why this is so; see also [Smith, 1962, pp. 8-10]. Smith [1962, p. 11] observes of his approach, "Essentially this is the sales realization method of cost accounting expressed in terms of expectations." This will be true only when no product is partly discarded.

[11] [Jensen, 1974, pp. 475-76] might be read as asserting an exception. When demand functions are less than completely known, companies may wish to experiment with prices of joint products, adjusting them (via a series of converging, iterative approximations) until their marginal revenues approximately equal their marginal costs. "In such cases, there is justification for an accounting procedure that assigns joint products their marginal costs."–[p. 476].

But, as in note 5, the only virtue of the joint-cost allocation method is its behavior-congruence, albeit what is now a relatively complex congruence.

CHAPTER FOUR

THE SHAPLEY APPROACH

...Molly retired to wet her pillow with a few remorseful tears, and to fall asleep, wondering if real missionaries ever killed their pupils in the process of conversion. —Louisa M. Alcott, *Jack and Jill*

One of the most interesting approaches to joint-cost allocation derives from the theory of cooperative games and, specifically, from the work of L.S. Shapley [1953].[1] [2] As this is written, several substantial articles on Shapley allocations have recently appeared in the accounting literature,[3] and at least one more is forthcoming.[4] But, prior to these, accounting references to Shapley's analysis were rare, indirect, and had little apparent impact.[5] Perhaps, as Littlechild and Owen [1973, p. 370] point out, this

---

[1] See also [Luce and Raiffa, 1957, esp. pp. 192-96, 245-52], [Shubik, 1962 or 1964], [Mossin, 1968], [Shapley and Shubik, 1969a], [Littlechild, 1970a], [Loehman and Whinston, 1971 and 1974], [Littlechild and Owen, 1973], [Hamlen, Hamlen and Tschirhart, 1977], [Jensen, 1977] and [Roth and Verrecchia, 1977]. For an elaboration and additional bibliographical references, see [Littlechild, 1975, esp. pp. 117, 121]; the pricing problems discussed by the author are easily recast as joint-costing problems. The related game-theory approaches are methods for determining distributions of resources in economic systems; for the relationship between these approaches and economists' traditional (competitive-market) approaches to resource-distribution, see [Scarf, 1967, pp. 50-51]. For a survey of game theory, aimed at the nonspecialist and offering a broad introduction to its literature, see [Lucas, 1972, esp. pp. P·12-15]; the basic work here, of course, is [Neumann and Morgenstern, 1953].

[Buchanan, 1965] and [Pauly, 1967] are excellent introductions to the problem that Shapley tackled, and to why his solution is appealing. For examples of the sorts of perplexities of economists out of which Shapley's approach arose, see [Coase, 1946, pp. 169-73] and [Wiseman, 1957, esp. pp. 64-68]. [Loehman and Whinston, 1971, p. 610] explains the former's relevance.

[2] Loehman and Whinston [1971, pp. 613n-14n] maintain that their work is independent of Shapley's. But the formula that they use is identical to his and, when implicit assumptions are considered, so are their axioms. Since Shapley has priority, Loehman and Whinston's 1971 and 1974 work is best perceived as an interpretation of his analysis beyond the game-theoretic context in which he performed it. For differences between the two approaches, see [Loehman and Whinston, 1974, p. 251]; for a derivation of their approach from axioms, see [pp. 239-46].

[Loehman and Whinston, 1976] is a generalization of both their 1971 and 1974 approach and Shapley's; for a comment on this generalization, see the end of Appendix E, below.

[3] For instance, [Hamlen, Hamlen and Tschirhart, 1977], [Hughes and Scheiner, 1977], [Jensen, 1977] and [Callen, 1978].

[4] [Roth and Verrecchia, 1977].

[5] See [Samuels, 1965, pp. 182, 191], [Bierman and Dyckman, 1971, p. 182], [Amey and Egginton, 1973, p. 266] and [Abdel-khalik and Lusk, 1974, pp. 21-22]. The references are all to [Shubik, 1964], not to Shapley's work *per se*.

was because of the approach's enormous computational demands in some situations.[6] Yet:

1. Computer capabilities continue to expand, and, anyway, computational difficulties have nothing directly to do with theory,[7]

2. As Littlechild and Owen [1973] and Jensen [1977, pp. 849-54] show, Shapley calculations can be much simplified in individual situations,

3. As traditionally conceived, joint-cost allocation often affords such a situation, and

4. Both the Shapley approach and its variants (one of whose calculations are childishly simple) have congruence properties that render them of considerable potential practical interest.

For brevity, this chapter will concentrate on a single variant (based on [Shubik, 1964]) whose properties are especially good.

Jargon

It will speed description of the Shapley approach to introduce some additional notation and terminology.[8] Figure 4-1 describes three discontinuous production functions for the same inputs and production period.[9] I'll begin by discussing only production functions 1 and 2, saving number 3 for later. Here, A and B are two inputs, with θ representing the null case of no input whatever. The C columns show all possible input combinations, or *coalitions* (where a coalition may have one or no member). The v's are the deterministic[10] *values* of each coalition, here the maximum[11] output that each can produce.

---

[6] See also [Davidson, 1964, pp. 238-39]. Anton [1964, pp. 233-36] raised another possible reason: Shapley's analysis is based on a theory of cooperative games in which players freely form coalitions to advance their joint interests, then bargain to divide the proceeds. This description doesn't fit the actual circumstances of business life as well as one might wish. However, that has nothing to do with the behaviour-congruence of Shapley allocations with respect to certain goals, decisions and circumstances (discussed in Chapter Six). As Jonathan Edwards put it, we judge by fruits, not roots.

[7] Calculation of Shapley values for two factors is trivial; calculation for three to five factors is within the capacities of card-programmable slide-rule calculators if, in some cases, one is willing to enter data repetitively or in unaesthetic ways.

[8] I'll follow [Mossin, 1968] loosely, using a simplified notation. The following discussion is intuitive, not rigourous, since several of the works cited in note 1 provide adequate rigour.

[9] This figure is based on [Thomas, 1971b, p. 475], where the inputs were graders and the output was graded examinations.

[10] For a literature in which coalition values aren't deterministic (but, rather, random variables with given distribution and functions) see [Granot, 1977].

[11] See, for instance, [Sorenson, Tschirhart and Whinston, 1976, p. 499].

Figure 4-1

Three Related Production Functions

Function 1		Function 2		Function 3	
C	$v'(C)$	C	$v''(C)$	C	$v(C)$
θ	0	θ	0	θ	0
A	5	A	0	A	5
B	3	B	0	B	3
AB	8	AB	4	AB	12

In production function 1, inputs A and B can individually produce 5 and 3 units of output per period; working together, they can produce 8. In function 2, neither A nor B generate anything individually, but together they can produce 4 units of output per period (situations where both inputs are essential are instances of this kind of production function). Readers will notice that I've concocted things so that all coalition values are non-negative, and so that in both functions output is zero whenever both inputs are absent (the null, θ case). I'll discuss these assumptions later.

Figure 4-1's tabulations of all possible coalitions and values are called the *characteristic functions* of these production functions. Because of the game-theoretic origins of this approach, what I call production functions other authors call *games* (or *games in characteristic function form*). Readers may verify that game 1 is *additive*: in it, output generated by the two inputs working together exactly equals the total of the outputs that they'd produce working separately (8 = 5 + 3). In contrast, game 2 is *superadditive*: the output of its two inputs working together exceeds the sum of their separate outputs (4 > 0 + 0), and results from positive interaction of the two inputs. I've argued elsewhere that almost all real-world, business production functions are superadditive to some degree; game 2 is wholly so.

We need one final concept to speed later analysis: a *0-additive game*.[12] Figure 4-2 illustrates such a game, which is superadditive. Here, coalitions of 0 and 1 member uniformly have zero coalition values, whereas the sum of the values of the three 2-member coalitions equals the value of the 3-member coalition (26 + 8 + 14 = 48). Generalizing this example, I'll call any n-loci game *0-additive* if, for $k < (n - 1)$, all values for coalitions of up through k members are zero, and all values for coalitions of $k + 1$ through n members are additive.

[12] The term *0-additive* is a neologism; some game theorists would, at the least, regard the concept defined below as aesthetically abominable.

Figure 4-2

A 0-Additive Game

Number of Coalition Members	C	v(C)
0	θ	0
1	K	0
	L	0
	M	0
2	KL	26
	KM	8
	LM	14
3	KLM	48

Shapley Allocation Rules

So much for notation and terminology. Applications of Shapley's analysis to business situations follow the [Barnard, 1938]–[Simon, 1957] strategy of perceiving companies to be coalitions of individual factor suppliers. In effect, Shapley and his followers ask what allocation rules will reliably encourage coalitions that benefit the company as a whole (we'll consider exceptions to this later). Two rules immediately suggest themselves:[13]

Rule 1. Allocate joint outputs of additive games according to the separate effects of their individual inputs. Thus, in production function 1, attribute 5 units of output to input A and 3 to B.

Rule 2. Allocate interaction effects of superadditive games evenly among fungible inputs. Thus, in function 2, attribute 2 units of output to A and 2 to B.

The simplest rationale for Rule 1 is the behavioural one that unless each input factor receives at least its separate effects it has no reason to remain in the coalition—and that, if forced to remain, this may be at a cost in dysfunctional behavior. Although Rule 2 is intuitively attractive (for reasons that parallel Bernoulli's Princi-

---

[13] For more rigourous rules, see [Mossin, 1968, pp. 464-66], [Loehman and Whinston, 1974, pp. 238-39] and, of course, [Shapley, 1953, p. 309]. See [Jensen, 1977, pp. 843-45] for a clear exposition of Shapley's and Loehman and Whinston's axioms. For an alternative (and superficially very different) set of axioms under which the Shapley approach can be applied to joint-cost allocations, see [Roth and Verrecchia, 1977, pp. 10-13]. In the draft of the latter cited, the authors' third assumption involves an additional, implicit assumption that no coalition values need to be raised to zero to satisfy the fifth rule given below. Since this latter assumption is apt to be counter-factual, their approach's applicability seems limited.

ple), three caveats are necessary. First, although Rule 2 is applicable to joint-cost allocations, it's not necessarily appropriate for all allocations to which the Shapley approach might be applied[14] (however, Appendix D shows that its applicability is greater than one might at first suppose). Second, the word *fungible* is vital to Rule 2. In function 2 nothing distinguishes the two inputs except their labels. We could switch these labels without affecting its characteristic function (something *not* true of function 1). Rule 2 applies only to such fungible situations.

In order to discuss Figure 4-1's function 3, we need a third rule:

Rule 3. Presuppose that Rules 1 and 2 indicate how to allocate the individual outputs of two games, and that some third game is the union of these two *constituent games.* Then the amount of output that should be allocated to each of the union game's inputs equals the sum of what should be allocated to that input in each of the constituent games.

Production function 3 is the union of functions 1 and 2. Following Rule 3, we should allocate $5 + 2 = 7$ units of output to function 3's input A, and $3 + 2 = 5$ to B.[15] If supplemented by additional rules (discussed below), Rule 3 makes it possible to calculate a Shapley allocation in any (traditional) joint-cost situation by decomposing it into additive and superadditive games, determining appropriate Rule 1 and Rule 2 allocations, then reuniting the games.[16] [17]

An Example

Here's a simple example. Figure 4-3 shows a three-product joint process. It's impossible, at least in the short run, for the company to buy any of these products externally, something that I reflect by setting all x_i's equal to infinity. As before, all proportions are fixed, but all joint costs can be escaped by total shutdown. The

---

[14] [Jensen, 1977] discusses, and [Shubik, 1964] illustrates, this.

[15] This is allocation procedure 4 in [Thomas, 1971b, p. 475].

[16] When decomposing games under the approach described here, it's essential that the resulting subgames be either strictly additive, like function 1, or strictly superadditive, like function 2. That's to say, either the inputs' separate effects should exactly add up to the total output or they should equal zero. Otherwise, it will "be impossible to obtain the solution to the original game as the sum of the solutions to the subgames." –[Mossin, 1968, p. 465].

[17] Be warned that this need not be true for interactions more complex than those traditionally considered in joint-cost allocation–for instance, see [Mossin, 1968, p. 462]. Moreover, my exposition deliberately disregards a difficulty discussed in [Luce and Raiffa, 1957, pp. 251-52].

left part of Figure 4-4 shows this process' characteristic function. (As a technical point, there are two ways to calculate coalition values here; we'll consider the other later in this chapter.)

Figure 4-3
A Three-Product Joint Process

J	n_i	f_i	p_i		x_i
	32	38	70	W	∞
12	62	24	86	X	∞
	14	30	44	Y	∞
	108				
	N				

Figure 4-4
Characteristic Functions for
Figure 4-3's Joint Process

The Original Function		Decomposition of the Original Function			
C	$v(C)$	C	$v'(C)$	C	$v''(C)$
θ	0^1	θ	0	θ	0
W	20	W	20	W	0^6
X	50^2	X	50	X	0
Y	2	Y	2	Y	0
WX	82^3	WX	70^4	WX	12^7
WY	34	WY	22	WY	12
XY	64	XY	52	XY	12
WXY	96	WXY	72^5	WXY	24

[1] By definition.
[2] $n_X \cdot J = 62\text{-}12 = \underline{50.}$
[3] $n_W + n_X \cdot J = 32 + 62\text{-}12 = \underline{82.}$
[4] $v'(W) + v'(X) = 20 + 50 = \underline{70.}$
[5] $v'(W) + v'(X) + v'(Y) = 20 + 50 + 2 = \underline{72.}$
[6] $v(W) - v'(W) = 20\text{-}20 = \underline{0.}$
[7] $v(WX) - v'(WX) = 82\text{-}70 = \underline{12.}$

For instance, the original function's £20 value for the single-member coalition W equals the revenue from making a single batch of product W (p_w = £70) less the cost of running the joint process to produce only that one product (discarding products Y and Z at split-off, much as when calculating Moriarity's y_i in Chapter Two): $J + s_w$ = £12 + £38 = £50. Figure 4-4 shows parallel calculations for v(X) and v(WX). Please note, for future reference, that it's important that a characteristic function always reflect the *maximum* (output, profit, whatever) that could be generated under each input combination.[18]

We may decompose this characteristic function into the additive, $v'(C)$, and superadditive, $v''(C)$, ones shown on the right. For $v'(C)$, Rule 1 allocates their £20, £50 and £2 separate effects to products W, X and Y and their combinations. Inspection of $v''(C)$ reveals the three products to be fungible: no change of labelling will alter this game's characteristic function. Therefore, Rule 2 indicates that we should allocate the WXY coalition's £96 - (£20 + £50 + £2) = £24 interaction effect equally among the three products: £8 apiece.[19] Using Rule 3 to reunite $v'(C)$ and $v''(C)$, the Shapley profit allocation for our original v(C) is:

$$
\begin{aligned}
b_W &= 20 + 8 = 28 \\
b_X &= 50 + 8 = 58 \\
b_Y &= 2 + 8 = \underline{10} \\
B &= 108 - 12 = \underline{\underline{96}}
\end{aligned}
$$

with an associated joint-cost allocation of £12 ÷ 3 = £4 per product:

Product	p_i	-	f_i	-	b_i	=	j_i
W	70		38		28		4
X	86		24		58		4
Y	44		30		10		4
Total	200		92		96		12

(This version of the Shapley approach allocates *book profits*; its assignments of joint costs are merely consequences of this.) Appendix C uses the canonical Shapley formula to reach the same result.

A Fourth Rule

All of the previous example's coalition values were nonnegative. Though it may initially sound rather abstract, the next rule will help us cope with situations where this isn't so:

---

[18] See [Shubik, 1964, pp. 207, 214].

[19] Please note that the only significance of the £0 and £12 values for $v''(C)$'s one- and two-product coalitions is to reveal product fungibility. Since the company is producing all three products, it's the £24 *three*-product interaction effect that we must allocate.

Rule 4. Any additive game of n loci (n > 1) may be decomposed into n additive games of n-1 loci. In turn, any corresponding n additive constituent games of n-1 loci may be reunited into the original n-loci additive game. The same holds true of any 0-additive game where n > 2.

For instance, let's consider the simple, additive game:

C	v(C)
θ	0
X	7
Y	9
XY	16

As long as we're assured that everything is additive, we obtain identical information from the two games:

Cl	v(Cl)	C2	v(C2)
θ	0	θ	0
X	7	Y	9

For, given additivity, v(XY) must equal 7 + 9 = 16.

Similarly, the 0-additive game:

C0	v(C0)	C0	v(C0)
θ	0	KL	26
K	0	KM	8
L	0	LM	14
M	0	KLM	48

may be decomposed into the three games shown at the top of Figure 4-5. Since the inputs to each of these three games are fungible, Rule 2 indicates that we should allocate their interaction effects as shown at the bottom of Figure 4-5. Finally, Rule 3 indicates that Figure 4-5's bottom right-hand column gives the Shapley allocation for the original, reunited game, 0 (once again, Appendix C reaches the same result via the canonical Shapley formula).

Nonnegativity of Coalition Values

Thus far, I've deliberately chosen examples whose coalition values are either zero or positive. This may be generalized:

Rule 5. All coalition values of union games must be nonnegative. This rule follows automatically from our dealing with coalitions of divisions managers (or other company actors), and from our earlier observation that a coalition value must be

Figure 4-5

Decomposition of a 0-Additive Game and
Allocation of Its Interaction Effects

		Decomposition			
Cl	v(C1)	C2	v(C2)	C3	v(C3)
θ	0	θ	0	θ	0
K	0	K	0	L	0
L	0	M	0	M	0
KL	26	KM	8	LM	14

Allocation

	Game			
Locus	1	2	3	Total
K	13	4		17
L	13		7	20
M		4	7	11
Total	26	8	14	48

the *maximum* that the coalition can produce.[20] Let's suppose
instead that we tentatively calculated a particular coalition value
to be negative. In the real world, the coalition could, at least potentially, always increase its value to zero simply by withdrawing from the process. Therefore, the negative value *can't* be the
maximum output that the related coalition can produce. And
from this it immediately follows that coalition values must be
nonnegative, and that those that initially are negative must be
raised to zero.[21]

Please note, though, that by the same logic this rule need apply
only to "real" games whose Shapley allocations we're trying to
calculate, and with whose players' behavior we're concerned. It
need not apply to any imaginary games into which we may decompose them. That's why the rule specifies that it pertains only to
union games.

An Example

Here's an example. The top part of Figure 4-6 shows a joint
process identical to the one in Figure 4-3 except that the joint cost

---

[20] It's also consistent with something mentioned earlier: the various modern theories
of organization and management that stem from [Barnard, 1938] –e.g., those in [Simon,
1957].

[21] See [Neumann and Morganstein, 1953, p. 240] and [Schmeidler, 1969, p. 1163].

Figure 4-6

Same as Figure 4-3, Except That J is
Now £40, and the Characteristic Function is Tentative

J	n_i	f_i	p_i		x_i
	32	38	70	W	∞
40*	62	24	86	X	∞
	14	30	44	Y	∞

*Changed from Figure 4-3.

C	v (C)	C	v (C)
θ	0	WX	54
W	(8)	WY	6
X	22	XY	36
Y	(26)	WXY	68

per batch is now £40 instead of £12. Except for $v(\theta)$, which always equals zero, its coalition values are all £40 − £12 = £28 less than they were in Figure 4-4. Alternatively, its £26 loss for v(Y) may be calculated as follows: Were Y the only division participating in the joint process it would incur a £40 joint cost plus a £30 further-processing cost, for a per-batch total of £70. This would be partly offset by a £44 revenue, for a net loss of £26 per batch.

But this single-member coalition could do better: it can refuse to engage in such an unprofitable activity at all, thereby cutting its loss to zero. Similar remarks apply to the (single-member) W coalition. Therefore, the correct characteristic function is really the

Figure 4-7

Correct Characteristic Function and Initial
Decomposition for Figure 4-6's Joint Process

The Correct Original Function		Initial Decomposition of This Original Function			
C0	v(C0)	C1	v(C1)	C2	v(C2)
θ	0	θ	0	θ	0
W	0	W	0	W	0
X	22	X	22	X	0
Y	0	Y	0	Y	0
WX	54	WX	22	WX	32
WY	6	WY	0	WY	6
XY	36	XY	22	XY	14
WXY	68	WXY	22	WXY	46

one shown in Figure 4-7's left-hand columns. Figure 4-7 also decomposes the correct original game 0 into additive game 1 and superadditive game 2.

Next, we decompose game 2 into super-additive game 3 and 0-additive game 4, as shown in Figure 4-8. Since the "real" (game 0) WXY coalition value is nonnegative, there are no possible perverse behavioural consequences to imaginary game 3's WXY coalition value being negative. Therefore, Rule 5 is irrelevant to game 3 (and to decomposition games, generally).

Figure 4-8

Decomposition of Figure 4-7's Game 2

C3	v(C3)	C4	v(C4)
θ	0	θ	0
W	0	W	0
X	0	X	0
Y	0	Y	0
WX	0	WX	32
WY	0	WY	6
XY	0	XY	14
WXY	(6)	WXY	52

Using Rule 4, it's now possible to decompose 0-additive game 4 into the three 2-loci subgames 5 through 7 shown in Figure 4-9. Finally, under Rules 1 through 3 we may calculate our original game 0's Shapley allocations, as shown in Figure 4-10. It is important to note that the Shapley values in the top right corner of Figure 4-10 are allocations (b_i) of the total batch *profit* (B = £32 + £62 + £14 − £40 = £68). The bottom part of Figure 4-10 shows the related Shapley total-cost (t_i) and joint-cost (j_i) allocations.

Figure 4-9

Decomposition of Figure 4-8's Game 4

C5	v(C5)	C6	v(C6)	C7	v(C7)
θ	0	θ	0	θ	0
W	0	W	0	X	0
X	0	Y	0	Y	0
WX	32	WY	6	XY	14

The Value of the Null Coalition Must be Zero

Readers who wish to experiment with Shapley values should be aware of an additional rule:

Rule 6. The value of the null coalition, $v(\theta)$, must equal zero. Here's a simple demonstration: A joint process costs £14 per batch and yields joint products, A and B, whose batch net realizable values are £15 and £20, respectively. Presuppose that $v(\theta) = \lambda$. We then have:

$v(\theta)$ $= \lambda$

$v(A)$ $= 15 - 14 = 1$

$v(B)$ $= 20 - 14 = 6$

$v(AB) = 20 + 15 - 14 = 21.$

Using Appendix C's canonical Shapley formula, we obtain:

$b_A = \tfrac{1}{2}[(1 - \lambda) + (21 - 6)] = \ \ 8 - \lambda \div 2$

$b_B = \tfrac{1}{2}[(6 - \lambda) + (21 - 1)] = \underline{13 - \lambda \div 2}$

Total $\underline{\underline{21 - \lambda}}$

This total will equal the global, £21, profit only when $\lambda = 0$. Thus, insofar as a company can't escape joint costs by total shutdown, *the Shapley approach can't allocate them.*[22]

Figure 4-10

Calculations of Shapley Values and Joint-Cost
Allocations for Figure 4-6's Joint Process (Game 0)

Locus	Game 1	3	5	6	7	Total Shapley Value
W		(2)	16	3		17
X	22	(2)	16		7	43
Y		(2)		3	7	8
Total	22	(6)	32	6	14	68

Product	b_i (from above)	t_i $(= p_i - b_i)$	j_i $(= t_i - f_i)$
W	17	53	15
X	43	43	19
Y	8	36	6
Total	68	132	40

[22] See [Loehman and Whinston, 1974, p. 239] for generalization of my example.

Even Division of Interaction Effects

By now, our intuitive approach to calculating Shapley allocations has become cumbersome; readers are invited to use the canonical one in Appendix C.[23] But before we leave the intuitive approach, we should focus on one important characteristic of Shapley allocations that's a consequence of Rule 2: *they always divide interaction effects evenly among loci.* For instance, we've seen them divide game 3's £(6) interaction effect evenly among the three loci that it involved, and game 7's £14 interaction effect evenly between *its* two loci. Similarly, the Shapley allocation for Figure 4-1's production function divided its £4 interaction effect evenly between inputs A and B. This will always be so,[24] even in the complex situations discussed in Appendix D. It has three important consequences:

1. Readers may verify from Appendix C that each time the number of loci increases by one, the number of terms used in canonical Shapley calculations doubles. Therefore, if a mere 20 inputs affected an output (or if a joint process generated 20 outputs), formula calculation of each factor's share would require dividing 20! into 2^{19} = 524,288 expressions, each of which was the result of multiplying two other factorial expressions by the difference between two coalition values.

However, as the foregoing and Appendix D illustrate, such enormous calculations can often be reduced to a much smaller number of assignments of separate effects and even divisions of interaction effects. That's why I'm confident that clever programming can overcome the Shapley approach's computational complexities. Loehman and Whinston [1971], Littlechild and Owen [1973] and Jensen [1977, pp. 849-54] discuss other circumstances in which Shapley calculations can be simplified, or in which they reduce to other, more familiar, allocation schemes.

---

[23] It should be emphasized again that I've described a *simplified* version of the Shapley approach, designed for joint-cost situations as we accountants traditionally conceive them. As an example of a less conventional conception, Shubik [1964, pp. 218-19] assigns profits to a central office as well as to the joint-product divisions. In any event, my simplifications aren't necessarily appropriate for other kinds of internal allocations or for such things as non-zero split-off values.

[24] See [Luce and Raiffa, 1957, p. 249] and [Jensen, 1977, p. 855].

2. Whenever all coalition values are nonnegative, the Shapley approach also splits *joint costs* evenly among divisions.[25] This makes intuitive sense, too: Shapley allocations specify nothing in advance about players or (non-negativity excepted) circumstances. Thus, we should *expect* results from them that parallel applications of Bernoulli's Principle. This basic naïveté and indifference to the facts of any given allocation situation should make us skeptical of the Shapley approach's utility in any decision situations outside of the relatively narrow game-theoretic ones for which it was designed. These suspicions will be verified in Chapters Six and Ten, and Appendix I.

3. In light of the foregoing, one is tempted to chuck Rule 5 and adopt the simple dictate: Divide all joint costs evenly among divisions. I denote this the *Democratic* approach. In Figure 4-6's situation, with its £40 joint cost, the Democratic approach allocates £40 ÷ 3 ≅ £13.33 of joint cost to each product, giving us:

Product	j_i	t_i	b_i
W	13.33	51.33	18.67
X	13.33	37.33	48.67
Y	13.33	43.33	0.67
Total	40.00	132.00	68.00

[25] For instance, using the notation developed in Appendix C and earlier chapters, if there are three loci, X, Y and Z:

$$v(XY) = v(X) + v(Y) + J$$
$$v(XZ) = v(X) + v(Z) + J$$
$$v(YZ) = v(Y) + v(Z) + J$$
$$v(XYZ) = v(X) + v(Y) + v(Z) + 2J$$
$$n_X = v(X) + J$$

$$b_X = n_X - j_X = v(X) + J - j_X; \text{ therefore,}$$
$$j_X = v(X) + J - b_X.$$

Substituting the Shapley value for b_X, we obtain:

$$
\begin{aligned}
j_X &= v(X) + J - [1 \div 3!] \cdot [0! \cdot 2! \cdot \{v(X) - v(\theta)\} + 1! \cdot 1! \cdot \{v(XY) - \\
&\quad v(Y)\} + 1! \cdot 1! \cdot \{v(XZ) - v(Z)\} + 2! \cdot 0! \cdot \{v(XYZ) - v(YZ)\}] \\
&= v(X) + J - [1 \div 6] \cdot [2 \cdot \{v(X) - 0\} + \{v(X) + v(Y) + J - v(Y)\} + \{v(X) + \\
&\quad v(Z) + J - v(Z)\} + 2 \cdot \{v(X) + v(Y) + v(Z) + 2J - v(Y) - v(Z) - J\}] \\
&= [1 \div 6] \cdot [6 \cdot v(X) + 6J - \{2 \cdot v(X) + (v(X) + J) + (v(X) + J) + 2 \cdot \\
&\quad (v(X) + J)\}] \\
&= [1 \div 6] \cdot [6 \cdot v(X) + 6J - (\{6 \cdot v(X)\} + 4J)] \\
&= J \div 3.
\end{aligned}
$$

It should be obvious from the foregoing that a full proof could be developed via mathematical induction.

(all totals adjusted for a 1¢ cumulative rounding error). Readers may verify that these results are identical to what the Shapley approach would generate were one to discard Rule 5.[26] Chapter Six compares the properties of the Shapley and Democratic approaches.[27]

Alternative External Sources for Products

Up to now, we've assumed that, for all products, $x_i = \infty$—that's to say, that the only way a company can acquire any joint product is to obtain it from the joint process itself. Thus, $v(X) = n_X - J$, $v(XY) = n_X + n_Y - J$, and so forth. In particular, were the company to acquire only product X, that would cost it $J + f_X = £40 + £24 = £64$, for a batch profit of $£86 - £64 = £22$, Figure 4-6's $v(X)$.

However, in Chapter Two we saw Moriarity [1975; 1976] suggest another, more likely, possibility: that it is possible for the company to buy joint products externally (presumably, in a market to which its own customers don't have access). Let's now suppose that it could do so for the following per-batch costs:

$$x_W = 52$$
$$x_X = 53$$
$$x_Y = 86.$$

For simplicity, we'll also continue Moriarity's implicit assumption that there are no cost savings to buying two or more different products together (though, actually, the Shapley approach has no difficulty in handling such savings).

Readers may verify that the company will still maximize its batch profits (at £68) by *not* buying any of the products. Nonetheless, the availability of these external sources of supply changes the company's coalition values. Figure 4-11 is a *tentative* calculation of the characteristic function for this new situation. Each coalition value attempts to reflect the maximum that its particular coalition could earn. However, Figure 4-11 overlooks something.

The WY coalition could earn more than £6 per batch by adopting a simple stratagem: have Division Y become inactive, thereby

---

[26]But continued to assume that all joint costs would be escaped by total shutdown.

[27]Since total profit on a joint process is also an interaction effect, one could apply a democratic rule to *it*: Divide global profits evenly among divisions. However, it turns out that this approach has few desirable properties for joint-cost allocation. To save time, interested readers are invited to verify this after they've read Chapter Six.

obtaining the W coalition's £18. Since, by definition, a coalition value is the maximum that a coalition can earn, this means that v(WY) really equals £18.[28] This may be generalized:

Rule 7. No coalition value is ever less than what the most profitable subcoalition of the coalition members could earn.

Figure 4-12 shows the corrected characteristic function and Shapley allocations (the latter being calculated according to Appendix C's formula).

Figure 4-11

Tentative Calculation of the Characteristic
Function for a Situation Where a
Company Can Buy a Joint Product Externally

Product	p_i	f_i	x_i	J
W	70	38	52	
X	86	24	53	
Y	44	30	86	
Total	200	92	191	40

C	v(C)	C	v(C)
θ	0^1	WX	54^5
W	18^2	WY	6^6
X	33^3	XY	36^7
Y	0^4	WXY	68^8

^{1}By Rule 6.

$^2\max|(p_w - J - f_w), (p_w - x_w), 0| = \max|(8), 18, 0| = \underline{18}.$

$^3\max|22, 33, 0| = \underline{33}.$

$^4\max|(26), (42), 0| = \underline{0}.$

$^5\max|(p_w + p_x - J - f_w - f_x), (p_w + p_x - J - f_w - x_x), (p_w + p_x - J - x_w - f_x),$
$(p_w + p_x - x_w - x_x), 0| = \max|54, 25, 40, 51, 0| = \underline{54}.$

$^6\max|6, (50), (8), (24), 0| = \underline{6}.$

$^7\max|36, (20), 7, (9), 0| = \underline{36}.$

$^8\max|68, 12, 39, 54, (17), (2), 25, 9, 0| = \underline{68}.$

[28]We can reach the same conclusion on behavioural grounds. Division W would never willingly engage in a two-member coalition with Division Y were it to be credited with less than what it could earn on its own. But at any coalition value less than £18, avoiding such diminishment of W's book profits would require assigning negative earnings to Division Y. Yet Rule 5 implies that no division need ever accept that, either. So, £18 must be the minimum value of the WY coalition. Since nothing in Figure 4-11 makes the coalition value *exceed* £18, this minimum must also be the maximum.

Figure 4-12

Correct Characteristic Function and Shapley
Allocations for the Situation in Figure 4-11

C	v(C)	C	v(C)
θ	0	WX	54
W	18	WY	18*
X	33	XY	36
Y	0	WXY	68

*Changed from Figure 4-11.

Product	j_i	t_i	b_i
W	8.83	46.83	23.17
X	22.33	46.33	39.67
Y	8.83	38.83	5.17
Total	40.00^1	132.00^1	68.00^1

[1] Corrected for a 1¢ cumulative rounding error.

Complications[29]

In all previous examples, for all products $f_i < x_i$. We need an additional rule if one or more $f_i \geqslant x_i$. To illustrate this, let's now suppose that x_W declines from £52 to £36. Figure 4-13 shows the resulting new characteristic function and Shapley allocations if both are calculated rather naïvely. In particular, please note that v(WXY) reflects that the most profitable thing that the company can now do is to manufacture products X and Y, but buy product W from outsiders, for a per-batch profit of $p_W + p_X + p_Y - x_W - J - f_X - f_Y = 70 + 86 + 44 - 36 - 40 - 24 - 30 = 70.$

It's immediately obvious that Figure 4-13's allocations just don't add up—for instance, $j_W + j_X + j_Y = 38 \neq 40 = J$. To resolve these inconsistencies, we add another rule, one that corresponds to what the Louderback, JIM and JIL approaches do whenever $f_i \geqslant x_i$:

Rule 8. Whenever $f_i \geqslant x_i$, set $j_i = 0$; apply Rules 1 through 7 to the remaining products only.

Figure 4-14 follows this rule (using the formula in Appendix C).

[29] I've deliberately chosen this section's examples so as to be able to delay discussion of certain additional complications until Chapter Six's discussions of its Cases C, D and E. Moreover, readers are warned that, in keeping with the simplification made at the beginning of this chapter, I have chosen Rules 8 and 9 purely so as to give Shapley allocations as good congruence properties as possible. For all I know, these rules would distress a game theorist; certainly, I'm unable to cite any authority for them.

Figure 4-13

Same as Figures 4-11 and 4-12,
Except That $f_w > x_w$

(Calculations are deliberately naïve)

Product	p_i	f_i	x_i	J
W	70	38	36	
X	86	24	53	
Y	44	30	86	
Total	200	92	175	40

C	v(C)	C	v(C)
θ	0	WX	67
W	34	WY	34*
X	33	XY	36
Y	0	WXY	70

*Figure 4-11's approach would give v(WY) = 8; but since v(W) = 34, Rule 7 specifies that v(WY) = 34.

Product	j_i	t_i	b_i
W	(2.00)	36.00	34.00
X	27.50	51.50	34.50
Y	12.50	42.50	1.50
Total	38.00	130.00	70.00
	$\neq$J	$\neq$T	$\neq$B

Figure 4-14

Correct Characteristic Function and Shapley
Allocations for the Situation in Figure 4-13

C	v(C)
θ	0
X	33
Y	0
XY	36

Product	j_i	t_i	b_i
W	0.00[1]	38.00[2]	32.00[3]
X	27.50	51.50	34.50
Y	12.50	42.50	1.50
Total	40.00	132.00	68.00
	J	T	B

[1] By Rule 8.
[2] $j_w + f_w = 0.00 + 38.00 = 38.00$.
[3] $p_w - t_w = 70.00 - 38.00 = 32.00$.

We should consider one final complication. In Chapter Two, three of the main example's joint products had positive net realizable values, but the fourth did not. We have yet to discuss the Shapley approach when a product's net realizable value is nonpositive.

Certainly, such products (or divisions) are undesirable members of joint-production coalitions: if their net realizable values are zero, these products do nothing to increase total profits; if negative, they actually *de*crease them. The rationale for our Rule 5 (that all coalition values of union games must be nonnegative) was that were they not, a coalition could increase its value to zero merely by disbanding. Similarly, no coalition would ever willingly include a product whose net realizable value is nonpositive;[30] therefore, such products should be treated as they are under the JIM and JIL approaches: assigned zero joint costs (and, consequently, zero or negative book profits), with the Shapley approach *per se* applied only to the remaining (positive-net-realizable-value) products.

Rule 9. Whenever $n_i \leqslant 0$, set $j_i = 0$; apply Rules 1 through 8 to the remaining products only.

To illustrate, let's add undesirable product Z to the three products in Figures 4-11 and 4-12:

Product	p_i	f_i	n_i	x_i	J
W	70	38	32	52	
X	86	24	62	53	
Y	44	30	14	86	
Z	42	49	(7)	78	
Total	242	141	101	269	40

Figure 4-15 gives the resulting characteristic function and Shapley allocations. Finally, Figure 4-16 presents these for the joint process that's illustrated in Figures 2-1 and 2-2.

Cost-Based Characteristic Functions

I mentioned earlier that several variations on the Shapley approach are possible. The version that we've pursued bases its characteristic functions on the net profits that coalitions and subcoalitions could earn. This, of course, requires attending both to selling

---

[30] For instance, this seems an obvious implication of the passage from [Shapley, 1953, p. 316] that's quoted at the beginning of Appendix E. For how could (or why would) a player, on admission to a coalition, demand a zero or negative amount that his/her admission contributed to that coalition?

Figure 4-15

Same as Figure 4-12, Except That
There Is Now Also an Undesirable Product

C	v(C)	C	v(C)
θ	0^5	WX	54^5
W	18^5	WY	18^5
X	33^5	XY	36^5
Y	0^5	WXY	68^5

Product	j_i	t_i	b_i
W	8.83^5	46.83^5	23.17^5
X	22.33^5	46.33^5	39.67^5
Y	8.83^5	38.83^5	5.17^5
Z	0.00^2	49.00^3	$(7.00)^4$
Total	40.00^1	181.00^1	61.00^1

[1] Corrected for a 1¢ cumulative rounding error.
[2] By Rule 9.
[3] $t_z = j_z + f_z = 0.00 + 49.00 = \underline{49.00}$.
[4] $b_z = p_z - t_z = 42.00 - 49.00 = \underline{(7.00)}$.
[5] Same as Figure 4-12.

Figure 4-16

Characteristic Function and Shapley Allocation
For the Joint Process in Figures 2-1 and 2-2

Product	p_i	f_i	n_i	x_i	J
R	21	7	14	18	
U	10	12	(2)	13	
V	18	15	3	11	
W	13	5	8	22	
Total	62	39	23	64	9

C	v(C)
θ	0
R	5
W	0
RW	13

Product	j_i	t_i	b_i
R	5.00	12.00	9.00
U	0.00^1	12.00	(2.00)
V	0.00^2	15.00	3.00
W	4.00	9.00	4.00
Total	9.00	48.00	14.00

[1] By Rule 9.
[2] By Rule 8.

prices and to costs of joint products. An alternative version, which may be developed from [Loehman and Whinston, 1971] and which seems particularly significant when joint products are used only internally, pays heed only to product costs (much as do the Moriarity and Louderback approaches).

For instance, if we return to the joint process described at the top of Figure 4-11, we could calculate the characteristic function shown in the middle of Figure 4-17, where $v(W) = \min | (J + f_W)$, $x_W|$, $v(WY) = \min | (J + f_W + f_Y)$, $(J + f_W + x_Y)$, $(J + x_W + f_Y)$, $(x_W + x_Y)|$, and so forth (*min*, of course, signifying *minimum*).[31] You will note that whereas up to now the Shapley approach calculated divisional batch book profits, from which one then determined total- and joint-cost allocations, here the Shapley approach calculates total costs, from which one determines joint costs and book profits.

(Readers who are interested in pursuing this version of the Shapley approach further are invited to verify that one can obtain the same arithmetic results as those in Figure 4-17 by allocating the total *cost savings* from producing products jointly rather than separately, thereby emulating the way in which Moriarity motivates his [1975] paper. We can calculate these cost savings from the amounts in Figure 4-17's characteristic function: As usual, $v(\theta) = 0$; $v(W) = v(X) = v(Y) = 0$, since there can be no savings from producing jointly if one produces separately. $v(WX) = (52 + 53) - 102 = 3$; $v(WY) = (52 + 70) - 108 = 14; v(XY) = (52 + 70) - 94 = 29$. Finally, since we are assigning cost savings to individual products (*not* to pairs of products):

1. $v(WXY) = (52 + 53 + 70) – 132 = 43$, and

2. The resulting Shapley values are cost-savings allocations, to be subtracted from 52, 53 and 70 to obtain the three products' respective total costs.

Remaining details of this gambit are left to the reader.)

To repeat a point made in Chapter Two, the crucial thing to recognize here is that all joint-cost allocations are radically arbitrary (incorrigible) and that therefore there is no "right" version of the Shapley approach. The best one can do is choose among versions in terms of their comparative congruence properties. Since this "cost" version of the Shapley approach turns out not to have as desirable congruence properties as the "profits" one that we have been considering,[32] I shall not refer to it again in this book, save when considering using Shapley allocations in transfer pricing.

---

[31]Although not illustrated by this example, our Rules 8 and 9 apply to this approach.

[32]Witness, for instance, its assigning a book loss to desirable product Y.

Figure 4-17

Same as Figure 4-11, Except That the
Characteristic Function is Based Solely on Costs

Product	f_i	x_i	J
W	38	52	
X	24	53	
Y	30	86	
Total	92	191	40

C	$v(C)$	C	$v(C)$
θ	0	WX	102
W	52^1	WY	108^3
X	53	XY	94
Y	70^2	WXY	132

$^1 \min|(40 + 38), 52| = \underline{52}.$

$^2 \min|(40 + 30), 86| = \underline{70}.$

$^3 \min|(40 + 38 + 30), (40 + 38 + 86), (40 + 52 + 30), (52 + 86)| = \underline{108}.$

Product	j_i	t_i	b_i
W	6.50	44.50	25.50
X	14.00	38.00	48.00
Y	19.50	49.50	(5.50)
Total	40.00	132.00	68.00

Some Final Caveats

(This section is technical; casual readers should feel free to disregard it.)

Shapley allocations are the unique consequences of the particular set of axioms that generate them and, on first blush, these
axioms are highly plausible as a "constitution" to which a company's divisional coalition members might agree.[33] However, Shapley
values are only one of a *group* of possible values that fall within a

[33]This is argued forcefully in [Luce and Raiffa, 1957, pp. 246-47].

game's core,[34] each of which has its own properties.[35] That Shapley values fall at the centre of this core has aesthetic appeal. But I'm unaware of any economic interpretation of this centrality that should make us favour Shapley allocations over these alternatives.[36] Thus, in a broader sense, Shapley allocations *aren't* unique. This is not to denigrate them. But it does indicate that, once again, a choice of them must hinge on their specific (congruence) properties rather than upon some broad matter of principle.

This conclusion is reinforced when we consider how little of a company's internal situation Shapley allocations really impound. Indeed, all that they reflect are the relative bargaining strengths of players, and these narrowly construed to include only the opportunity-cost[37] data that characteristic functions incorporate (and,

[34] And then only when the game is convex—see, for instance, [Roth and Verrecchia, 1977, p.4]. Mention of the core of the game and these alternative values raises issues that go beyond both the scope and the mathematical sophistication of this book. [Sorenson, Tschirhart and Whinston, 1976, pp. 499-502, 504, 513] offers a brief introduction to these matters. For the core of a game, generally, and for related notions of a game's kernel, see also [Scarf, 1967], [Shapley and Shubik, 1969a and b] and [Shapley, 1971]. For the range of possible alternative procedures and their stability and equitable properties, see also [Pauly, 1967, pp. 318-21], [Schmeidler, 1969, e.g. p. 1164], [Shapley, 1971, p. 11], [Maschler, Peleg and Shapley, 1972, p. 73], [Loehman and Whinston, 1976] and [Butterworth, Hayes and Matsumura, 1977, p. 37.]. The Loehman and Whinston article is especially valuable for suggesting the variety of other "equitable" allocation schemes that could be developed from game theory and welfare economics. Again, readings of [Lucas, 1972] and [Littlechild, 1975] also make it obvious that the Shapley approach is only one of many game-theoretic ones that could be applied to managerial (or financial) accounting's allocations. A parallel here is my [1974, pp. 167-68] demonstration that the NRV approach is merely one of a family of allocation approaches that are behaviour-congruent ("sterilized") with respect to further-processing decisions.

[35] Chapter Six includes discussion of the equitable (and other congruence) properties of Shapley allocations. Two examples of their limitations will suffice for now. In Shubik's [1964, p. 219] pioneering exercise in Shapley joint-cost allocation, his two operating divisions are each charged approximately the entire joint cost—indeed, one is charged slightly *more* than the joint cost. If the managers were to catch on, they'd scarcely be apt to regard this as equitable.
Again, although the Shapley approach insures that coalition members can't improve their situations by forming different coalitions, ordinarily some will be credited with higher book profits than others, and the latter may still regard this as inequitable—compare [Wiseman, 1957, pp. 64-66]. This is merely to say that the equitability of Shapley allocations is the notoriously limited equitability of Pareto optima.

[36] Contrast [Sorenson, Tschirhart and Whinston, 1976, p. 504].

[37] For a quick example of the Shapley approach's being an opportunity-cost one, see [Shubik, 1964, p. 220]. Readers may verify that all three loci's book profits are affected by the costs of the two processes, α_2 and β_1, that were never undertaken. This example may be generalized.

thus, to disregard all the behavioural–"psychological"–factors that affect real-life bargaining strengths.)[38] Again, we'll see in Part Two that the Shapley approach's assumption (Rule 5) that players cannot be forced to accept negative book profits is counterfactual in transfer pricing. More interesting for present purposes, whenever this assumption *is* correct *it's unlikely that players would be willing to accept miniscule book profits, either.* But Shapley allocations don't allow for this.[39] Nor, as we have seen, do they allow for the lively possibility that some costs of the joint process cannot be escaped by total shutdown (thereby violating Rule 6).

Finally, despite Jensen's [1977, *passim*] claims to the contrary, Shapley allocations don't solve the expansion-path problem raised in [Thomas, 1969; 1974]. This is partly because, as Loehman and Whinston [1976, pp. 88-89] and [Roth and Verrecchia, 1977, pp. 2-3] point out, Shapley allocations make the often-implausible assumption that all coalitions of players are equally likely.[40] But, far more important, it's because (as Loehman and Whinston [1971, pp. 611-12] also point out), Shapley allocations implicitly assume that each player must receive either all or none of its demands. Appendix E demonstrates that as soon as we (realistically) relax this assumption, an infinite number of other allocations become available.

All of the foregoing, as well as other matters discussed in Chapter Six, suggest that accounting theorists should be cautious in advancing claims for Shapley allocations. They're important, but they're no panacea. I'll return to this point briefly at the end of Chapter Ten, and in Appendix I.

---

[38]They disregard other things, too–for instance, see Shapley's [1971, p. 11*n*] point that they consider only constructive aspects of bargaining strength, and completely ignore the powers of coalitions to *ob*struct.

[39]Please note that these criticisms, as well as Butterworth, Hayes and Matsumura's [1977, p. 34] point that the Shapley approach assumes additive utilities, are immune to Mossin's [1968, p. 469] reply to superficially similar criticisms. I would be equally glad to complain of the assumptions made by, say, Schmeidler's [1969] nucleolis approach–especially the pertinence of its central ethical criterion (maximize the welfare of the least well-off coalition memeber) to ordinary, real-life companies. But since the nucleolis approach hasn't yet been actively proposed as a cure for accounting's ills, this would be beating a straw man.

[40]This assumption should be evident from inspection of the canonical Shapley formula at the beginning of Appendix C, which resembles the formula for an expected value in statistics. See also [Shapley, 1953] on this point.

CHAPTER FIVE

A NAIVE SURVEY
OF POSSIBLE CONGRUENCE PROPERTIES

> An allocation method will be *behaviour-congruent* if it reliably en-
> courages actors to act in ways that are consistent with whatever it is
> that the central office can be discovered to want (in a context of speci-
> fic decisions to be made and particular surrounding circumstances).

Having surveyed all of the main approaches to joint-cost allocation that are to be found in the literature, we may now survey
their possible congruence properties. I will do so by listing all characteristics of joint-cost allocations that economists and accountants have proposed as being desirable, as best as I can discern these
from the works cited in the References. Proponents advance each
such characteristic as being beneficial to the company as a whole.
Thus, they imply that each either is or should be consistent with
central-office wants and, therefore, is at least a *possible* congruence property.

This, of course, is a naïve way to conduct such a survey (for instance, the central office may not cooperate by wanting what it
"should" want), but I have been unable to devise any other. To
avoid inordinate footnoting,[1] I shall make no specific citations to
works wherein individual properties are proposed. Instead, readers
are invited to peruse the References and determine whether I have
omitted anything important or misrepresented anything discussed.

On the other hand, some readers may wish to skip ahead to
Chapter Six, where I take a large sample (though hardly all) of
these properties and use them to contrast the allocation approaches discussed in Chapter Two through Four. But I ask them at least
to *skim* the rest of this chapter, in order to gain some apprehen-
sion[2] of the sheer variety of properties that authors have proposed
for joint-cost allocations. Finally, such readers should look closely
at what (toward the end of this chapter) I summarize as
"ISROPM" properties—for Chapter Six will make frequent mention of them.

---

[1] And lengthy, pedantic demonstrations that observations made by individual authors
do indeed imply particular properties.

[2] In both of this word's senses: intuitive understanding and dread.

Assumptions and Simplifications

Unless otherwise specified, I shall continue to perceive companies as coalitions of their divisions,[3] and will take the point of view that joint-cost allocations influence such coalitions. This is important, for one suspects that causation often runs in the opposite direction (coalitions that happen to have formed for other reasons determining what allocation approaches the company uses). But where it does, joint-cost allocations become mere epiphenomena: foam on the waves, *symptoms* (of the company's organizational structure), without decision significance and, therefore, outside this book's span.

For brevity, I shall use an additional bit of jargon. Instead of saying "consistent with whatever it is that the central office can be discovered to want (or that a proponent of an allocation property explicitly or implicitly assumes that it wants or should want)," I shall merely say *central-office optimal* (and shall call its opposite *central-office dysfunctional*).

Readers are warned that some purportedly desirable characteristics of joint-cost allocations are mutually inconsistent; we'll see examples. On the other hand, many are interconnected in complex intellectual webs. Because of this, the order in, and the headings under, which I discuss them are necessarily somewhat arbitrary.[4] For convenience of exposition, I'll begin with some relatively general properties, then will flesh these out by describing more specific ones.

General Properties

A. *Efficiency.* Joint-cost allocations will be behaviour-congruent with respect to divisional efficiency if they reliably encourage divisions to do things that improve the company's overall profitability, and discourage divisional actions that harm it.[5] Some specific efficiency properties are:

---

[3] And, for ease of exposition only, will treat all measurements as error-free.

[4] Indeed, I fear that much depends on the unsystematic order in which I happened to read books and articles.

[5] I use *profitability* language here (instead of words suggestive of more general goals) in order to capture the sense of *efficiency* intended by my sources. However, I've tried to leave things vague enough to allow for central offices that wish to maximize profits, those content to satisfice them, and those for which profits are only one of many concerns.

1. *Further-processing.* Divisions must decide whether to discard joint products[6] at their split-off points or process them further. When they base such decisions on allocated data, the allocations should reliably generate central-office-optimal decisions.

a. *By-product recovery.* If divisions base decisions whether or not to recover by-products on allocated data, the allocations should satisfy the same criterion. In particular, if selling a by-product (and giving it such additional processing as is necessary for sale) improves the company's overall profits, divisional book profits on its sale should also be positive, in order to provide incentive for going to the trouble of dealing in the by-product.

b. *Partial discarding.* It sometimes happens that a company's overall profits will be improved by discarding some, but not all, of one or more joint products at split-off.[7] If so, and divisions base related decisions on allocated data, the allocations should reliably encourage the central-office-optimal degree of such discarding (which, as this property is discussed in the literature, will be the degree that maximizes short-run global profits).

2. *Scale.* Allocations used in decisions about the levels of total inputs and outputs of joint processes should reliably lead to divisions making central-office-optimal decisions.

a. *Mix.* Whenever a company can alter the output mix from its joint processes (as in oil refining), allocations used in decisions whether or not, and how, to do so should also reliably lead to central-office-optimal decisions.

3. *Coalition-forming.* Whether or not divisions are actually free to form or refuse to form joint-production coalitions (without central-office interference), joint-cost allocations should reliably encourage divisional coalition preferences that are central-office optimal.[8]

a. *Discretionary usage.* Whenever internal utilization of joint products is discretionary (as it is when production departments may use or refrain from using the outputs of service depart-

---

[6] Or sell them, an alternative that (as Chapter Two indicated) extends beyond the scope of this book.

[7] As Chapter Three indicated, this can happen when product marginal costs or marginal revenues are non-horizontal.

[8] If they don't, divisions either may form perverse coalitions or, prevented from doing so, may suffer from perverse élan effects. Such notions of coalition forming are central to Chapter Four's Shapley allocations.

ments), joint-cost allocations should reliably encourage central-office-optimal utilizations.

b. *Alternative acquisition.* Sometimes divisions have the opportunity to acquire their joint products in more than one way: either internally, by alternative processes or divisional coalitions, or externally, by purchase.[9] If the divisions' acquisition decisions are based in part on joint-cost allocations, these allocations should reliably result in central-office-optimal decisions.

c. *Input prices.* Relatedly, any allocations used in deciding how much divisions can afford to pay for raw materials, labour or other input factors should reliably lead to central-office-optimal decisions.

B. *Pricing and marketing.* If a company bases its product pricing (or other marketing) decisions in part on allocated data (as when pricing at full cost plus an "equitable" markup), the allocations should reliably generate central-office-optimal decisions.

1. *Promotion.* If a company bases decisions on how much to spend for promotion and other marketing of joint products in part on their allocated costs, these allocations should reliably encourage these decisions to be central-office optimal.

2. *Hold or sell.* When companies have inventories of joint products on hand, they must decide whether to hold or sell them. If they use joint-cost allocations in making such decisions, these allocations should reliably encourage hold-or-sell decisions that are central-office-optimal.

C. *Evaluation.* Joint-cost allocations will be behaviour-congruent with respect to central-office evaluations of products, product lines, sales territories, divisions and division managers if they reliably lead the central office to make such evaluation decisions in central-office-optimal ways.

1. *Discontinuance.* If a company bases its decisions whether or not to discontinue products or divisions in part on allocated data, the allocations should reliably generate central-office-optimal decisions.

2. *Waste.* If a company uses joint-cost allocations in its decisions whether or not to investigate (or to correct) waste, these allocations should reliably encourage central-office-optimal decisions.

D. *Elan effects.* To summarize Chapter One's discussion, a company's allocations will be élan congruent if division managers regard

---

[9] Such situations inspired Chapter Two's Moriarity, Louderback, JIM and JIL approaches.

them as equitable, and if they don't deem them to be destructive of divisional autonomy or manipulative. The literature implies that such élan congruence is globally optimal. Whenever it arises as an issue, I take it to be central-office optimal, too. We'll see that equity is a particular problem with joint-cost allocations, and autonomy with transfer prices.

(In this context, please note that all congruence properties may, in some manner or another, be perceived to be "equitable" ones, designed to generate "fair" or "reasonable" allocations of joint costs, in one or more of the many senses of these marvellously vague words.[10] However, I shall confine equity language to a particular group of properties, so labelled in the next section, that seem especially related to lay notions of fairness.)

More Detailed Properties

I gave each of the previous section's possible congruence properties a descriptive name, and explicitly related each to satisfaction of central-office wants. It will speed things up to be less formal hereafter, and to allow Chapter Six (which uses these descriptive names) to suggest how some of this section's more detailed properties might advance particular central-office goals. Throughout, unless indicated otherwise, I shall continue to assume that, whatever else they want, central offices seek to improve the company's overall profits and division managers seek to improve their book profits.

E. *Opportunity properties.* The next group of possible congruence properties may be styled *opportunity* ones, since each has something to do with opportunities available to the company and its divisions. (Marginal and incremental cost and revenue calculations also reveal opportunities, of course, but, with one exception, it's convenient to reserve properties directly related to marginal and incremental analysis until the next subsection.)

1. The total cost assigned to a joint product (t_i) should exceed the cost of acquiring it in the next best alternative way (x_i or y_i) if and only if it is central-office optimal to adopt this alternative (which might involve acquiring the good either externally or via

---

[10]Cf. [Anthony, 1975, p. 16] and [Financial Accounting Standards Board, 1976, p. 6].

some revised coalition of the company's divisions).[11] As a corollary:

a. No division should be assigned a joint cost that exceeds the total joint cost unless it's central-office optimal that the division not be part of the joint-production coalition.

2. A parallel property is: Divisions involved in joint-production coalitions should be able to improve their book profits by forming different coalitions if and only if their doing so would be central-office optimal. Equivalently, the allocation method(s) used in calculating their book profits should encourage divisions to form central-office-optimal joint-production coalitions—and if they already occupy such an optimum, the allocation method should ensure that the divisions cannot improve their book profits by deviating from this optimum.[12] This rule has two corollaries:

a. Allocations of book profits to divisions (in consequence of joint-cost allocations) should depend only on these divisions' incremental impacts on the company's total profitability, as reflected in the various contraction (or expansion) paths that would result from withdrawing (or adding) each division's services.

b. Divisions that make the same demands, receive the same services, and otherwise are fungible should be assigned identical joint costs. More formally, joint-cost allocations should be independent of how we label divisions and in what order we consider them.

3. All divisions that receive joint products should pay some of their joint costs. There should be no free riders[13] (and no cross-subsidization of products), nor should any such divisions be assigned negative joint costs. As a corollary,[14] where output propor-

---

[11] For instance, let's suppose that a joint process and a particular product, i, are both profitable and that $f_i < x_i$. If an allocation method were to allocate joint costs so that $j_i + f_i = t_i > x_i$, the i-division manager could increase the i-division's book profits by buying product i externally, even though doing so would decrease per-batch global profits by $x_i - f_i$.

[12] Except, perhaps, by forming another coalition that is *also* central-office optimal. For instance, no division or combination of divisions should find it financially advantageous to expell the previous note's division i from the joint-production coalition.

[13] Free-rider situations can develop whenever the incremental cost of adding a user of a joint product or service is zero, the classic example being radio and TV broadcasting.

[14] Another corollary is: The *total* cost assigned to a good should never be less than the incremental cost of obtaining it internally. As an exception: Waste is a joint product; whenever it is planned and unavoidable, all joint costs should be assigned to other products.

A less strict version of property E3 is: No divisions should be assigned zero or negative joint costs except those that should be assigned zero or negative book profits for reasons given in this or the next subsection. Alternatively, *only* the users of a joint process should pay its costs—or, equivalently, users must pay the full costs of the joint process (since, after all, these must be paid by *someone*).

tions of joint products can be altered (as, for instance, is true of most service departments), fixed joint costs of capacity should be allocated in proportion to:

a. The extent that different users actually consume output, or

b. The extent to which the company incurred these joint costs to satisfy users' *anticipated* output consumptions.

4. As the obverse of property E3, each member of a joint-production coalition should obtain some positive share of the cost savings resulting from acquiring goods jointly instead of separately (or, at least, each member whose presence in the coalition is central-office-optimal should).

F. *Marginal and incremental properties.* We may now turn to a group of closely related, possible congruence properties that are founded on marginal or incremental analyses (or on parallel accounting notions of product contributions).

1. An allocation method should yield book profits proportionate to each product's incremental contributions to global profits and joint costs. That's to say, if we let H signify total contributions and let λ be a constant, then for any product i, b_i should equal $\lambda \cdot h_i \div H$. Thus, products should have positive book profits if and only if their contribution margins on traceable costs and revenues are also positive. An equivalent of this property is:

1'. Allocate joint costs according to each product's ability to bear them, where this ability is measured by the product's contribution margin, and each dollar of margin receives equal weight.[15] Either form of this property has the corollary:

a. Were the company to give all joint products further processing, those whose further processing is central-office optimal should be credited with positive book profits, those whose further processing is central-office dysfunctional should be charged book losses, and those whose further processing is neither should be assigned zero book profits.[16]

----

[15] It's striking that no theorists have condemned this even-handed rule as "regressive" and proposed progressive joint-cost allocations styled after those used in income taxation—especially allocations designed to give positive book profits to products whose contributions are negative.

[16] Assuming that the central office seeks profits but adopts some sort of materiality standard, a plausible variant would be: Were the company to give all joint products further processing, those whose further processing has a positive effect on the company's global profits that exceeds a specified positive threshold should be credited with positive book profits, those whose further processing has an effect that exactly equals this threshold should be assigned zero book profits, and those whose further processing has effects falling short of this threshold should be assigned book losses.

2. As a stricter version of property F1, whenever decisions should be based on marginal costs or marginal revenues but instead are based on allocated magnitudes, these magnitudes should exactly equal the marginal ones (however they may be labelled).

G. *Equitable properties.* Finally, several properties reflect aspects of what lay persons deem to be "fair" or "reasonable".[17] Indeed, we might list this as a property in its own right: Joint-cost allocations should satisfy lay notions of equity. Here are some ways to implement this:

1. Actions (or inaction) by one division should not affect other divisions' book profits. (This is a central aspect of responsibility accounting.) Four corollaries follow:

a. Amounts of joint costs and book profits assigned to a division should not be affected by changes in other divisions' separate costs, revenues, or profitabilities.

b. If one division makes an erroneous further-processing decision, other divisions' book profits should be unaffected.

c. If one division splits up into two or more divisions, the book profits of other divisions should be unaffected.[18]

d. If one division discovers a less expensive alternative source of supply for a joint product than any previously known to the company, other divisions' book profits should be unaffected (whether or not it's to the company's advantage to adopt this alternative, and whether or not the company does adopt this alternative source).

2. Divisions should benefit from increases in their own efficiencies and be penalized for decreases in their own efficiencies. Under our continuing assumption that both the central office and the divisions are profit-seekers, corollaries include:

---

[17]A comment by Schlenker [1976, p. 1326] reveals the poverty of most accountants' imaginations in these matters:

> . . .an equity norm is only one of several possible allocation rules that can be employed in groups. Instead of being based upon the relative magnitudes of members' inputs to the group (equity rule), rewards can be dispensed on the basis of an e-quality or parity norm, where participants receive equal rewards irrespective of their inputs; on the basis of a reciprocity norm, where participants receive from an allocator amounts commensurate with what they have given him as an individual; or on the basis of participants' needs, wherein resources are meted out in accord with a norm of Marxian justice (to each according to his needs) or a norm of social responsibility (he who requires help should receive it from those who are able to provide it.).

Compare note 14, above.

[18]This property doesn't happen to appear in the literature; I use it for didactic purposes in Chapter Six.

a. If a division's separate costs decrease (increase), its book profits should increase (decrease). Variants on this rule could have the change in book profits be either temporary or permanent and might either limit its application to changes in separate costs resulting from the division's own actions or allow some that resulted from external events.

b. If a division discovers a less expensive alternative source of supply for a joint product than any previously known to the company, its book profit should increase. Variants on this rule could have the increase in book profits be either temporary or permanent and could have it hinge on whether or not adoption of the alternative source was to the company's advantage, or on whether or not the company did adopt it.

c. Divisions whose efficiencies increase (decrease) should not be penalized (rewarded) by having the joint costs that are allocated to them increase (decrease).

3. If total joint costs increase or decrease, the joint costs allocated to each division should increase or decrease in the same proportion.

4. Joint costs or book profits should be proportionate to easily measured phenomena associated with joint products. I shall mention only two of the many corollaries to this popular rule:

a. Each product's book profit should be a uniform percentage of its selling price.

b. The joint cost assigned to each product should be in uniform proportion to that product's weight (or volume).

Because of the widely acknowledged theoretical defects of such rules, I shall disregard them hereafter.

5. Allocations should be impersonal. Joint costs should be divided evenly ("democratically") among products. If there are n joint products, each should be charged $1/$nth of the joint cost. As variants:

a. Equity should be preserved among customers (either external or internal): each should bear its pro-rata share of joint overheads.

b. Joint costs should be so allocated that each product bears the same percentage markup.

c. See property E3: There should be no free riders.

d. If a division has an opportunity to do something that's central-office optimal but fails to seize it, the division should not be rewarded anyway.

Of course, this survey isn't exhaustive. For instance, joint-cost allocations might conceivably be behaviour-congruent with respect to certain capital-budgeting decisions,[19] or with respect to the manner in which the central office wishes to recover costs in the company's selling prices. But what I've listed will suffice for present purposes.[20]

ISROPM Properties

I mentioned at the outset that this chapter's taxonomy is unavoidably arbitrary. The next chapter, organizing matters slightly differently, pays particular attention to a combination of properties A1, A3b, E1, E2 and F1b. If a company and its divisions wished to maximize their immediate, short-run, overall profits, an ideal joint-cost allocation method would ensure that:

1. Whenever the company's immediate, short-run, overall profits were maximized by manufacturing a product, that product's total book cost should be less than both its selling price and its external cost (so that its division manager wouldn't be tempted to discontinue the product or to buy it externally),

2. If the company should be indifferent to whether or not it manufactured a product, then that product's total book costs should equal either its selling price or its external cost, and

3. If manufacture of a product would be *contrary* to immediate, short-run, overall profit maximization, then that product's total book costs should exceed either its selling price or its external cost, so as to encourage its division manager to discontinue its manufacture (after which, the division manager would decide whether or not to discontinue the product itself by comparing its selling price and external cost).

The foregoing repeatedly refers to *immediate, short-run* maximization because, of course, a joint-cost allocation method might have other properties that, indirectly or in the long run, harmed global profits. To keep this in mind, I shall refer to the foregoing properties collectively as *ISROPM* ones (for immediate, short-run, overall profit maximization).

---

[19] See [Thomas, 1974, p. 167].

[20] To save time, I've avoided listing a few properties that all joint-cost allocation methods discussed in Chapter Six share. Of these, one of the more interesting is: For specified production and demand functions, there should be no way that all divisions could improve their book profits—or that one (or more) could improve its book profits without reducing those of the others. This implies:

1. That the allocation method should be an additive partitioning of the total joint cost, no more and no less, and
2. Pareto optimality.

Relationships Among Properties

By and large, the relationships between what I've called detailed and general properties are obvious and straight-forward. The opportunity properties (E) are usually means to attaining efficiency (A) and evaluation (C) ones; so are the marginal and incremental properties (F). Equitable properties (G) are intended to obtain desirable élan effects (D). The previous section's ISROPM properties reflect a close relationship between six other properties.

Sometimes such relationships are quite explicit, as between the coalition-forming properties E2 and A3 and the further-processing properties F1a and A1. In other cases, one property is significant for *several* others. For instance, property F1 (book profits to be proportionate to incremental contributions) is related to further-processing, by-product recovery, mix, evaluation and discontinuance properties, besides having an equitable dimension that might have élan effects.

Indeed, as mentioned earlier, *most* congruence properties have such equitable dimensions; thus under unfavourable circumstances failure to attain a property could generate alienation. This is important, because some properties are mutually contradictory: Allocating joint costs according to ability to bear (F1′) is inconsistent with impersonal even-handedness (G5); total cost not exceeding alternative costs (E1) can conflict with joint costs being allocated in proportion to actual or anticipated output consumptions (E3a or E3b)—which, in turn, can conflict with each other.

There are other ways in which such conflicts can arise. Most if not all allocation methods with desirable efficiency properties risk failure to be fully élan-congruent. For division managers who have even minimum awareness of which side their bread is buttered on may be expected to perceive that these methods are designed to manipulate them—and therefore are apt to become a little skeptical of the company's internal reports, their true autonomies, and the like. I can't believe that resulting dysfunctional élan effects would be as severe for joint costing as we'll see them to be for parallel transfer-pricing manipulations. But, nonetheless, they may be significant.[21]

Chapter Six provides other examples of conflicts between congruence properties. It would be valuable for someone to work out the details systematically. More generally, as previous remarks

---

[21]Obviously, this is a potential topic for empirical investigation.

were intended to suggest, I fear that this chapter has only begun to develop a satisfactory framework for considering joint-cost allocation methods' congruence properties. The matters to be classified are diverse and confusing, demanding some of the talents of an Aristotle or Buffon. I earnestly invite some other, abler researcher to improve on what I've essayed here.

Meanwhile, for present purposes, this section's discussion does suggest something crucial: It is impossible for any one joint-cost allocation method to possess all desirable properties. Chapter Six will illustrate this in considerable detail.

CHAPTER SIX

CONGRUENCE PROPERTIES OF NINE ALLOCATION METHODS

Our nine joint-cost allocation methods offer different properties to potential users. This chapter will explore some of these differences.[1] I shall make no attempt to rank approaches on the basis of some properties being more desirable than others—for such desirability depends on the central office's wants, the particular decisions that the company may base on allocated data and the company's surrounding circumstances. However, it will turn out that some approaches offer significantly more congruence properties than others; this suggests that they can be ranked in a different sense, akin to versatility. I shall also demonstrate that judicious combinations of a few of these approaches yield hybrids that rank higher (in this sense) than can any individual approach alone.

Because its assumption of declining marginal costs or marginal revenues conflicts with other approaches' implicit assumptions that these are horizontal, it will be convenient to discuss Chapter Three's marginal approach to joint-cost allocation separately, and last. For brevity, unless stated otherwise I shall continue to make Chapter Five's assumption that central offices and divisions seek to improve their immediate, short-run profits. Finally, in order to focus on the properties of the nine allocation methods *per se*, I shall disregard such things as the possibility of a company's supplementing them with analyses of variances in divisional book profits.

Preliminary Considerations

First, a few preliminary considerations. Readers are invited to verify that there are five reasons why it might not be to a company's overall profit advantage to process an individual joint product, i, past its split-off point:

A. $f_i \geqslant p_i$; the product's further-processing costs equal or exceed its selling price.

B. $f_i \geqslant x_i$; the company can buy the product in an external market for less than its further-processing costs, or for the same sum.

---

[1]But not all. Besides the G4 properties mentioned in Chapter Five, brevity requires disregarding properties A1a, A2, A3, C2, E1a, E2a, E4, F1' and G5; however, some of these are corollaries to properties that I do discuss.

C. $f_i < \min|p_i,x_i|$, but $F + J > P$; each product's further-processing cost is less than both its selling price and its external cost, but the joint cost is large enough to render the joint process as a whole unprofitable.[2]

D. $f_i < \min|p_i,x_i|$, but $F + J > X$; each product's further-processing cost is less than its selling price and its external cost, but the joint cost is large enough to render it *most* profitable to buy all products externally.[3]

E. $f_i < \min|p_i,x_i|$; $F + J \leq \min|P,X|$; but $\Sigma(p_k - x_k) \geq P - F - J$, where k signifies all products whose $x_k < p_k$. Each product's further-processing cost is less than both its selling price and its total external costs. Yet the joint cost is large enough that were the company to discontinue those products whose external costs equal or exceed their selling prices, then buy all remaining products externally, its resulting profits would equal or exceed the maximum that it could attain by manufacturing products.[4]

We shall consider each of these cases in what follows.

Codes

All of this chapter's Figures will use the following code:

[1] Corrected for a 1¢ cumulative rounding error.

[2] Violates the ISROPM properties—i.e., could lead division managers to make an inappropriate decision to continue or discontinue a product or its manufacture.

[3] A correct decision to discontinue this product will harm at least one other division's book profits.

[2] As an example:

Product	p_i	f_i	x_i	J
A	70	55	75	
B	30	25	33	
Total	100	80	108	27

[3] As an example:

Product	p_i	f_i	x_i	J
A	70	55	61	
B	40	25	31	
Total	100	80	92	27

[4] As an example:

Product	p_i	f_i	x_i	J
A	70	55	81	
B	40	25	31	
Total	110	80	112	27

Whenever in this chapter I compare joint-cost allocation methods, I shall parenthetically cite Chapter Five's codes for the congruence properties under consideration, using square brackets. Thus, in comparison (1), below, I cite [Al, Fla] because these are the Chapter-Five properties that relate to further-processing decisions. (The one exception here is the ISROPM properties taken as a group, which Chapter Five did not code.)

Of course, I shall cite properties more than once when they are relevant to more than one kind of decision. Also, I cite some properties more than once when exploring how different allocation approaches fare under changing circumstances.

The Central Example

I'll base most comparisons of the NRV, SV, Moriarity, JIM, Louderback, JIL, Shapley and Democratic approaches on variations upon the example shown in Figure 6-1. A joint process that costs £100 per batch yields four products, A, B, C and D with the respective batch selling prices (p_i), further-processing costs, (f_i) and net realizable values (n_i) there indicated.

I'll initially assume that, within the applicable time horizon, it's impossible to buy any of the four products externally; I represent this by setting all external costs (x_i) equal to infinity.[5] Once again assuming (for brevity) that each product's lowest alternative cost is $J + f_i$, this will also be Moriarity's y_i here. In this example and in those that follow, I've chosen all figures for didactic purposes, though economic interpretations *could* be provided.

The lower parts of Figure 6-1 give the batch joint-cost allocations (j_i), total book costs (t_i) and book profits (b_i) under each of these eight approaches. Interestingly, at this limiting case of $x_i = \infty$, the Louderback and Democratic approaches give identical results.

Suboptimal Production Decisions

On inspection of Figure 6-1, it's readily apparent that the company *should* discontinue product D—dispose of it at split-off. Why, then, do I use an example in which the company errs and gives this product further processing?

The answer is fundamental to this chapter. There are two ways that an allocation method can fail to be behaviour-congruent, corresponding to the familiar Type I and II errors of statistics:

I. It can lead a decision maker to reject a possible decision that is central-office optimal, or

---

[5] Actually, to avoid undefined expressions I used 10^{98} as a surrogate for infinity.

Figure 6-1. Comparison of Eight Different Allocation Methods When It's Impossible to Buy Joint Products Externally

Product	n_i	f_i	p_i	x_i	y_i	J
A	154	41	195	∞	141	
B	79	3	82	∞	103	
C	1	54	55	∞	154	
D	(5)	24	19	∞	124	
Total	229	122	351	∞	522	100
	N	F	P	X	Y	J

	Allocation Method							
Joint-Cost Allocation	NRV	SV	Moriarity	JIM	Louderback	JIL	Shapley	Democratic
A	67.25	82.33	18.97	59.42	25.00	65.81	60.00	25.00
B	34.50	48.86	40.80	55.40	25.00	33.76	39.50	25.00
C	0.44	(19.21)	11.49	(14.83)	25.00	0.43	0.50	25.00
D	(2.18)	(11.98)	28.74[3]	0.00	25.00[3]	0.00	0.00	25.00[3]
Total	100.00[1]	100.00	100.00	100.00[1]	100.00	100.00	100.00	100.00
Total Cost								
A	108.25	123.33	59.97	100.42	66.00	106.81	101.00	66.00
B	37.50	51.86	43.80	58.40	28.00	36.76	42.50	28.00
C	54.44	34.79	65.49[2]	39.17	79.00[2]	54.43	54.50	79.00[2]
D	21.82	12.02[2]	52.74	24.00	49.00	24.00	24.00	49.00
Total	222.00[1]	222.00	222.00	222.00[1]	222.00	222.00	222.00	222.00
Book Profit								
A	86.75	71.67	135.03	94.58	129.00	88.19	94.00	129.00
B	44.50	30.14	38.20	23.60	54.00	45.24	39.50	54.00
C	0.56	20.21	(10.49)	15.83	(24.00)	0.57	0.50	(24.00)
D	(2.82)	6.98	(33.74)	(5.00)	(30.00)	(5.00)	(5.00)	(30.00)
Total	129.00[1]	129.00	129.00	129.00[1]	129.00	129.00	129.00	129.00

II. It can lead a decision maker to accept a possible decision that is *not* central-office optimal.

Unless we explore what allocation methods do when companies err, we will end up considering only their propensities to Type I errors—that's to say, tell only half the story about them. (For similar points, see the end of Chapter Two and [Johnson and Thomas, 1979].)

Accordingly, although I'll consider central-office-optimal production situations presently, we should begin with suboptimal ones.

Case A: All $x_i = \infty$, one $f_i > p_i$, $F + J < min|P, X|$, $\Sigma(p_k - x_k) < P - F - J$

(1) *Further processing* [Al, Fla]. Since Figure 6-1 allows no way to buy joint products from outsiders, there's no way that an allocation method can violate the ISROPM properties relating to make-buy (external acquisition) decisions. But it is still possible for allocation methods to tempt division managers into inappropriate further-processing decisions. This can happen whenever:

a. $t_i < p_i$ (and, therefore, $b_i > 0$) for an unprofitable product, as with product D under the SV approach, or

b. $t_i > p_i$ (and, therefore, $b_i < 0$) for a profitable product, as with product C under the Moriarity, Louderback and Democratic approaches.[6]

Only the NRV, JIM, JIL and Shapley approaches are reliably behaviour-congruent with respect to such further-processing decisions.[7] [8]

---

[6] Once again, these two failures correspond to Type I and Type II errors.

[7] The NRV approach is because, as we saw in Chapter Two, its $b_i = n_i \cdot (B \div N)$, and therefore its b_i's must always have the same algebraic signs as its n_i's. Appendix F gives the proofs for the JIM and JIL approaches.

Rather than essay proofs for this and similar positive assertions about the Shapley approach, I refer readers to its literature (its congruence properties being consequences of the method's axioms), again reminding these readers that the version of the Shapley approach that I use here is based on [Shubik, 1964]. I will, however, illustrate the Shapley approach's *perversities*.

[8] If, instead, we were to follow a suggestion made in Chapter Five's footnote 16, and require a product's positive contributions to exceed a specified threshold, Δ, before positive book profits should be reported, then none of these approaches will be reliably behaviour-congruent. However, we may tinker with the NRV approach. If this threshold is an absolute amount, the following allocation formula will suffice:

$$b_i = B \cdot (n_i - \Delta) \div (N - [m \cdot \Delta]),$$

where m is the number of joint products. Of course, Δ might also be expressed as a percentage of sales, a percentage of net realizable value or a rate of return on book investment, each of which would require a different allocation approach for behaviour-congruence.

I suspect (but have not yet verified) that one could tinker with the JIM and JIL approaches in similar ways.

(2) *Efficiency; Elan effects* [A, D, Fla]. From (1), it follows that all save the NRV, JIM, JIL and Shapley approaches either reward divisions for doing things (like processing product D further) that reduce the company's immediate, short-run global profits or penalize them for doing things (like processing product C further) that enhance such profits. Assuming that such enhancement is desirable, these perversities could have dysfunctional élan effects.

(3) *Evaluation* [C, Fl]. Only the NRV method's book profits are proportionate to each product's contribution to global profits and joint costs[9] —a property significant for evaluating products, divisions and division managers, and all related decisions.

(4) *Mix* [A2a]. Relatedly, sometimes a company can alter the proportions of its joint outputs. When so, a profit-seeking central office may want output-mix decisions to be based on analyses of whether increases in contributions of those products whose outputs might be expanded would exceed decreases in contributions of products whose outputs would thereby be contracted. But if the decision maker instead bases such decisions on relative book profits, it will nonetheless make them central-office optimally if each product's book profit is in uniform proportion to its contribution. Since this will be so only under the NRV approach, only that approach offers this congruence property.

(5) *Coaltion forming; Discontinuance; Elan effects* [A3, C1, D, G1]. In Illustration 6-1 the company could improve its immediate, short-run, global profits by discontinuing product D. Yet, this

---

[9] Again, because the NRV method ensures that $b_i = n_i \cdot B \div N$, these contributions will, of course, equal the n_i's. For extreme instances of the JIM, JIL and Shapley approaches *not* possessing this property, if we change Figure 6-1 so that $f_A = £165$, we will have:

Product	Individual Contribution ÷ Total Contribution	Book Profit ÷ Total Profit		
		NRV	JIM	JIL	Shapley
A	28.57%	28.57%	117.47%	54.55%	96.67%
B	75.24	75.24	49.40	143.64	96.67
C	0.95	0.95	33.13	1.82	6.67
D	(4.76)	(4.76)	(100.00)	(100.00)	(100.00)

product receives a positive joint-cost allocation under the Moriarity, Louderback and Democratic approaches. As Figure 6-2 illustrates, if the company does discontinue product D this allocated joint cost must be reallocated *somewhere*; doing so inevitably reduces the book profits of other divisions.

To the extent that (as sometimes is proposed by theorists) the company is a coalition of its divisions and these divisions (as sometimes is assumed in game theory) are free to decide which coalitions to joint, this encourages what an immediate, short-run profit-seeking central office would regard as dysfunctional coalition forming and discontinuance decisions. To the extent that the central office can override divisions' coalition preferences, this is a potential source of negative élan effects: For instance, why should other divisions be penalized for something over which they have neither responsibility nor control (and that actually increases the company's profits)?

In contrast, the NRV approach always assigns negative joint costs to products whose $f_i > p_i$, thereby encouraging central-office-optimal coalition-forming and discontinuance decisions.[10]

---

[10]We've seen that under the NRV approach:

$$b_i = n_i \cdot B \div N$$

Also, since B = N - J, for all positive J, N > B. Let's suppose that some division's $n_i = \lambda$. If the company discontinues product i, then for every remaining division, with net realizable value and book profit of n_j and b_j, respectively:

$$b_j = n_j \cdot (B - \lambda) \div (N - \lambda)$$

Let's first assume that n_j is positive. Then simple algebra tells us that:

1. If λ is positive, $b_j < b_j$,
2. If $\lambda = 0$, $b_j = b_j$, and
3. If λ is negative, $b_j > b_j$.

If $n_j = 0$, $b_j = 0$, regardless of λ's algebraic sign. Finally, if n_j is negative, the effects of λ's sign will be the exact opposite of those described *supra*. But b_j will be negative (thus indicating that the product shouldn't receive further processing anyway)—so this lacks decision significance.

Accordingly, the NRV approach is behaviour-congruent with respect to such coalition-forming decisions under the assumed circumstances that, for all products, $f_i < x_i$. (Readers who are following the analysis closely may wish to note that these results aren't confined to situations where $x_i = \infty$, but extend to the situation that we'll examine in the next subsection, where x_i is finite.)

Figure 6-2

Same as Figure 6-1, Except That
The Company Discontinues Product D

Product	n_i	f_i	p_i	x_i	y_i	J
A	154	41	195	∞	141	
B	79	3	82	∞	103	
C	1	54	55	∞	154	
Total	234	98	332	∞	398	100

	Allocation Method							
Joint-Cost Allocation	NRV	SV	Moriarity	JIM	Louderback	JIL	Shapley	Democratic
A	65.81	75.30	29.15	59.42	33.33	65.81	60.00	33.33
B	33.76	45.90	48.24	55.40	33.33	33.76	39.50	33.33
C	0.43	(21.20)	22.61	(14.83)	33.33	0.43	0.50	33.33
Total	100.00	100.00	100.00	100.00[1]	100.00[1]	100.00	100.00	100.00[1]
Total Cost								
A	106.81	116.30	70.15	100.42	74.33	106.81	101.00	74.33
B	36.76	48.90	51.24	58.40	36.33	36.76	42.50	36.33
C	54.43	32.80	76.61	39.17	87.33	54.43	54.50	87.33
Total	198.00	198.00	198.00	198.00[1]	198.00[1]	198.00	198.00	198.00
Book Profit								
A	88.19	78.70	124.85[4]	94.58	120.67[4]	88.19	94.00	120.67[4]
B	45.24	33.10	30.76[4]	23.60	45.67[4]	45.24	39.50	45.67[4]
C	0.57	22.20	(21.61)[4]	15.83	(32.33)[4]	0.57	0.50	(32.33)[4]
Total	134.00	134.00	134.00	134.00[1]	134.00[1]	134.00	134.00	134.00[1]

[4] Decreased from Figure 6-1.

The SV,[11] JIM, JIL and Shapley[12] approaches assign zero joint costs to such products and, therefore, are also behaviour-congruent here.

Later, we'll see what happens when a company discontinues a product whose manufacture increases immediate, short-run overall profits.

(6) *Promotion* [B1]. None of the eight approaches reports joint products at their marginal costs. Therefore, none is behaviour-congruent with respect to decisions on how much promotional effort to devote to different products, if these decisions are based on absolute book profitabilities. However, the NRV approach is behaviour-congruent for decisions based on *relative* book profitabilities.[13]

[11]Under the SV approach, j_i = $[(T \div P) \cdot p_i] - f_i$. Assuming that $P > T$, if $f_i > p_i$ then j_i must be negative. But P must exceed T; otherwise at least one product's book profit must be negative, guiding the company to discontinue that product.

[12]For brevity, I disregard a few technical points here. First, the Shapley approach doesn't necessarily yield *long-run* optima—see [Loehman and Whinston, 1974, pp. 248-50]. Second, although the Shapley approach is behaviour-congruent with respect to co-alition forming in the textbook joint-cost allocation situations that we've been considering, it need not be in situations having what, technically, is called an *empty core*—see [Luce and Raiffa, 1957, pp. 192-96], [Shubik, 1964, p. 225], [Pauly, 1967, pp. 314-19], [Mossin, 1968, pp. 469-70], [Ellickson, 1973, p. 420] and [Hamlen, Hamlen and Tschirhart, 1977, pp. 617-18]. In such circumstances, although it's still possible to calculate Shapley allocations there's no way to allocate book profits so that it won't be advantageous for some divisions to form central-office-dysfunctional subcoalitions.

Mossin [1968, p. 470] gives an example of why our joint-cost situations escape this difficulty: for a three-product joint process to have an empty core it's necessary that:

$$v(ABC) \leqslant v(AB) + v(AC) + v(BC)] \div 2.$$

Now, it's easily proved that, as long as there are no demand dependencies or technological dependencies (other than those of the joint process itself), all coalition values are nonnegative, and all $x_i = \infty$, for any three-product joint process:

$$v(ABC) = v(A) + v(B) + v(C) + (2 \cdot J)$$
$$> v(A) + v(B) + v(C) + (1.5 \cdot J) = [v(AB) + v(AC) + v(BC)] \div 2.$$

For the core to be empty, negative externalities exceeding ½ J must result from processing and selling all three products (as compared with selling just two). Situations with negative coalition values or finite x_i's, though more complicated, lead to similar conclusions.

Readers wishing to explore further might well begin by interpreting a solution falling within a game's core as one possessing Pareto optimality vis-à-vis divisions and their coalitions—see, for instance, [Pauly, 1967, p. 317]. However, they're warned that Mossin [1968, p. 470] also discusses situations with *non*-empty cores that can't yield satisfactory Shapley allocations; once again, these involve externalities. Mossin doesn't regard them as having much practical importance.

[13]See footnote 9 for why—and for an example of why it isn't true of the JIM, JIL and Shapley approaches.

(7) *Pricing and marketing; Hold or sell* [B, B2]. It should be immediately evident that none of these approaches is behaviour-congruent with respect to pricing decisions, nor with respect to decisions whether to hold or sell units carried in stock.

Case A (continued): All $f_i < x_i$; one $f_i > p_i$; $F + J < min|P,X|$; $\Sigma(p_k - x_k) < P - F - J$

Figure 6-3 reflects a new set of circumstances. Each product's further-processing cost still is less than its external cost, but each x_i is now finite. We should reconsider some of the previous properties under these new circumstances.

(8) *ISROPM.* Inspection of Figure 6-3 reveals that all but the JIM, JIL and Shapley approaches violate the ISROPM properties. The NRV approach would tempt its manager to buy product A. So would the SV approach, as well as encourage manufacture of product D. Moriarity's and Louderback's approaches encourage discontinuing manufacture of product B; Louderback's does this with product C, too. And the Democratic approach encourages external purchase of product C. All of these approaches thereby tempt division managers to make decisions that would reduce the company's immediate, short-run, overall profits.

(9) *Efficiency; Elan effects* [A, D, G2]. Accordingly, under all approaches except JIM, JIL and Shapley divisions will be rewarded for doing things that a central office wishing to maximize its immediate, short-run profits would find dysfunctional. And if the central office *prevents* divisions from doing so, the result would be arbitrary-seeming prevention of divisions from maximizing *their* immediate, short-run profits, something that could have dysfunctional élan consequences.

(10) *Coalition forming; Elan effects* [A3, A3b, D, E1, E2]. Inspection of the joint costs allocated to Figure 6-3's product C reveals that under the SV, Moriarity and JIM approaches, buying product C externally must improve the book profits of at least one other division[14] —despite that a company wishing to maximize its immediate, short-run profits would deem such behaviour to be perverse.

Figure 6-4 illustrates this, and reveals that Division D's profits increase under the NRV approach.[15] The Louderback, JIL, Shapley and Democratic approaches escape these perversities because their j_i's can never be negative.

---

[14] The reasoning here is: The negative amount of joint cost assigned to product C by each of the three methods must be reallocated *somewhere*; doing so must reduce at least one other division's joint costs and, thereby, increase its book profits.

[15] From £(2.8166) to £(2.8070).

Figure 6-3. Same as Figure 6-1, Except That It's
Possible to Buy Products Externally (For all products, $f_i < x_i$)

Product	n_i	f_i	P_i	x_i	y_i	$\min|p_i,x_i|$	J
A	154	41	195	68	68	68	
B	79	3	82	210	103	82	
C	1	54	55	58	58	55	
D	(5)	24	19	31	31	19	
Total	229	122	351	367	260	224	100
	N	F	P	X	Y	MIN	J

Allocation Method

	NRV	SV	Moriarity	JIM	Louderback	JIL	Shapley	Democratic
Joint-Cost Allocation								
A	67.25[2]	82.33	17.06	24.68	11.02	25.23	23.67	25.00
B	34.50	48.86	84.95	76.20	84.49	73.83	75.67	25.00
C	0.44	(19.21)	(4.48)	(0.88)	1.63	0.93	0.67	25.00
D	(2.18)	(11.98)	2.47	0.00	2.86	0.00	0.00	25.00
Total	100.00[1]	100.00	100.00	100.00	100.00	100.00[1]	100.00[1]	100.00
Total Cost								
A	108.25[2]	123.33[2]	58.06	65.68	52.02	66.23	64.67	66.00
B	37.50	51.86	87.95[2]	79.20	87.49[2]	76.83	78.67	28.00
C	54.44	34.79	49.52	53.12	55.63[2]	54.93	54.67	79.00[2]
D	21.82	12.02[2]	26.47	24.00	26.86	24.00	24.00	49.00
Total	222.00[1]	222.00	222.00	222.00	222.00	222.00[1]	222.00[1]	222.00
Book Profit								
A	86.75	71.67	136.94	129.32	142.98	128.77	130.33	129.00
B	44.50	30.14	(5.95)	2.80	(5.49)	5.17	3.33	54.00
C	0.56	20.21	5.48	1.88	(0.63)	0.07	0.33	(24.00)
D	(2.82)	6.98	(7.47)	(5.00)	(7.86)	(5.00)	(5.00)	(30.00)
Total	129.00[1]	129.00	129.00	129.00	129.00	129.00[1]	129.00[1]	129.00

Figure 6-4. Same as Figure 6-3, Except That
The Company Discontinues Product C

Product	n_i	f_i	p_i	x_i	y_i	$\min\lvert p_i,x_i\rvert$	J
A	154	41	195	68	68	68	
B	79	3	82	210	103	82	
D	(5)	24	19	31	31	19	
Total	228	68	296	309	202	169	100

Allocation Method

Joint-Cost Allocation	NRV	SV	Moriarity	JIM	Louderback	JIL	Shapley	Democratic
A	67.54	69.68	15.55	24.28	11.20	25.47	24.00	33.33
B	34.65	43.54	82.66	75.72	85.89	74.53	76.00	33.33
D	(2.19)	(13.22)	1.78	0.00	2.90	0.00	0.00	33.33
Total	100.00	100.00	100.00[1]	100.00	100.00[1]	100.00	100.00	100.00[1]

Total Cost								
A	108.54	110.68	56.55	65.28	52.20	66.47	65.00	74.33
B	37.65	46.54	85.66	78.72	88.89	77.53	79.00	36.33
D	21.81	10.78	25.78	24.00	26.90	24.00	24.00	57.33
Total	168.00	168.00	168.00[1]	168.00	168.00[1]	168.00	168.00	168.00[1]

Book Profit								
A	86.46	84.32[4]	138.45[4]	129.72[4]	142.80	128.53	130.00	120.67
B	44.35	35.46[4]	(3.66)[4]	3.28[4]	(6.89)	4.47	3.00	45.67
D	(2.81)[4]	8.22[4]	(6.78)[4]	(5.00)	(7.90)	(5.00)	(5.00)	(38.33)[1]
Total	128.00	128.00	128.00[1]	128.00	128.00[1]	128.00	128.00	128.00[1]

[4] Increased from Figure 6-3.

An Increase In Efficiency

Before going any further, let's contrast a situation in which a company that wishes to maximize its immediate, short-run profits should process *all* joint products further. To obtain these new circumstances we need merely modify Figure 6-3 by supposing that Division D increases its efficiency and reduces its further processing costs to £16. Figure 6-5 shows the results. First, we note in passing that all approaches except the JIM, JIL and Shapley ones continue to violate the ISROPM properties, even in what might be considered to be the most ideal circumstances for joint-cost allocation.

(11) *Elan effects* [D, E3, G5c]. Readers will note that here, as in Figure 6-3, the SV, Moriarity[16] and JIM approaches allow free riders—i.e., credit negative joint costs to products that it's to the company's profit advantage to process further. This can also occur under the Shapley approach.[17]

Division managers who are being charged positive joint costs are apt to regard the existence of free riders as unfair—just as one might be distressed if a neighbour had to pay no taxes. When, as here, profitable neighbours are actually "paying" *negative* taxes, the perceived unfairness and possibilities of perverse élan effects become even stronger. Readers are invited to verify, from Chapter Two's formulas, that the NRV, Louderback, JIL and Democratic approaches are reliably behaviour-congruent here, in the sense that they will charge any product whose further processing is central-office optimal a positive portion of the joint costs.

(12) *Efficiency; Evaluation; Elan effects* [A, D, G2, G2a]. Comparison of Figures 6-3 and 6-5 reveals that, as is central-office optimal, all eight approaches reward Division D for its increased efficiency.

(13) *Evaluation; Elan effects* [C, D, Gl, Gla]. However, all save the Democratic approach *also* reward divisions whose efficiencies didn't increase. Here, because impacts on other divisions' book profits are positive, this muddle might be defended by those who also defend contemporary tax and welfare systems. But a *de*crease in one division's efficiency (corresponding to a move from Figure 6-5 to Figure 6-3) will, of course, *reduce* book profits of other di-

---

[16]Cf. the fourth advantage claimed by Moriarity [1975, p. 794] for his approach.

[17]For an extreme instance, readers are invited to substitute some very large number, such as 10^{95}, for p_D. The book profits of products A, B and C each converge to zero, resulting in $j_D \simeq £(134)$. To them that hath shall it be given.

Figure 6-5. Same as Figure 6-3, Except That
Division D's Efficiency Has Improved (For all products, $f_i < \min|p_i x_i|$)

Product	n_i	f_i	p_i	x_i	y_i	$\min|p_i x_i|$	J
A	154	41	195	68	68	68	
B	79	3	82	210	103	82	
C	1	54	55	58	58	55	
D	3	16	19	31	31	19	
Total	237	114	351	367	260	224	100

Allocation Method

Joint-Cost Allocation	NRV	SV	Moriarity	JIM	Louderback	JIL	Shapley	Democratic
A	64.98	77.89	14.97	23.96	10.67	24.55	22.67	25.00
B	33.33	46.99	81.78	75.34	81.82	71.82	74.67	25.00
C	0.42	(20.47)[4]	(6.26)[4]	(1.46)	1.58	0.91	0.67	25.00
D	1.27[4]	(4.42)[4]	9.52[4]	2.15[4]	5.93[4]	2.73[4]	2.00[4]	25.00
Total	100.00	100.00[1]	100.00[1]	100.00[1]	100.00	100.00[1]	100.00[1]	100.00

Total Cost	NRV	SV	Moriarity	JIM	Louderback	JIL	Shapley	Democratic
A	105.98[2]	118.89[2]	55.97	64.96	51.67	65.55	63.67	66.00
B	36.33	49.99	84.78[2]	78.34	84.82[2]	74.82	77.67	28.00
C	54.42	33.53	47.74	52.54	55.58[2]	54.91	54.67	79.00[2]
D	17.27	11.58	25.52[2]	18.15	21.93[2]	18.73	18.00	41.00[2]
Total	214.00	214.00[1]	214.00[1]	214.00[1]	214.00	214.00[1]	214.00[1]	214.00

Book Profit	NRV	SV	Moriarity	JIM	Louderback	JIL	Shapley	Democratic
A	89.02[4]	76.11[4]	139.03[4]	130.04[4]	143.33[4]	129.45[4]	131.33[4]	129.00
B	45.67[4]	32.01[4]	(2.78)[4]	3.66[4]	(2.82)[4]	7.18[4]	4.33[4]	54.00
C	0.58[4]	21.47[4]	7.26[4]	2.46[4]	(0.58)[4]	0.09[4]	0.33	(24.00)[4]
D	1.73[4]	7.42[4]	(6.52)[4]	0.85[4]	(2.93)[4]	0.27[4]	1.00[4]	(22.00)[4]
Total	137.00	137.00[1]	137.00[1]	137.00[1]	137.00	137.00[1]	137.00[1]	137.00

[4] Increased from Figure 6-3.

Figure 6-6. Same as Figure 6-3, Except That Product D's Selling Price Has Increased

Product	n_i	f_i	P_i	x_i	y_i	$\min|p_i,x_i|$	J
A	154	41	195	68	68	68	
B	79	3	82	210	103	82	
C	1	54	55	58	58	55	
D	3	24	27	31	31	27	—
Total	237	122	359	367	260	232	100

Allocation Method

Joint-Cost Allocation	NRV	SV	Moriarity	JIM	Louderback	JIL	Shapley	Democratic
A	64.98	79.58	17.06	24.07	11.02	24.55	22.67	25.00
B	33.33	47.71	84.95	75.47	84.49	71.82	74.67	25.00
C	0.42	(19.99)	(4.48)	(1.37)	1.63	0.91	0.67	25.00
D	1.27	(7.30)	2.47	1.84	2.86	2.73	2.00	25.00
Total	100.00	100.00	100.00	100.00[1]	100.00	100.00[1]	100.00[1]	100.00

Total Cost	NRV	SV	Moriarity	JIM	Louderback	JIL	Shapley	Democratic
A	105.98	120.58	58.06	65.07	52.02	65.55	63.67	66.00
B	36.33	50.71	87.95	78.47	87.49	74.82	77.67	28.00
C	54.42	34.01	49.52	52.63	55.63	54.91	54.67	79.00
D	25.27	16.70	26.47	25.84	26.86	26.73	26.00	49.00
Total	222.00	222.00	222.00	222.00[1]	222.00	222.00[1]	222.00[1]	222.00

Book Profit	NRV	SV	Moriarity	JIM	Louderback	JIL	Shapley	Democratic
A	89.02[4]	74.42[4]	136.94	129.93[4]	142.98	129.45[4]	131.33[4]	129.00
B	45.67[4]	31.29[4]	(5.95)	3.53[4]	(5.49)	7.18[4]	4.33[4]	54.00
C	0.58[4]	20.99[4]	5.48	2.37[4]	(0.63)	0.09[4]	0.33	(24.00)
D	1.73	10.30	0.53	1.16	0.14	0.27	1.00	(22.00)
Total	137.00	137.00	137.00	137.00[1]	137.00	137.00[1]	137.00[1]	137.00

[4] Increased from Figure 6-3.

visions in response to something that they didn't do and over which they had no control, phenomenon generally deemed less desirable. As a result of this bookkeeping externality (as it were), all but the Democratic approach are perverse for evaluation decisions under these circumstances—and, of course, for any élan decisions that might stem from such things as resentment that one's book profits are at the mercy of another division's ineptitudes.[18]

(14) *Evaluation; Elan effects* [C, D, Gl, Gla]. Things are slightly different if Division D's sales price increases instead of its further-processing cost decreasing. Figure 6-6 is the same as Figure 6-3, save for an increase in p_D. The Democratic approach is still behaviour-congruent. But so now are the Moriarity and Louderback ones, and reliably so, too.[19]

(Figure 6-6 is especially interesting as an instance of something mentioned in Chapter Two: There will be occasional decisions and circumstances for which the Moriarity approach is preferable to JIM, and the Louderback to JIL.)

(15) *Evaluation; Elan effects* [C, D, Gl, Gld, G2b]. Next, let's consider something that does *not* involve an increase in a division's efficiency. Figure 6-7 is identical to Figure 6-6 except that x_A has fallen from £68 to £60, perhaps from Division A's uncovering a cheaper source of supply, perhaps for reasons having nothing to do

---

[18]For another instance of the Shapley approach's violating this rule, the reader might consider the example in [Loehman and Whinston, 1971, pp. 611-12]. Let's suppose that, due to inefficiency, their second division's marginal costs change from 0.50 to 0.75. Then, using their notation:

$C(K_1)$	=	6		
$C(K_2)$	=	99 + 750	=	849
$C(K)$	=	100 + 751.5	=	851.5
@ (1)	=	[6 + (851.5 - 849)] ÷ 2	=	4.25
@ (2)	=	[849 + (851.5 - 6)] ÷ 2	=	847.25
@ (1) + @ (2) =		4.25 + 847.25	=	851.5.

The allocation of total costs to the first division increases from 4.00 to 4.25, while its book profits decline by 0.25.

[19]Moriarity's $t_i = T \cdot y_i \div Y$, where $y_i = \min|(J + f_i), x_i|$. Louderback's $j_i = J \cdot (x_i - f_i) \div (X - F)$. Since neither of these expressions is affected by a change in any p_i, the two approaches are reliably behaviour-congruent here.

Kreps [1930, pp. 422-23] tells a nice anecdote in which the cost of a joint product (figured for tariff purposes) declined because its selling price had declined relative to fellow joint products due to competition from massive imports. The essential arbitrariness of any joint-cost allocation approach based on sales values (i.e., all but the Moriarity, Louderback and Democratic) is evident. See also Kreps' illuminating-gas example on [pp. 424-25].

Figure 6-7. Same as Figure 6-6, Except That Product A's External Cost Has Decreased

Product	n_i	f_i	p_i	x_i	y_i	$\min|p_i,x_i|$	J
A	154	41	195	60	60	60	
B	79	3	82	210	103	82	
C	1	54	55	58	58	55	
D	3	24	27	31	31	27	
Total	237	122	359	359	252	224	100

Allocation Method

	NRV	SV	Moriarity	JIM	Louderback	JIL	Shapley	Democratic
Joint-Cost Allocation								
A	64.98	79.58	11.86	18.46	8.02	18.63	18.42	25.00
B	33.33	47.71	87.74	78.27	87.34	77.45	78.42	25.00
C	0.42	(19.99)	(2.90)	0.51	1.69	0.98	0.75	25.00
D	1.27	(7.30)	3.31	2.76	2.95	2.94	2.42	25.00
Total	100.00	100.00	100.00[1]	100.00	100.00	100.00	100.00[1]	100.00
Total Cost								
A	105.98	120.58	52.86	59.46	49.02	59.63	59.42	66.00
B	36.33	50.71	90.74	81.27	90.34	80.45	81.42	28.00
C	54.42	34.01	51.10	54.51	55.69	54.98	54.75	79.00
D	25.27	16.70	27.31	26.76	26.95	26.94	26.42	49.00
Total	222.00	222.00	222.00[1]	222.00	222.00	222.00	222.00[1]	222.00
Book Profit								
A	89.02	74.42	142.14[4]	135.54[4]	145.98[4]	135.37[4]	135.58[4]	129.00
B	45.67	31.29	(8.74)[4]	0.73[5]	(8.34)[5]	1.55[5]	0.58[5]	54.00
C	0.58	20.99	3.90[5]	0.49[5]	(0.69)[5]	0.02[5]	0.25[5]	(24.00)
D	1.73	10.30	(0.31)[5]	0.24[5]	0.05[5]	0.06[5]	0.58[5]	(22.00)
Total	137.00	137.00	137.00[1]	137.00	137.00	137.00	137.00[1]	137.00

[4] Increased from Figure 6-6.
[5] Decreased from Figure 6-6.

with Division A's actions. Please note first that under all but the NRV, SV and Democratic approaches (whose failures to be affected by x_i's render them reliably behaviour-congruent here) this decline in the external cost of one product reduces the book profits of at least one other division—penalizing such other divisions in ways that are likely to be perceived as unfair and that certainly confound evaluations of their successes.

(16) *Evaluation* [C, G2b]. Moreover, under all but the NRV, SV and Democratic approaches Division A is rewarded for something that's useless to the company. (With a further-processing cost of only £41, it should no more buy at £60 than it should at £68.) The increases in Division A's book profits are mere artifacts of the algorithms used. Besides, this encourages gaming (fiddling) by division managers unless they have no influence over what x_i's are reported to the central office—something that, under typical information-flow arrangements, seems unlikely.

Similarly, Division A would be penalized for an irrelevant *increase* in x_A.

Case B: All $f_i < p_i$, one $f_i > x_i$, $F + J < min|P,X|$, $\Sigma(p_k - x_k) < P - F - J$

(17) *Efficiency: Evaluation* [A, C, G2b]. In contrast, Figure 6–8 reflects a decrease in product D's external cost that could benefit the company.[20] All approaches except the NRV, SV and Democratic reward Division D—something that certainly will be appropriate if Division D's actions caused the decline, and which could be defended as a legitimate attribution of a windfall profit, otherwise.

(18) *Evaluation; Elan effects* [C, D, G1, G1d]. Unfortunately, it is also evident from Figure 6–8 that under all but the NRV, SV and Democratic approaches at least two other divisions are penalized for this change in product D's external cost.

(19) *Efficiency; Evaluation* [G5d]. Moreover, please note that under all but the NRV, SV and Democratic approaches Division D will be rewarded *even if it takes no advantage of the lower external cost.*

(20) *Efficiency* [A, A3b, F1a]. Worse, the SV and Moriarity approaches actually dissuade it from doing so: Under each, Division D's book profits from processing Product D further exceed the £4 book profit that it would obtain from buying.

---

[20]For brevity, I shall disregard such considerations, relevant to real-world decisions to buy externally, as continuity of this external supply at an attractive price.

Figure 6-8. Same as Figure 6-6, Except That Product D's External Cost Has Decreased (And is now less than f_D)

Product	n_i	f_i	p_i	x_i	y_i	$\min|p_i,x_i|$	J
A	154	41	195	68	68	68	
B	79	3	82	210	103	82	
C	1	54	55	58	58	55	
D	3	24	27	23	23	23	
Total	237	122	359	359	252	228	100

Allocation Method

	NRV	SV	Moriarity	JIM	Louderback	JIL	Shapley	Democratic
Joint-Cost Allocation								
A	64.98	79.58	18.90	24.68	11.34	25.23	23.67	25.00
B	33.33	47.71	87.74	76.20	86.97	73.83	75.67	25.00
C	0.42	(19.99)	(2.90)	(0.88)	1.68	0.93	0.67	25.00
D	1.27[3]	(7.30)	(3.74)	0.00	0.00	0.00	0.00	25.00[3]
Total	100.00	100.00	100.00	100.00	100.00[1]	100.00[1]	100.00[1]	100.00
Total Cost								
A	105.98[2]	120.58[2]	59.90	65.68	52.34	66.23	64.67	66.00
B	36.33	50.71	90.74[2]	79.20	89.97[2]	76.83	78.67	28.00
C	54.42	34.01	51.10	53.12	55.68[2]	54.93	54.67	79.00[2]
D	25.27	16.70[2]	20.26[2]	24.00	24.00	24.00	24.00	49.00
Total	222.00	222.00	222.00	222.00	222.00[1]	222.00[1]	222.00[1]	222.00
Book Profit								
A	89.02	74.42	135.10[5]	129.32[5]	142.66[5]	128.77[5]	130.33[5]	129.00
B	45.67	31.29	(8.74)[5]	2.80[5]	(7.97)[5]	5.17[5]	3.33[5]	54.00
C	0.58	20.99	3.90[5]	1.88[5]	(0.68)[5]	0.07[5]	0.33	(24.00)
D	1.73	10.30	6.74[4]	3.00[4]	3.00[4]	3.00[4]	3.00[4]	(22.00)
Total	137.00	137.00	137.00	137.00	137.00[1]	137.00[1]	137.00[1]	137.00

[4] Increased from Figure 6-6.
[5] Decreased from Figure 6-6.

(21) *Coalition forming* [A3, E2]. Figure 6–8 also shows that if the company does make a central-office-optimal decision to buy product D, at least one other division's book profits must suffer under the NRV and Democratic approaches.[21] Nor is the SV approach reliably behaviour-congruent here, either, as may be seen by supposing a decline in x_A to, say, £33.

(22) *Elan effects* [D]. There's a behavioural aspect to coalition-forming properties (10) and (21). In each, if the central office insists on further-processing decisions that maximize the company's immediate, short-run profits, some division managers will be frustrated in their book-profit seeking (since their book profits would be higher under other joint-production coalitions). Only the Louderback, JIL and Shapley approaches reliably escape this problem.

(23) *ISROPM.* Finally, inspection of Figure 6–8 reveals that, once again in these new circumstances, all but the JIM, JIL and Shapley approaches violate the ISROPM properties with other products.

We may now conclude this phase of our discussion by briefly considering the three situations (Cases C through E) in which the company should process no products further.

Case C: $f_i < min|p_i, x_i|$, but F+J > P

(24) *ISROPM.* As Figure 6–9 shows, the Shapley approach displays vigourous *TILT* signals here, by refusing to make any joint-cost allocation whatever. The other methods pose no difficulties as far as the ISROPM properties go, either, as long as the central office permits divisions to cease further processing of products with negative book profits. For, since $F + J > P$, there must be at least one product, i, such that $j_i + f_i > p_i$. Once its division has ceased its further processing, the remaining $J + F$ must still exceed the remaining P (since, for all i, $f_i < p_i$). Therefore there must be at least one *other* product, k, such that $j_k + f_k > p_k$ ...and so forth until the company has discontinued further processing of all products.

(25) *ISROPM.* But if the central office does *not* permit divisions to cease further processing of products with negative book profits, the Moriarity, Louderback and Democratic approaches can yield $j_i + f_i < min|p_i, x_i|$ for some products, as demonstrated in Figure

---

[21] See comparison (5)'s discussion for why this must be so.

Figure 6-9. Same as Figure 6-6, Except That F+J>P (Case C) (All $f_i < \min|p_i,x_i|$)

Product	n_i	f_i	p_i	x_i	y_i	$\min|p_i;x_i|$	J
A	9	41	50[4]	68	68	50	25.00
B	79	3	82	210	103	82	25.00
C	1	54	55	58	58	55	25.00
D	3	24	27	31	31	27	25.00
Total	92	122	214	367	260	214	100
		F	P				

[4] Changed from Figure 6-6.

Allocation Method

Joint-Cost Allocation	NRV	SV	Moriarty	JIM	Louderback	JIL	Shapley	Democratic
A	9.78	10.87	17.06	10.87	11.02	9.78	0.00	25.00
B	85.87	82.07	84.95	82.07	84.49	85.87	0.00	25.00
C	1.09	3.06	(4.48)	3.06	1.63	1.09	0.00	25.00
D	3.26	4.01	2.47	4.01	2.86	3.26	0.00	25.00
Total	100.00[1]	100.00[1]	100.00	100.00[1]	100.00	100.00	0.00	100.00
Total Cost								
A	50.78	51.87	58.06	51.87	52.02	50.78	Not applicable	66.00
B	88.87	85.07	87.95	85.07	87.49	88.87		28.00[5]
C	55.09	57.06	49.52[5]	57.06	55.63	55.09		79.00
D	27.26	28.01	26.47[5]	28.01	26.86[5]	27.26		49.00
Total	222.00	222.00[1]	222.00	222.00[1]	222.00	222.00		222.00
Book Profit								
A	(0.78)	(1.87)	(8.06)	(1.87)	(2.02)	(0.78)		(16.00)
B	(6.87)	(3.07)	(5.95)	(3.07)	(5.49)	(6.87)		54.00
C	(0.09)	(2.06)	5.48	(2.06)	(0.63)	(0.09)		(24.00)
D	(0.26)	(1.01)	0.53	(1.01)	0.14	(0.26)		(22.00)
Total	(8.00)	(8.00)[1]	(8.00)	(8.00)[1]	(8.00)	(8.00)		(8.00)

[5] $t_i < \min|p_i;x_i|$.

6-9.[22] [23] Here, the most profitable thing that the company could do would be to discontinue all four joint products, but these three approaches each encourage further processing by at least one division. This could mislead the central office, too, if, besides making joint products, divisions also engage in other, profitable activities.

Case D: $f_i < min|p_i, x_i|$, but $F + J > X$

(26) *ISROPM.* As you can see from Figure 6-10, the Shapley approach supplies more subtle *TILT* signals here—$\Sigma b_i \neq B$, and the approach allocates only part of the joint cost. Still, this should more than suffice to prevent erroneous decisions. An argument that parallels that for comparison (24) indicates that this case also poses no difficulties under any of our other approaches as long as the central office permits divisions to cease further processing of products whose $j_i + f_i > x_i$.

(27) *ISROPM.* Figure 6-10 demonstrates what happens if the central office *doesn't* permit this. Here, the most profitable thing that the company can do is to by all products externally (for a batch profit of P-X = £359-£207 = £152). But the NRV, SV and Democratic approaches encourage further processing. It can be proved that the other five approaches are reliably behaviour-congruent.[24]

[22] Inspection of their algorithms indicates that the NRV and SV approaches will be reliably behaviour-congruent here (with $t_i = j_i + f_i > p_i$ for all products). Proofs that the JIM, JIL and Shapley approaches are also reliably behaviour congruent are more complicated. See Appendix F for the first two of these.

[23] Readers are invited to note that, just as the Louderback approach becomes the Democratic one when joint products can't be purchased externally, so the JIM approach becomes the SV one when all $f_i < p_i$ and all $p_i < x_i$. So will Moriarity's when all $p_i = x_i$.

[24] For instance, under Moriarity's approach:

$t_i = (J + F) \cdot min|(J + f_i), x_i| \div \Sigma min|(J + f_i), x_i|$.

But $J + f_i$ can't be less than x_i; otherwise, in order for $F + J > X$ there would have to be some product, Ψ, such that $f_\Psi > x_\Psi$. But this violates our initial assumption that, for all products, $f_i < min|p_i, x_i|$. Therefore:

$t_i = (J + F) \cdot x_i \div X$. But, since $F + J > X$,

$t_i > x_i$.

Similarly, under Louderback's approach:

$t_i = J \cdot (x_i - f_i) \div (X - F) + f_i$.

Let's suppose that for some product, Ψ, $t_\Psi < x_\Psi$; then,

$J \cdot x_\Psi \div (X-F) - J \cdot f_\Psi \div (X-F) + (X-F) \cdot f_\Psi \div (X-F) < (X-F) \cdot x_\Psi \div (X-F)$;

therefore,

$(J + F - X) \cdot x_\Psi < (J + F - X) \cdot f_\Psi$; therefore,

$x_\Psi < f_\Psi$

But this violates our initial assumption that, for all products, $f_i < min| p_i, x_i |$.

See Appendix F for proofs that the JIM and JIL approaches are reliably behaviour-congruent here, too.

Figure 6-10. Same as Figure 6-6, Except That F+J > X (Case D) (All $f_i < \min|p_i,x_i|$)

Product	n_i	f_i	p_i	x_i	y_i	$\min|p_i,x_i|$	J
A	154	41	195	68	68	68	
B	79	3	82	50[4]	50	50	
C	1	54	55	58	58	55	
D	3	24	27	31	31	27	
Total	237	122	359	207	207	200	100
		F	P	X			

[4] Changed from Figure 6-6.

	Allocation Method							
Joint-Cost Allocation	NRV	SV	Moriarity	JIM	Louderback	JIL	Shapley	Democratic
A	64.98	79.58	31.93	34.48	31.76	34.62	27.00	25.00
B	33.33	47.71	50.62	52.50	55.29	60.26	47.00	25.00
C	0.42	(19.99)	8.20	7.05	4.71	1.28	1.00	25.00
D	1.27	(7.30)	9.25	5.97	8.24	3.85	3.00	25.00
Total	100.00	100.00	100.00	100.00	100.00	100.00[1]	78.00	100.00
Total Cost								
A	105.98	120.58	72.93	75.48	72.76	75.62	68.00	66.00[5]
B	36.33[5]	50.71	53.62	55.50	58.29	63.26	50.00	28.00[5]
C	54.42[5]	34.01[5]	62.20	61.05	58.71	55.28	55.00	79.00
D	25.27[5]	16.70[5]	33.25	29.97	32.24	27.85	27.00	49.00
Total	222.00	222.00	222.00	222.00	222.00	222.00[1]	200.00	222.00
Book Profit								
A	89.02	74.42	122.07	119.52	122.24	119.38	127.00	129.00
B	45.67	31.29	28.38	26.50	23.71	18.74	32.00	54.00
C	0.58	20.99	(7.20)	(6.05)	(3.71)	(0.28)	0.00	(24.00)
D	1.73	10.30	(6.25)	(2.97)	(5.24)	(0.85)	0.00	(22.00)
Total	137.00	137.00	137.00	137.00	137.00	137.00[1]	159.00	137.00

[5] $t_i < \min|p_i,x_i|$.

Case E: $f_i < min|p_i, x_i|$, $F + J \leqslant min|P,X|$, but $\Sigma(p_k, x_k) \geqslant P\text{-}F\text{-}J$

(28) *ISROPM*. Finally, Figure 6-11 illustrates Case E. Here the company would maximize its per-batch profits (at £195-£50 = £145) by buying product A and discontinuing the other three. The JIM and JIL approaches reliably guide all division managers to this decision.[25] So, by a *TILT* signal similar to that in comparison (26), does the Shapley approach. The other methods are not reliably behaviour-congruent here.

Other Properties

(29) *Evaluation; Elan effects* [C, G5b]. Only the SV approach assigns each product the same percentage markup (approximately 38.16% in Figure 6-11).[26] [27]

(30) *Elan effects* [D, G]. Some of the foregoing properties have additional behavioural dimensions. For instance, each approach is "equitable," "fair" or "reasonable" in a different sense: the NRV and SV methods for their uses of ability-to-bear or ability-to-generate-revenues criteria based respectively on net realizable values and selling prices,[28] the Shapley approach for being uniquely consistent with its particular axioms, the Democratic approach for its even-handedness[29] (a property that, as we saw in Chapter Four, the Shapley approach shares when all coalition values are nonnegative),[30] and so forth.

---

[25] See Appendix F for the proofs that they do.

[26] Be it noted, though, that Bierman and Dyckman [1971, p. 174] contend that, far from being a virtue, this renders an approach misleading for evaluation decisions—and object to the NRV method's tendencies in its direction.

[27] Relatedly, Lorig [1955, pp. 635-36] claimed that, under the SV approach, a negative j_i indicates that the company should discard product i without further processing and devote the funds released to buying more of the joint process and proportionately more further processing of the remaining products. I disregard this claim, for the reasons given in [Hill, 1956, esp. p. 205] and [Lawson, 1956, 1957]; see also [Lorig, 1956; 1958].

[28] Another possibility here would be net realizable values less a normal profit margin—see [Vatter, 1945, p. 171].

[29] Similarly, if the company bases its prices on book costs, the NRV, SV and Democratic approaches each, in different senses, offer the property [G5a] that equity should be preserved among customers by having each bear a pro-rata share of joint cost.

[30] Not that an even division of joint costs will necessarily be perceived to be equitable if some divisions are larger than others and thereby seem to make greater use of joint facilities (or greater contributions to the savings that result from producing goods jointly)—see [Hamlen, Hamlen and Tschirhart, 1977, p. 624]. Again, both the Democratic and Shapley approaches' even divisions of joint costs might be deemed not so much equitable as merely *indifferent to the facts* of the joint-cost situation.

Figure 6-11 Same as Figure 6-6, Except That $\Sigma(p_k-x_k)$ > P-F-J (Case E) (All f_i < min$|p_i,x_i|$)

Product	n_i	f_i	p_i	x_i	y_i	min$|p_i,x_i|$	J
A	154	41	195	50[4]	50	50	
B	79	3	82	210	103	82	
C	1	54	55	58	58	55	
D	3	24	27	31	31	27	
Total	237	122	359	349	242	214	100
		F	P	P			

[4] Changed from Figure 6-6.

Joint-Cost Allocation	Allocation Method							
	NRV	SV	Moriarity	JIM	Louderback	JIL	Shapley	Democratic
A	64.98	79.58	4.87	10.87	3.96	9.78	9.00	25.00
B	33.33	47.71	91.49	82.07	91.19	85.87	79.00	25.00
C	0.42	(19.99)	(0.79)	3.06	1.76	1.09	1.00	25.00
D	1.27	(7.30)	4.44	4.01	3.08	3.26	3.00	25.00
Total	100.00	100.00	100.00[1]	100.00[1]	100.00[1]	100.00	92.00	100.00

Total Cost								
A	105.98	120.58	45.87[5]	51.87	44.96[5]	50.78	50.00	66.00
B	36.33[5]	50.71[5]	94.49	85.07	94.19	88.87	82.00	28.00[5]
C	54.42[5]	34.01[5]	53.21[5]	57.06	55.76	55.09	55.00	79.00
D	25.27[5]	16.70[5]	28.44	28.01	27.08	27.26	27.00	49.00
Total	222.00	222.00	222.00[1]	222.00[1]	222.00[1]	222.00	214.00	222.00

Book Profit								
A	89.02	74.42	149.13	143.13	150.04	144.22	145.00	129.00
B	45.67	31.29	(12.49)	(3.07)	(12.19)	(6.87)	0.00	54.00
C	0.58	20.99	1.79	(2.06)	(0.76)	(0.09)	0.00	(24.00)
D	1.73	10.30	(1.44)	(1.01)	(0.08)	(0.26)	0.00	(22.00)
Total	137.00	137.00	137.00[1]	137.00[1]	137.00[1]	137.00	145.00	137.00

[5] t_i < min$|p_i,x_i|$.

(31) *Elan effects* [D, G]. And each *fails* to be equitable in ways characteristic of other approaches.

(32) *Evaluation* [C, Glc]. Figure 6-12 illustrates an unusual situation. The company reflected in Figure 6-6 has split its Division B into two equal divisions, B1 and B2, each of which continues to process and sell product B, but at half Division B's output. This shouldn't affect other divisions' book profits, and under the NRV, SV, Louderback and JIL approaches it reliably won't. But as readers may verify, this split does affect other divisions' book profits under the Moriarity, Shapley and Democratic approaches; moreover, while the JIM approach is behaviour-congruent here, it isn't reliably so.[31]

(33) *Elan effects* [D, G2c]. Comparison of Figures 6-3 and 6-5 suggests a possible perverse behavioural property of all but the Democratic approach. We're all familiar with complaints of homeowners who paint or otherwise improve their houses only to find their property tax assessments increase. Similarly, although it's true that Division D is rewarded for its increase in efficiency by an increase in its book profits, under all but the Democratic approach its joint costs increase, too (indeed, under the NRV approach they change from a subsidy to a charge). This could dampen enthusiasm for improving efficiency, just as dangers of moving into higher income tax brackets are reputed to discourage productivity in the professions.

(34) *Evaluation; Elan effects* [C, D, G1b]. As we have previously noted, ideally, divisions' book profits shouldn't be affected by other divisions' inefficiencies. The same applies to their errors. We may interpret Figure 6-3 as one in which Division C made a correct decision to process product C further, and Figure 6-4 as one in which it erred. Under all eight approaches this error affected the book profits of other divisions.

(35) *Partial discarding* [A1b]. Similarly (for reasons given in Chapter Three), since all eight approaches implicitly assume horizontal marginal costs and marginal revenues, none are behaviour-

---

[31] As an example, let's suppose that a company is in the following situation:

Product	P_i	f_i	x_i	J
E	320	60	280	
F	80	50	70	
Total	400	110	350	100

and splits Division E evenly. Under the JIM approach, Division F's book profit will change from £16.09 to £35.45.

Figure 6-12 Same as Figure 6-6, Except That the Company Has Made Two Divisions Out of Division B

Product	n_i	f_i	p_i	x_i	y_i	$\min|p_i, x_i|$	J
A	154.0	41.0	195	68	68.0	68	
B1	39.5	1.5	41	105	101.5	41	
B2	39.5	1.5	41	105	101.5	41	
C	1.0	54.0	55	58	58.0	55	
D	3.0	24.0	27	31	31.0	27	
Total	237.0	122.0	359	367	360.0	232	100

	Allocation Method							
Joint-Cost Allocation	NRV	SV	Moriarity	JIM	Louderback	JIL	Shapley	Democratic
A	64.98	79.58	0.93	24.07	11.02	24.55	24.00	20.00
B1	16.67	23.85	61.09	37.73	42.24	35.91	36.50	20.00
B2	16.67	23.85	61.09	37.73	42.24	35.91	36.50	20.00
C	0.42	(19.99)	(18.23)	(1.37)	1.63	0.91	0.75	20.00
D	1.27	(7.30)	(4.88)	1.84	2.86	2.73	2.25	20.00
Total	100.00[1]	100.00[1]	100.00	100.00	100.00[1]	100.00[1]	100.00	100.00
Total Cost								
A	105.98	120.58	41.93	65.07	52.02	65.55	65.00	61.00
B1	18.17	25.35	62.59	39.23	43.74	37.41	38.00	21.50
B2	18.17	25.35	62.59	39.23	43.74	37.41	38.00	21.50
C	54.42	34.01	35.77	52.63	55.63	54.91	54.75	74.00
D	25.27	16.70	19.12	25.84	26.86	26.73	26.25	44.00
Total	222.00	222.00[1]	222.00	222.00	222.00[1]	222.00[1]	222.00	222.00
Book Profit								
A	89.02	74.42	153.07[4]	129.93	142.98	129.45	130.00[4]	134.00[4]
B1	22.83	15.65	(21.59)	1.77	(2.74)	3.59	3.00	19.50
B2	22.83	15.65	(21.59)	1.77	(2.74)	3.59	3.00	19.50
C	0.58	20.99	19.23[4]	2.37	(0.63)	0.09	0.25[4]	(19.00)[4]
D	1.73	10.30	7.88[4]	1.16	0.14	0.27	0.75[4]	(17.00)[4]
Total	137.00[1]	137.00[1]	137.00	137.00	137.00[1]	137.00[1]	137.00	137.00

[4] Changed from Figure 6-6.

congruent with respect to decisions on the extent to which the company should *partly* discard certain joint products.

(36) *Input prices* [A3c]. None of these approaches report joint products at book costs equal to the maximum amounts that the company could afford to pay outside suppliers for them.

(37) *Opportunity properties; Elan effects* [E2b, G5a]. Presuppose that two divisions receive the same amounts of the same joint product and have identical separate costs. One sells domestically, the other overseas (at a lower price). The Moriarity, Louderback and Democratic approaches will allocate the same amount of joint costs to both divisions, but the others will allocate less joint costs to the overseas division than to the domestic one, thereby violating the equitable rule that users who make the same demands on a joint process should be charged the same joint costs.[32]

(38) *Elan effects* [G3]. As readers may verify by substituting a £100 joint cost for the £50 one in the last footnote's example, if total joint costs increase or decrease, under the NRV, Louderback, JIL and Democratic approaches the joint cost allocated to each product will increase or decrease in the same proportion, whereas this need not be true under the other five approaches.

(39) *Miscellaneous.*[33] None of these approaches is reliably behaviour-congruent when used as an input to such things as capital-budgeting and taxation decisions, or to decisions made within a framework of anti-dumping or other regulatory laws.

The Marginal Approach

In this section, I shall rate the marginal approach on the same 39 properties as above. For brevity, much must be left to the reader, who is invited to verify what follows, using Appendix B's analysis and the examples in Chapter Three as starting points.

---

[32] Readers may verify this by the following example, where d and o respectively signify *domestic* and *overseas*:

Product	p_i	f_i	x_i	J
S_d	90	23	78	
S_o	50	23	78	
T	54	46	63	
U	23	3	20	
Total	217	95	239	50

[33] In Chapter Five, I didn't code the first of these properties, and didn't discuss the remaining ones.

Code numbers in round brackets will refer to the previous section's comparisons.

(1,2) *Further processing when joint products aren't available externally; related efficiency and élan properties.* In Chapter Three's second example ($f_i = 5$, $f_k = 9$), the central-office-optimal solution was to produce and sell 9.5 i's, discard 4.5 k's and sell 5.0 k's. Readers may verify that doing so generates respective £90.25 and £12.50 book profits for products i and k.

Let's now suppose that Division k makes an erroneous further-processing decision and sells six units. Division i's book profits will be unaffected, but Division k's will fall to £12.00,[34] thereby reducing global profits by £0.50. Since £12.00 is still positive, the marginal approach lacks these congruence properties.

(3,4) It follows that it's also not behaviour-congruent with respect to evaluation and mix decisions, in the particular senses of these developed in the previous section and Chapter Five.[35]

(5) *Discontinuing an unprofitable product.* Under the marginal approach, discontinuing a product that it is profitable to eliminate

[34] $TR_k = 14q_k - \tfrac{1}{2} \cdot (q_k^{\,2})$

$= 14 \cdot 6 - \tfrac{1}{2} \cdot 6^2 = 66$

Total book cost $= 6f_k = 6 \cdot 9 = 54$

$b_k = 12$

[35] As to the first of these, readers might also ponder the following. Under the marginal approach a product's "contributions" can be ambiguous, depending on the expansion or contraction paths by which the company is deemed to add to or delete from its stock in trade. Returning to Chapter Three's second example, were the company to process and sell only product i, it would maximize its profits at £90.25 per period. The optimal output of product k, in isolation, is zero, with a zero profit. Producing both yields a maximum of £90.25 + £12.50 = £102.75 per period. Therefore, the individual contributions of these two products may be deemed to be either:

	Expansion/(Contraction) Path Assumed		
Product	i Added First (k Deleted First)	or	k Added First (i Deleted First)
i	90.25		102.75
k	12.50		0.00
Total	102.75		102.75

The £90.25 and £12.50 book profits are consistent with the products' contributions only if we assume a particular expansion or contraction path for outputs. Here, the left-hand path is appropriate for decisions about adding to stock in trade, but not for decisions involving possible discontinuance (the cost of deleting product i would be £102.75, not £90.25). Again, the right-hand path is appropriate for decisions about deleting product i, but not for deleting product k, and so forth. Similar, more complex, ambiguities occur with three or more outputs.

won't affect joint costs assigned to other products—because this sort of product will have received a zero joint-cost allocation.

(6,7) *Promotion, pricing, hold or sell.* To the degree that the marginal approach generates product book costs that equal their marginal costs, it will be behaviour-congruent to these decisions. But, as we saw in Chapter Three, it does so only for products that should be partly discarded.[36] Therefore, its behaviour-congruence isn't reliable.

(8,9) *ISROPM and related properties when all $f_i < x_i$.* For a simple instance of the marginal approach's violating these properties, let's suppose that x_i = £20 and x_k = £30 in Chapter Three's first example: t_i = £24 will exceed x_i, despite that it is not to the company's immediate, short-run profit advantage to buy this product.

(10) *Buying a product that the company should manufacture.* Under the marginal approach, products that the company should partly discard receive a zero joint-cost allocation; all other products that the company should manufacture receive positive ones. Therefore, buying such products cannot increase another division's book profits, and the marginal approach is behaviour-congruent here.

(11) Under the marginal approach, any product that's partly discarded is a free rider.

(12) Readers may verify that the marginal approach rewards divisions for their efficiencies and penalizes them for their inefficiencies. For instance, in Chapter Three's first example if f_i increases from £9 to £12, b_i declines.

(13,14) However, the same increase in f_i results in doubling the amount of joint cost assigned to product k. Similarly, if the first constant in product i's demand function increases from 40 to 50, the joint cost allocated to product k drops to zero. Thus, the marginal approach isn't behaviour-congruent here.

(15,16) *Useless decrease in an external cost.* The marginal approach's failure to be affected by external costs renders it reliably behaviour-congruent here.

(17) *Useful decrease in an external cost.* Returning to Chapter Three's first example, let's suppose that product i's and k's exter-

---

[36]Book costs of products do equal their marginal *revenues*, but only under the very assumptions of business-as-usual that promotion, pricing and hold-or-sell decisions question.

nal costs were initially £14 and £6, respectively. Subsequently, x_k falls to £3. Under the marginal approach this won't improve the book profits of the division that manufactures product k.

(18,19) *Related evaluation, élan and efficiency properties.* The marginal approach's failure to be affected by external costs renders it reliably behaviour-congruent here.

(20) *Dissuasion of buying when doing so is globally profitable.* The marginal approach's making of nonnegative joint-cost assignments renders it reliably behaviour-congruent here.

(21) *Effect of such buying on other divisions.* In the example given for (17), immediately above, if the division responsible for product k does buy it, the other division's book profits will suffer.

(22) Thus, related élan effects could be dysfunctional.

(23) *ISROPM.* The marginal approach's failure to be affected by external costs prevents it from being reliably behaviour-congruent here.

(24,25) *Case C.* If there is no selling price at which a joint process will be profitable, the marginal approach will reveal this by specifying negative quantities of output.

(26) *Case D, divisions free to buy.* If total costs to manufacture exceed total costs to buy, the marginal approach will reliably generate book costs that exceed external costs for at least one product.

(27,28) *Case D, otherwise; Case E.* The marginal approach's failure to be affected by external costs prevents it from being reliably behaviour-congruent here.

(29) The marginal approach does not assign each product the same percentage markup.

(30,31) *Fairness.* Like the other eight approaches, the marginal approach will appear equitable on some dimensions, inequitable on others.

(32) *Splitting a division.* Under the marginal approach, this won't affect other divisions' book profits.

(33) *Increase in efficiency increasing joint costs.* Let's return again to the first example in Chapter Three, and suppose that Division i's further-processing costs drop from £9 to £8. If so, joint costs allocated to it will increase from £15.00 to £15.33.

(34) An incorrect decision to manufacture a product will have no effect on other division's book profits, since the joint cost assignment to the incorrect product will be zero. But an incorrect decision, say, to buy product k in Chapter Three's first example would reduce product i's book profits.

(35) *Partial discarding.* The marginal approach was designed to be reliably behaviour-congruent here. However, see (1) above: its failure reliably to report negative book profits when a company makes incorrect decisions on partial discarding prevents this.[37]

(36) As Chapter Three indicated, the marginal approach reliably reports products at book costs equal to the maximum amounts that the company could afford to pay an outside supplier for them.

(37) *Domestic and overseas divisions.* The marginal approach isn't behaviour-congruent here, as readers may verify from the following example (see Appendix B for its notation):

$$J = 16 \qquad \alpha_i = 40$$
$$f_i = f_k = 7 \qquad \alpha_k = 28$$
$$\beta_i = \beta_k = 1.5$$

Here, j_i = 12 and j_k = 4. (However, under such circumstances, the marginal approach assigns both divisions the same book *profits*, something that may or may not be a desirable property.)

(38) *Impact of increase in total joint cost on allocated joint costs.* The marginal approach isn't reliably behaviour-congruent here. For instance, if we return to Chapter Three's final example and increase joint costs by 25%, the proportion of joint costs allocated to the two products changes from 15:1 to 7.6:1, j_i increasing by 18% and j_k by 133%.

(39) *Capital budgeting, taxation and regulatory decisions.* The marginal approach is not reliably behaviour-congruent here.

Summary

Figure 6-13 is a tabular summary of all 39 comparisons of our nine joint-cost allocation methods. A plus indicates that an approach is reliably behaviour-congruent with respect to the particular decision and circumstances described, a minus that it is not.

Restriction of the discussion to textbook joint-cost situations, lack of randomness in my choices of comparisons and congruence properties, inability to resolve the possibility that some properties may be more desirable than others, and my disregarding such things as supplementary analyses of variances in book profits, demand interdependencies and other issues all limit Figure 6-13's sig-

---

[37] As we saw in Chapter Two (in connection with the Moriarity and Louderback approaches), a procedure's being designed to help decision makers make central-office-optimal decisions doesn't guarantee its ringing alarm bells if these decisions err. A tool need not be a control.

nificance. Yet three conclusions may legitimately be drawn from it:

1. It's obvious that no individual allocation method even approaches being reliably behaviour-congruent with respect to all decisions and circumstances. In particular, given the recent excitement about them in the accounting literature, readers are asked to note that this is true of Shapley allocations.[38]

2. Authors who henceforth propose novel joint-cost allocation schemes should specify the main dimensions on which their methods are superior and inferior to, say, the NRV, JIL and Shapley approaches.

3. As is evident from Figure 6-14, if the central office is willing to use different methods in different situations, then a judicious combination of approaches (using one method for decisions, and in circumstances, where it's behaviour-congruent and another where it isn't) can yield better results that any one method can alone. Indeed, of the ten comparisons that the JIL/ Democratic combination fails, only five are ones that *any* other approach passes.[39] The suggested combinations of the NRV, JIL, Shapley and Democratic methods seem operationally feasible and (assuming use of a computer) inexpensive.

---

[38] And I repeat that the version of the Shapley approach used in this chapter was the one with the best congruence properties.

[39] In this context, it is interesting to consider how ideal analyses based on allocation-free data might score on our 39 comparisons. In theory, if we continue to assume that the central office wants immediate, short-run, global profit maximization, they could do quite well. Allocation-free marginal analyses would reliably lead to central-office-optimal ISROPM and related decisions (1, 5, 8, 10, 22-28, 35, 36) and should promote proper evaluations of divisions and products, and product-mix, promotion and hold-or-sell decisions (3, 4, 6, 7). Rewardings and penalizings of divisions should be appropriate (since operating results couldn't be confused by joint-cost assignments) (2, 12-21, 33, 34). There would be no difficulties with such things as splitting divisions in two (32), domestic versus overseas divisions (37) or increases in total joint costs (38)–and, on some levels anyway, results would appear equitable (30).

Of course, on other dimensions they might not (31), there's no reason to expect that allocation-free data would be appropriate for tax or regulatory purposes (39), allocation-free approaches allow free riders (11) and they don't ensure that each product has the same percentage markup (29). Still, 35 out of 39 is respectable, especially when one reflects that equality of percentage markups may not be desirable, that the free-riders issue's severity is limited when *no* products are charged joint costs, and that it would be possible to make supplementary, expedient joint-cost allocations for tax and regulatory purposes without using these for internal decision making.

If so, still assuming that allocation-free decision making is feasible, the only remaining problem is that division managers might deem an otherwise appropriate allocation-free approach to be significantly less fair than some allocated one. One can imagine extreme situations in which that could render this allocated approach preferable (just as some will contend, though I believe incorrectly, that conventional, allocated *financial* accounting is preferable on economic-consequences grounds to any allocation-free approach). But I cannot see this happening very often. And, when it does, it should be amenable to education.

Figure 6-13

Summary of Congruence Properties

Property	NRV	SV	Moriarity	JIM	Louderback	JIL	Shapley	Democratic	Marginal
1	+	−	−	+	−	+	+	−	−
2	+	−	−	+	−	+	+	−	−
3	+	−	−	−	−	−	−	−	−
4	+	+	−	+	−	+	+	−	+
5	+								
6	+	−	−	−	−	−	−	−	−
7	−	−	−	−	−	−	−	−	−
8	−	−	−	+	−	+	+	−	−
9	−	−	−	+	−	+	+	−	−
10	+	−	−	−	+	+	+	+	+
11	+	−	−	−	+	+	−	+	−
12	+	+	+	+	+	+	+	+	+
13	−	−	−	−	−	−	−	+	−
14	−	−	+	−	+	−	−	+	−
15	+	+	−	−	−	−	−	+	+
16	+	+	−	−	−	−	−	+	+
17	−	−	+	+	+	+	+	−	−
18	+	+	−	−	−	−	+	+	+
19	+	+	−	−	−	−	−	+	+
20	+	−	−	+	+	+	+	+	+

Property	NRV	SV	Moriarity	JIM	Louderback	JIL	Shapley	Democratic	Marginal
21	−	−	+	+	+	+	+	−	−
22	−	−	−	−	+	+	+	−	−
23	−	−	−	+		+	+	−	−
24	+	+	+	+	+	+	+	+	+
25	+	+	−	+	−	+	+	−	+
26	+	+	+	+	+	+	+	+	+
27	−	−	+	+	+	+	+	−	−
28	−	−	−	+	−	+	+	−	−
29	−	+	−	−	−	−	−	−	−
30	+	+	+	+	+	+	+	+	+
31	−	−	−	−	−	−	−	−	−
32	+	+	−	−	+	+	−	+	+
33	−	−	−	−	−	−	−	−	−
34	−	−	−	−	−	−	−	−	−
35	−	−	−	−	−	−	−	−	−
36	−	−	−	−	−	−	−	−	+
37	−	−	+	−	+	−	−	+	−
38	+	−	−	−	+	+	−	+	−
39	−	−	−	−	−	−	−	−	−
Total +	20	12	9	16	15	21	18	16	14
−	19	27	30	23	24	18	21	23	25

Limitations of Behaviour-Congruence

> At the bachelor dinner Shloimele spoke brilliantly. First of all he propounded ten questions which seemed to be absolutely basic, and then he answered all ten with a single statement. But after having disposed of these essential questions, he turned around and showed that the questions he had asked were not really questions at all, and the enormous facade of erudition he had erected tumbled to nothing. His audience was left amazed and speechless. —[Singer, 1961]

But that may be the most that can be said. Whenever it's possible for a company to make central-office-optimal decisions without using joint-cost allocations, doing that requires no more knowledge of such things as the company's production and demand functions than does selection of behaviour-congruent allocation methods. Thus, whenever allocation-free decision making is feasible, behaviour-congruence seemingly has no merit beyond rescuing decision makers from side effects of doing something that's unnecessary. Of course, as Chapter One indicated, the great question is: How often *is* joint-cost allocation unnecessary?

Certainly, empirical research can help answer this.[40] But, as Part Two's discussion of transfer pricing (culminating in Chapter Twelve) will try to show, so can analysis.

---

[40] Similarly, empirical researchers are invited to investigate whether companies actually do adopt allocation methods that are behaviour-congruent with respect to central-office wants, surrounding circumstances and any decisions that the company bases on allocated joint costs.

Figure 6-14

Properties of Judicious Combinations of Methods

Property	NRV and JIL	NRV and Shapley	JIL and Democratic	Shapley and Democratic
1	+	+	+	+
2	+	+	+	+
3	+	+	−	−
4	+	+	−	−
5	+	+	+	+
6	+	+	−	−
7	−	−	−	−
8	+	+	+	+
9	+	+	+	+
10	+	+	+	+
11	+	+	+	+
12	+	+	+	+
13	−	−	+	+
14	−	−	+	+
15	+	+	+	+
16	+	+	+	+
17	+	+	+	+
18	+	+	+	+
19	+	+	+	+
20	+	+	+	+
21	+	+	+	+
22	+	+	+	+
23	+	+	+	+
24	+	+	+	+
25	+	+	+	+
26	+	+	+	+
27	+	+	+	+
28	+	+	+	+
29	−	−	−	−
30	+	+	+	+
31	−	−	−	−
32	+	+	+	−
33	−	−	+	+
34	−	−	−	−
35	−	−	−	−
36	−	−	−	−
37	−	−	+	+
38	+	+	+	+
39	−	−	−	−
Total +	28	28	29	28
−	11	11	10	10

PART TWO

TRANSFER PRICING

There is possibly no single accounting topic that consumes more management time and energy in multi-profit center companies than the business of establishing acceptable transfer prices. The expenditure of energy in this area far exceeds that expended on pricing products sold to outside customers. −[Seed, 1970, p. 10]

With the computer and with the much better understanding of the nature of business we now have, significant improvements in techniques of cost allocation are possible. Methods of assigning more items of cost directly to cost objectives will be developed. Better transfer prices will be constructed. −[Anthony, 1975, p. 16]

CHAPTER SEVEN

PRELIMINARY CONSIDERATIONS

An administrative organization is centralized to the extent that decisions are made at relatively high levels in the organization; decentralized to the extent that discretion and authority to make important decisions are delegated by top management to lower levels of executive authority. —[Simon et al., 1954, p. 1; original entirely in italics]

The essence of divisionalization is delegated profit responsibility. —[Solomons, 1977, p. 44·2]

Transfer pricing[1] is a major aspect of company decentralization into profit centres. Combined, the two foregoing quotations provide a good working definition of *decentralization* as it's perceived in contemporary practice.[2] Later, though, we shall make three qualifications:

1. The authority of division managers to make important decisions may be illusory: the central office may "force" particular divisional decisions in much the way that a magician forces a card on the subject of a card trick.

---

[1] For general background on transfer pricing, see [National Association of Accountants, 1957a], [Whinston, 1962], [Shulman, 1966], [Livesey, 1967], [McCulloch, 1967], [Rook, 1971], [Williamson, 1971], [Centre for Business Research, 1972], [Tomkins, 1973, Ch. 1-4, 8], [Milburn, 1977] and, especially, [Solomons, 1965]. The CASB's research project on transfer pricing was still in process at date of writing. Whinston's book is particularly valuable for its consideration of problems involving externalities that are fundamental to transfer pricing. Williamson's article discusses why companies integrate vertically (as contrasted to why, having done so, they then decentralize and use transfer prices). However, many of the things described by him that encourage vertical integration (e.g., vertical integration's making it difficult for independent companies to strike bargains) also make it hard to set behaviour-congruent transfer prices. Finally, the first footnote in [Menge, 1961, p. 215] lists three early accounting discussions of transfer pricing.

Here are some additional works on transfer pricing that I shan't discuss specifically in what follows because, as readers are invited to verify, the points that they make are made better elsewhere, they're directed to highly specialized issues, they're unconcerned with theory or, in a few cases, they're generally inadequate: [Stone, 1956], [Mattessich, 1961], [Shillinglaw, 1964], [Thompson, 1964], [Sartoris, 1971], [Cupples, 1972], [Crompton, 1972] (see [Tastor, 1972] and [Williamson, 1973]), [Vendig, 1973], [Cushing, 1976] and [Edwards and Roemmich, 1976]. In particular, I largely disregard Goetz's [1967; 1969] writings, which other authors have revealed to be confused and which have not proved to be influential—see [Wells, 1968, pp. 174, 176-77, 181; 1971, p. 55], [Fremgen, 1970, p. 27] and [Lemke, 1970, pp. 182-83].

[2] For an alternative definition of decentralization that recognizes a possible multiplicity of company goals, perhaps with different actors having different priorities, see [Charnes, Clower and Kortanek, 1967, p. 295].

2. Such divisional autonomy is often incompatible with other things that central offices expect of decentralization. (Indeed, one of the next few chapters' main purposes will be to *demonstrate* this.)

3. Division managers may be judged by criteria additional to their divisions' book profits.

Nonetheless, divisional autonomy and profit responsibility are the essence of decentralization as it is viewed in both the business world and the theoretical literature.

A *profit centre* is any division of a company for which its accountants calculate book profits (or losses) that the central office uses in evaluating the success of this division and its management.[3]

A *transfer price* is a monetary representation of a good or service exchanged between divisions, this price being internally reported either as a revenue of the supplier division or a cost of the receiver division, or both.[4] Hereafter, I'll often refer to the product or service as an *intermediate product* or a *transfer good,* and the supplier and receiver as *transferor* and *transferee*, respectively.

There are two ways in which transfer pricing may involve one-to-many allocation. First, the transfer price *per se* may be an allocated magnitude, such as the "full" (absorption) cost of a manufactured intermediate product to its manufacturing division. Second, and more important for our purposes, a company that engages in transfer pricing will always earn an overall profit. If it treats both transferor and transferee as profit centres, inevitably the transfer price used affects how much of that overall profit it attributes to each division. That's to say, the transfer price inevitably involves a one-to-many (at least one-to-two) allocation of global profits even if, in itself, the transfer price is a one-to-many-allocation-*free* tracing of direct costs.[5]

> To take a standard example, let's suppose that a manufacturing division sells to an assembly division that, in turn, sells to the public. A batch of product costs £20,000 to manufacture, £4,000 to assemble, and sells for £40,000, a total margin of £16,000. If the transfer price is £20,000, the total margin goes to the assembly division; if it's £28,000, the margin is allocated 50/50 between the divisions and so forth.[6]

---

[3] See [Reece and Cool, 1978, p. 28].

[4] Loosely based on [Wells, 1968, p. 175].

[5] See [Bierman, 1959, p. 429], [Caplan, 1971, p. 99] and [Thomas, 1971a, pp. 44-47 and *passim*]. Of course, since profit is a residual we accountants never allocate it directly. Instead, we always allocate it by allocating either revenue or cost.

[6] Please note that £16,000-£0 is just as much a one-to-many allocation as is £8,000-£8,000.

Must Decentralization Be Into Profit Centres?

It's evident from the foregoing that a company's decision whether or not to treat divisions as profit centres can have a major impact on the quality of its transfer prices. Where divisions are *not* profit centres, obviously there's no need for one-to-many profit allocations to them, and one-to-many cost allocations might be avoided by what corresponds to direct costing. From this, it follows that the theoretical difficulties of transfer pricing that we shall explore are consequences of the use of profit centres, not of transfer pricing as such.[7]

The next several chapters will assume decentralization into profit centres, for three reasons:

1. This book's concern is with such theoretical difficulties,

2. As will become evident, most of the literature that it reviews makes the same assumption, and I intend to analyze this literature on its own terms, and

3. Available empirical studies[8] indicate that real-world decentralization mostly *is* into profit centres.

Perhaps one reason for the last is that, as we'll soon see, companies wish division managers to act as much as possible as independent entrepreneurs would. Such entrepreneurs *are* judged by their profits. Again, outside investors evaluate companies in terms of their profitabilities. When companies decentralize their central offices must, in turn, evaluate the performances of divisions and division managers. Mistakenly or not, it is only natural to evaluate them on the same, profitability, basis. Indeed, unless companies do evaluate divisional performances in terms of divisional book profits, they can easily experience serious problems of comparability and consistency.[9]

In summary, although Chapter Twelve will reconsider the matter, until then I shall analyze transfer pricing in a context of profit centres.

---

[7]Horngren [1975, p. 23*n*] comments:

> ...profit centers and decentralization are sometimes erroneously used as if they were synonymous terms. Decentralization is the relative freedom to make decisions. Although it seems strange at first glance, profit centers can be coupled with a highly centralized organization, and cost centers can be coupled with a highly decentralized organization. So the labels of *profit center* and *cost center* can be deceptive as indicators of the degree of decentralization. [Boldface instead of italics in the original.]

This, of course, is also essentially the position repeatedly taken by Wells [e.g., 1968; 1971].

[8]Such as [National Association of Accountants, 1957a], [Livesey, 1967], [McCulloch, 1967], [Mautz and Skousen, 1968], [Rook, 1971], [Centre for Business Research, 1972], [Tomkins, 1973, Ch. 8] and [Emmanuel, 1977c].

[9]A familiar, parallel problem occurs in accounting education whenever professional associations and employers judge our programs by criteria that differ from those (perhaps more conceptual or theory-oriented) criteria that *we* use in evaluating our students.

Ubiquity of Transfer Pricing

Although few authors perceive transfer-price allocations to be as *radically* arbitrary as the term *incorrigible* implies, most concede their arbitrariness.[10] The essential point here is that whenever the transferor and transferee are profit centres, transfer pricing's book-profit allocations have exactly the same form as that of a two-product, joint-cost allocation:

Subject ──────── ┤ ────→Object
                   └────→Object

Thus, transfer prices can be of no higher quality than joint costs. Readers who agree that joint-cost allocations are incorrigible should have no difficulty accepting that the same is true of such transfer prices.[11]

All of a company's internal cost allocations (and all of the parallel cost allocations of centrally planned economies[12]) may be perceived as transfer prices of related goods and services. To use our previous example, any joint-cost allocation may be deemed to be a transfer of costs from the joint process to the divisions that receive the joint products.[13] [14] But this ubiquity of transfer pricing extends much further—even to such things as calculations of internal

---

[10]For instance, see [Simon et al., 1954, pp. 40-42], [Henderson and Dearden, 1966, p. 146], [Fremgen, 1971, p. 25], [Horngren, 1972, p. 729], [Holstrum and Sauls, 1973, pp. 29, 33] and [Milburn, 1977, pp. 60-63, 80-83, 201]. Wiseman [1957, pp. 58-59] makes the fundamental point that any transfer-pricing system is simultaneously a system of income distribution between divisions, and that there exists no underlying theory of welfare for this division to which all parties will subscribe. To be sure, at the global optimum the distribution will be Pareto optimal. But, as usual, Pareto optimality is a joint phenomenon that gives no support to the book profits credited to *individual* divisions. (See also [pp. 60-61].)

[11]Readers who *disagree* are directed to Part One and [Thomas, 1974, esp. pp. 15-16, 51-57].

[12]See [Kornai and Lipták, 1965], Malinvaud, 1967], [Kornai, 1967a; 1967b; 1973], [Gordon, 1970], [Horwitz, 1970] and the various earlier works indirectly cited in footnote 25, below.

[13]This is especially evident for allocations of service-department costs to production departments, and is explicit in [Shubik, 1962 and 1964]. This overlap has caused some difficulties in the organization of this book. For instance, as noted earlier, [Kaplan and Thompson, 1971] and [Kaplan and Welam, 1974] could be discussed in either context. Convenience of exposition dictated their discussion's falling under the joint-cost heading, whereas Shapley allocations and related notions from game theory appear in both Parts of this book, though mainly in Part One. Any artificiality in this is mitigated by my fundamental critiques of both joint-cost allocations and transfer pricing being identical.

[14]Here's additional evidence on the ubiquity of joint costs and, thus, of transfer pricing: Because they're also one-to-many, allocations of what we accountants call *common* costs are identical for our purposes with joint-cost allocations. Mautz and Skousen [1968, pp. 16-17] empirically determined that even the *noninventoriable* portion of such costs is quite significant to industry: on average it exceeded profit.

interest rates.[15] (Similarly, any externalities created by one division can, in theory at least, be controlled by transfer prices—again, central-government use of taxes to control such things as pollution offers a parallel.)[16]

Why Do Companies Use Transfer Prices?

> I think it is fair to say that internal price systems...have not been introduced into practical business operations as desirable innovations in their own right. Rather, they have been the by-product of the institution of decentralized "profit centers." —[Hirshleifer, 1964, p. 27]

Why do companies use transfer prices? Some of the most obvious reasons have to do with tax-minimization[17] and compliance with anti-trust regulations.[18] But these, though often of great

---

[15] See [Arrow, 1959, pp. 14-15].

[16] Practice-oriented literature on transfer pricing takes a somewhat less catholic view of its ubiquity, but one that remains impressive. In particular, readers are directed to such empirical surveys as [National Association of Accountants, 1957a], [Livesey, 1967], [McCulloch, 1967], [Mautz and Skousen, 1968], [Rook, 1971], [Centre for Business Research, 1972], [Tomkins, 1973, Ch. 8] and [Emmanuel, 1977c], where transfer prices are highly significant. Again, we may use profits as our index. Milburn's [1976, esp. p. 24; 1977, pp. 19-34, 77-80] empirical study provides indirect evidence of the magnitude of real-world transfer prices when compared to what correspond to divisional profits. Of the Canadian industry groupings that he studied, subsidiary-corporation 1971 imports or exports from foreign affiliates exceeded total subsidiary net incomes in 15 out of 22 cases, and were roughly of the same magnitude in 4 more. In only one industry grouping (Other manufacturing) did *total* transfers fail to exceed total subsidiary profits by less than 71%; in the median remaining case the excess was 450%, and, for all subsidiaries combined, 740%. Moreover, it's to be noted that these figures include only *merchandise* transfers; they don't include amounts assigned to transfers of capital goods, interest, royalties, management fees and research and development charges—which would have raised the excess by another 42% of profits.

Canada is an extreme case, both in degree of foreign ownership and in the extent to which affiliates trade with each other. But the conclusion remains that where transfers do occur the allocations used to price them can greatly influence divisional profits. As Milburn [1976, p. 22] mildly observes:

> Clearly, in certain industries major companies' operating results are highly sensitive to even moderate amounts of variability in the valuation of merchandise transfer transactions.

Even compared with the much larger magnitude, sales, transfer prices can be significant. For British empirical evidence, see [Rook, 1971, pp. 1, 3-4], [Centre for Business Research, 1972, pp. 3-4] and [Tomkins, 1973, pp. 179-80].

[17] See [Stone, 1960] for an introduction. The literature summarized in [Thomas, 1971a] and [Milburn, 1976 and 1977] reflects the importance of taxation in multi-national transfer pricing (the bibliography in the last is especially valuable). Companies use similar transfer-pricing strategies to minimize the total taxes levied by different jurisdictions *within* individual nations. See also [Solomons, 1965, p. 74].

[18] See [McCulloch, 1967, pp. 12-13].

practical significance, are outside the scope of this primarily theoretical study. (Similarly, reasons stemming from financial accounting's need for inventory figures raise issues that I've discussed elsewhere.)[19]

The other main reason was implied by our earlier discussion: Companies wish to decentralize into profit centres. Whenever profit centres trade with each other, transfer pricing is essential to calculating their profits, which, in turn, is deemed essential to their evaluation. Thus, in this profit-centre context, asking why companies use transfer prices is equivalent to asking why they decentralize.

Solomons [1977, p. 44·2] summarizes what the literature as a whole suggests are the main answers to this last question:[20]

> First, decentralized decision making is likely to result in better decisions because the people who make them are closer to the scene of action and have a smaller area of responsibility to worry about. Second, greater efficiency results from the sense the divisional managers have that they are running "their" businesses. In motivating these managers, divisional profit plays an important part. Third, giving a person responsibility for running a division is perhaps the best way of providing preparation for a top management role at the corporate level.

In effect, I'll subsume discussion of Solomons' third reason in discussing his second. But let's begin by briefly considering his first reason.

Information Economies

This, of course, is the familiar explanation of information economies, also reflected in the following two early observations:

> ...*given realistic limits on human planning capacity* the decentralized system will work better than the centralized. −[March and Simon, 1958, p. 203]

> [Decentralization] is advantageous in economizing on the transmission of information. In particular, the detailed technical knowledge of the process need not be transmitted to a central office but can be retained in the department...we may regard it as close to an impossibility for individuals in close contact with the productive processes to transmit their information in all its details to another office. This proposition,

---

[19] Milburn's [1977] bibliography is also useful for such financial accounting aspects.

[20] Though see [Heflebower, 1960, pp. 7-13] for some interesting, earlier answers.

long recognized in practice, is the basis of the management literature on the questions of centralization and decentralization. —[Arrow, 1959, p. 11][21]

Watson and Baumler [1975, pp. 467-68] broaden these notions, in their discussion of decentralization's role in helping complex organizations cope with uncertainty, and my lay opinion is that this broader context is essential to the fruitfulness of subsequent research on the topic. However, except for gaming (divisions giving *mis*information to central offices), those matters aren't central concerns of this study.

Autonomy of Division Managers

Solomons' second reason why companies decentralize is that division managers supposedly perform better when given the autonomy to run their divisions as though they were entrepreneurs running their own businesses. Certainly (as readers may verify) the economics, management-science and accounting literatures agree here: All see divisional autonomy as a means to get division managers to work harder and more efficiently, tenaciously, imaginatively and creatively—as well as to foster in them a general awareness of the profit dimensions of their decisions. Moreover, as Tomkins [1973, p. 5] notes, by making the division managers' positions more challenging and interesting, such autonomy attracts more capable people to fill their posts.

Appendix G reviews psychological theories and empirical evidence on these matters. Although neither theories nor evidence entirely satisfactory, on balance one seems entitled to conclude that the literature is usually right here. I will so presume in what follows.[22] But this *is* a crucial presumption, if only because (as mentioned earlier), one of the next several chapters' main concerns will be to argue that divisional autonomy is often incompatible with other things that central offices expect of decentralization.

---

[21] Hass [1968, p. B·310] adds avoidance of data time lags as another virtue of decentralized systems. For more on these matters, see [Hayek, 1944, pp. 48-50], [Koopmans, 1957, pp. 22-23], [Arrow and Hurwicz, 1960, p. 36], [Dearden, 1962a, p. 88], [Arrow, 1964, p. 317], [Hirshleifer, 1964, p. 28], [Marschak, 1964, p. 86], [Shubik, 1964, p. 208], [Whinston, 1964, pp. 418-19], [Dearden, 1967, pp. 100-01], [Malinvaud, 1967, pp. 170, 174-75], [Hass, 1968, p. B·311], [Kriebel and Lave, 1969, p. 186], [Ronen and McKinney, 1970, p. 99], [Simon, 1957, pp. 81-82], [Freeland, 1973, pp. 7-9], [Tomkins, 1973, pp. 4-5], [Dopuch, Birnberg and Demski, 1974, pp. 651, 654-55] and [Solomons, 1977, p. 44·2].

[22] Given my earlier-mentioned strategy of analyzing the transfer-pricing literature on its own terms, I'd be pretty well forced to do this, anyway.

In particular, other main goals of decentralization, implicit in Solomons' surrounding discussion, now need to be made explicit. Central offices often wish to eat their cakes and have them. They want to obtain the information economies and divisional élan of decentralization without sacrificing the coordination associated with centralization. They would decentralize, yet have the decentralized units behave exactly as the central office would direct them to behave were information economies and élan not considerations. Or, in Part One's language, they would decentralize into profit centres yet have any consequent allocations universally behaviour-congruent with respect to related decisions, circumstances and central-office wants. Here are three examples (two of which assume that the company has a single goal of profit-maximization):

> By coherent decentralization of a system we mean that the system is so coupled or organized that with the provision of prices and possibly certain additional information to its units, the unit's drive to individual profit goals will result in overall optimal profit. —[Charnes, Clower and Kortanek, 1967, p. 296]

> ...an appropriate transfer price would be one which results in the division manager making the same decision that corporate management would make in viewing the overall benefit to the firm. —[Larson, 1971, p. 20n]

> Ideally, transfer prices should guide each manager to choose his inputs and outputs in coordination with other subunits so as to maximize the profits of the organization as a whole. —[Horngren, 1977, p. 679] [23]

As the final quotation suggests, such decisions include ones on divisional outputs and the company's internal resource allocations. Division managers are to make the same output and resource-allocation decisions as, ideally, the central office would make itself. Yet divisional autonomies are to be preserved. How are companies to accomplish all this?

The Visible Hand

In traditional *macro*economic theory, price systems and market-clearing mechanisms achieve this (while simultaneously providing information economies and inspiring entrepreneurial élan):

---

[23] Three other examples, chosen merely because they lay ready to hand, may be found in [Goetz, 1967, p. 438], [Fremgen, 1970, p. 26] and [Holstrum and Sauls, 1973, pp. 29, 33]. [Horwitz, 1970, pp. 2, 26-28, 58] indicates that the Russians also seek behaviour-congruent transfer prices, though often without success [e.g., pp. 61-65].

> Economists have long recognized that demand and supply schedules in a market (simple price and quantity relations) summarize enormous amounts of information with respect to the costs of producing and benefits derived from obtaining the good in question. If a market device can be introduced, planning and control can be left to the market clearing mechanism... —[Hass, 1968, p. B·311]

Much of the rationale of such market devices lies in that they supposedly do preserve the autonomies of the macro actors while rendering their outputs, and the allocations of society's resources to them, globally optimal. The essential ideas here appear in [Smith, 1776, e.g., Bk. I, Ch. 1; Bk. IV, Ch. II]:[24] The only dependable human motive is self interest; yet, a system of prices and markets can ensure that if people follow their self interests they'll be led by an invisible hand to promote an end that was no part of their intentions: maximization of society's annual product.

The invisible hand is invisible because no one consciously coordinates economic actors to achieve this global optimum. But for generations writers on collectivism have suggested similar price and market devices to help central planners attain the same results consciously.[25] It was only natural to propose applying such visible hands to companies' *internal* economies, with divisions substituted for the macroeconomy's firms.[26] And that's precisely what most economists, management scientists and accountants writing on transfer-pricing theory have done.[27]

Unfortunately, Smith's invisible hand reliably achieves the general weal only when certain restrictive assumptions hold true. In particular, we must assume that there are no *externalities*: effects

---

[24]The rest of this sentence follows [March and Simon, 1958, p. 200]; see also [pp. 202-03].

[25]For example, see the pre-1940 works cited in [Hayek, 1944], [Koopmans, 1957, pp. 37-43, 63-64, 66-68 and *passim*], [March and Simon, 1958, pp. 201-10], [Marschak, 1959, pp. 399-400] and [Gordon, 1970, pp. 427-30]. (I am aware that this sentence simplifies a complex intellectual history, and that the simplification has its roots in the general philosophy of Hayek.)

[26][Dean, 1955, pp. 66-68] is a good example of the optimism with which such proposals were initially made. For instance, [p. 68] opines that the problems of transfer pricing can be solved by "three simple principles": (1) transfer prices should be negotiated, (2) negotiators should have perfect access to information and (3) buyers and sellers should be completely free to deal outside the company. Oh, it were bliss in that dawn to be alive.

Similar oversimplifications abound in today's accounting literature, especially in the practitioner-oriented journals (as, for instance, a review of the last few years' issues of *Management Accounting* will reveal).

[27]For explicit recognition of this analogy, see [Arrow, 1959, pp. 9, 17], [March and Simon, 1958, pp. 201-202], [Gould, 1964, p. 61], [Charnes, Clower and Kortanek, 1967, pp. 297-300], [Hass, 1968, pp. B·311-12], [Abdel-khalik, 1971, p. 787] and [Ronen, 1974, pp. 71-73, 76-77].

of one economic actor's actions upon other actors, where such effects escape the price and market mechanisms.[28] The very existence of such externalities on the real world's macro level (especially negative externalities, such as pollution) explains many conscious interventions into the economy made even by governments that are ideologically committed to allowing the invisible hand to function as freely as possible.

Similarly, we'll find that externalities of various sorts pose severe problems for decentralization at the micro level, often requiring overt or covert central-office intervention for their resolution.[29] And, just as central-government intervention is destructive of company autonomy on the macro level, so these central-office interventions are destructive of divisional autonomy on the micro level. The upshot, as noted in Part One, is that the visible hand often becomes a visible ham-hand.[30]

Transfer Pricing in the Real World

The question naturally arises: How successful have theorists been in selling their visible-hand approaches to practitioners? There's a convenient index of this: as we'll see in detail later, most

---

[28]See [March and Simon, 1958, p. 202], [Shapley and Shubik, 1969b, p. 678], [Ronen, 1974, p. 72] and [Heller and Starrett, 1976].

[29][Whinston, 1964, pp. 441-45] discusses other ways in which the realities of companies' internal economies fail to correspond to what the Smith model assumes. We'll consider some of these in later chapters.

[30]Besides the classical literature of economics, it's clear (e.g., from [Wiseman, 1957, pp. 57-59], [Hirshleifer, 1964, p. 28] and [Lin, 1976]) that the literatures of public-utility pricing, indirect taxation (and welfare economics generally), theory of teams, input-output analysis and externalities are highly pertinent to transfer pricing. For instance, as Hirshleifer [1964, p. 28] observes of transfer pricing:

> This question is really a special case of a classical problem of welfare economics: under what conditions, and in what senses, does goal-maximization on the micro level lead to a macro optimum?

Here "micro" and "macro" refer to the divisional and global-company levels, respectively. Would that I were at present capable of bringing these literatures effectively to bear upon the problems discussed in subsequent chapters, but that must be left to other researchers.

One such literature deserves particular mention. Inspired by [Marshall, 1972], [Demski, 1973; 1974], [Beaver and Demski, 1974], [American Accounting Association, 1977] and [Demski and Feltham, 1977], I had hoped to crown this book's analyses by showing that Arrow's Possibility Theorems render it impossible simultaneously to attain global optima and preserve divisional autonomy. But several months of sporadic labour failed to provide a logically tight proof (or to satisfy me with what seems to have satisfied certain other accountants in this area), and, in any event, I'm now beginning to fear that some of Arrow's assumptions are questionable. Readers interested in pursuing this might want to begin with [Arrow, 1950 and 1963], [Vickrey, 1960], some of the works cited in [Niemi and Riker, 1976 (see p. 132)], and [Cushing, 1977, esp. pp. 312-15].

such approaches proposed since the 1950s involve setting transfer prices equal to transfer goods' short-run opportunity costs (in one of the specific ways of measuring these: marginal costs, shadow prices, etc.). Thus, a rough test of practical acceptance of visible-hand approaches to decentralization is to ask how widespread is the use of such opportunity-cost transfer pricing.

Real companies do use it in one, limited sense. When there's a perfect external market for a transfer good, in theory its opportunity cost for transfer-pricing purposes will be the price that it will command in this external market. Here (or in circumstances that approximate such perfect intermediate markets), companies often do use such external prices (or slight modifications of them) as transfer prices. But this should offer little comfort to theorists. For, as I'll argue in the next chapter, when intermediate markets are perfect such use of external prices boils down to a form of al-location-*free* current-value accounting. Although theorists should delight in companies doing this, it hardly puts the seal of practical approval on their theories—for the latter were intended to cope with more difficult situations where perfect intermediate markets don't exist (and transfer prices are bona-fide one-to-many allocations).

In these more difficult circumstances, all available empirical evidence indicates that in the U.K. and North America *practical men usually shun the sorts of opportunity-cost transfer prices recommended by theorists.* Most U.S. evidence on this is over ten years old,[31] but there's some relatively recent U.K. research.[32]

The Purposes of Part Two

This is a striking phenomenon. One purpose of the next few chapters is to try to explain it. A major reason may be sketched in now. Chapter Five listed congruence properties that the literature proposes for joint-cost allocations; without trying to be as compre-

---

[31] [National Association of Accountants, 1957a, esp. pp. 28-36], [McCulloch, 1967, pp. 1-19, esp. p. 9], [Dearden, 1973, pp. 364-73, 375-78] and [Okpechi, 1976, esp. pp. 101-10].

[32] [Livesey, 1967, p. 99], [Rook, 1971, p. 9], [Centre for Business Research, 1972, pp. 15-18, 30-31] and [Emmanuel, 1977c, p. 12]. For parallel conclusions, see [Piper, 1969, p. 734] and [Gordon, 1970, p. 429]. Readers might wish to verify the matters summarized in the last two paragraphs by perusing the actual studies cited: my conclusions are necessarily based on considerable reading between the lines. But surely Watson and Baumler [1975, p. 473] overstated the case when they claimed that "... little empirical evidence has been gathered on how transfer prices are established in various organizations."

hensive or detailed, the next chapter tries to do the same for transfer pricing. Here are a few of the main ones: Transfer-price approaches should:

    1. Encourage divisions to operate at central-office-optimal output levels,

    2. Promote evaluations of products, divisions and division managers that will lead the central office to make consequent decisions that best satisfy its wants and have central-office-optimal élan effects, and

    3. Preserve divisional autonomies and the positive élan effects that these supposedly generate.

I'll argue that no transfer-pricing approach offered by the visible-hand theorists escapes major perversities here—indeed, that there are good behavioural reasons why most won't work at all.[33] Thus, it's only sensible for companies to use less sophisticated approaches, even though these have their own perverse consequences. A sort of Sow's Ear explanation applies here: if all approaches are dysfunctional, we should at least try to keep things simple.

My AAA studies [1969, 1974] of financial accounting's allocations had two main goals: (a) comprehension of many, seemingly insoluble, problems faced by such bodies as the FASB and (b) cleaning away intellectual dead wood—specifically, our theories of matching and realization. Of course, all this had policy implications. Similarly, my concerns here are (a) to understand why transfer pricing has proved to be as troublesome as Seed claims (in the quotation introductory to this Part) and (b) to demonstrate that elaborate and mathematically complex theories of transfer pricing to be found in the literature should be regarded skeptically.[34] [35]

---

[33] It's important to stress this, because prestigious academic accountants sometimes seem to imply that there exists a managerial-economics/management-science literature in which the main problems of transfer pricing have been solved. See, for instance, [Demski and Feltham, 1977, p. 156].

[34] One possible exception is the literature on marginal-cost transfer pricing in the French electric industry, summarized (for the 1950s and early 1960s) by [Nelson, 1964], which was called to my attention too late for me to deal with it thoroughly. I suspect, but have not proved, that the structure and circumstances of this nationalized industry (which produces an intermediate product for other nationalized industries), with its network of numerous separate production centres for an homogenous product, what correspond to substantial internal freight costs, and above all, its political need to subsidize large portions of consumption, sharply differentiate its characteristics from those envisaged in most of the other literature that we shall examine. See, in particular, [Boiteux, 1964, pp. 16-27] and [Dessus, 1964, pp. 33-40]. As I noted in Part One, research must be brought to term at one point or another. But this *is* a loose end, and I could be wrong here.

[35] For a different style of behavioural research into transfer pricing, conducted via a series of business games, see [Arvidsson, 1973].

Of course, this has policy implications, too—for instance, that we should be equally skeptical of the enthusiasms expressed by Anthony in *his* introductory quotation.

Assumptions

In the next few chapters, I'll make several assumptions and exclusions:

1. For brevity, discussions will follow the almost universal practice of disregarding inventories.[36] Doing otherwise would only reinforce the conclusions that we shall reach. Similarly, I disregard inflation.

2. These discussions usually don't distinguish between long- and short-run central-office optimization (instead, they implicitly adopt whatever concept authors under consideration are using).[37]

3. Unless stipulated otherwise, all economic functions considered will be convex[38] and continuous (this implies complete divisibilities of inputs and outputs). In Chapters Eight and Nine I'll assume that there are no capacity constraints to prevent production of what otherwise would be central-office-optimal outputs.[39] (I'll relax this assumption in Chapter Ten.)

4. Usually, I'll disregard studies at the level of abstraction of, say, [Demski, 1972], for their lack of specific allocation proposals.[40] At an opposite extreme, I shall disregard the use of matrix

[36] Readers may assume either that they don't exist or that inventory levels and prices remain constant.

[37] See [Godfrey, 1971, pp. 286-87, 287n]. Abdel-khalik and Lusk's [1974] concern over whether or not a division's marginal costs are calculated to allow for replacement of investments and profit depends on whether long- or short-run optimization is at stake. Contrast [Heflebower, 1960, pp. 13-14].

[38] See [Koopmans, 1957, pp. 23-25] for a good, intuitive discussion of what this implies, and [pp. 47, 50-51], generally. As the diagram on [page 50] indicates, if we're unable to assume convexity there's no guarantee that Pareto optima can be sustained by any price mechanism—nor, therefore, that those forms of central-office optimization commonly sought in the literature can be achieved via transfer prices. How serious the practical implications of this are might be an interesting subject for empirical research.

[39] [Tomkins, 1973, pp. 58-62] analyzes situations where this assumption is inappropriate.

[40] See [pp. 243-44, 254-55] for the level of Demski's discussion. He comments [p. 243]:

> Optimal systems are not derived, nor is the existence issue addressed. Instead, I focus on a statement of the optimization problem. The more mundane questions of existence of and search for an optimum can only be addressed within a context far too specific for what is required for a general statement of the class of problems.

algebra to allocate costs of service departments when these transfer goods reciprocally. For such matrix techniques offer no attempted theoretical solutions to problems of transfer pricing but are merely mechanical expedients to process numbers efficiently *given a prior decision on how to allocate.*[41]

5. I'll assume that any externalities generated by one division's activities are *immediately* reflected in global profits and in the book profits of any other divisions affected by them[42] (as well as similar instantaneous impacts on anything else of concern to our discussions). Again, if anything, assuming this loads the dice against my conclusions.

6. My perception of human motivations and the ways that people within organizations make decisions is essentially that of the behavioural assumptions of modern organization theory. For brevity of exposition I'll often follow traditional, profit-maximization, assumptions, but only where doing this doesn't affect the argument.

7. Our discussions will make the other traditional assumptions, identified by Butterworth, Hayes and Matsumura [1977], of a consensus of divisional and central-office beliefs with respect to costs and market prices,[43] the availability at some point or points within the organization of all relevant information, adequate exchange of information among subunits (except when gaming is explicitly considered), the existence of a sufficient power base to enforce a profit-maximizing (or other desiderata-maximizing) solution, and a deterministic market environment.[44]

Butterworth, Hayes and Matsumura's [1977; 1978] relaxation of these assumptions leads to conclusions for transfer pricing that are quite as gloomy as mine. Under their analysis, transfer prices lose all significance except as symptoms of environmental and organizational conditions. The realities of the company's situation (in particular, of its internal distribution of power) dictate resource allocations, output decisions and divisional book profits. Transfer prices are consequent upon these, but only as epiphenomena—the foam on the surface of the clashing waves.

---

[41] See [Thomas, 1969, p. 40*n*].

[42] See [Paik, 1975, pp. 82-86] for a relaxation of this assumption.

[43] Insofar as they simultaneously have beliefs, something that information economies might dictate against.

[44] For transfer pricing under *un*certainty, see also [Kornai, 1967b], [Jennergren, 1971, Ch. V], [Hurwicz, Radner and Reiter, 1975], [Demski, 1976b], [Ismail, 1977] and, to a limited degree, [Ruefli, 1969]; [Arrow, 1964, pp. 406-07] is a good introduction here. Surely, relaxation of this certainty simplification would do nothing to ease the problems discussed in the next several chapters—compare [Wiseman, 1957, pp. 68-72].

Therefore, the authors' analysis falls out of this book's area of concern: theories under which transfer prices are taken seriously as decision variables. I agree that wherever possible they shouldn't be, but, as mentioned before, will try to prove this on these theories' own ground—try to show that, even given the assumptions of *traditional* analysis, transfer prices are bound to be unsatisfactory for decision purposes and, thus, of only symptomatic import.

8. Finally and relatedly, I shall assume that a presumption that control is exercised downwards through a company's organizational hierarchy isn't so unsound behaviourally as to defeat my analysis.[45]

---

[45] Again, should one assume otherwise, I anticipate that the conclusions that we'll reach in later chapters would only be reinforced.

CHAPTER EIGHT

THE EASIEST CASES

The next few sections will centre upon a very simple transfer-pricing situation discussed by Hirshleifer [1956], Gould [1964] and Naert [1973] :[1] a company has two divisions; one manufactures a product then transfers it to the other, which packages and distributes it.[2] I'll initially confine the discussion to the simplest of the models that these authors propose for dealing with this situation; subsequent chapters will apply the insights gained from these discussions to more complicated situations and models.

Decisions That Might Be Based on Transfer Prices

As was true of joint costs, our discussions will investigate whether or not proposed transfer-price methods are behaviour-congruent. This, of course, requires identifying decisions that might be based on transfer prices. In order to buttress its gloomy conclusions about multiple congruence, Part One surveyed all decisions that might be based on joint-cost allocations. Here, though, we need not be as exhaustive: The literature indicates that the following are the main decisions that might be based on transfer prices:[3]

Output: How much of a particular transfer good should the company produce?

Use or sell: How much should it utilize internally? Sell externally?

Make or buy: How much should it make internally? Buy externally?

---

[1] Also, of course, by other, subsequent authors, most notably Solomons [1965;1977] and Tomkins [1973] –both of whom, for brevity, I'll not otherwise cite here. Hirshleifer's discussion continues in [Hirshleifer, 1957 and 1964]. The Hirshleifer, Gould and Naert papers supercede part or all of several earlier works, such as [Cook, 1955 and 1957].

[2] Dopuch, Birnberg and Demski [1974, pp. 651-52, 662, 666] observe that in such cases there's little likelihood of divisionalization's leading to information economies (though see p. 663 and *n*10). But this needn't trouble us as long as we perceive these simple cases as exemplars of more complex ones.

[3] Compare [Simon et al., 1954, p. 3]'s score-card, attention-directing and problem-solving questions (discussed in [Golembiewski, 1964]). I'll mention some additional, minor decisions in later chapters.

The specific works drawn upon in compiling the following list happened to be [Simon, et. al., 1954, pp. 32-33], [Dean, 1955, pp. 66, 72], [Cook, 1957, p. 74], [Dearden, 1960, p. 118], [Shubik, 1964, *passim*], [Solomons, 1965, *passim*], [Fremgen, 1970, p. 26], [Onsi, 1970, pp. 537-38], [Watson and Baumler, 1975, pp. 471-72] and [Cushing, 1976, p. 48]. Readers are encouraged to verify from these and other works listed in the References that I haven't omitted any major decisions.

Divisional evaluation: How well is each division doing?

Expand or contract: Should the company increase its investment in the division? Hold its investment steady? Contract
its investment? Discontinue the division?

Resource allocation: How much of its resources (e.g., working
capital, equipment) should the company physically allocate
to each division?[4]

Managerial evaluation: How effective is each division manager?[5]

Elan: In addition, division managers base the various personal
decisions identified in Chapter One on transfer prices: The
seriousness with which they take the company's internal
accounting data, their trust in the equitability of its system
of internal evaluation and control (or their alienation),
how much time they waste in unproductive efforts to improve their book profits rather than global profits, and the
host of decisions that stem from general managerial creativity and élan. In particular, transfer pricing may encourage
or discourage such things as innovation by division managers
and divisional conflict resolution.[6]

Perfect Competition in Intermediate Markets

The simplest possible transfer pricing situation is the null case
of no interdivisional transfers at all. The next simplest occurs

---

[4] Discussion of resource-allocation decisions will be delayed until we consider complex
situations involving three or more divisions and mathematical-programming transfer-price
approaches.

[5] These last four decisions are often given the alternative orientation:

Profitability: Which products, activities and managerial units are profitable?
Which aren't?

[6] [Centre for Business Research, 1972, p. 5], a fairly recent (apparently non-random)
empirical survey, indicated that 42 U.K. companies reported the following weights for
transfer-pricing objectives (4 is high):

To foster awareness of profit implications of decision[s]	3.0
To identify the contribution of each main operating unit to total company performance	3.0
To assist in the longer run allocation of resources in the company	2.3
To assist in the evaluation of managerial performance	2.0
To achieve short term coordination of main operating units	1.5

The last chapter indicated that transfer-pricing theory and practice differ sharply. Evidently, the difference here lies in practice's being relatively unconcerned with output decisions. (The questionnaire used is opaque to élan decisions.)

when a manufacturing division (hereafter, *Mfg*) produces a product[7] for which there is a perfect (fully competitive) intermediate market. A distribution division (hereafter, *Dst*) packages and sells this good. Save for this relationship, the two divisions are technologically (cost) and demand independent.

Here, theorists usually agree that the transfer price should be the price to be found in the intermediate market.[8] However, it should be readily evident that in such situations the central office and divisions should be indifferent whether the latter actually trade with each other: Mfg could sell all of its output, and Dst buy all of its inputs, externally without affecting global profits.[9] Really, there's no transfer pricing problem here at all, for the company isn't allocating costs: instead, it's using allocation-free current-market values, of the sorts recommended by [Edwards and Bell, 1961], [Chambers, 1966; 1970; 1974; 1979], [Sterling, 1970; 1975], [Wells, 1973a; 1976], [Johnson and Bell, 1976], [Anderson, 1979], [Bell and Johnson, 1979], [Boatsman and Hite, 1979], [Carsberg, 1979], [Kay and Johnson, 1979], [Mosich and Vasarhelyi, 1979] and [Stamp, 1979][10] Thus, the perfect-intermediate-market case is, effectively, the *null* case, and we're left with Henderson and Dearden's [1966, p. 145] comment that, when a company has two divisions, their:

...integrated performance should exceed the performance achieved when the two operations are kept separate. If it does not, why integrate?[11]

[7]Few service departments have *any* external markets for their transfer products, much less perfect ones. Solomons [1965, p. 205] suggests that a trucking department might be an exception. So might a computer department that offered rather routine services externally and internally.

[8]Presumably, ignoring any distress prices that might result from minor, temporary market imperfections. See, for instance, [Arrow, 1959, p. 11], [Dopuch and Drake, 1964, p. 12], [Solomons, 1965, pp. 171-74, 212-28], [Henderson and Dearden, 1966, p. 150] and [Onsi, 1970, p. 538]. [Naert, 1973, pp. 101-10] is an efficient exposition of the underlying economic analysis.

[9]As Hirshleifer [1956, p. 176] says, the two divisions are effectively independent firms with common ownership. See also [Shubik, 1964, p. 210].

[10]This point is made by Wells [1971, p. 56]; see also [Henderson and Dearden, 1966, p. 150].

[11]See also [Solomons, 1965, p. 160; 1977, p. 44•19]. Technically, there's an alternative answer to Henderson and Dearden's question: Integration could reduce global risk if the profits of the two operations had a negative covariance. But this doesn't seem pertinent here.

Finally, perfection in the intermediate market requires that:

All traders have perfect knowledge of the intermediate market price and other pertinent characteristics of the transfer goods.

These prices are deterministic,[12] and the activities of individual buyers and sellers can have no significant impact upon them.[13]

There are no transportation costs, transfer taxes, bad debt losses, brokerage fees or other transactions costs for either Mfg or Dst.

Unfortunately, these conditions are hard to satisfy. Often it's difficult to discover from published market prices what actual current-market values would be.[14] Some degree of oligopoly is common. Transportation costs, bad debts and other transactions costs are ubiquitous.[15] Solomons [1965, pp. 177-78] was presumably right to conclude that instances of perfect intermediate markets are rare.

No Intermediate Market

Though we'll find it far more complex than the foregoing, the next simplest situation arises when there's no intermediate market

---

[12]Ismail [1977] has pointed out that when external market prices for transfer products are known only stochastically, Mfg may rationally prefer a certain internal transfer price to an uncertain, though higher, external market price—and that the latter is no longer Mfg's opportunity cost and, therefore, no foundation for global optimization. Calculation of a transfer price may yet be feasible here, though: the difference between the internal and external prices is a risk premium. Its calculation need involve none of the incorrigibilities involved in one-to-many allocations.

[13]These intermediate market prices must also be real alternatives; access to that market mustn't be barred by company policy. See [Cook, 1955, p. 89; 1957, p. 75], [Naert, 1973, pp. 101*n*, 113] and Problem 10-31 in [Louderback and Dominiak, 1978, p. 341]. The latter implicitly assumes such a barrier (along with assuming that the transferor division has sufficient capacity to meet all demands placed on it), and shows the sort of difficulty that can arise when this characteristic of a perfect market is violated.

[14]See [Dean, 1955, pp. 67, 69] and [National Association of Accountants, 1957a, pp. 25-30]. Branded products pose special difficulties—see [Cook, 1955, p. 89]. [Milburn, 1977, pp. 72-75] provides an excellent discussion of difficulties in developing surrogate arms-length prices for internal transfers even when there *is* an external market. The author concludes [p. 75]:

> In summary, it seems unlikely that there could be many situations in which transfer transactions are directly equivalent in all significant price-determining respects to transactions between unrelated parties. Direct equivalency would seem to be a possibility only when there are virtually no savings resulting from affiliation—that is, where there is insignificant integration of operations.

Readers will note the parallel to the [Henderson and Dearden, 1966, p. 145] quotation, above.

[15]See [McCulloch, 1967, pp. 18-19] and [Horngren, 1977, pp. 681-83] for other problems that can arise when companies set transfer prices equal to intermediate-market prices.

whatever for transfer goods. Individually, neither Mfg nor Dst can earn anything by dealing in the transfer product; together, they earn its global profit. Any transfer price will divide this profit between them; the problem is to determine which division will be appropriate.[16]

As we've seen, any such division must be a radically arbitrary, one-to-many one.[17] Thus, we have here a classic instance of the sort of situation, analyzed in Part One, where choice among different possible allocation methods must be based on asking: For what kinds of decisions is each method behaviour-congruent? Where can each generate dysfunctional results?[18]

Specifically, when there is no intermediate market we must ask whether any proposed transfer pricing approach generates behaviour-congruent or perverse output, divisional evaluation, managerial evaluation and élan decisions. In particular, since, as we've seen, divisional autonomy is the key to many élan decisions of division managers, we must also ask whether any proposed transfer pricing approach preserves divisional autonomy.

The Simplest Hirshleifer Approach

In the absence of external markets to provide a measuring stick for prices, the organization is beset internally with all the problems of monopoly and imperfect competition in general.

However, there is a . . . modern theorem, due to Barone, which states that the invisible hand will operate satisfactorily without perfect competition but still assuming the absence of external economies or diseconomies, provided we substitute for profit-maximizing the rule that each subpart of the organization sets marginal cost . . . equal to price for each of the variables it can control. This rule will clear markets . . . and will, under the given assumptions, lead to profit maximization for the firm (but not, in general, for the individual subparts) . . . — [March and Simon, 1958, p. 202]

---

[16]Compare [Henderson and Dearden, 1966, p. 145].

[17]We'll soon see that either division might maximize its own book profit on the transfer good (at the expense of global profits) by acting as an internal monopolist or monopsonist. For instance, in Appendix H's Figure 1, the first situation considered results in a globally optimal periodic profit of £ 3,520.00. Were Mfg to act as an internal monopolist it could attain book profits of £ 2,277.65 per period; were Dst to act as an internal monopsonist it could attain periodic book profits of £2,420.00 Upon reflection, it should be evident that allocation of at least £ 2,277.65 (the lesser maximum) of the globally optimal £ 3,520.00 is totally ambiguous [Thomas, 1974, p. 22]. This example is conservative: readers may verify from the same Figure that the totally ambiguous portion of the central-office-optimal profit may equal, or even *exceed*, that profit.

[18]For fairly clear recognitions of this, see [Shubik, 1964, p. 208] and [Larson, 1971, p. 20n; 1974, p. 32].

Where there's no intermediate market, textbooks emphasize two ways of setting transfer prices: (a) ones in which divisions negotiate transfer prices with each other and (b) a method that's usually associated with [Hirshleifer, 1956].[19] I'll delay discussion of the former for a later chapter, and will here discuss only the simplest form of Hirshleifer's approach.[20]

The key to the latter approach is its specifying that the transfer price must be Mfg's marginal cost for the transfer product at the globally optimal output.[21] Here's an example. A company's revenue and cost functions are:

$$R = 205 - 0.5Q$$
$$C_m = 19 + Q$$
$$C_d = 10 + 0.7Q$$

—where R signifies unit revenue, C is unit cost, Q is quantity of output, and the m and d subscripts respectively signify *Mfg* and

---

[19] It's only proper, though, to credit a major precursor. As March and Simon point out in the passage just quoted, the origins of much of Hirshleifer's analysis (and, for that matter, of the Gould-Naert and mathematical-programming approaches that we'll consider in later chapters, too) may be found in a 1908 theorem by Barone—see [Barone, 1935, pp. 265-74, 281-82, 289]. Barone [pp. 246-74] in turn attributes many of his ideas to Pareto and Walras, but not those with which we shall wrestle. I'll not mention Barone again, but piety for the memory of one who planted much of the vineyard in which we shall labour requires saying here that when I speak of such things as Hirshleifer's approaches to transfer pricing, or even ones based on the decomposition principle, I'm really discussing elaborations of Barone's work.

[20] [Abdel-khalik and Lusk, 1974, pp. 10-14] offers a parallel discussion of this and the Gould-Naert approach discussed in the next chapter. Readers should be warned, though, that its language is potentially confusing: its *selling division* is Mfg and its *processing division* Dst; indeed, in the right column of p. 10 the authors seem to have confused themselves (*seller* should be *buyer*). There are several other minor confusions in this influential paper:

    Page 10, note: this gives an erroneous title for Gould's article.

    Page 11, left column, bottom line: *processing* should be *selling*.

    Page 13, Figure 3: this diagram is misleading. Despite what's said on page 12, $q_3 \neq q_1 - q_2$; similarly, TMR $\neq$ MR(O) + MR(s).

    Page 14: the authors use $P(s)$ and $P(b)$ in different senses than in the Figures on page 12.

    Passim: they misspell *Hirshleifer.*

[21] We may delay consideration of such things as the central office's possible need to audit these marginal costs (assuming that they're reported to it by Mfg).

For instances in the literature of this rule besides the earlier quotation from [March and Simon, 1958], see [Hirshleifer, 1956, pp. 172-75, 183] and [Solomons, 1965, pp. 181-82]. For general background on difficulties of guiding division managers by the rule that price should equal marginal cost, see [Lewis, 1946, pp. 236-58, esp. pp. 236-46].

If we limit ourselves to short-run time horizons (ones insufficient to permit acquisition of additional productive capacity), these marginal costs equal the opportunity costs of supplying units of the transfer product—see [Dopuch and Drake, 1964, p. 13].

Dst. Elementary calculus reveals that the company will maximize its global profits (at £3,520) at a periodic output of 40 units of transfer product.[22] The question then becomes: What will induce Mfg to produce exactly 40 units? Since we're assuming that Mfg's manager is a book-profit maximizer, we may rephrase this question to: At what transfer price will Mfg maximize its book profits by producing exactly 40 units of output?[23]

Economic theory tells us that this maximum occurs where Mfg's marginal cost equals its marginal revenue. But (making the additional assumption, discussed below, that Dst pays the same transfer price on all units), Mfg's unit, average, and marginal revenues all equal this transfer price. Thus, it immediately follows that this transfer price must equal Mfg's marginal cost at an output of 40 units per period. This equals £99,[24] so the central office specifies a £99 transfer price.

Simultaneously, at this transfer price Dst's marginal revenue equals *its* marginal costs of processing and selling the globally optimal 40 units per period (which include the £99). This is the familiar market-clearing behaviour of any price system. Further calculation reveals that the transfer price divides the company profit of £ 3,520 into book profits of £1,600 and £1,920 for Mfg and Dst, respectively.[25]

The foregoing has slightly simplified Hirshleifer's [1956, pp. 176, 178-80] actual approach. He would have Mfg and Dst exchange supply and demand schedules then supposedly autonomously determine their outputs and transfer prices from these. However, in both the simple case described here and in more complex ones involving imperfect markets, Hirshleifer's central office imposes restrictions to prevent one division's exploiting the other. It's easily shown that these restrictions have the effect of specifying the

---

[22] Letting T signify *total* and M signify *marginal*, the calculations here are:

$$TR = 205Q - 0.5Q^2 \qquad MR = 205 - Q$$
$$TC = 19Q + 10Q + Q^2 + 0.7Q^2 \qquad MC = 29 + 3.4Q$$

When MR = MC:
$$205 - Q = 29 + 3.4Q$$
$$Q = 40$$

[23] For notions of information inductance that seem fundamental to the ways transfer prices affect division-manager behaviour, see [Prakash and Rappaport, 1977, pp. 29-35].

[24] $TC_m = 19Q + Q^2$ and $MC_m = 19 + 2Q$; therefore, at $Q = 40, MC_m = 19 + (2 \cdot 40) = 99$.

[25] At a transfer price of £ 99 and an output of 40, Mfg's book profits will be:
$$(99 \cdot 40) - (19 \cdot 40) - (40^2) = \underline{1,600}$$

while Dst's book profit will be:
$$(205 \cdot 40) - (0.5 \cdot 40^2) - (99 \cdot 40) - (10 \cdot 40) - (0.7 \cdot 40^2) = \underline{1,920}.$$

transfer price.[26] Therefore, for brevity I'll just say hereafter that the central office dictates the central-office-optimal transfer price.

Internal Monopsony or Monopoly

I've deliberately avoided customary, loose ways of phrasing things here. Many would say that at the central-office-optimal transfer price the division managers maximize their book profits by producing the globally optimal output, and that this transfer price is *the* marginal cost. But this is misleading, for two reasons:

1. £99 is but *Mfg's* marginal cost, and it's that only at the optimal output. For instance, readers may verify that Mfg's marginal costs at outputs of 39 and 41 are £97 and £101, respectively.

2. Moreover, the divisions maximize their book profits via this transfer price only in a very limited sense. To appreciate this, let's suppose that Dst can act as an internal monopsonist and pay Mfg only whatever transfer price is necessary to summon forth an output that's selfishly optimal for Dst. It can be shown that at this selfish optimum Mfg will produce only 27.5 units per period, in response to a £74 transfer price. This reduces global profits and Mfg's book profits to £3,176.25 and £756.25, respectively, but increases Dst's book profit, by £500, to £2,420.00.

Similarly, if Mfg can act as an internal monopolist, it would maximize *its* book profits (at £2,277.65) at an output of 25.88 units, a transfer price of £132.88, and global and Dst profits of £3,081.52 and £803.88, respectively.[27] Figure 8-1 summarizes this example.[28]

(What we're dealing with here is, of course, a special case of a classic problem of welfare economics: Under what conditions, and in what sense, does optimization of want satisfaction on the micro level lead to a macro optimum?)[29]

---

[26]Contrast [Gordon, 1964, p. 22]. Similar things hold true for Hirshleifer's still more complex tax and subsidy proposals, to be discussed later.

[27]For more extended discussions of such situations, see [Hirshleifer, 1956, pp. 175, 179; 1964, p. 32], [Gould, 1960, pp. 346-48], [Solomons, 1965, pp. 165-71] and [Onsi, 1970, pp. 535-36]. [Butterworth, Hayes and Matsumura, 1977] discusses circumstances in which divisions, left to their own devices, attempt to dominate each other.

[28]I repeat the point, made early in Chapter Seven, that the phenomena we're considering here are consequences of decentralization into profit centres, rather than of transfer pricing *per se*. Cost centres would have no impetus to act as internal monopsonists or monopolists. Again, though, we are dealing with a literature that, in this context, takes decentralization into profit centres as a given.

[29]See [Hirshleifer, 1964, p. 28].

Figure 8-1

A Case of Increasing Marginal
Manufacturing and Distributing Costs

		Optima	
	Central-Office	Mfg	Dst
Output	40.00	25.88	27.50
Transfer price	99.00	132.88	74.00
Total profit	3,520.00	3,081.52	3,176.25
Mfg's book profit	1,600.00	2,277.65	756.25
Dst's book profit	1,920.00	803.88	2,420.00

Horizontal or Declining Marginal Costs

The previous example assumed increasing marginal costs (decreasing returns to scale) in both the manufacturing and distributing divisions. Of course, over the relevant range for output decisions marginal costs might instead be approximately horizontal—or might even decline. We'll see, though, that these conditions have little effect upon the analysis.

For instance, let's alter Figure 8-1 so that Mfg's marginal costs are horizontal. This can be done by making C_m = 99 (instead of 19 + Q). Readers are invited to verify the results, shown in Figure 8-2.

I designed this example so that the central-office optimal output and transfer price are still 40 and £ 99, respectively. But now, instead of the global profit being split between the two divisions at this optimum, as in Figure 8-1, all of it is allocated to Dst's book profits, with none to Mfg. This is characteristic of the Hirshleifer

Figure 8-2

A Case of Horizontal Marginal Manufacturing
Costs and Increasing Marginal Distributing Costs

		Optima	
	Central-Office	Mfg	Dst
Output	40.00	20.00	40.00
Transfer price	99.00	147.00	99.00
Total profit	1,920.00	1,440.00	1,920.00
Mfg's book profit	0.00	960.00	0.00
Dst's book profit	1,920.00	480.00	1,920.00

approach: when one division's marginal costs are horizontal the other is credited with all the profit from their synergy.

This means that Dst cannot improve its book-profit position: even were it to act as an internal monopsonist the most it could do would be to hog the entire global profit. Therefore, Dst's selfish optimum is identical with the global optimum. Not so, though, with Mfg. Were it to act as an internal monopolist it could raise its book profits to £ 960 by reducing output (and global profits). At least one division always can so improve its book profits over those allocated to it at the central-office optimum. (Appendix H's Figure 1 illustrates this.)

Next, let's change Figure 8-1 so that Mfg's marginal costs decline (in response to economies of scale over the relevant range of output).[30] This can be done by having $C_m = 107 - 0.1Q$. Figure 8-3 shows the result. Again, I've rigged things to give a central-office-optimal output and transfer price of 40 and £ 99. Here, at this central-office-optimal output Mfg's book profits are *negative*, something characteristic of Hirshleifer's manufacturing divisions whenever their marginal costs decline.[31] In this instance, though, both divisions can improve their book profits at the company's (and other division's) expense if they are free to act selfishly. (Please

Figure 8-3

A Case of Decreasing Marginal Manufacturing
Costs and Increasing Marginal Distributing Costs

	Optima		
	Central-Office	Mfg	Dst
Output	40.00	19.13	44.00
Transfer price	99.00	149.09	98.20
Total profit	1,760.00	1,280.91	1,742.40
Mfg's book profit	(160.00)	841.74	(193.60)
Dst's book profit	1,920.00	439.17	1,936.00

[30] A public utility is a standard example of a decreasing-cost company; a power plant might be a within-company parallel. See [Hirshleifer, 1957, pp. 101-02, 102*n*] for a plausible, if slightly more complex, situation in which a manufacturing division's marginal costs decline as output increases. See also [Hirshleifer, 1956, pp. 180, 183-84; 1964, pp. 29, 37] and [Arrow, 1964a, p. 319].

[31] This is *not* characteristic, however, of distribution divisions with declining marginal costs, as readers may verify by substituting $C_d = 70 - 0.5Q$ in Figure 8-1, or by examining the right-column examples in Appendix H's Figure 1. Nor need it necessarily be so during a period of inflation—see [Boiteux, 1964, pp. 25-26]. But, as noted in Chapter Seven, this book disregards inflation.

note that selfish action by Dst in this case results in output *greater* than the optimal one.)[32]

Significance of Marginal-Cost Transfer Prices

Recognizing all this should dissipate some of the mystique of such transfer prices that arises from the bona fide importance of marginal costs in other disciplines. Sure, the transfer price is a marginal cost, but only one of an infinite number of possible ones.[33] Sure, it results in optimal divisional book profits, but only in a special sense in which both divisions have made the best of what, for them, is usually a decidedly *sub*optimal situation.[34]

In external markets, it's often (though not always) the practice for vendors to charge, and buyers to pay, equal amounts for each unit of product (or service). The transfer-pricing literature makes a parallel assumption for internal pricing. Yet doing so hardly seems necessary.[35] Were one to relax this assumption, there would be an infinite number of (linear and nonlinear) nonhorizontal transfer-price curves that would yield the central-office-optimal output, each with its own allocation of profits. In particular, a greedy distribution division might pay Mfg only enough to summon forth *successive* units of output,[36] therby hogging most of the profit

[32] Once again, I remind readers that I'm writing from the context in which Hirshleifer wrote. From another context, Watson and Baumler [1975, pp. 471-72, 472n] comment:

> . . .within a complex organization conflict is going to be multidimensional. In a highly differentiated organization this will at times involve the transfer of goods and services within the organization. But it may also include design and engineering changes, production and delivery schedules, and quality control. Seen in this light, the transfer pricing question becomes one facet of a multidimensional conflict resolution process . . . Hence, it makes little sense to be concerned about a possible monopoly by one department. It is unlikely, if at all possible, in uncertain environments or reciprocally independent situations (or both) that one department will have a monopoly position on all dimensions of the conflict.

Despite strong sympathy for what Watson and Baumler are saying here, I distrust its applicability to Hirshleifer's output problem, since the parallel argument that's sometimes applied to the economy as a whole is dubious. "Natural" macro monopsonies and monopolies do manage to distort output over extended periods.

[33] For instance, any within a range of £74.00 to £132.88 in Figure 8-1 or £99.00 to £147.00 in Figure 8-2.

[34] See [Hirshleifer, 1956, pp. 175, 178-79], [Solomons, 1965, pp. 178-79, 181] and [Tomkins, 1973, pp. 54-55].

[35] On the external level, the assumption of equal prices for all units is regularly violated by such things as volume discounts. On the internal level, at least one work, [Onsi, 1970, p. 538], has made modest suggestions toward relaxing this assumption.

[36] It would pay $19 + 2Q$ for each successive unit: £21 for the first, £23 for the second, and so forth.

even when all marginal costs increase with output. This is as much allocating in terms of marginal costs as is Hirshleifer's approach.

Finally, there's nothing sacred—or even very specific—about marginal costs even were we to ignore the foregoing ambiguities. Marginal costs will vary, depending on the time period selected, from zero (instantaneous period, during which all factors are fixed) to full absorption cost (long enough run that all factors are variable).[37] Therefore, the only really solid virtue of the central-office-optimal transfer price here is that it is behaviour-congruent with respect to output decisions: If the company uses Hirshleifer's approach, division managers who base their output decisions on its transfer-price allocations will always make decisions that satisfy central-office desires to maximize global profits.[38] Similar things are true of other authors' opportunity-cost transfer-pricing schemes, for instance those of the decomposition procedures that we'll examine in Chapter Ten.

Divisional Autonomy

> The socialists believe in two things which are absolutely different and perhaps even contradictory: freedom and organization. —Élie Halévy (quoted in [Hayek, 1944, p. 32])

> "What do I look like?"
> "You look like a Bear holding on to a balloon," you said.
> "Not," said Pooh anxiously, "—not like a small black cloud in a blue sky?"
> "Not very much."
> "Ah, well, perhaps from up here it looks different. . ."
> After a little while he called down to you.
> "Christopher Robin!" he said in a loud whisper.
> "Hallo!"
> "I think the bees *suspect* something!"
> "What sort of thing?"
> "I don't know. But something tells me that they're *suspicious!*"
> "Perhaps they think that you're after their honey." —[Milne, 1926, pp. 12-13]

The question therefore becomes: Is Hirshleifer's approach also behaviour-congruent with respect to *other* decisions: divisional evaluation, managerial evaluation and élan? Unfortunately, it clearly isn't. Let's begin with divisional autonomy, since this affects all of these decision areas. It is widely recognized in the

---

[37]Compare [Wiseman, 1957, pp. 60-61].

[38]See [Hirshleifer, 1956, pp. 174-75, 178] and [Solomons, 1965, pp. 191-92].

literature that achievement of the global profit maximization that we have taken to be central-office optimal threatens divisional autonomy and vice-versa,[39] and that, in particular, the simple, Hirshleifer approach can't simultaneously maintain both.[40]

We've seen why: Given their heads, division managers may try to maximize their book profits by setting central-office-perverse output levels and transfer prices. There is no way to prevent this save by having the central office intervene in one way or another.[41] Under Hirshleifer's approach, this intervention takes the form of using transfer prices to manipulate division managers to seek local optima offering lower book profits than they could attain were they free to follow their selfish interests.

In Wiseman's [1957, p. 66] words, the central office can allow division managers' decisions here to be ". . .'voluntary' only in the special sense that a malefactor voluntarily goes away to prison after a judge has sentenced him; he chooses the best alternative still available." The autonomy is only Appendix G's *ceremonial* autonomy. In reality, the divisions are merely the central office's tools. The latter seeks to maintain an illusion that it doesn't dictate output decisions, much as Pooh would have had the bees believe that he was an innocent cloud. But division managers are at least as adept as economic theorists are in seeing which side their bread is buttered on, and the illusion is unlikely to persist beyond the first budget period.[42] The central office is after their honey; the division managers will recognize this and act accordingly.

There's a strong analogy here to Argyris' [1957, pp. 145-46] pseudo-participation in budgeting. Caplan [1971, pp. 87-88] comments:

[39] For instance, see [Henderson and Dearden, 1966, p. 145], [Abdel-khalik and Lusk, 1970, pp. 8-9], [Godfrey, 1971, p. 286] and, more generally, [Hayek, 1940, esp. pp. 145-49].

[40] For instance, see [Hirshleifer, 1964, pp. 30, 32, 34], [Ronen and McKinney, 1974, pp. 100, 102-03] and [Bailey and Boe, 1976, p. 560].

[41] Be it noted that even if the problems of internal monopsony and monopoly that we've discussed could somehow be avoided, there would still be problems of divisions trying to exploit each other that only central-office intervention could cure. Fremgen [1970, p. 27] comments:

> Unless enjoined by top management from doing so, buying divisions might use the selling division as a materials stocking point. They might place only minimum quantity orders at frequent intervals so as to reduce their own inventory carrying costs.

Similarly, buying divisions could cause inefficiencies in selling divisions by "rush orders or excess set-up costs on nonstandard production runs."–[p. 27]

[42] Similarly, one would expect them to see through the taxes, subsidies, exchanges of price schedules and iterative algorithms of Hirshleifer's more complex proposals; we'll return to this point later.

It is doubtful that pseudo-participation provides any benefits to an organization; rather it can be expected to create serious morale and motivation problems. Indeed, if for some reason a firm is unable to use true participation effectively, it would probably be much wiser to follow authoritarian budget practices—and honestly admit it—than to engage in the pretense of pseudo-participation.

Similarly with pseudo-participation in output decisions. Again, manipulation is something that one does to children;[43] ethical issues aside, the élan consequences of doing it to adults in circumstances where one is bound to get caught are apt to be unfortunate.

A Contrary View

Here, we should pause for an opposed view. Solomons [1965, pp. 193-94, 233; 1977, p. 44·3] argues that the central office's setting of the transfer price may not be a serious infringement of divisional autonomy after all. Everyone, including division managers, recognizes that divisions can't just be given free hands to do whatever they please—otherwise, the divisionalized company would degenerate into a sort of investment trust. (Indeed, *some* such constraints are essential to preserve freedom in society generally, as well as within companies—thus traffic laws) Requirements, say, that divisions charge full costs plus a specified return on capital for *non*-transfer goods are rarely thought of as dictation. And certainly a transfer-pricing system is less likely to be perceived as dictation than would be direct central-office specification of outputs. To this one might add that, in the perfect-intermediate-market situation division managers experience no loss of autonomy from the central office's dictating the use of market prices as transfer prices, because they *expect* to be constrained by market prices. Why shouldn't they expect to be constrained by *internal* market prices here?

As for the last question (which was *not* raised by Solomons), it soon would become obvious to division managers that the central office's transfer prices differ from external-market prices in one vital respect: the external prices are impersonal, the internal ones personal, manipulative and administered. Since their administration is designed to satisfy someone else's goals—goals that often *conflict* with those of the division managers—the latter are bound to

---

[43]Compare [Argyris, 1957, pp. 50-53, 66]. Alternately, this sort of transfer pricing is an application of McGregor's [1966, pp. 5-6] Theory X to division managers—see [McGregor, 1960, pp. 54-55] for such applications.

regard them as arbitrary. (As an extreme instance, how else would Mfg's division manager regard Mfg's negative book profits in Figure 8-3's central-office optimum?)

Sure, divisions can't be allowed to do whatever they will, but the central office's administered prices don't merely constrain division managers, they also turn divisional book profits (insofar as these result from dealing in transfer goods) into administered profits and in effect stipulate some of the most important things over which truly autonomous managers might expect to have control: the quantities of their inputs and outputs.[44]

The central office's manipulation may be more diplomatic than *direct* stipulation of outputs would be, but any élan advantages of diplomacy are apt to be swamped by the consequences of division managers becoming aware that the company's internal accounting data aren't to be taken seriously and that, as a result, its system of internal evaluation and control will be equitable only by coincidence (and will be likely to play favourites, as it clearly does whenever Mfg's marginal costs are constant or declining, and as it's apt to be *perceived* to do whenever one division's book profits on transfer goods are less than the other's). This is likely to affect motivation and élan.[45] Since transfer prices and book profits are known to be administered, rational division-manager behaviour is to do whatever counter-manipulation may be available (if one's profits are to be a fiction, let's at least try to make them a pleasing fiction); later, we'll consider the implications of this for gaming.

One must be careful not to overdo these observations. As Hopwood [1976, e.g., pp. 89-90] repeatedly emphasizes, people are far too complex and diverse for any simple model of their behaviour when confronted by particular organizational stimuli to be universally valid. Doubtless some division managers wouldn't be affected by administered transfer prices in these ways at all. But it would be most surprising if the reactions to such transfer prices weren't often behaviourally perverse.

In summary, under Hirshleifer's approach division managers lose autonomy over their outputs. Its allocation of global profits between divisions is defensible only as a side effect of satisfying the wants of a third party, the central office. From the standpoints of

---

[44] Similarly, Solomons [1965, p. 24] himself observes, "A good test of the degree of real autonomy divisions have is to ask whether they are free to set selling prices for their products."

[45] Or generate other perverse managerial reactions, such as those described by [Larson, 1974, p. 30].

the division managers this allocation is grossly arbitrary and the whole procedure blatantly manipulative.

Evaluations of Divisions and Their Managers

> Since the transfer price is the price at which the selling division sells and the buying division buys, most authors have explicitly or implicitly assumed that divisional performance can be measured on the basis of the profit made by the divisions. In order for divisional profit to be an appropriate measure of divisional performance, profit of one division should not be affected when the performance of the other division deteriorates or improves. Indeed, if profit of one division depends on the performance of the other division, the first purpose of decentralization is not served, since decentralization does not result then in a better means of controlling managerial performance. Neither will the second purpose of decentralization, namely, to improve motivation, be realized and for the same reason. Divisional performance should then be measured on a cost performance rather than on a profit performance basis.
> —[Naert, 1973, p. 100]

Similarly, Hirshleifer's approach is far from behaviour-congruent when it comes to evaluating divisions and their managers. In Part One, we saw that allocations should have the following properties with respect to such decisions:

1. Divisions should benefit from increases in their efficiencies and be penalized for decreases in their efficiencies.

2. Actions (or inactions) by one division shouldn't affect other divisions' book profits.[46] In particular, one division's book profits shouldn't be affected by changes in another division's separate costs.

Readers are invited to verify that the Hirshleifer approach lacks these properties by making the changes in our earlier examples that are indicated in Figure 8-4. In particular, when Mfg's marginal costs are increasing as output increases, decreases in its efficiency will decrease Dst's book profits (Cases A and B), whereas an increase in its efficiency can both increase Dst's book profits and *decrease* its own (Case C). Similarly, if Dst becomse less efficient this reduces Mfg's book profits (Cases D and E)—in the second of these cases by far more than Dst's book profits are reduced!

If Mfg's marginal costs are constant, any inefficient increases in that constant term has no effect on its book profits, but reduces Dst's (Case F). If Mfg becomes less efficient by having its marginal costs increase with output (in the manner of Case G), its own book profits increase while Dst's decrease.

---

[46] See [Shillinglaw, 1957, pp. 84-85] and [Larson, 1971, *passim*].

Figure 8-4

Changes in Earlier Examples

Case	Example	Change
A	8-1	$C_m = 23+Q$
B	8-1	$C_m = 19+1.5Q$
C	8-1	$C_m = 19+0.65Q$
D	8-1	$C_d = 12+0.7Q$
E	8-1	$C_d = 10+0.9Q$
F	8-2	$C_m = 115$
G	8-2	$C_m = 99+0.15Q$
H	8-3	$C_m = 107-0.2Q$
I	8-3	$C_m = 125-0.1Q$
J	8-3	$C_m = 107$
K	8-3	$C_m = 107+0.3Q$
L	8-3	$C_d = 12+0.7Q$
M	8-3	$C_d = 10+0.45Q$

Finally, if Mfg's marginal costs decline, changes in efficiency have generally perverse consequences. For instance, if Mfg becomes more efficient this can reduce its book profits and increase Dst's (Case H), whereas if it becomes less efficient the reverse happens (Cases I, J and K). Similarly, if Dst becomes less (more) efficient Mfg's book profits will increase (decrease) (Cases L and M). Figure 8-5 gives check figures for those who wish to verify these conclusions. Similar phenomena occur when Dst's marginal costs are horizontal or decline with output.

Figure 8-5

Check Figures for Figure 8-4

Case	Central-Office-Optimal Output	Central-Office-Optimal Transfer Price	Central-Office-Optimal Profit Total	Central-Office-Optimal Profit Mfg	Central-Office-Optimal Profit Dst
A	39.05	101.18	3,361.82	1,528.10	1,833.72
B	32.59	116.78	2,868.15	1,593.42	1,274.73
C	47.57	80.84	4,185.95	1,470.74	2,715.21
D	39.55	98.09	3,440.45	1,563.84	1,876.61
E	36.67	92.33	3,226.67	1,344.44	1,882.22
F	33.33	115.00	1,333.33	0.00	1,333.33
G	35.56	109.67	1,706.67	189.63	1,517.04
H	44.00	89.40	1,936.00	(387.20)	2,323.20
I	31.82	118.64	1,113.64	(101.24)	1,214.88
J	36.67	107.00	1,613.33	0.00	1,613.33
K	29.33	124.60	1,290.67	258.13	1,032.53
L	39.09	99.18	1,680.91	(152.81)	1,833.72
M	51.76	96.65	2,277.65	(267.96)	2,545.61

Under these circumstances, individual evaluation of divisions and their managers based on allocated transfer-price and book-profit data is rendered meaningless—and it should be emphasized again that the *only* significance of Hirshleifer's transfer prices lies in their being behaviour-congruent with respect to divisional output decisions. They just aren't meaningful for evaluating divisional and managerial performances,[47] both because (as we saw in the last subsection) they're administered and because (as we've seen here) either division's book profits are affected by actions, efficiencies and inefficiencies of the other.[48]

Effects on Other Decisions

The foregoing analysis leads to what may be the most fundamental weakness in Hirshleifer's approach. We've just concluded that, insofar as they're affected by transfer prices, divisional book profits are meaningless for evaluating division managers. But the central office's use of book profits *in* evaluating them is precisely what's supposed to motivate these managers to make central-office-optimal output decisions. I'll denote this as *the evaluation paradox*; we should consider this paradox's behavioural implications.

To recapitulate, the way that the Hirshleifer approach evaluates division managers doesn't reflect their successes in operations. Nonetheless, it *is* the way that they are evaluated, and if they don't do what the central office wants them to do they will receive less favourable arbitrary evaluations than if they conform. Therefore, one would expect them to conform but to suffer élan dysfunctions (much as would students whose grades don't reflect their understandings of a course but who, nonetheless, do what they can to enhance these grades): they would feel manipulated, distrust the company's accounting data and its system of internal accounting and control, believe that their contributions were being underrated (or, what can be just as bad, *over*rated), lose some of the very profit consciousness that transfer pricing is supposed to encourage[49]

---

[47] At least, they're not meaningful evaluations in any sense that a lay-person would give to that phrase. One reader of an earlier version of this book suggested an alternative: that in such cases the allocation method used *defines* the divisional profits. If so, the definition is excessively ambiguous.

[48] For similar conclusions, see [Hirshleifer, 1956, p. 180; 1957, pp. 105-08] and [Emmanuel, 1977b]. Contrast [Cook, 1955, p. 88] and [Abdel-khalik and Lusk, 1974, p. 23].

[49] Compare [Dearden, 1960a, p. 118].

and, generally, suffer from lowered élan.[50] Moreover, of course, in all those situations where inefficiency increases divisional book profits or efficiency decreases them, division managers will be tempted to make decisions that are central-office perverse.[51]

Finally, since it should be apparent to all actors that divisional book profits on transfer goods are administered and that they don't reflect division managers' performances, how, in the long run, could they be taken seriously enough for the company to continue to use them to motivate central-office-optimal output decisions? The evaluation paradox threatens the one area in which Hirshleifer's approach supposedly is behaviour-congruent.[52] In later chapters, I'll refer to this as his approach's tendency to *self-destruct.*[53]

Just as important for our purposes, the evaluation paradox also seems bound to be destructive of any sense of divisional autonomy that a manager might retain after becoming aware of the matters discussed in previous subsections. To appreciate this, let's perform a simple mental experiment. Suppose that the central office were to determine either division's maximum possible book profits by drawing a *random number* from, say, the range 25% to 75% of the central-office-optimal global profit on the transfer good. However, this division would be credited with this book profit only if it operated at some specified output level; at any other, the central office would reduce its book profit from this arbitrarily determined maximum to some lower arbitrary amount.[54]

If division managers knew that evaluations of their performances would be based on such arbitrary numbers, doubtless they would do what they could to maximize these numbers—and would, therefore, comply with the central office's wishes. But

---

[50]Dean [1955, p. 72] observes of internally arbitrated transfer prices: "... the results do not satisfy either party. Everyone feels cheated, and everyone has an alibi for his profit...results." Hirshleifer's administered transfer prices are an extreme instance of internally arbitrated ones: the arbitrator simply takes over and sets prices to suit itself. See also [Dearden, 1960a, p. 123].

[51]See [Bierman, 1963, pp. 100-01].

[52]As far as I can tell, the closest that prior literature comes to noticing this may be found in [Dopuch and Drake, 1964, pp. 13-14, 20-21].

[53]Similarly, as Solomons [1965, p. 9] points out, the extent to which the central office will be willing to grant divisional autonomy will be heavily influenced by its ability to evaluate divisions' individual performances. Therefore, those problems of evaluation would strike at the roots of divisional autonomy, too—were there anything significant to strike at here.

[54]In any event, the other division (with which we are temporarily unconcerned) would be assigned whatever global profit was left over, as *its* book profit.

would they be under any illusion of acting as bona-fide profit centres here? or that "their" output decisions were anything but centralized? or that they were doing anything but following orders? The orders are indirect, but patently orders all the same. To suppose otherwise is to suppose the managers to be too gullible ever to have attained their positions.

Yet, things are even worse with Hirshleifer's approach:

1. As we've seen, Hirshleifer's book profits can be negative, not merely held to a lower limit of zero, and

2. Hirshleifer's maximum book profits lack the even-handed impersonality of random numbers; instead, they're manifestly designed to serve the central office's purposes.

Accordingly, it's evident that the evaluation paradox would (a) generate substantial behavioural perversities and (b) destroy division managers' senses of autonomy as far as dealings in transfer goods are concerned—something that, as we've seen, would be apt to generate further behavioural dysfunctions. These conclusions will be important in subsequent chapters.

Other Defects

Here are a few more, related, properties of Hirshleifer's approach to transfer pricing. First, let's suppose that divisions deal in other goods besides the transfer good, but that book profits on the latter materially affect total divisional book profits. For reasons that parallel those given above, Hirshleifer's transfer prices won't be behaviour-congruent with respect to decisions whether to increase, hold constant, or decrease investments in (and related resource allocations to) individual divisions if the central office bases such decisions wholly or partly on total divisional book profits.[55]

Obversely, Abdel-khalik and Lusk [1974, p. 13] correctly observe that, in the economic-theory context in which Hirshleifer wrote, marginal costs include returns to all factors of production, including capital. Therefore, a division that is allocated zero book profits need not feel distressed on that account alone, for zero is a capital-attracting return. Nonetheless, whenever divisions have constant or declining marginal costs and, therefore, zero or negative book profits they have no reason to propose new capital-bud-

---

[55] See [Hirshleifer, 1957, pp. 105-06, 108] for similar conclusions in a situation where there are two distribution divisions.

geting projects, or otherwise innovate.[56] And, of course, whenever Mfg's marginal costs decline Hirshleifer's transfer prices lead to the classic problems that arise when marginal-cost pricing fails to cover the costs of producing a product or service.[57]

Some of the behavioural perversities of Hirshleifer's approach, mentioned above, stem from problems of equity. There are numerous equity theories of motivation; here, it's plausible to assume that matters will depend as much on how equitable transfer prices are *perceived* to be as upon the actual circumstances.[58] We've already seen how Hirshleifer transfer prices violate lay perceptions of equity (e.g., lack of impersonality, assignment of book losses to essential divisions, one division's profits being lowered by another's inefficiencies or its own efficiencies). Usually, the approach will yield what ordinary people would regard as "fair" rates of return on each division's investment[59] only by coincidence.[60]

The central problem here is that the interests of the two divisions inevitably are opposed and, aside from the limited consequences of their driving things to a Pareto optimum, Hirshleifer's transfer prices do nothing to resolve this internal conflict[61] and the associated tensions that can be major sources of dysfunctional behaviour.[62] In particular, Hirshleifer's transfer prices encourage gaming. When division managers perceive the company's accounting methods to be inequitable, it is only natural for them to do a bit of counter-manipulation, expending time, energy and creativity

[56] See [Onsi, 1970, pp. 537-38].

[57] See [Loehman and Whinston, 1974, pp. 236-37] and, more generally, [Coase, 1946].

[58] See [Steers and Porter, 1975, pp. 135-37, esp. p. 136].

[59] [Dean, 1955, p. 70].

[60] I qualify, with *usually*, only because I haven't thoroughly analyzed [Tomkins, 1973, pp. 58-62], which raises the possibility of capacity constraints being operative at a level of output below what otherwise would be the central-office-optimal level. Tomkins argues that when this occurs a mutually fair rate of return may be possible.

[61] As a specialized instance of failure of conflict resolution, readers might imagine a slightly more complicated situation: By exhausting its capacity, Mfg can make a different product and sell it externally; similarly, Dst could buy and distribute some other product externally. It is easy to confect situations where one division's profits from such a change will exceed its Hirshleifer book profits on the transfer good, yet where its doing so would be central-office dysfunctional. Here, Hirshleifer's approach will lack Part One's central-office-optimal coalition-forming properties.

[62] Compare [Seed, 1970, p. 10], [Caplan, 1971, pp. 37-38] and [Watson and Baumler, 1975, pp. 471-72].

in efforts to improve their book profits (rather than those of the company as a whole).[63]

Under Hirshleifer's approach, an excellent way for division managers to do this is to misrepresent their cost curves.[64] Prakash and Rappaport's [1977, p. 32] discussion of Campbell's two "laws" gives the essence of this:

> The more any quantitative indicator is used for social decision-making, the more subject it will be to corruption pressures, and the more apt it will be to distort and corrupt the social processes it is intended to monitor.

For instance, readers may verify that if, in Figure 8-1, Mfg could only fool the central office into believing that its cost function was really $C_m = 20.9 + 1.1Q$ (a 10% increase over the truth), it would attain a £1,790.86 book profit (12% higher than before) at an output of 37.85 and a £104.17 transfer price (Dst and the company as a whole suffering lower profits in consequence).

As Shubik [1964, pp. 210-11] points out, besides improving their book profits such fiddling also offers division managers a way of capturing some of the autonomy that Hirshleifer's approach otherwise denies them. Were Hirshleifer's approach to be used in practice, one would expect gaming to be as popular under it as anecdotal literature suggests it is, say, in the Russian economy.[65] It's hard to see how the central office could prevent this without becoming so knowledgeable about the details of divisional operations as to defeat the fundamental, information-economies rationale of transfer pricing itself.[66] [67]

---

[63] Simon et al., [1945, p. 32] comment:
> When the operating man is placed in the position of justifying his performance in terms of a standard that he doesn't regard as fair he has two choices: to change the performance, or to change the measurement of it. And since he regards the measurement of his performance as unfair, he almost inevitably chooses the second alternative.

See also [McGregor, 1960, p. 9] and [Bailey and Boe, 1976, p. 560].

[64] See [Cook, 1955, p. 87], [Gould, 1964, pp. 66-67], [Hirshleifer, 1964, pp. 32, 34-36], [Gordon, 1970, pp. 428-29], [Onsi, 1970, p. 537] and [Abdel-khalik and Lusk, 1974, pp. 15, 20, 23].

[65] Not that gaming is unique to situations involving transfer prices or other allocations; any time and motion study system must contend with it—see [Cook, 1955, p. 87]. Similarly, as [Dean, 1955, p. 69] notes, when transfer prices are based on allocation-*free* published market prices, managers may be tempted to manipulate these prices.

[66] Compare [Gordon, 1970, pp. 428-29].

[67] Finally, be it noted in passing that Hirshleifer's marginal-cost transfer prices aren't apt to be satisfactory for financial- and tax-accounting purposes, and may violate anti-dumping and other laws and regulations. See [National Association of Accountants, 1957a, pp. 22-23, 30] for the tax aspects of this.

Failure of the Simple Hirshleifer Approach

> The more important...interdivisional transactions become, the more dependent is the whole system of profit measurement on the system of transfer pricing. Unfortunately, as the performance of one division becomes increasingly bound up with the affairs of other divisions, it also becomes more doubtful whether separate profit responsibility, the hallmark of a full-fledged division, continues to be feasible. —[Solomons, 1965, p. 161]

Evidently, then, the simple version of Hirshleifer's approach just won't work—even in theory and when approached on its own terms. It displays not merely joint-cost allocations' failure of universal behaviour-congruence, but a nearly universal *perversity*: dysfunctions so severe as to render the notion of separate divisional profit centres meaningless.[68] This renders its popularity in accounting textbooks somewhat disturbing.

Even more important, we'll soon see (though, necessarily, in less detail) that the main conclusions that we've reached here apply with equal vigour to *any* system of marginal or opportunity-cost transfer prices, even the mathematical-programming ones so prominent in the management-science journals. This is why I've devoted so much space to what otherwise might seem to be an overly simplified model: its defects illuminate a huge corpus of literature whose mathematical complexity might otherwise blind us to its faults.

---

[68] See [Simon, et al., 1954, p. 41], [Dean, 1955, pp. 67-68], [National Association of Accountants, 1957a, p. 8] and [Henderson and Dearden, 1966, p. 145].

CHAPTER NINE

MORE COMPLICATED SITUATIONS

This chapter explores what happens when we relax some of the assumptions made in Chapter Eight, specifically that:

1. The central office specifies the transfer price directly,

2. When there's an external market for the transfer good, the company pays the same price as a buyer as it commands as a seller in that market,

3. Demand and supply curves in this intermediate market are horizontal,

4. The company's divisions are demand-independent: Mfg's sales in the intermediate market don't affect Dst's sales in the final market, and vice versa, and

5. The company's divisions are technologically independent: changes in Mfg's output don't affect Dst's costs if its output remains unchanged, and vice-versa.[1]

I'll also mention situations involving more than two divisions, though these are more the next chapter's province. For brevity, I'll hold analysis to the bare minimum necessary to demonstrate that relaxing these assumptions doesn't alter Chapter Eight's main conclusions. Even so, readers who aren't following the argument closely may wish to skim what follows.

Indirect Specification of the Transfer Price

In his description of the simple situation discussed in Chapter Eight, Hirshleifer [1956, pp. 174-175] does not have the central office specify use of the central-office-optimal transfer price directly. Instead, one or the other division dominates the internal exchange. If it's Mfg, it obtains Dst's demand schedule; if it's Dst, it obtains Mfg's supply schedule. In either event, the dominant division then bases the transfer price on this schedule, seemingly in the same way that an autonomous seller or buyer would respond to external demand and supply curves.

---

[1]Please note the difference between this last assumption and the situation described in the latter part of Chapter Eight. There, because the internal market always had to be cleared, changes in one division's costs affected the other division's marginal costs and profits via a change in the latter's output.

But there's a catch: The central office stipulates that Dst must not exploit its dominant position by acting like a monopsonistic buyer, or that Mfg must not exploit its dominant position by acting like a monopolistic seller [p. 175]. Since, in context, any departure from the central-office-optimal transfer price counts as exploitation, in effect the central office has dictated use of that transfer price.

Different Prices in the Intermediate Market

Chapter Eight assumed that whenever an external market existed for the transfer good, Mfg commanded the same price in it as Dst would have to pay—that's why the company was indifferent to whether its divisions dealt internally or externally. In reality of course, such things as transportation costs[2] and institutional arrangements result in the price that the company would have to pay to acquire the transfer good externally exceeding the price for which it could sell it externally. Another common instance occurs when Mfg can escape external promotion and bad-debts costs by selling internally.[3]

Here, the company can't merely follow Chapter Eight's rule of setting transfer prices equal to external market prices. For the appropriate market price is, at least initially, unclear. Gould [1964] introduced, and Naert [1973, esp. pp. 103-14] refined, what writers on transfer pricing now regard as the standard marginal analysis of such situations.[4] Not surprisingly, their recommendations for these situations are hybrids of what marginal analysis recommends in the two extreme, Chapter Eight, cases that bracket them: Sometimes the company should use allocation-free current market val-

---

[2]Conceivably, this could take a form as simple as the following: The company faces a perfect intermediate market but is located at a distance from it, so that it must pay freight whether buying or selling. As [Cook, 1955, p. 89] and [Gould, 1964, p. 61] point out, such situations engender vertical integration and, therefore, the circumstances of transfer pricing itself.

[3]For examples of those and the other intermediate-market imperfections discussed in the remainder of this chapter, see [Cook, 1955, p. 89], [Hirshleifer, 1956, pp. 173, 176, 178-80; 1964, pp. 27-28], [Gould, 1964, pp. 62-63], [Whinston, 1964, p. 411], [Solomons, 1965, pp. 174-77; 1977, pp. 44·21-22], [McCulloch, 1967, pp. 15-16, 22] and [Naert, 1973, p. 103].

[4][Hirshleifer, 1964, pp. 33-34] discussed the aspect of this analysis that we'll soon call Case I. With reference to the last part of this chapter, one notes in passing that Hirshleifer [1956, p. 173] also observed that the phenomena under discussion here could arise from technological dependence.

ues as transfer prices, other times it should use allocated transfer prices identical with those stipulated by the simple Hirshleifer approach.[5]

One would expect the price that Dst has to pay to buy the transfer good externally to be greater than or equal to the price that Mfg could command by selling it externally. We may denote these prices as P_n and P_x, for the transfer good's current-*entry* and current-*exit* prices, respectively. Since $P_n \geqslant P_x$, these prices bear only three possible relationships to Chapter Eight's central-office-optimal, no-intermediate-market, transfer price, $P*$:

Case I: $P_n \geqslant P_x > P*$
Case II: $P* > P_n \geqslant P_x$
Case III: $P_n \geqslant P* \geqslant P_x$

We'll be concerned here with situations where these inequalities are absolute.[6]

Gould and Naert prove that in Case I the company will maximize global profits by having Mfg sell Dst whatever the latter demands at a transfer price of P_x, then allowing Mfg to sell additional transfer goods to outsiders (at P_x, of course) until its marginal costs equal P_x.

Similarly, in Case II the company will maximize global profits by having Dst buy from Mfg all that the latter will produce at a transfer price of P_n, then allowing Dst to buy additional transfer goods from outsiders (at P_n) until its marginal revenues equal its marginal costs.

Finally, in Case III the company will maximize global profits at a transfer price of $P*$, with neither division dealing in the external market. (As the market for an intermediate product becomes progressively thinner, this situation is more and more likely to prevail.) Thus, the Gould-Naert transfer pricing rules are:[7]

---

[5] Readers who wish a detailed discussion of the Gould-Naert approach should consult [Naert, 1973]. As I did with the Hirshleifer approach in Chapter Eight, I'll slightly simplify the Gould-Naert approach's exposition here. For instance, [Gould, 1964, p. 66] uses an iterative procedure (ultimately derived from Arrow [1959]) to avoid direct central-office dictation of transfer prices. But, as we'll soon see, such iterative procedures don't remedy an approach's dysfunctional properties.

[6] Whenever $P_n = P_x$, we have Chapter Eight's perfect-intermediate-market situation. We'll see that the Gould-Naert approach stipulates use of this single current-market price as the transfer price. Contrawise, Chapter Eight's no-intermediate-market situation is merely an extreme instance of Case III, where, P_n equals infinity and P_x equals zero. We'll see that, here, the Gould-Naert approach stipulates use of $P*$. Thus, the Gould-Naert approach impounds both approaches discussed in Chapter Eight, subsuming perfect competition in the external market and the simple Hirshleifer situation as limiting cases.

[7] Compare [Tomkins, 1973, p. 55].

Case	Central-Office-Optimal Transfer Price
I	P_x
II	P_n
III	$P*$

Monopsonistic and Monopolistic Behaviour

A complete analysis of the ways monopsonistic and monopolistic divisions could be expected to behave when $P_n > P_x$ turns out to be surprisingly complex, but the following generalities will suffice for our purposes:

1. In Case I, it would be selfishly advantageous for Mfg to set a transfer price just (barely) enough less than P_n that it would persuade Dst to buy internally rather than from outsiders. This would reduce Dst's output and, thereby, global profits, but would increase Mfg's book profits. (Though the proportion it sells to outsiders increases, Mfg will sell the same total volume as before, its units sold to Dst bear higher prices, and the price for which it sells its other units remains unchanged.)

2. Similarly, in Case II it would be selfishly advantageous for Dst to set a transfer price just enough higher than P_x that it would persuade Mfg to sell to it rather than to outsiders. This would reduce Mfg's output and global profits, but would increase Dst's book profits.

3. In Case III, Mfg would want to increase, and Dst want to lower, the transfer price, subject to restrictions imposed by Dst's and Mfg's abilities to deal in the external intermediate market.

The availability here of external alternatives to an exploited division often leaves dominant divisions less latitude for exploitation than in the simple Hirshleifer situation. But, otherwise, attainment of central-office-optimal profits requires just as active central-office intervention as it did there, and with just as great threats to divisional autonomy. And since the central-office-optimal solution to Case III is identical with the one under the simple Hirshleifer approach, it shares all of the latter's crippling dysfunctional properties.[8]

---

[8] Compare [Naert, 1973, pp. 105, 107].

In the other two Cases (excepting threats to autonomy), the Gould-Naert approach suffers from fewer perversities than does Hirshleifer's. But this is hardly surprising: the former often uses allocation-free current-exit and -entry values as transfer prices and, as emphasized in Chapter Eight, I have no quarrel with these. However, even when the company uses these current values the Gould-Naert approach doesn't entirely escape perversities. In Case I, the central-office-optimal transfer price that Dst pays for its inputs is less than what it would have had to pay in the market; therefore, Dst's book profits are higher than they would have been had it used the external market. In Case II, the revenues (and book profits) that Mfg receives from its output are greater than what it would receive in the market; in both cases the other division's profits are lower than they would be had they been free to deal exclusively in the market. Accordingly, divisional profits are administered ones, and this creates difficulties for central-office evaluation decisions similar to (if not as intense as) those faced under the simple Hirshleifer approach.

The upshot of all this is that insofar as the Gould-Naert approach is an allocation method it's as fallible as Hirshleifer's, whereas insofar as it's allocation-free it still diminishes divisonal autonomy and displays other perversities.

Non-Horizontal External Demand and Supply Curves

Let's turn now to another sort of imperfection: situations where the intermediate market has a downward-sloping demand curve. Here, Mfg is in a position similar to that of a discriminating monopolist that sells in two different markets (here, internal and external ones).[9] As is typical of such cases, the company will maximize global profits by equating:

> ...the joint marginal cost of production with the net marginal revenue in each separate market. The word "net" means that we must adjust the market marginal revenue by the incremental cost of delivering to the market concerned...
>
> The solution just discussed would be arrived at directly by a central decision agency with the appropriate information.—[Hirshleifer, 1956, p. 178]

Once again, though (despite Hirshleifer's [p. 178] talk of maintaining divisional autonomy), it's clear from the paragraph that overlaps [pp. 178-79] that the central office dictates the central-

[9] Readers are reminded that we continue to assume demand independence.

office-optimal transfer price here to the same degree that it does in Chapter Eight's simple Hirshleifer situation. Naert [1973, pp. 109-10, 112] extends this to situations where the external market's supply curve is upward-sloping, with Dst a monopsonist in that market.[10] All of the perversities of the simple Hirshleifer situation follow;[11] indeed, Naert concludes that divisions shouldn't even be treated as profit centres.

Demand Dependence

Two products will be demand-dependent whenever sales of one affect sales of the other.[12] These effects can be positive (e.g., self-developing film and cameras) or negative (e.g., upright and horizontal home freezers). Much of Hirshleifer's [e.g., 1957, pp. 97-98] discussion of demand dependence involves divisions that aren't selling goods to each other, but his analysis is applicable to situations where Mfg is selling both to an external intermediate market and to Dst; here:

> Generally speaking, the firm's two markets will be connected in that an additional internal sale to a distributing subsidiary would be expected to lead to some reduction of external demand on the part of purchasers of the intermediate commodity who compete with the distributing subsidiary in the market for the final good.—[Hirshleifer, 1956, p. 180]

In such situations, earlier proposals for attaining central-office optima break down, since:

> Whenever demands are related, the apparent marginal revenue of each of the separate divisions...is not the marginal revenue for the firm as a whole...Let us denote the apparent marginal revenues MR_1 and MR_2, and the corrected or true marginal revenues MR_1^* and MR_2^*. Then each division acting autonomously to maximize its separate profit would try to equate marginal cost to MR when it should be trying to equate marginal cost to MR^*...
>
> What institutional device can we establish so that each of the divisions will take into account the effect on the revenues of the others while still retaining as many of the advantages of autonomous decision-

---

[10] Naert [p. 110] also points out, though, that as long as the division under consideration is an external price-taker (and there is an external price-leader), Chapter Eight's recommendation for transfer pricing in a perfect market remains correct, in the sense that the transfer price should be whatever market price is set by that price leader.

[11] For a rather specialized instance, see [Dearden, 1960, p. 118].

[12] Hass [1968, pp. B· 311-12] mentions the sorts of externalities discussed in the next two sections, along with other situations in which the central office must coordinate the activities of divisions. See also [Bailey and Boe, 1976, p. 559].

making as possible? The most natural solution is to set up a system of "taxes" (in the case of competitive demands) and "bounties" (in the case of complementary demands) so as to correct the MR for each division and make it equal to MR*. —[Hirshleifer, 1957, pp. 99, 100] [13]

The catch here though (despite Hirshleifer's concern for autonomy) is that, as he explicitly notes [1964, pp. 34-35], the central office must intervene to prevent Mfg from behaving as an external monopolist. Again readers are invited to verify that this intervention boils down to central-office dictation of the transfer price, and that, accordingly, all the dysfunctions of Chapter Eight's simple Hirshleifer situation arise here, too. The simplest reason why this is so is that Hirshleifer imposes his taxes and subsidies *in addition* to his other proposals, not as substitutes for them. Thus, whenever an external, declining demand (or increasing supply) curve for the transfer good would lead to the perversities discussed in the last section, the taxes and subsidies do nothing to relieve things. Whereas whenever circumstances would have led Hirshleifer to recommend use of a current-exit or -entry transfer price for two demand-*in*dependent divisions, his transfer prices will now be administered ones specified by the central office. Similarly, the purchasable sales rights that, on information-economy grounds, Hirshleifer [1957, p. 100] proposes as a possible alternative to his taxes and subsidies are only modifications of the transfer-price procedures that he proposes for demand-independence.

The only exception occurs when [1956, p. 181] Mfg is the sole supplier of the transfer good to the entire economy, Hirshleifer's other conditions for what he calls "perfect demand dependence" are met, and long-run equilibrium has been attained. Simultaneous satisfaction of these conditions is apt to be rare. Thus, all that demand-dependence usually does is to make matters worse: Where the central office intervened to dictate transfer prices it still does so (in more complex ways), while now it must also intervene in situations that previously were allocation-free. Otherwise, demand-dependence doesn't change our earlier conclusions one iota.

Technological Dependence

The same is true of technological dependence. Just as demand dependence prevents the divisions' marginal revenues from sum-

---

[13] See also [Hirshleifer, 1956, pp. 173, 176, 178, 180-82; 1964, pp. 33-35]. Curiously, subsequent writers have largely disregarded Hirshleifer's proposals for demand dependence, despite his arguments that it's apt to be quite common.

ming to the company's marginal revenue, so technological dependence prevents the divisions' marginal *costs* from summing to the company's marginal costs.[14] Hirshleifer [1956, pp. 182-83] initially commented that:

> ...a beginning approach to the problem of transfer pricing under conditions of technological dependence would involve establishment of an internal "tax" or "subsidy" to make the autonomous calculations of the separate divisions take into account the effects on the margin of impaired or enhanced productivity in the other divisions.

Unfortunately, in context it's clear that the same thing is true of these taxes and subsidies as was of those that he proposed for demand dependence: they are modifications of his earlier proposals, involving additional central-office dictation of transfer prices and administration of divisional book profits.

Later, Hirshleifer [1957, pp. 103-05; 1964, pp. 30, 32] suggested an alternative approach to deal with the technological dependence of two distribution divisions that obtain the same transfer good from a single manufacturing division (whose marginal costs aren't horizontal). These costs will depend on the combined demands of both Dsts. In order for the latter to reach mutually consistent output decisions, he proposes an iterative procedure whereby Mfg sets a tentative transfer price and output, the Dsts react with their tentative separate outputs, and Mfg checks to see whether these sum to its tentative output. If not, Mfg adjusts its transfer price and output until, by successive iterations, it discovers a transfer price that clears the internal market.[15]

Readers are left to verify that the same possibilities for exploitation (by Mfg individually, or by a collusion of the Dsts) exist here as in Chapter Eight's simple Hirshleifer situation. Since Hirshleifer's only barrier to exploitation is central-office intervention,[16] we're back to the familiar dysfunctional properties of that situation. In addition, the iterative approach is itself a source of further perversities that we'll discuss in the next chapter.[17] Identical conclusions follow for Hirshleifer's [1957, pp. 104-05] situation where there is more than one transfer good.

---

[14] See [Onsi, 1970, p. 537*n*].

[15] For instance, if total Dst demand exceeds Mfg's tentative output, it would raise its transfer price and output in the next iteration.

[16] For an explicit statement of such intervention, see [1964, p. 34].

[17] Other iterative proposals at this chapter's level of organizational complexity, to which identical conclusions apply, may be found in [Gould, 1964, p. 66] and [Marschak, 1964, pp. 85-86]. Paik [1975] discusses situations where one division's activities generate externalities of the same sorts as those we've considered in the last two sections, and reaches similarly gloomy conclusions—see especially his figure on page 81.

Relationship to Joint-Cost Allocations

One reason for all these difficulties is that, as Hirshleifer [1956, pp. 182-83; 1957, pp. 96-97] points out, technological dependence is the joint-cost phenomenon.[18] More generally, we saw in Chapter One that whenever a transferor division makes other goods besides the transfer one, or makes transfer goods for two or more transferees, transfer pricing involves joint-cost allocation. What contribution does the last two chapters' analysis make to Part One's discussions of joint-cost allocations?

If joint products have positive split-off values prior to further processing, Hirshleifer's analysis implies that the joint process itself should be treated as a profit centre and that the transfer prices for its products should be the external market prices. If memory serves, the (scanty) literature on this topic agrees.[19] Be warned, though, that imperfections in this intermediate market could easily generate one of the situations discussed earlier in this chapter.

When split-off values are zero, the situation resembles Chapter Eight's simple Hirshleifer one, save that there are now two or more distribution divisions. Such situations suffer from all of the dysfunctional properties of the simple Hirshleifer one, plus perversities of their own.[20] Negative split-off values would complicate matters even further. From this perspective, it's not surprising that the marginal approach to joint-cost analysis (and the related NRV method) aren't universally behaviour-congruent, nor that each of the other joint-cost approaches discussed in Part One has various dysfunctional properties. Hirshleifer [1956, p. 183] may be given the last word here:

> Where technological dependence exists, the situation is so complex that we have not been able to indicate even the nature of the general solution. We suspect that the prospects for divisional autonomy may be poor under these conditions.

[18] See especially his oil refinery example on [1957, p. 97].

[19] I apologize for having mislaid my bibliographical notes on specific discussions of this matter.

[20] Independently, Shillinglaw [1977b, p. 863] observes that marginal cost is indeterminate when a transferor sells to two or more transferees, and that attainment of what correspond to central-office-optimal profits in such situations requires central-office dictation to divisions. Readers should reach identical conclusions from close study of [Hirshleifer, 1956, pp. 182-83; 1957, pp. 102-05, 108].

Summary

> "Sonny Liston has a lot of good points. It's his bad points that aren't so good." —quoted by Buckley [1978]

By now it's all too evident that the prospects for avoiding the crippling dysfunctional properties of Chapter Eight's simple Hirshleifer approach are grim in almost any situation save where there's a perfect intermediate market for the transfer good,[21] and that such conditions are rare.[22]

Thus, despite the esteem in which accounting theorists hold them, Hirshleifer's, Gould's and Naert's transfer-pricing proposals fail theoretically. No wonder that companies don't adopt them in practice. The next chapter shows that identical conclusions apply to mathematical-programming approaches to transfer pricing, and for identical reasons.

---

[21]Dopuch and Drake [1964, p. 20] reach similar conclusions. Analogously, Hayek [1944, pp. 48-50] argues that a price system is essential to decentralization at the macro level, but that price systems will do their jobs "... only if competition prevails..." [p. 49].

[22]Contrast [Lemke, 1970, p. 186]; would that something as mild as mere failure of his "perfect goal congruence" were really the issue here.

CHAPTER TEN

MATHEMATICAL PROGRAMMING APPROACHES

The failure of the marginal cost pricing models to deal with pricing of transfer goods in a multidivision, multiproduct, decentralized organization prompted the introduction of other models to determine transfer prices that will achieve efficient allocation of resources while maintaining autonomy.—[Abdel-khalik and Lusk, 1974, p. 15]

Many accountants and almost all economists argue that any allocation of joint costs (including overhead and depreciation over time) is arbitrary and serves no useful purpose. Yet, over the last fifteen years, mathematical programming models of a firm's decision problem have yielded, in addition to the optimal decision rule, allocations based on the dual variables from the programming model. These allocations permit an overall or global decision problem to be decomposed into a series of much smaller problems. By using the allocations derived from the global model, managers solving their local or suboptimal problem will be motivated to achieve the solution that is globally optimum for the firm. —[Kaplan, 1977, p. 30]

The foregoing quotations offer several themes for the early parts of this chapter, as well as provide continuity with our previous discussions. For, the mathematical programming approaches that we'll now consider simultaneously:

1. Extend Hirshleifer's efforts into arenas that are far more complex (and realistic) than those with which his, Gould's and Naert's methodologies could cope,

2. Prescribe specific, detailed ways in which companies should physically allocate their resources among divisions (in contrast to the—at best—only general guidance provided by the Hirshleifer, Gould and Naert approaches), and

3. Develop rationales for internal cost (and profit) allocations that, as Kaplan points out, we may equally perceive as transfer prices and as assignments of joint costs.[1]

---

[1] Readers of [Thomas, 1969; 1974] might take particular interest in the joint-cost-allocation aspects of these mathematical programming approaches. As the quotation from [Kaplan, 1977] suggests, some believe that they can be used to defend the internal choice of, say, a particular depreciation method. From this, it seems only a short step to saying: If this is the depreciation method that management should be using internally, isn't it thereby also the depreciation method that the company should use in its external reports? I've been disappointed that none of my critics have raised this question—especially given Callen's [1978] similar attempt to found financial accounting on (far more arcane) Shapley allocations (see Appendix I).

This chapter notes that mathematical programming approaches generate two kinds of allocations: distributions of resources and notional assignments of costs and profits. I've

Unlike most discussions of these matters, wherever possible this chapter will avoid going into mathematical details of programming approaches.[2] There are three reasons:

1. My own lack of mathematical maturity,

2. A suspicion that this lack is shared by many of my potential readers, and

3. A belief (also influential in Chapters Four, Eight and Nine) that concentration on mathematical minutia tends to obscure important aspects of the procedures that we shall examine.

As to the last, it's vital that mathematical programming approaches be developed rigourously. But *once others have done so,* it is equally vital to explore these methods' key properties (and the main issues to which they give rise) without getting tangled in the sorts of detail that have been the besetting sin of much recent literature.[3] This is what this chapter and Appendix J attempt, using the analytical framework developed in the last two chapters.

Why Mathematical Programming?

Mathematical programming techniques are far more complex and demand far greater user sophistication than the transfer-pricing methods discussed in Chapters Eight and Nine. These are disadvantages. What compensating advantages do the techniques offer?

As I've suggested in Appendix G, part of the answer may lie in their setting a very elegant mathematical problem for economists

no quarrel with the former, but will try to show that the latter, though the former's duals, are far from behavior congruent with respect to companies' internal decisions. Indeed, in the typical instance they suffer from all the perversities of the allocations generated by the simple Hirshleifer approach. From this it follows that their extension to financial accounting would be misguided.

[2]But one need not desert ones readers here. For elementary background on mathematical programming approaches to decentralization, their customary implicit assumptions (such as convexity), and the relationships of such approaches to models of competitive equilibrium, see [Koopmans, 1957]. For general background, see [Whinston, 1962], [Solomons, 1965, pp. 196-97], [ten Kate, 1972b], [Kornai, 1973, esp. pp. 522-30] and, should a copy be available, [Freeland and Baker, 1972, esp. pp. 22-23]. [Tomkins, 1973, pp. 34-36, 71-100, 105-08] gives good expositions of several of the more prominent mathematical programming approaches.

For other surveys of approaches, and bibliographies, see [Ruefli, 1969, Ch. II; 1974], [Geoffrion, 1970a; 1970b], [Jennergren, 1971] and [Freeland, 1973]. For entry into the literature on certain resource-allocation procedures that brevity forces me to disregard, see [Hurwicz, Radner and Reiter, 1975, pp. 187-88, 190]. Finally, for *physical* (structural and productive) decompositions of production systems, rather than the informational and decisional decomposition algorithms that we'll consider, see [Weil, 1968a], whose bibliography offers entry into another literature that, for brevity, this book must disregard.

[3]Of course, this presupposes that the broad discussion doesn't materially violate what a rigourous one would have concluded. Here's another matter whose verification I must leave to the readers' industry.

and management scientists, one all the more alluring because its solution always seems nearly within reach. But, leaving this aside, there are some solid explanations. Here's the simplest, verification of which may be left to the reader: Whenever economic realism encourages us to relax Hirshleifer's, Gould's and Naert's simplifying assumptions and to try to extend their analyses to, say situations involving:

1. Two or more transfer goods or three or more divisions, and
2. Two or more limitations on resource capacities

one usually ends up in an unholy computational mess. Now, anyone who has taken a course in linear programming[4] should at least vaguely recall that:

1. It is designed to cope with just the sorts of multiple constraints that are characteristic of such situations.

2. Like Chapter Eight's and Nine's marginal costs, its shadow prices are opportunity costs,[5] and

3. These can play much the same roles as those marginal costs did earlier.[6]

In particular, it should be possible to use these shadow prices to coordinate divisional operations.[7] Accordingly (slightly simplifying the actual, historical sequence of events), it's hardly surprising that economists and management scientists would use linear programming to extend Hirshleifer's analysis.[8]

Unfortunately, linear programming has its own limitations:

1. Central-office use of it to calculate central-office-optimal transfer prices requires such detailed knowledge of divisional af-

---

[4]Both [Barron, 1972] and [Jennergren, 1972, pp. 1407-08] provide clear expositions of the basic linear programming procedures that underlie most of the literature discussed in this chapter.

[5]Which equal marginal ones at stable equilibria—see [Abdel-khalik and Lusk, 1974, p. 20]. See also [Samuels, 1965, pp. 182-83] and [Solomons, 1965, pp. 186-97].

[6]Readers who wish to pursue these points further might consider the similarity between the zero profit that linear programming assigns to a non-bottleneck resource and the zero book profit that (non-bottleneck) manufacturing divisions earn in the linear (constant-marginal-cost) instance of the simple Hirshleifer situation. However, as Emmanuel [1977b] points out, the two allocate the internal profit in opposite ways: to the transferor in the linear-programming case and to the transferee in the Hirshleifer one. (Emmanuel generalizes this conclusion.)

[7]Thus (and especially relevant to what follows), Jennergren [1971, p. 15] comments that ". . . the Lagrange multipliers of mathematical programming problems can be interpreted as prices and thus have an informational value which can sometimes be used to achieve coordination of decentralized operations in organizations." See also [Abdel-khalik and Lusk, 1974, pp. 15-16].

[8]As a technical point, to turn shadow prices into transfer prices one must add to them variable costs incurred up to the point of transfer—see [Solomons, 1965, p. 191], repeated in [Manes, 1970, pp. 569-70].

fairs and circumstances as to defeat the information-economies rationale for decentralizing,

2. Imposition of such transfer prices, along with linear programming's concomitant specifications of divisional inputs and outputs, would be at least as destructive of divisional autonomies as was Hirshleifer's specification of transfer prices,[9]

3. If applied to realistically complicated situations, such linear programming analyses overwhelmed the capacities of then-existing computers, and

4. Important real-world economic phenomena violated various implicit assumptions of linear programming—such as convexity, single-goal utility functions, simple, two-level organizational structures and, above all, linearity itself (which implies horizontal demand and supply curves, and bars consideration of certain kinds of demand and supply interdependencies and various other externalities).[10]

A major breakthrough occurred here when Dantzig and Wolfe [1960; 1961] discovered the decomposition principle and Baumol and Fabian [1964] demonstrated that it could be used to break up complex optimization problems into sets of smaller problems solvable by divisions and the central office exchanging information iteratively.[11] Such iterative processes resulted in great information economies, *seemed* to allow greatly increased autonomies

---

[9] On these first two points, and for several other technical difficulties that faced linear programming approaches, see [Abdel-khalik and Lusk, 1974, pp. 16-17].

[10] See [Hass, 1968, p. B· 312] and [Abdel-khalik and Lusk, 1974, p. 16].

[11] Please note the word *optimization*. The decomposition algorithm assured the same global (short-run, direct, overall profit-maximization) optimum that the original, complex linear programming problem would have led to had it been computationally feasible. This is what distinguished Dantzig and Wolfe's procedures both from the earlier iterative algorithms developed to coordinate divisions in complex circumstances and from more traditional kinds of bargaining (where each division merely tries to maximize its book profits, with no assurance of central-office optimality).

I mentioned earlier that my descriptions simplified the historical facts. Actually, writers on collectivism prior to the Second World War recognized that it was impossible for a central planning body to process all pertinent information available at (and to) the operating levels of State enterprises. This led several to suggest some sort of iterative exchanges between these enterprises and the central planners—see the works cited in [Hayek, 1940], [Koopmans, 1957, pp. 37-43, 63-64, 66-68 and *passim*], [March and Simon, 1958, pp. 201-10], [Marschak, 1959, pp. 399-400] and [Gordon, 1970, pp. 427-30].

Later, as we've seen, Hirshleifer [1957] also suggested such an iterative approach for a simple decentralization situation. Similarly, Arrow and Hurwicz's [1960] iterative procedures were independent of the decomposition principle. Nonetheless, the real revival of interest in such procedures didn't begin until Dantzig and Wolfe's contribution, which, along with Kornai and Liptak's [1965], has dominated recent mathematical programming research on decentralization.

to divisions, and made much less demand on computer capacities.[12] Subsequently (as Appendix J indicates) refinements on early, linear decomposition algorithms have relaxed many of linear programming's restrictive assumptions.

What makes the mathematical programming literature so formidable to lay readers like me[13] is authors' needs to (a) solve various technical problems (such as assuring finite convegence to optima) or (b) to extend procedures to progressively more realistic situations: goal conflict, multi-level hierarchies, nonlinear and nonconvex[14] functions and (as in some recent work) uncertainty. (There's an aesthetic barrier, too: a few authors seem to favour mathematical elegance over easy communication with nonmathematicians.) But we've seen a thread that can guide us here: most of these approaches may be perceived as extensions of Hirshleifer's marginal analysis, extensions that calculate globally optimal transfer prices and internal resource distributions (as duals) and give at least lip service to maintenance of divisional autonomies.

How They Work

Recent mathematical programming approaches to decentralization involve considerable back-and-forth interchanges of information between a company's hierarchical levels (central office, divisions and, sometimes, operating levels subordinate to divisions). In all versions, one hierarchical level begins each period's iterations by communicating information to another hierarchical level. Typically, there are only two levels, the central office is the one that makes this first move, and the information is a set of constraints on divisions. The divisions respond to these constraints, their responses cause the central office to promulgate a revised set of constraints, that generate new divisional responses, and so forth in a sequence of iterations.[15] Each iteration advances (or, at least,

---

[12] For a different rationale for such iterative approaches, see [Kriebel and Lave, 1969, pp. 184-90].

[13] Besides its depending upon a mathematical literature that's evolved from the Kuhn-Tucker [1951] Theorem—see [Pfouts, 1961, p. 654].

[14] See [ten Kate, 1972a] on these.

[15] Analogies to the iterative nature of this procedure may be found in participative budget setting, the successive tableaus of the Simplex method of linear programming, the iterations of the Cobweb Theorem, beloved of elementary economics courses (though these lack finite convergence) and, I'm reliably informed, certain manuals on how sexual partners may attain Pareto optima that meet the additional (e.g., Schmeidlerian [1969]) welfare criterion of maximizing the satisfaction of the least satisfied coalition member. Alternatively, one may perceive these iterations as the Walrasian *tâtonnement*, as does [Malinvaud, 1967, p. 173].

doesn't diminish) whatever utility or utilities the approach is designed to maximize. Typically, things end when a final iteration either attains a feasible central-office optimum or gives the central office the last bits of information needed to specify *how* to attain such an optimum.

The last paragraph was a bit abstract because it tried to embrace a variety of possible algorithms. First of all, most mathematical programming approaches allow only one goal, shared by all hierarchical levels: profit maximization. However, goal programming permits complex utility functions and (weighted) hierarchies of goals, while other approaches (discussed towards the end of this chapter) allow divisions and the central office to have different (if overlapping) goals, and yield satisficing, rather than central-office-optimal, solutions. *For brevity, the next two sections will assume a single, shared goal of profit maximization.*

All reported accounting magnitudes are consequences of multiplying quantities by prices. Accordingly, the central office can express the constraints that it communicates to divisions as either prices that it charges for resources (including, but not restricted to, transfer goods) or quantities of each resource (again including, but not restricted to, transfer goods) that it allows each division to use.[16] These prices and quantities are duals of each other in the same sense (and for the same reasons) that shadow prices and quantities are duals in linear programming. One consequence is that there are two basic styles of mathematical programming for optimizing decentralized systems; Geoffrion [1970a, p. 376] calls these *price-directive* and *resource-directive*.[17] Henceforth, I'll consistently distinguish physical allocations of resources from notional (bookkeeping) allocations of costs and profits by calling the former resource *distributions* and the later cost and profit *allocations.*

Here's how a resource-directive approach might work:[18] The central office begins a series of iterations by, say, announcing the quantities of each scarce resource to be distributed to each division.[19] Divisions respond with operating plans under which they

---

[16] See [Freeland and Baker, 1974, pp. 3-7, 10-13] for a very general mathematical model of this resource-distribution problem that underlies the transfer-pricing problem.

[17] The former stem from Dantzig and Wolfe's [1960] work, the latter from Kornai and Lipták's [1965]. For alternative nomenclatures and background, see [Jennergren, 1972, p. 1408], [ten Kate, 1972b, pp. 883-84, 890], [Freeland, 1973, pp. viii, 34], [Burton, Damon and Loughridge, 1974, pp. 297-303], [Freeland and Baker, 1974, pp. 10-11] and [Freeland and Moore, 1975, pp. 1-2, 8].

[18] See [Freeland, 1973, pp. 20-24] for a good, generalized description of such procedures.

[19] See [ten Kate, 1972b, p. 884] for an alternative opening gambit.

arrange their outputs so as to maximize the book profits that they can earn under these resource constraints. The programming approach allows the central office to detect both that these outputs aren't central-office optimal and how to change its resource distributions so as to move things closer to the as-yet-unknown central-office optimum.[20]

The second iteration begins with the central office reporting revised resource distributions to the divisions, which respond with revised plans that generate a third iteration, and so forth. Throughout, shadow prices of resources (including transfer goods) are available as duals of the primal resource distributions.[21] Indeed, it's these that divisions use in pricing out their operating alternatives and determining (by separate linear or other mathematical programming models) how to maximize their book profits under each iteration's resource distributions.

In contrast, a price-directive approach might begin with the central office providing divisions with a tentative schedule of the prices of all inputs or outputs (including transfer goods).[22] Divisions might respond with the quantities of each resource that they will "buy" and the quantities of each output that they will produce. The central office detects goods whose internal markets haven't been cleared (goods whose demands either exceed or fall short of supply) and adjusts individual prices[23] up or down accordingly. The divisions respond to those new prices, each successive iteration bringing things closer to a feasible solution that, ideally anyway, the method assures will also maximize global profits.[24]

---

[20] *How* the programming approach does this varies from system to system, and generates the sorts of mathematical complexities that this discussion attempts to circumvent.

[21] See, for example, [Kornai, 1973, p. 536].

[22] Or, conceivably, by the central office directly specifying the profits that divisions can earn on each output, or its using some system of taxes and subsidies that has the same effect as either of these approaches (see [Baumol and Fabian, 1964, pp. 3-5]).

[23] Or tariffs and subsidies, etc.

[24] As the foregoing tries to suggest, once again different price-directive approaches differ substantially in how they go about things, and I'm deliberately fudging over complexities. I'm also temporarily disregarding the possibility that under either a resource- or price-directive approach the central office may have to make a final, terminal intervention after the last iteration to ensure central-office-optimal divisional behaviour.

Arrow and Hurwicz [1960, pp. 35-36] anticipated the basic rationale of these programming algorithms. Notice its origins in Pareto's work:

> Since welfare economics assures us that under certain assumptions as to the utility function and the productive process...a competitive equilibrium can be identified with an economic optimum, we may conclude that the method of successive approximations which solves the problem of market equilibrium is also a computational method for solving the problem of optimal resource allocation. Indeed, it was seen in precisely this light by Pareto...who compared the market to a computing machine.

Recent thinking tends to favour resource- over price-directive approaches because each of the former's iterations yield feasible solutions to the primal problem. This means that if, for whatever reason, the company were to cease iterating before reaching the optimal solution, the resulting, suboptimal solution could be implemented. This isn't true of most price-directive approaches, which can be implemented only at the optimum.[25]

Nonetheless, both kinds of mathematical programming approaches end up distributing the company's resources to its divisions in central-office-optimal ways. I have no quarrel with these distributions, just as I have none with the short-run, overall-profit-maximization optimality of the consequent divisional output decisions under these approaches (or under the Hirshleifer approach, for that matter).

Under both resource- and price-directive approaches, any transfer prices *per se* are allocations. These allocations are usually intended (though with what success remains to be explored) to be behaviour-congruent with respect to output decisions and Chapter Eight's use or sell, make or buy and expand or contract decisions. Unfortunately, we shall see that these approaches violate divisional autonomies and encourage perverse evaluation and élan decisions. In particular, all suffer from Chapter Eight's evaluation paradox:

> If a company uses such a method, it will be evident to all actors that resulting divisional book profits are administered ones that don't reflect division-manager performances. Besides being destructive of any sense of meaningful divisional autonomy, we saw that this threatens the very means of motivating division managers (*via* these book profits) that's necessary to these approaches' success—threatens their mainspring, as it were.[26]

Divisional Autonomy

Most planners who have seriously considered the practical aspects of their task have little doubt that a directed economy must be run on more or less dictatorial lines. That the complex system of interrelated activities, if it is to be consciously directed at all, must be directed by a

---

[25] I tried to write the generalized descriptions of both styles of programming to make this evident on reflection. Nonetheless, Baumol and Fabian's [1964] price-directive algorithm is an exception—see [Freeland, 1973, pp. 110, 114] and [Burton, Damon and Loughridge, 1974, p. 310].

[26] For other deficiencies of some of these mathematical programming approaches (especially price-directive ones) that I don't discuss in what follows, see [Freeland, 1973, pp. 58-59, 76-77] and [Abdel-khalik and Lusk, 1974, pp. 17, 20].

> single staff of experts, and that ultimate responsibility and power must rest in the hands of a commander-in-chief whose actions must not be fettered by democratic procedure, is too obvious a consequence of underlying ideas of central planning not to command fairly general assent.
> —[Hayek, 1944, p. 88]

> More often than not it is . . . necessary for the central headquarters to decide upon the optimal plan for the whole company and then give the divisional managers sufficient information so that they can, independently, decide upon *the same plan as that already decided upon centrally.*
> —[Tomkins, 1973, p. 8]

Before attempting any direct consideration of divisional autonomy under mathematical programming approaches to decentralization, it will be helpful to make two distinctions. The first is familiar from our earlier analysis: as Marschak [1959, pp. 400-01] pointed out, under any mathematical programming approach divisions will possess considerable *informational* autonomy, in the sense that fundamental considerations of information economy prohibit the central office from having detailed knowledge of such things as market prices of many divisional inputs and outputs, divisional production functions and the like. But this has nothing whatever to do with whether such things as divisional output and transfer-price decisions are autonomous.

Second, it's notorious that many mathematical programming approaches require explicit central-office stipulation of divisional decisions after their final iterations have been completed, and that such *terminal interventions* are destructive of divisional autonomies.[27] This difficulty is a grave one,[28] and affects most of the approaches surveyed in Appendix J. However (and here my language

---

[27]See [Ruefli, 1971a, p. B·510], [Barron, 1972, esp. pp. 52-54], [Kornai, 1973, pp. 522-524], [Kydland, 1975, p. 1029] and the first page of [Butterworth, Hayes and Matsumura, 1977]. Technical matters are involved here that make it dangerous to generalize. Nonetheless, [Jennergren, 1972, pp. 1408-09] explains one major reason why this is so. (His p^o is the optimal price vector):

> It is now well known that suboptimization by divisions on the basis of the price vector p^o on corporate resources will not be overall optimal, in general...i.e., it is not possible to decentralize on the basis of constant prices in a linear system...In view of this, it suffices to say that the basic difficulty encountered in trying to decentralize on the basis of constant prices in a linear system is that the divisional subproblems may have many optimal solutions, some of which may not be consistent with overall optimality. In fact, under the nondegeneracy assumption made above...that for at least one division, there will be an infinite number of optimal solutions to its divisional subproblem...This may lead to a violation of the corporate restrictions and hence to a nonfeasible overall solution. It may also lead to underutilization of the corporate resources. In either case, the resulting solution is not overall optimal.

[28]As Littlechild [1970b, p. 325n] points out, the indeterminacy of optimal divisional outputs implied in the previous note's quotation from [Jennergren, 1972] is the dual of the indeterminacy of joint-*cost* allocations—i.e., is subject ot all of Part One's ambiguities.

must be guarded), if one takes authors' representations at their face values, it doesn't affect *all* mathematical programming approaches to decentralization. Therefore, in order to reach as broad conclusions as possible (and to avoid some mathematics), I shall disregard this difficulty hereafter (though not in Appendix J's comments on individual mathematical programming approaches).

Instead, I'll try to show that the very nature of the iterative processes common to all mathematical programming approaches is destructive of divisional autonomy *if it's required that such iterations converge to global optima.* I italicize the final clause because, as we'll see later, things aren't as simple when algorithms satisfice instead of optimize.

Why Algorithms Whose Iterations Converge to Global Optima Destroy Divisional Autonomies

. . . the principal objective of the [mathematical programming] model. . . is to allocate scarce corporate resources. The crux of the issue is that since these resources are assumed to be scarce, it is *impossible* to allow complete autonomy by the divisions in their decisions about using these resources. There is a natural conflict between the concept of autonomous decision making in a decentralized organization and the usage of common, scarce, corporate resources. Therefore, a centralized coordinating mechanism is *necessary* for these resources to be distributed among competing divisions . . . .

The point is, however, let us not attempt to conceal the need for the intrusion by central headquarters under the facade of an internal market mechanism. – [Godfrey, 1971, p. 293] [29]

The first limitation of these approaches is that they maintain only the facade of decentralized decision making. The last phase of the process is usually directed by central management . . . .

There seems [sic] to be two explanations for this problem. The first is that many authors of the programming solutions are primarily interested in the mathematical properties (or elegance) of their solutions and only secondarily in the model's organizational implications. The second is that most authors in the transfer price literature are asking the question, "What transfer price will result in the decentralized firm maximizing joint (or corporate) profits?" Since the emphasis is on the maximization of joint profits whenever conflict arises between this goal and the decentralization philosophy, the latter tends to be sacrificed. The solution is always centralized decision making whether this is through some

---

[29] A hasty reading of [Godfrey, 1971, p. 289] might make one think that he claims that Hass [1968] solved these difficulties. But his description of Hass' approach [p.289] reveals, indeed *says* otherwise.

> stated price rule, a wishful appeal to competitive market prices and their surrogates, or to mathematical programming solutions.—[Watson and Baumler, 1975, p. 470]

A basic autonomy problem is easily stated. Divisions generate what we might call "internal" externalities: their actions directly or indirectly affect other divisions.[30] As the quotations indicate, if the central office is to guide the company to global optima it must control these effects. Almost by definition, that requires direct or indirect intervention—for reasons that parallel why, lacking some code of conduct that the entire society respects, *governmental* intervention is usually the only remedy for such "external" externalities as air and water pollution.[31] In particular, there's the same potential here as in the simple Hirshleifer situation that, left to their own devices, divisions will attempt to exploit each other by acting like internal monopsonists or monopolists.[32] And, because the situations now under consideration are more complex, there are additional ways that divisions could prevent realization of central-office optima by attempting to maximize their book profits: divisions will be tempted to make central-office-perverse decisions to sell internally or externally, make or buy products, or hog scarce resources, to mention just a few of the many possibilities.

Mathematical programming's iterative algorithms are designed to prevent as much of this as is possible, but succeed only by indirectly forcing divisions to behave in the same ways as they would had the central office somehow obtained all relevant information, performed one large optimization, then dictated its results to the divisions.[33] Thus, the resulting divisional decisions are, once more, "voluntary" only in Wiseman's [1957, p. 66] melancholy sense of making the best of situations over which divisions have little control.[34] Freeland [1973, pp. 114-15] gave the definitive description of all such globally optimizing approaches, whether price- or resource-directive:

> . . . merely schemes by which the subordinate decision makers can be manipulated to attain the same decision at which the superordinate

---

[30] See, for example, [Whinston, 1964, pp. 406, 408, 427-31].

[31] I'm aware that some would deem this last clause to be gravely oversimplified.

[32] See, [Hass, 1968, p. B·313], for instance.

[33] [Hayhurst, 1976, p. 100]. Freeland and Baker [1974, pp. 3-7, 10-13] provide a very general mathematical model of such schemes that, as is evident from [p. 6], could easily be made the basis of a formal proof of those matters—an exercise left to the reader.

[34] Or, in the sense that, living in a city with minimal dog ordinances, I'm free to learn how to complete this book to the accompaniment of my neighbours' dogs' hysterical barking.

would have arrived, had he known all the constraints. Thus, a subordinate exists as a tool for carrying out the desires of the superordinate . . . .The subordinate in effect has no autonomy and no impact on the final allocation decision. His purpose is to process information and solve problems. Under these circumstances pricing and resource [directive] methods certainly do not enhance the motivational aspects of decentralized decision making. The superordinate's task is really to create an environment in which the subordinate believes he is participating in the decision making process.[35]

and, in an earlier, co-authored work, observed that such schemes are:
. . . often called decentralized decision making, but it would appear that the subordinate has no impact on the final decision. Thus, in this case the subordinate has no autonomy, he is nothing more than an information processor and problem solver.—[Freeland and Baker, 1972, p. 31].

Reconsideration of a Contrary View

Our definition of autonomy would include one aspect which is not dealt with adequately in the accounting literature: An independent supplier is not perfectly autonomous nor does he control all the variables which determine his profits. Among other things, he depends on his demand curve which in turn partially depends on the efficiency of his buyers. Thus, his profitability is partially a function of variables controlled by his buyers and his suppliers. Probably the maximum autonomy we can hope for in the case of divisionalization is the freedom which an independent supplier or an independent buyer enjoys in deciding on his quantity-price combinations. In other words, the degree of similarity or dissimilarity to the conditions under which independent buyers and sellers operate should be the criterion by which the extent of autonomy of a divisionalized profit center is measured.—[Ronen and McKinney, 1970, p. 101][36]

Here, Ronen and McKinney object to the previous subsection's conclusions in ways similar to objections by Solomons [1965] that I summarized in Chapter Eight. Ronen [1975, pp. 352-53] later added that, under the Ronen-McKinney approach to transfer pricing, divisions dealt directly with the central office as though they were independent buyers and sellers facing external supply and demand curves in monopolistic or monopsonistic markets. If *company* autonomies are behaviourally meaningful here, why should this change just because the buyers and sellers become divisions and all the monopolists and monopsonists happen to be their central office?

---

[35] See also [p. ix]. These point are repeated in [Freeland and Baker, 1974, p. 13; 1975, p. 676].

[36] [Ronen, 1975, p. 352] repeats these points.

Indeed, to repeat a point made earlier with regard to the Cobweb Theorem, even under perfect competition ". . . the market place solves the economic problem of equating supply and demand by successive approximations to the equilibrating price or prices..."[37] in a manner similar to mathematical programming's iterations. Why should divisional autonomy be any less under the latter than company autonomy under the former? No economic entity can escape *some* constraints on its actions. Why are those of mathematical programming algorithms for central-office optimization significantly more coercive than those of the external market?[38]

One might begin a reply by noting, with Whinston [1964, p. 408], that division managers suffer from all the restrictions on their autonomies of managers of independent companies, plus, almost inevitably, a few more resulting from the "internal" externalitites discussed in the last subsection. But a critic could rightly reply that this just makes divisional autonomy a matter of degree, without demonstrating that central-office-optimizing, mathematical programming approaches restrict divisional autonomy to any behaviourally harmful extent.

The remainder of my reply is similar to the one given in Chapter Eight. First, please note that the degree of autonomy is surely a low one. In effect, Ronen and McKinney are saying that we shouldn't expect divisions to possess any more autonomy than is present in those extreme cases of imperfect competition where buyers are at the mercy of a seller and sellers at the mercy of a buyer. Nor is this a peculiarity of Ronen and McKinney's approach: The same can be said of all mathematical programming approaches that seek global optimization.

Moreover, as in Chapter Eight, the *nature* of the restrictions on a division is significantly different from those on a company facing external market forces. Except in rare, pathological cases of underhanded dealing with relatives or affiliates, or one individual's attempts to ruin another, the market's reactions are impersonal—whereas, as we saw, a central office's reactions inevitably are either personal or perceived to be so. As Hayek [1944, p. 106] pointed out a third of a century ago, the élan impacts of impersonal and personal restrictions are apt to be quite different. Chamberlain [1944, pp. vi] expressed those differences well. His remarks, though directed to the economy as a whole, seem equally applicable to the micro-economy of the individual company:

[37] [Arrow and Hurwicz, 1960, p. 35].
[38] [Jennergren, 1972, p. 1414] makes a similar point.

> The threat of state "dynamism" results in a vast, usually unconscious fear among all producing interests that still retain a conditional freedom of action. And the fear affects the springs of action. Men must try to outguess the government as yesterday they tried to outguess the market. But there is this difference; the market factors obeyed at least relatively objective laws,while governments are subject to a good deal of whim. One can stake one's future on a judgment that reckons with inventories, market saturation points, the interest rate, the trend curve of buyers' desires. But how can an individual outguess a government whose aim is to suspend the objective laws of the market whenever and wherever it wishes to do so in the name of "planning"?[39]

The essence of the administered prices and resource distributions generated by mathematical programming procedures is a suspension of objective laws of the market (which would tempt divisions into exploitative behaviour) in order to accomplish the central office's goals by *manipulating* division managers. There's no way to prevent the managers from detecting this: if, in Chapter Eight, they were as adept as economists in determining which side their bread was buttered on, here one could expect them also to be quite as adept as management scientists.[40] The visible hand will remain visible, however fancy the glove it may wear, and even if it operates a computer console. Division managers will know that their autonomy is the freedom to draw from a stacked deck—indeed, with these iterative approaches it's the freedom to draw then keep redrawing from a deck that's repeatedly *re*stacked until finally its manipulator is pleased with what one has drawn.[41]

The patently dictatorial nature of such processes is further emphasized by the gyrations of prices, book profits and resource distributions characteristic of successive iterations (discussed in the next section) and the *slowness* of these iterative processes (even when conducted via modern computers) when compared with external market clearing mechanisms.[42] Chapter Eight's unfortunate élan consequences may be expected to follow from division managers' awarenesses that the company's internal accounting

---

[39] See also [Whinston, 1962, p. II·47] on the difference between the social welfare function generated by a market and one generated by a central office.

[40] On this point, see [Burton, Damon and Loughridge, 1974, pp. 298-302, 304-05] and [Abdel-khalik and Lusk, 1975, pp. 356-58].

[41] Not that there can't be exceptions. The sorts of marginal-cost transfer prices charged by Electricité de France to other nationalized French companies (see [Nelson, 1964]) are probably no more personal-seeming than are many other things that business enterprises must deal with when coping with encroaching (and increasingly dominant) central governments—and, thus, no greater (though no lesser) threats to autonomy.

[42] See [Hayek, 1940, pp. 135-36].

data are administered, and not to be taken as honest indicators of their successes.

What else would one expect? The mathematical programming algorithms weren't *designed* to evaluate divisions, but ". . . as a learning process whereby the center iteratively comes to understand more and more exactly the relevant parts of the production possibilities sets without ever requiring any [division] to transmit the entire set."[43] As in the long quotations of the last subsection, the algorithms are designed solely to advance the interests of *the central office*. We can only extend Abdel-khalik and Lusk's [1974, p. 20] verdict on [Hass, 1968] to all such approaches:

> It is doubtful that divisional decision-makers will perceive these communication manipulations as representing decentralized decision-making.[44]

Evaluation of Divisions

As the previous section's quotation from [Ronen and McKinney, 1970] pointed out, any analysis of the behaviour-congruence of mathematical programming algorithms with respect to decisions involving evaluation of divisions and their managers should recognize that even an independent company doesn't control all the variables that affect its profits. These profits may, for instance, be affected by how efficient the company's suppliers and customers are. Yet this doesn't make us abandon profits evaluations, it merely indicates that we shouldn't make them naïvely.

Similarly, so the argument goes, it isn't a crippling defect in a mathematical programming algorithm that one division's book profits should be influenced by efficiencies or inefficiencies of other divisions (or by other considerations over which the division manager has no control). As with the previous section's discussion of the Ronen-McKinney quotation, I would agree that independent companies' situations differ only in degree from those of divisions participating in mathematical programming algorithms were it not that the distorting impact of such uncontrollable factors is so vastly greater under mathematical programming algorithms than it is in all but the most pathological external markets that the difference in degree again becomes a major difference in kind. The next subsection develops this point.

[43] [Weitzman, 1970, p. 54].

[44] On the same point, see [Godfrey, 1971, pp. 289-90] and [Tomkins, 1973, pp. 100-101]. For others who agree with some or all of these conclusions, see [Horngren, 1972, p. 753], [Hayhurst, 1976, pp. 100-01], [Okpechi, 1976, p. 35] and [Shillinglaw, 1977b, p. 868].

A Reply

> In the linear programming context, if dual prices are used to allocate scarce resource cost to goods, the net profit of each good produced in the optimal mix will be zero. (Negative profits will occur with a nonoptimal product mix.)—[Kaplan and Welam, 1974, p. 478]

A reply might begin by considering a common situation: a manufacturing division that, under the resource distributions and utilizations determined by a mathematical programming approach's final iteration, isn't pressing up against any capacity constraints. Depending on the approach followed, such a division will receive either zero transfer prices or zero book profits on its dealings in transfer goods. Similar things can hold true for distributing divisions.[45] (The reasons here parallel those why a manufacturing division with constant marginal costs earns zero book profits in the simple Hirshleifer situation.) Indeed, under several systems, such as the Kaplan and Welam one quoted above, *all* divisions report zero book profits at the central-office optimum.[46] These phenomena are *artifacts of the algorithms used,* not reflections of divisional efficiencies or inefficiencies—as can be easily verified by noting that if such a division's efficiency changes, even enough to generate a new final outcome to the iterative process, its transfer price or book profit can easily remain at zero.

Now, zero book profits here don't necessarily mean what they do in financial accounting—we must recall that the economists' "profit" is net of recovery of fixed costs and a capital-attracting return on investment. But that doesn't make the zero book profit any the less arbitrary. This arbitrariness parallels that of Part One's SV approach that gave uniform markups to all joint products. In fact, whenever the book profit (or the transfer price) is zero, it's obvious that it has been administered (fiddled) to such an extreme degree as to be worthless for evaluating the effectiveness of a division manager.

The same conclusion follows from the instability of such book profits and transfer prices under mathematical programming approaches. What Kaplan [1977, p. 40] has to say of linear programming models is true of more sophisticated algorithms, too:

---

[45] See [Manes, 1970, pp. 570-71], [Onsi, 1970, p. 541], [Barron, 1972, pp. 62-63], [Tomkins, 1973, pp. 75-76], [Hayhurst, 1976, pp. 98-99] and [Emmanuel, 1977b, p. 4].

[46] See also the approach apparently favoured by Whinston [1964], and Kornai [1967b, p. 385]. As Kornai points out, the reason for zero book profits *here* is ". . . the proposition, well-known from the literature on the subject, according to which in the case of optimal distribution the marginal returns of resources will be equal in all domains of utilization . . ."

Large changes in transfer prices occur as divisions reach or recede from capacity. Also, small changes in the firm's opportunity set lead to dramatic reallocations of intra-firm profitability.[47]

(One consequence, as readers may verify, is that no division manager should ever willingly plan to have excess plant capacity—even when doing so would be to the company's long-run global advantage. For factors in excess supply are allocated zero book profits while scarce factors command premiums.[48])

Given these extreme instabilities, it's evident that changes in efficiencies (or other actions) of other divisions—even divisions with which one doesn't trade—influence divisional book profits under these mathematical programming approaches to a far greater degree than changing external market forces are apt to affect an independent company.[49] The only exceptions occur under systems where all divisions are assigned zero profits (and such exceptions hardly help).

Generalizing the foregoing, the Pareto optima attained by the final iterations of these mathematical programming approaches are accompanied by transfer prices and book profits that these approaches happen to generate.[50] But the latter are no more meaningful for evaluation of divisions and their managers than the distribution of wealth in a Pareto social optimum necessarily satisfies standards of social equity. Instead, transfer prices and divisional book profits on transfer goods will be largely matters of luck. Certainly, they are useless for evaluating any dimension of division managers' performance save (as we saw in Chapter Eight) *their abilities to carry out indirect orders.* This last is hardly in the authentic spirit of decentralization.

---

[47]Kaplan goes on to observe, "Further, it is not clear who should get credit for the imputed profits (dual variables) associated with constraints other than production or capacity constraints." See also [Manes, 1970, pp. 571-72] and [Godfrey, 1971, p. 294]. Hayhurst [1976, p. 98] observes:

> If a dominant constraint is seen to be especially restrictive, expenditure may be authorized for its relaxation. At once, a second constraint will normally become dominant. This will set a new "ruling" shadow price for the sub-system. There is nothing in a sub-system model to say that this new shadow price will be in even the same range as the old—or in that range adjusted (in "reasonable" cost accounting terms which will be understood by management) for the costs and gains accruing to the relaxation expenditure. The two shadow prices may be completely different. This may be mathematical logic, but it will scarcely be readily acceptable. [Corrected for a minor typographical error]

[48][Manes, 1970, p. 571].

[49]For examples of such influences, see [Manes, 1970, p. 571], [Onsi, 1970, pp. 537-38], [ten Kate, 1972b, p. 884], [Abdel-khalik and Lusk, 1975, p. 358] and, reading between the lines [Ronen and McKinney, 1970, pp. 103-11]. See also [Hayhurst, 1976, p. 98].

[50][Hayhurst, 1976, p. 98] says "incidentally generate[d]."

It need only be said in conclusion that, under most proposed algorithms, rampant gaming could be expected to render divisions' book profits on transfer goods meaningless for evaluation of division managers, even in the absence of the other problems discussed in this section:

> To function successfully the models we have outlined all depend on the active and honest cooperation of the decision-makers in the organization. While this may be a noble expectation its occurence in practice is somewhat dubious. To expect managers not to overstate or understate prices or requirements, or not to hoard resources is to fly in the face of much experience. Yet the solution of each of the models reviewed earlier depends on the absence of such behavior.—[Ruefli, 1974, p. 361] [51]

As in Chapter Eight, the only remedy would usually be a control system destructive of both divisional autonomy and the information-economies rationale for decentralization.

The Evaluation Paradox

Therefore, we're back to the same evaluation paradox that, in Chapter Eight, afflicted the simple Hirshleifer approach. Analysis paralleling that conducted there would reveal that the meaninglessness of mathematical programming approaches' divisional book profits on transfer goods for evaluating division managers' performances threatens the very division-manager motivation that's needed to make such approaches work (as well as generating other élan perversities).

On first consideration one might wonder whether the much greater complexity of these mathematical programming approaches might not greatly delay division managers' recognitions of the phoniness of their book profits—or even delay it indefinitely for managers who are overawed by computers. But the extreme instability of these artifactual profits—both from iteration to iteration and in response to small changes in other divisions' activities and efficiencies—should more than overcome any confusions that mathematical complexities might engender as to their true, manipulative nature.

So, we emerge with conclusions similar to Part One's conclusions for joint-cost allocations (something that's not at all surprising,

---

[51] See [Abdel-khalik and Lusk, 1974, pp. 15, 20, 23], [Jennergren, 1971, Ch. IV], [Tomkins, 1973, p. 103], [Burton, Damon and Loughridge, 1974, pp. 304-310], [Bailey and Boe, 1976, pp. 562, 570] and [Kaplan, 1977, p. 41]. For an apparent exception, see [Jennergren, 1971, pp. 50-51, 115-16].

considering the way that the two kinds of allocations overlap). The mathematical programming transfer-price allocations are either behaviour-congruent with respect to divisional input and/or output decisions or can be *made* behaviour-congruent by central-office terminal interventions that override transfer prices as bases for division managers' decisions. They aren't behaviour congruent with respect to evaluation decisions made by the central office, nor with respect to a host of élan decisions that may be made by division managers.[52] And these approaches run the same risk of self-destruction that the simple Hirshleifer approach did in Chapter Eight: it's hard to fathom how, in the long run, approaches that depend on evaluation can survive their inabilities to provide meaningful evaluations. Indeed, in this long run the mathematical programming approaches may be behaviour congruent with respect to no major decisions whatever, save where terminal interventions override them.[53]

The next section explores whether those melancholy conclusions also hold true for recent algorithms designed merely to satisfice.[54]

Satisficing Approaches

Freeland [1973, pp. 195-96] makes a helpful distinction between *cooperative* and *non-cooperative* organizations:

> There may exist conflict between subordinate decision making units over sharing limited resources. An organization where this is the only source of conflict is referred to as a "cooperative organization." On the other hand, the breaking up of the organization into several different decision making entities can cause conflict between levels in the hierarchy over what objectives should be pursued. An organization which has both kinds of conflict is referred to as a "non-cooperative organization."[55]

The mathematical programming approaches to decentralization that we've considered thus far have all implicitly assumed cooperative organizations.[56] For example, in most, all hierarchical levels

---

[52] It's widely alleged that massive, macro-level income redistribution reduces producers' incentives to work, at least when such redistribution is designed to serve goals set by the central government (rather than by producers). If so, division-manager élan presumably is dampened by the mathematical programming approaches' parallel income redistributions at the micro level. See [Hayek, 1944, pp. 107-08] for macro implications.

[53] For other difficulties with these approaches, see [Likert, 1961b, p. 387], [Arrow, 1964a, pp. 319-21], [Cooper, 1964, pp. 338-39], [Hass, 1968, pp. B·312-13], [Barron, 1972, pp. 60-68] and [Hayhurst, 1976, p. 98].

[54] In the sense of that term to be found in [March and Simon, 1958, pp. 140-41].

[55] See also [Freeland and Baker, 1974, pp. 7-9; 1975, pp. 675-76].

[56] See, for instance, [Bailey and Boe, 1976, pp. 561-62].

share the single goal of profit maximization. Even algorithms, such as Charnes, Clower and Kortanek's [1967] that allow multiple goals assume agreement at all levels on what combination of goals should be pursued. Yet non-cooperative organizations may well be far more common than cooperative ones. Freeland and Baker [1974, pp. 12-19] argue that price-directive mathematical programming approaches are apt to break down for non-cooperative organizations.[57]

What *would* be apt to work with such organizations? Many academic accountants have had classroom experiences that provide a clue. One begins a course with particular goals: perhaps for students to appreciate some aspects of theory, sharpen their analytical abilities, digest certain important concepts and learn a few models and procedures. Students enter the course with goals that partly overlap the instructor's, but partly conflict with them. For instance, students may be more concerned with what is immediately "practical" than their teacher is. Often, over the term there's an iteration between instructor and students (via classroom discussions, quizzes and their subsequent reviews, office-hour arguments) wherein actors gradually modify their goals until, ideally, the upshot is satisfactory, though not optimal, to everyone. The result is also non-dictatorial: students retain a significant degree of autonomy and work better for having retained it.

Both Freeland [1973, Ch. VI][58] and Bailey and Boe [1976] offer satisficing mathematical programming approaches to decentralization that operate in an analogous manner. These, in turn, are based on works by Ruefli [1969; 1971a; 1971b; 1974]; indeed, Bailey and Boe's article may serve as an introduction to Ruefli's work.[59] All three approaches are generalizable to an n-level hierarchical organization, where each level has its own goals that only partly overlap those of its superordinate or subordinates. Freeland's algorithm leads to "...a resource allocation plan being selected which is different from one which would be selected by the superordinate or the subordinates acting in isolation; however, it will lead to a program which reflects both the goals of the superordinate and the goals of the subordinates."[1973, p. x][60] Simi-

---

[57]In light of the last section's conclusions, recapitulation of their arguments seems pointless; however, they provide something to fall back upon should those conclusions somehow turn out to be overstated.

[58]See also the other single- and co-authored works by Freeland in the References.

[59][Bailey and Boe, 1976, pp. 563, 565-67]. For Ruefli's approach see [Ruefli, 1969, pp. 2 of Synopsis, iii, 76].

[60]See also [pp. 176-77, 183-85].

larly, Ruefli's approach, as described by Bailey and Boe [1976, p. 568], results in a solution that is "...a function of the multiple competing utilities of the divisions. It is a satisficing solution."[61]

Under such approaches, divisions possess far more autonomy than under any transfer pricing approach that we've considered previously (save for Hirshleifer's divisions facing a perfect, external intermediate market).[62] There's a price, of course: a failure of universal behaviour-congruence, similar to those of the joint-cost methods discussed in Part One. In particular, the price of the desirable élan decisions that may flow from bona-fide divisional autonomy is output and resource-distribution decisions that are no longer central-office optimal. But, again as in Part One, perhaps this is the most for which we can legitimately hope.

(This reaction is reinforced when one considers that central-office optimality is unlikely under the optimizing mathematical programming approaches, too. A major reason for using such approaches is that the central office cannot know all costs, prices and production and demand functions. Therefore, it cannot hope, say, to maximize global profits if division managers game. Yet, ordinary experience and various works cited earlier indicate that they *will* game. Auditing whatever division managers report to the central office could help alleviate this problem, but I doubt that it could eliminate it—though here is another potential topic for further research.)

Difficulties

Unfortunately, these satisficing approaches have other characteristics that, by now, are all too familiar. First, under Ruefli's approach (and, therefore, under Bailey and Boe's) the central office may have to make what I earlier called a "terminal" intervention in which, at the end of the iterative process, it specifies final outputs and resource distributions, to the detriment of divisional autonomies.[63] Moreover, as Watson and Baumler [1975, p. 470n] comment, Ruefli's way of coordinating divisions' behaviours, a liason arrangement or joint planning committee, "...seems to act very similarly to the central management unit and consequently be subject to the same 'centralization' criticism..." of depriving divi-

---

[61]See [pp. 566-68, 571], generally.

[62]See, for instance, [Bailey and Boe, 1976, p. 571].

[63]See [Freeland, 1973, pp. 143-65; 1976, pp. 101-02] and [Bailey and Boe, 1976, p. 569].

sions of autonomy—see [Ruefli, 1971b, pp. B·650, B·653-54] for details. Gaming is also clearly a problem under Ruefli's approach and, given the information autonomy that Freeland's divisions possess, is presumably one under his system, too.[64]

However, the main difficulty with those satisficing approaches is the one that also cuts to the roots of the central-office-optimizing mathematical programming, and simple Hirshleifer, approaches: Transfer prices and divisional book profits are just as unstable as they were in the last section and just as much *artifacts* of the particular algorithm used. They aren't meaningful for evaluating the successes of division managers and are most unlikely to be perceived as meaningful. Thus, once again we're faced with (a) the evaluation paradox and its train of dysfunctions and (b) the strong possibility of these approaches' eventually self-destructing. Finally, if Chapter Eight's analysis is correct, *the evaluation paradox will destroy the very divisional autonomies that the satisficing approaches are designed to preserve.*

Readers who are having difficulties here might consider the following analogy, though it understates the severity of the dilemma. Let's give Chapter Eight's simple Hirshleifer situation an additional wrinkle: the central office is prepared to satisfice—prepared to negotiate with the manufacturing and distributing divisions on transfer prices and outputs. The parties end up agreeing upon a price and output that's more pleasing to, say, the manufacturing division than the globally optimal one would have been.

Transfer prices and divisional book profits are still administered—only now they are jointly administered by the central office and one of the divisions. For evaluating division managers' performances, they still have all the weaknesses that they had before, plus they are now additionally confusing because they reflect the relative bargaining situations or abilities of the managers. (Bargaining strengths arising from accidents of organizational position or history seem entirely irrelevant to evaluation; those arising from abilities in negotiation will be double-counted, already having been reflected in results from dealings with outsiders—as when Mfg buys inputs or Dst sells outputs. In any event, even were these strengths relevant, the weights implicitly given them in transfer prices and book profits would be arbitrary.) Thus, although this satisficing, simple-Hirshleifer approach would seemingly allow greater autonomy (to one division, anyway), it would still lead to the evaluation paradox.

---

[64] See [Freeland, 1973, p. 194] and [Bailey and Boe, 1976, pp. 568-70].

As in Chapter Eight, division managers would know that evaluations of their performances were based on artifacts of the particular transfer pricing approach chosen. These artifacts would now be negotiated, but would appear no less arbitrary for that—at least to the division (here, the distributing one) whose evaluation was harmed by the superior negotiating position or skills of the other. That division would, as before, comply with the central office's indirect orders. But it would hardly be under any illusion of acting as an independent profit centre.

The satisficing mathematical programming approaches are this variation on the simple Hirshleifer approach writ large, with transfer prices and book profits that are far less stable, far easier affected by changes in other divisions' activities and efficiencies, and even more obviously artifacts of the algorithms used in obtaining them than were transfer prices and book profits under the simple Hirshleifer approach. The satisficing approaches may enhance the perceived autonomies of some divisions—any who consistently negotiate things to their selfish advantage. But the evaluation paradox will destroy the autonomies of the rest. Hence, our conclusions for these satisficing approaches should be essentially the same as those for the central-office-optimizing approaches.

A Special Difficulty of All Opportunity-Cost Approaches

Before concluding this discussion, we should consider one final reason why all of these opportunity-cost approaches generate divisional book profits that are inappropriate for evaluating division managers (and thus fall prey to the evaluation paradox). It's of the essence of all such approaches that they calculate the book profit attributed to a resource, division or other locus as either (a) the amount by which the company's global profits increased when that locus was added to the company's productive processes or (b) the amount by which global profits would decrease were that locus to be withdrawn. In both cases, it's implicitly assumed that all other loci are held constant. The result is that any scheme of book-profit assignments based on opportunity costs inevitably assumes a particular expansion or contraction path (or a family of such paths) for the company to follow.

This is easily seen for a company that has three essential inputs.[65] To keep things simple, let's imagine a pipeline company

---

[65] Analysis parallel to what follows appears in [Thomas, 1969, p. 47; 1974, pp. 141-44] and in the respective bread and bus company examples of [Thomas, 1975 and 1979].

that exists to pump oil from an interior field to a coastal loading facility, and that the three essential loci are pumping stations, denotated *A, B* and *C*, each of which is run by a separate division. Were any station to be withdrawn from the system, the oil wouldn't reach the coast and the company's global profits would fall to zero. There are six (3!) ways in which these three stations could be withdrawn from service:

ABC   BAC   CAB
ACB   BCA   CBA

Corresponding to each of these contraction paths is an opportunity-cost assignment of the global profit to these divisions. Since the stations are essential, in the first two of these all profit is assigned to Division A and none to the other two divisions; in the third and fourth all profit goes to Division B, while in the last two the global profit is allocated exclusively to Division C.

Since this global profit is clearly the result of *all three* inputs, each of those allocations is manifestly meaningless for evaluating division managers (for instance, under the first two Division B and C are credited with no profits whatever, despite that their activities are essential—and these are zero profits in the *accounting* sense, not the benign sense of economic theory). Identical results occur if we add, rather than withdraw, stations.

Generalization of this to the various mathematical programming approaches discussed in this chapter and Appendix J is left largely to those readers who are following the analysis closely. But four things should be evident:

1. As the pipeline example makes obvious, under opportunity-cost approaches book profits of one essential locus will be extremely responsive to changes in the efficiencies and activities of other loci—after all, these book profits are the profits of the company as a whole.

2. Similar problems arise when one deals with *non*essential inputs; the only differences are ones of degree. Any opportunity-cost approach must inevitably allocate the global profit according to a particular assumed contraction (or expansion) path. Even if we ignore the possibility of averaging such paths,[66] there will be n! of these, where *n* is the number of loci. Different paths will generate different allocation patterns as their artifacts. Each pattern will be as legitimate (or illegitimate) as the others. The only difference

---

[66]The material on Shapley allocations in Part One and Appendix I suffices to demonstrate that Jensen's [1977] choice of the particular averaged contraction (or expansion) path implicitly stipulated by the Shapley approach doesn't solve the problems discussed here.

from simpler situations in which all loci are essential is that there will be less zero allocations and the results may *appear* to be plausible.

3. Anyone familiar with the Simplex method of linear programming should be aware of how its exclusive assignments of the global profit to resources for which there are binding capacity constraints corresponds to the pipeline example's assignment of them to the first essential input to be withdrawn. This parallel extends to all mathematical programming approaches, even satisficing ones.

4. It doesn't help matters to credit each locus with the decrease in global profits that would result were it to be the first to be withdrawn from the company's productive processes. I'll denote such approaches as *everyone-first* ones. In the first place, such a procedure would be internally inconsistent, a simultaneous assertion of mutually incompatible alternatives.[67] Moreover, the procedure does nothing to improve the quality of the amounts allocated to each locus: for instance, in the pipeline example it would result in allocating the entire global profit to each division. That was arbitrary when done in series; it's no less arbitrary when done in parallel.

This last point is important to emphasize, because several of the mathematical programming algorithms mentioned in Appendix J are everyone-first ones, as is Ronen and McKinney's [1970] oft-cited[68] approach.[69] All such approaches are particularly vulnerable to the evaluation paradox.

Shapley Transfer Prices?

Another opportunity-cost approach, that we studied in Part One, suffers from related difficulties. Chapter Six concluded that although Shapley joint-cost allocations had many desirable congru-

---

[67]See [Shubik, 1964, p. 208].

[68]Let the enthusiastic [Tomkins, 1973, pp. 62-68, 78-81] serve here as proxy for all other works.

[69]Ronen and McKinney's proposals need little further comment, having been mortally wounded in the exchange between Abdel-khalik and Lusk [1974, pp. 13-15; 1975] and Ronen [1975]. Readers might note, though, that Ronen and McKinney use a device of providing divisions with supply and demand schedules that's similar to Hirshleifer's device discussed at the beginning of Chapter Nine. As we saw earlier, they assert that doing so will place the divisions in positions comparable to those of independent companies dealing with external monopsonists and monopolists. But this will be true *only* if the divisions somehow never discover that they're really dealing with a manipulative central office, a most unlikely state of affairs. See [Abdel-khalik and Lusk, 1975, pp. 356-58].

ence properties they also had many dysfunctional ones. Similar conclusions are warranted for any proposal of Shapley transfer prices. Since this possibility has received scant attention in the literature, my discussion will be brief. We've already seen that:

1. What I denoted as the Shapley approach's Rule 5 (coalition values must be nonnegative) is inconsistent with real-world transfer-pricing situations (except, perhaps, as an ethical criterion). Real divisions *are* required to operate at book losses on transfer goods. To be sure, Rule 5 is unnecessary under the variation on the Shapley approach that uses cost-based characteristic functions. But since, as we've seen, the really troublesome transfer-pricing allocation is of global *profits,* I'm skeptical of this variation's congruence properties.

2. Similarly, the Shapley approach's Rule 6 (all costs can be escaped by total shutdown) is often counter-factual in real-world transfer-pricing situations. Whenever it *is* counterfactual, the Shapley approach cannot allocate these costs and its allocated book profits don't add up to the global profit on the transfer good.

3. The Shapley approach offers none of the information economies that mathematical programming approaches provide. Indeed, the same problems of the central office's having to obtain and cope with enormous amounts of detailed data that rendered mathematical programming approaches infeasible until Dantzig and Wolfe invented the decomposition procedure, would also afflict Shapley transfer pricing. In this context, be it noted that, as [Shubik, 1964, p. 224] points out, gaming would be a problem for the Shapley approach.

4. There is no reason to expect Shapley transfer prices to result in divisions making central-office-optimal output decisions, except by coincidence.

5. Given the artifactual nature of Shapley allocations (as illustrated in Appendices E and I) and the sensitivity of one division's book profits to events involving other divisions that (as we saw in Chapter Six) characterizes the Shapley approach, its transfer-prices and book profits could be expected to be as meaningless for evaluating performances of division managers as are the allocations generated by the mathematical programming approaches.

6. This, in turn, exposes the Shapley approach to all the long-run dangers of self-destruction that result from the evaluation paradox.

Except for [Hughes and Scheiner, 1977], Shubik's [1962; 1964] article is still the only substantial example in print of Shapley allocations being proposed for transfer pricing. Thus, it probably is significant that his first [1964, pp. 219-20] example of transfer pricing *doesn't* use the Shapley approach to calculate transfer prices. Instead, he uses a linear programming one to represent the Dantzig-Wolfe [1960; 1961] decomposition-procedure transfer prices that he favours [1964, p. 213]. This is easily verified: Shubik's transfer prices always leave his manufacturing divisions with zero book profits, whereas were we, say, to evaluate his example as follows:

$$\pi_1 = 27 \quad \alpha_1 = 15 \quad \beta_1 = 18$$
$$\pi_2 = 23 \quad \alpha_2 = 14 \quad \beta_2 = 8$$

a Shapley allocation would assign them £45 and £60 book profits. From this, in turn, it is evident that Shapley allocations could easily lead Shubik's manufacturing divisions to make central-office-dysfunctional output decisions.

The all too understandable unwillingness of Shubik himself to use Shapley allocations in transfer pricing here is obscured by his next [1964, p. 220] using them in a *side* calculation of the impact of a cost-saving change in technology instituted by a manufacturing-division manager, then his actually using the Shapley approach in his transfer-pricing Example 4 [1964, pp. 221-22]. In both of the latter examples, the Shapley approach changes the book profits of both divisions in response to savings generated by a single division.

All in all, Shubik's examples inadvertently reveal that Shapley transfer-price allocations would generate many of the perversities that transfer-pricing theorists are most anxious to avoid (for instance, readers are invited to explore their implications for divisional autonomy). And no realistic refinement of Shubik's simple, linear examples, to allow for demand declining, or costs increasing, with increased output could remedy these defects.[70] Therefore, the Shapley approach just doesn't look promising for transfer pricing.

---

[70] Although, on balance, favouring Shapley transfer prices, [Hughes and Scheiner, 1977] reveals further difficulties.

Conclusions

> A healthy vine does not ordinarily assume the properties of a upas tree. — [Wingfield-Stratford, 1934, p. xiv]

All central-office-optimizing mathematical programming approaches to transfer-pricing are, in the short run, either behaviour-congruent with respect to division managers' input or output decisions or can be rendered so by terminal interventions that effectively negate these allocations' imports for decision making. None of these approaches are behaviour-congruent with respect to decisions that division managers base on their perceived autonomies (or lacks thereof). None are behaviour-congruent with respect to evaluations of division managers' performances. All are perverse with respect to numerous possible élan decisions. All are threatened by self-destruction—by the unlikelihood that, over the long haul, approaches that depend on being able to evaluate performances of division managers can survive if they can't make such evaluations meaningfully.

The satisficing approaches that stem from Ruefli's [1969, 1971a, 1971b, 1974] work trade off behaviour-congruence with respect to input and output decisions for greater perceived autonomies of dominant divisions (but not of divisions that aren't consistently successful in internal negotiations). We'll see that the same is true of the negotiated approaches to transfer pricing discussed in the next chapter. Otherwise, these satisficing approaches suffer from the same evaluation paradox and behavioural dysfunctions that plague the central-office-optimizing ones. Finally, upon detailed analysis readers would discover that individual mathematical programming approaches also suffer from some of the simple Hirshleifer approach's other defects, described in Chapter Eight. But this point need not be pursued here.

Part One concluded that no joint-cost allocation method was universally behaviour-congruent. Based on the last three chapters, we may equally conclude that no opportunity-cost transfer-pricing method is universally behaviour-congruent, either.[71] But two things render the situation here worse than in Part One (despite that joint-cost allocation is often regarded as the less tractable problem):

---

[71] Save for the marginal approach in perfect intermediate markets. And this, as we've seen, is an instance of allocation-*free* current-exit- or current-entry-value accounting.

1. The joint-cost approaches tended to be behaviour-congruent and perverse with respect to different decisions. In contrast, these transfer pricing approaches are more alike. They just don't allow the use of one approach for one decision and another approach for another decision that was described at the end of Chapter Six.

2. All of those approaches suffer from an evaluation paradox that, in the long run, threatens them with self-destruction.

Accordingly, I submit that, despite their popularity in the economics, management-science and accounting literatures, *these opportunity-cost approaches are intellectual dead ends.* To be sure, each approach offers some desirable congruence properties. Yet, none is able to provide what all seek: decentralization into meaningful profit centres. I'm only too aware that any non-mathematician is reckless to assert such conclusions. But *someone* should.

CHAPTER ELEVEN

OTHER APPROACHES

The establishment of transfer pricing methods and the administration of these methods should rank very high as the most difficult tasks that divisional managers face. Consider for instance the establishment of transfer prices which will involve in most cases three parties: the two divisional managers who represent their divisional interests and the corporate management that represents overall corporate interest. A price determined in a three party session such as the one described above may take into consideration the idle capacity in each division, the quantity of materials involved, the availability of supplies outside the organization and the effect of the agreed price on profitability measures of each division. These variables that go into the establishment of transfer prices are difficult to weigh in order to determine an equitable price. Consequently, simple and proven methods such as cost, cost plus, and negotiated prices, even though inefficient, are retained.—[Okpechi, 1976, pp. 90-91] [1]

The economics and accounting literature of the nonmathematical programming type generally falls into one of four broad categories in the way appropriate transfer prices or transfer pricing structures are suggested: (1) market pricing, (2) negotiated pricing, (3) accounting pricing (approximate full cost) and (4) marginal cost pricing . . . .—[Bailey and Boe, 1976, p. 559]

It remains to discuss a few other approaches to transfer pricing that, on the one hand, are far less ambitious theoretically than the ones that we've been considering and, on the other, are far more representative of actual practice. Where there are external markets for transfer goods, companies often use prices drawn from them as transfer prices. We considered the advantages and disadvantages of doing so in Chapters Eight and Nine and, with one exception, will not consider such situations here. When there are no such intermediate markets, real companies use transfer pricing approaches that may be sorted into two (somewhat overlapping) groups, *negotiated* and *administered,* that correspond to the last chapter's satisficing and central-office-optimizing approaches. In turn, a review of the literature suggests that most administered approaches fall into one of the following categories:

---

[1] In context, "inefficient" denotes "not central-office optimal."

1. So-called "marginal" approaches that charge variable manu-facturing costs as transfer prices. These are often *standard* vari-able costs, and usually are supplemented by either:

a. Periodic lump-sum charges to transferees to cover trans-ferors' fixed costs, or their fixed costs plus profit, or

b. Some kind of subsidy credited to transferors.

2. Approaches that charge transferees full (absorption) manu-facturing costs (often standard costs) or full costs plus a profit markup.

At least in theory, under each of these approaches the central office may use tariffs or subsidies (similar to those proposed by Hirsh-leifer) in order to control externalities. Besides these procedures, a few proposed administered approaches allocate profits to divisions directly.

Finally, we shall consider a few methods that are designed to be behaviour-congruent with respect to relatively specialized decisions involving taxes and timings of requests for centralized services. Two themes will regularly recur in our discussions:

1. None of these approaches is universally behaviour-congru-ent; each is designed to be behaviour-congruent with respect to some decisions and circumstances but can have perverse con-sequences in others.

2. In particular, none is reliably behaviour-congruent with respect to decisions involving evaluations of division managers.

Negotiated Approaches

There are at least five senses in which one might speak of a com-pany's divisions negotiating transfer prices:

1. Where there's an external market for the transfer good, the divisions may negotiate adjustments to its market price to reflect such things as reduced freight, marketing, and credit costs on in-ternal sales.[2] Such negotiations were considered (though not ex-plicitly *as* negotiations) in Chapters Eight and Nine.

---

[2] As in [Cook, 1955, p. 89].

2. Relatedly, they might negotiate to create an internal market that simulated an already existing external market for a transfer good. This was Joel Dean's [1955, pp. 67-69, 73-74] proposal.[3] Once again, it is impounded in the ideas discussed in Chapter Eight.

3. They might engage in iterative exchanges with the central office as part of a mathematical programming algorithm. This was discussed in Chapter Ten.

4. Where a single transferor serves two or more transferees and the transfer good is in short supply, the transferees may bid against each other. Chapter Ten implicitly considered some such situations; Dopuch, Birnberg and Demski's [1974, pp. 653-54] brief analysis suggests that others lead to familiar problems of exploitation of some divisions by others with consequent needs for central-office intervention.

This situation is essentially that of Hirshleifer's [1957, pp. 103-05; 1964, pp. 30, 32] manufacturing division serving two distribution divisions, discussed toward the end of Chapter Nine—bidding iterations conducted by transferees are no more likely to prevent exploitation (with its output perversities and evaluation ambiguities) than are Hirshleifer's iterations conducted by the transferor. Other problems arising under such circumstances are similar to those discussed below, so further separate discussion of this situation seems unnecessary.

5. Lacking an external market for the transfer good, the divisions might try to act like independent buyers and sellers setting mutually agreeable prices for specialized products.[4] Thus, we have Fremgen [1970, pp. 28-29] asserting:

> Some products are custom-made for the requirements of a single customer. Thus, there is no market price in the usual meaning of that term. Rather, the buyer and the seller must negotiate and agree upon a price that each feels is acceptable in terms of his own goals and constraints. This is true whether the parties to these negotiations are independent companies or divisions of the same company. Negotiations about price are inevitable in such a situation, and there is no reason why negotiations between affiliated divisions should be any less effective for both than would similar discussions between separate firms.

---

[3] See [Watson and Baumler, 1975, p. 471].

[4] See, for instance, [National Association of Accountants, 1957a, p. 24].

It's this last sort of transfer-price negotiation that we'll consider in this section.[5]

Advantages of Negotiated Transfer Prices

Let's begin by returning to the simple Hirshleifer situation in which there are two divisions, Mfg and Dst, and no external market for the transfer good. Let's initially also assume an approximate parity of bargaining strengths between the two divisions so that one cannot freely exploit the other to any significant degree. These circumstances differ from those imagined toward the end of Chapter Ten in that the central office now keeps its hands off the price-output decisions. Certainly, abandoning the simple Hirshleifer approach in favour of this negotiated one would enhance perceived divisional autonomies, with all of the positive élan consequences that that might entail.

More subtly, Watson and Baumler [1975, pp. 470-73] argue that behavioural research indicates that a general key to business success

---

[5] A reader of an earlier draft of this book commented here:

> . . . mutually satisfactory allocations initiated by negotiations that precede the incurrence of cost are possessed of a necessity that other allocations may lack. It is perfectly reasonable to characterize allocations as necessary or unavoidable in such settings. Moreover, implementation of the agreed upon allocation scheme, in this context, cannot be divorced from the negotiation process from which it springs. Yet our usual discussions of allocations proceed as if the allocated cost were already incurred and as if we didn't need to worry about the consequences of ignoring agreements entered at or prior to incurrence. In my view, this is a rich "behavioral" problem. Implementation of an allocation after the incurrence of cost is an artifact of a prior negotiation—a settlement process in which at least two decision makers exhibit behaviors that resolve, among other things, the amount to be incurred and its distribution. Accountants participate in such processes in a variety of ways but usually (perhaps ideally) as neutral figures. Sometimes their participation may be implicit in the sense that negotiants rely on the accountant to perform the "generally accepted" allocation. Subsequent implementation of the negotiated settlement also involves accountants. They calculate the allocation. Moreover, they may be subject to pressure to alter the allocation function—particularly if the negotiants didn't specify it unambiguously. The consequences of altering the allocation function may take the form of sanctions against the accountant or against participants in the joint economic activity. The point is that the structure of negotiation and subsequent implementation offer a promising setting in which to examine allocation. Perhaps this is a very special class of allocations that doesn't deserve much attention, but it's also an intriguing one. In short, I am inclined to see negotiation as a distinct *setting* for the allocation problem rather than as a *treatment* of the general allocation problem.

I find this convincing, despite its possible confusion of resource-distribution and notional (bookkeeping) senses of allocation. Obviously, such an interpretation of negotiated transfer prices would have to be conducted at the empirical level—here is another fruitful topic for research.

Nonwithstanding, it remains legitimate to continue pursuit of this book's limited, analytical concern for the congruence properties (or lacks thereof) of the resulting allocations. For these properties (or lacks) will emerge whatever the temporal sequence of negotiation and cost-incurrence may be.

is resolution of interdepartmental conflicts by negotiation. Negotiated transfer prices would be only one element of this, but perhaps a valuable one.[6] As Chapter Ten's discussion suggested, these advantages persist in far more complicated situations.

Disadvantages[7]

However, negotiated transfer prices won't always offer these advantages. A review of examples in Chapter Eight suggests that the range of possible transfer prices can often be great enough to give considerable scope for divisional conflict (fueled by (a) the zero-sum nature of the game involved and (b) the major effect that comparatively small changes in transfer prices can have on divisional book profits). The managers may never agree, or may agree only after acriminous argument.

Moreover, whenever divisions do *not* have approximately equal bargaining strengths, negotiated transfer prices open the door to exactly the sorts of exploitation by dominant divisions that necessitate central-office dictation in the simple Hirshleifer situation.[8] Lacking such dictation, only one division will have autonomy, and that will be the unhealthy autonomy of the monopolist or monopsonist.[9]

---

[6]Shillinglaw [1977b, Ch. 26] is another strong advocate of negotiated transfer prices. If memory serves, this is also predominantly true of other articles on transfer pricing (besides Fremgen's) that have appeared in the practitioner's journal, *Management Accounting*.

[7]Paraphrasing slightly, the same reader as in footnote 5 observed here:

The following discussion treats negotiated transfer prices as though their only role were to bollix things up, and as though we could determine a unique global optimum if we only chose to do so. But the concept of the core, as reviewed by [Hamlen, Hamlen and Tschirhart, 1977], suggests that that global optimum may not always be unique. In fact, in some cases the negotiants may have wide latitude to horse around without disrupting things from an efficiency or profitability point of view.

Yet, when the negotiation is unimportant from an efficiency viewpoint it may be important from a distributional viewpoint: In order to continue, the organization must distribute profits. Within the core, there seems to be no way to *choose* distribution, save by negotiation or an "equivalent" allocation procedure.

Once again, I'm primarily concerned with congruence properties. If the negotiants end up behaving in ways that are central-office optimal, then, by definition, to that extent any allocations involved will be behaviour-congruent (or will have been ignored—which, in Chapter One, we saw was one way, if a degenerate way, to attain behaviour-congruence). But the discussion that follows shows that negotiated allocations will not be reliably, much less universally, behaviour-congruent.

(Both here and in footnote 5, were the reasons already given insufficient, I would disregard the reader's interpretations of negotiated transfer prices for the same reasons that, at the end of Chapter Seven, I felt it important to disregard Butterworth, Hayes and Matsumura's [1977; 1978] related interpretations of transfer pricing as a whole.)

[8]Or, at the least, necessitate the central office's setting some sort of bounds on transfer prices—see [Watson and Baumler, 1975, pp. 472-73].

[9]Hirshleifer [1956, pp. 175, 179] explicitly mentions such exploitation in a context of bilateral bargaining.

More generally, just as in earlier chapters we saw that there was considerable élan difference between independent companies dealing in external markets and divisions dealing with the central office, so there are great differences between independent companies negotiating prices and quantities of a specialized good and these kinds of internal bargaining. First in the external case the independent companies usually have the alternative of buying and selling elsewhere, and at the very least have the option of refusing to do business in the particular good at all. In contrast, the divisions know that they must deal with each other. Thus, Fremgen [1970, p. 28] himself comments that negotiated transfer prices:

> . . . can function effectively only if the division managers have the authority to deal either with sister divisions or with outside companies. If the divisions are required by policy to deal only with each other, there is no point to their entering into negotiations about price. Both parties would know that the transfer was going to be made internally in any event. Price negotiations then would be nothing but an exercise in gamesmanship. As such, they might be stimulating to the contestants, but they would be worse than useless from the point of view of the corporation.

Accordingly, I just don't see how the illusion of genuine bargaining could be preserved. Any division manager should be able to recognize the differences between this sort of exercise and real negotiation with outside parties.

As Chapter Ten noted, negotiated transfer prices confuse evaluation of division managers' performances in another way by confounding the results of their negotiating skills with the results of operations.[10] Now Fremgen [1970, p. 31] is quite correct in observing that skill in negotiations is one attribute of a good manager. But the implicit weight given this characteristic will, from an evaluation standpoint, inevitably be quite arbitrary. Even more important (as Chapter Ten also noted) division managers' successes in internal bargaining may depend far less on their negotiating skills than on accidents of their divisions' organizational position or history—for instance, if the company's internal situation parallels one that, in the external world, would generate monopoly, the manager of a manufacturing division is apt to possess great internal bargaining strength, regardless of his or her personal skills at negotiation.

Other dysfunctional properties of negotiated transfer prices need only brief mention. As we saw in Chapter Ten, and as is ob-

---

[10]Of course, many others have noted this, too—for instance, [Dopuch and Drake, 1964, p. 13], [Amey and Egginton, 1973, p. 530] and [Abdel-khalik and Lusk, 1974, p. 23].

vious in the simple Hirshleifer situation, negotiated transfer prices will generate central-office-optimal output decisions (and, in more complicated situations, resource distributions) only by coincidence.[11] For like reasons, they will afford the central office no reliable assistance in controlling externalities. By their very nature they are subject to vigourous gaming.[12] And, finally, to a degree unique among transfer pricing approaches, their determination can waste scarce executive time in bargaining activities that make no contribution to the company's real-world success.[13]

Roth and Verrecchia's Surrogates for Bargaining

Recently, Roth and Verrecchia [1977] have suggested a way to obtain some of the benefits of division managers bargaining cost (and profit) allocations without suffering from central-office-perverse output decisions and division managers wasting time trying to improve their book profits rather than the company's overall profits. The central office is to:

> . . . implement *a priori* the cost assignment such that each manager would be indifferent between receiving that cost assignment for certain or actually bargaining toward an uncertain outcome. The outcome of a bargaining process is uncertain because it depends on the strategic interaction of rational managers . . . . Recent work in game theory . . . has suggested that, depending on managers' attitudes toward risk, their expected utility for bargaining can be determined in a fashion that is equivalent to evaluating the expected utility of a (probabilistically) uncertain event. Therefore, if a firm can evaluate each manager's expected utility for bargaining, it can use this figure as a costless surrogate for the bargaining process itself.
>
> * * *
>
> We would not expect all managers to have a neutral attitude toward both probabilistic and strategic risk in all situations. But there may be circumstances in which a firm would find it convenient to assume that managers behaved *as if* their preferences obeyed these assumptions . . .
> —[pp. 6-7, 19]

The authors [e.g., p. 5] suggest Shapley allocations as one way to attain this "costless surrogate."

The idea is intriguing. Certainly, putting division managers in situations where they *could* bargain, but decide on self-interested

---

[11] See, for example, [Henderson and Dearden, 1966, pp. 145-46].

[12] [Solomons, 1965, p. 193].

[13] See, for instance, [Cook, 1955, p. 93]. The iterations of mathematical programming approaches don't waste time in the same sense. For at least the central office is learning something from them, and doing so in what's designed to be a highly efficient way.

grounds to accept the central office's allocations instead, allows for more divisional autonomy than does central-office dictation of these same allocations. Once again, élan effects presumably would depend in part on whether division managers caught on to the rather sophisticated way that they were being manipulated. One suspects that they usually would—if only because if the approach initially worked descriptions of it would be bound to crop up in business journals. However, it may nonetheless be a better compromise than most—where it is applicable.

But it would seem to be applicable only when the range of possible transfer prices (and related outputs) was fairly narrow. Whenever a division could substantially increase its book profits by monopolistic or monopsonistic behaviour, I don't see how the surrogation could succeed. This implies that Roth and Verrecchia's proposal (with or without use of Shapley values) applies mostly to those comparatively easy situations where contending divisions have approximately equal bargaining strengths.

Finally, readers are asked to note that gaming, evaluation of divisions' and division managers' performances and the evaluation paradox remain problems under Roth and Verrecchia's approach.

Summary

The foregoing has deliberately disregarded the possibility mentioned in [Emmanuel, 1977c, p. 5], that division managers might subordinate their personal interests to those of the company as a whole.[14] Certainly, both the motivation literature reviewed in Appendix G and our personal (anecdotal) experience indicate that such selflessness is possible. It would solve some of the problems discussed above (though, notably, not those of evaluation). But it would do so by, in effect, division managers choosing to disregard the messages that the company's transfer pricing (and accounting) system gave them, and thus drops out of our purview.[15]

Otherwise, when divisions are of approximately equal bargaining strengths, negotiated transfer prices (or Roth and Verrecchia's surrogates for these) can preserve divisional autonomies and, perhaps, help reduce divisional conflict. When they aren't, negotiated transfer prices aren't reliably behaviour-congruent in this sense. On other

---

[14] It's interesting to speculate how the managers would *determine* these global interests, but that need not trouble us here.

[15] Except, of course, as another instance of one-to-many allocation methods being behaviour-congruent only because they are ignored.

dimensions they usually will be perverse—though not, one might suspect from the foregoing, quite as virulently so as marginal- and other opportunity-cost approaches are. Nevertheless, one is tempted to accept the National Association of Accountants' [1957a, p. 29] verdict:

> Sometimes transfer prices...are arrived at by negotiation between the divisions concerned, but such bilateral bargaining usually does not produce satisfactory results in the absence of market prices applicable either to present products or to alternative products which could be made with existing facilities. [Corrected for minor typographical error in original]

But we shall be cautious here. As Cyert and March [1963, pp. 275-76] point out, many companies' transfer prices *are,* at least in part, results of long histories of bargaining between divisions. Cyert and March may have been right in regarding these transfer prices as notoriously arbitrary to all actors. But since there are alternative ways of calculating transfer prices, companies' choices of negotiated ones[16] suggest that these have *some* virtue, even if it's only the virtue of being the best of a very bad lot. I'll expand on this (admittedly rather thin) point in the next chapter.

Administered Approaches

We've seen that the main merit of using negotiated transfer prices lies in the central office's not administering divisional book profits. In contrast, the next series of approaches involves implicit or explicit profit administration. At first I shall continue to assume that transfer goods are ones for which there are no external markets.[17]

Service Departments[18]

These approaches are especially apt to be proposed for pricing the outputs of service departments; we'll begin by considering them

---

[16]The empirical studies cited in Chapter Seven's footnotes 31 and 32 also support a conclusion that negotiated transfer prices are fairly common.

[17]Though this won't always be true of some of the works cited as illustrations, when existence of such an external market doesn't affect the argument.

[18]This study isn't concerned with the detailed mechanics of how one goes about allocating, but only with end results. Therefore it disregards the literature on applications of linear algebra to reciprocal service-department cost allocations that's summarized in [Kaplan, 1977, pp. 27-29]. (See also [Kaplan, 1973], whose discussion of decision properties of different linear approaches seems consistent with my analysis.)

in this context[19] (and will therefore speak of production and service *departments* instead of our usual *divisions*). Analyses similar to that of Chapter Eight indicate that, in the absence of capacity constraints,[20] a company will maximize its global profits by pricing service departments' services to equal their marginal costs at whatever output levels are demanded by the levels of activity that the company finds optimal for its production departments. In practice, companies instead price these services at their standard variable costs.[21] (I'll disregard the difference between marginal and variable costs temporarily, since we shall soon see that doing so doesn't affect the argument.)

A multiplicity of transferees and the difficulty of defining global profits on service departments' outputs makes analysis difficult here, but it's still possible to make a few *general* comments on how such approaches allocate book profits:

1. If companies treat service departments as profit centres, variable-cost transfer prices will often result in service departments' book profits being negative: If their marginal costs are horizontal, their book losses will approximate their fixed costs; if their marginal costs decline with increasing output,[22] their book losses will exceed these fixed costs. Only if their marginal costs increase with output might the service departments report positive book profits (and then only if their fixed costs are comparatively small or the rate by which marginal costs increase with ouput is comparatively rapid).

2. It follows that *whether or not service departments are treated as profit centres,* and regardless of how profits are allocated among individual production departments,[23] if the global profit on a service department's services is definable the production departments *as a group* will be credited with book profits on the transfer good that quite often will exceed that global profit. Clearly, such a profit

---

[19]For general background here, see [Dopuch, Birnberg and Demski, 1974, pp. 579-81, 588, 652-54, 658].

[20]With the possible exception of [Tomkins, 1973, pp. 58-62], I know of no literature explicitly directed to service departments whose capacities have been exceeded. Instead, one finds such situations subsumed in the mathematical programming literature surveyed in Chapter Ten and Appendix J.

[21]See [Shillinglaw, 1957, esp. pp. 83, 85, 92-93] for a modification of this that also charges certain incremental costs to production departments.

[22]As may happen if the service department functions as an internal public utility.

[23]For brevity, I'll not discuss such allocations between production departments. Suffice to say that Solomons' [1965, pp. 68-71] analysis reveals that this is another area where one division's actions can affect other divisions' book profits, gaming is possible, evaluations of division managers' performances become difficult, and other dysfunctions can arise.

allocation between service and production departments is arbitrary. Arguments similar to those in Chapter Eight also indicate that such an allocation would be behaviour-congruent only with respect to decisions on service departments' outputs and production departments' utilizations of those outputs. In particular, such profit allocations would not reflect relative efficiencies of production and service departments and, therefore, would be useless for evaluation purposes.

3. Obviously, perversities of these implicit book-profit allocations aren't alleviated if the global profit on a service department's services is *un*definable. Nor would the allocations be any less arbitrary were the transfer prices to be the true marginal costs rather than variable costs. Therefore, we may conclude that marginal- or variable-cost pricing of service departments' services may be behaviour-congruent with respect to output and service-utilization decisions, but will otherwise usually be so only by coincidence.

4. Finally, the foregoing applies even more forcefully to the extreme case of not charging *anything* for the services of a service department, something that is occasionally recommended to encourage innovative use of these services by production departments (or to discourage production departments from buying services externally when a service department is first establishing either itself or new capacity, or to prevent wealthy divisions from hogging services). Here, although the allocations may be behaviour-congruent with respect to the innovation (or other specialized) decision, they'll generate central-office-dysfunctional output and utilization decisions and won't be reliably behaviour-congruent on other dimensions.[24]

Lump-Sum Approaches

> . . . any method that entails an arbitrary markup is of little value for purposes of evaluating corporate profit, divisional profit, or managerial performance. If divisional profit is predetermined by policy (i.e., by establishing a markup over cost), it is meaningless for managerial review. Worse, it may induce management to believe that a division is profitable when, in fact, it is not.—[Fremgen, 1970, p. 27]

If service departments are to be profit centres, most authors are uncomfortable with variable-cost transfer prices' condemning them to perpetual losses. Yet, increasing the transfer price would result in perverse output and utilization decisions. The most popular

---

[24] See [Krasney, 1971, esp. pp. 17-18], [Schaller, 1974, pp. 41-42, 44] and [Cushing, 1976, pp. 47-48, 50].

remedy, associated in the literature with [Solomons, 1965, e.g., pp. 200-03], is to use a two-part transfer pricing scheme.[25] The company continues to charge production departments variable costs for individual units of the service department's services. But, in addition, production departments also "pay" the service departments lump-sum periodic fees to cover either their fixed costs or their fixed costs plus a profit margin.[26] This fee may be proportional to the production departments' actual or normal usages of service-department services[27] or, in slightly more sophisticated versions, the percentage of service-department total or peak[28] capacity that the company provided for each production department when it first established the service department.[29] Finally, this approach may be modified by first charging production departments with all service-department fixed costs that are directly traceable to them.[30]

Whatever form of lump-sum approach the company uses, book profits of service departments are obviously administered. For instance, if the service departments' marginal costs are horizontal (and actual costs equal standard costs), their book profits will be zero if the lump sum covers only fixed costs—or will be some arbitrary ("play money") amount if the lump sum provides for a profit. On reflection, it's equally apparent that therefore the book profits of production departments must be administered, too.[31]

Once again, the resulting transfer prices are behaviour-congruent with respect to output and utilization decisions. They now also try to be behaviour-congruent with respect to élan decisions made by service-department managers (decisions that stem from their supposed perceptions of running autonomous departments at break-even or profits). But since departmental book profits *are* patently administered, this appearance of autonomy seems fragile at best,

---

[25] [Jensen, 1977, p. 853] discusses circumstances in which Shapley [1953] allocations yield Solomons' two-part transfer prices. For other anticipations of these, see [Dearden, 1960a, p. 124] and the next note.

[26] This approach is sometimes attributed to [Coase, 1946]. But as Coase [pp. 171, 174*n*, 181-82] and Loehman and Whinston [1971, p. 610] make clear, Coase's lump-sum fee covers only *traceable* fixed costs.

[27] As in [Solomons, 1965, pp. 201-02], [Dopuch, Birnberg and Demski, 1974, pp. 580-81, 588] and [Ferrara, 1976, p. 14].

[28] See [Heins, 1972].

[29] See [Amey and Egginton, 1973, pp. 420-23].

[30] See [Ferrara, 1976, pp. 14-15]. Be it noted that one can't legitimately determine what fixed costs are traceable to production departments by asking how these costs would decline if each production department were the first to be discontinued; I've discussed the fallacy in such everyone-first approaches elsewhere in this book—contrast [Solomons, 1965, pp. 80-81].

[31] See [Wiseman, 1957, p. 63] for a similar conclusion, and [Dean, 1955, pp. 70-72].

and the evaluation paradox of Chapters Eight and Ten is apt to arise. In any event, there's no reason to expect such transfer prices to be behaviour-congruent on other dimensions.[32]

The same is true of approaches that charge full absorption costs, or full absorption costs plus a "normal" markup, on transfer goods.[33] The only difference is that such "accounting" transfer prices won't be behaviour-congruent with respect to output and utilization decisions, either,[34] unless one uses a sort of lump-sum procedure here, too.[35]

Any or all of these approaches may be modified by use of tariffs or subsidies to control externalities or to provide service departments with positive book profits,[36] but doing so in no way affects the foregoing conclusions. Finally, some of the approaches mentioned in this section are used (or, at least, proposed) for transfers between manufacturing divisions or manufacturing and distribution divisions. That's to say, although I've conducted their discussion in a service-department context, it has a more general significance.

Gordon's Approach

One example will suffice. Gordon [1970] has a central office lay down the rules under which divisions (here, firms of a socialist economy) set transfer prices.[37] But since, as his discussion [e.g., p. 430] makes clear, all technically competent actors should come up with practically the same prices if they follow the rules, the central office indirectly dictates these transfer prices just as surely as it did in the simple Hirshleifer situation.[38]

This transfer price is an accounting one:
$$V + (F + Y) \div N,$$
where V equals standard variable cost per unit, F is standard fixed cost, Y is a standard profit and N is standard output, as slightly

---

[32] For difficulties of evaluation, and a few other problems with lump-sum approaches, see [Gordon, 1964, pp. 23-24].

[33] See, for instance, [Dearden, 1960, pp. 122-23] and [Caplan, 1971, p. 100].

[34] See [Dean, 1955, p. 72], [Cook, 1957, pp. 74-76, 78-79] and [Dopuch and Drake, 1964, p. 14].

[35] One might model this on [Baughman, 1970, p. 43], even though Baughman's proposals really pertain to the next section's situations where there are external markets for transfer goods. See also [Hughes, 1971] and [Ferrara, 1976, pp. 14-17].

[36] See, for instance, [Hirshleifer, 1957, pp. 100-01; 1964, p. 29], [Dopuch and Drake, 1964, pp. 12-13] and [Amey and Egginton, 1973, p. 530].

[37] For background, see [Most, 1971], [Abdel-khalik, 1971] and [Gordon, 1971].

[38] Contrast [Gordon, 1970, p. 437].

adjusted up or down to clear internal markets.[39] By these adjustments, the central office effectively controls divisional output decisions.[40] Familiar problems of autonomy and evaluation inevitably arise. Besides evaluation problems stemming from the central office's indirect administration of prices and outputs, others are generated by its allocations to divisions of fixed costs (insofar as these are nontraceable)[41] and the standard profits. Abdel-khalik and Lusk [1974, p. 21] comment:

> Pricing at full-cost-plus implies willingness to incorporate inefficiencies that may be passed on to the consumer—a function of consumer demand inelasticity. This "pass it on" perspective may negate the operational controls used to evaluate divisional performance.

They also note [1974, p. 21]:

> The allocation of joint and fixed costs to products is necessarily arbitrary. It is true that in some situations, such as those assumed by Gordon, there are no joint costs; but even then the transfer price will vary according to volume. As a matter of fact, even under Gordon's assumptions, joint costs exist—e.g., the cost of the central administration.

Much the same point could be made using internal externalities instead of joint costs.[42]

Other Administered-Profit Approaches

We may conclude this discussion by mentioning a few other approaches, whose book profits are *blatantly* administered. The central office may credit goodwill fees or royalties to a division in order to make it "comparable" with other divisions,[43] "budget" transfer prices to divisions on some sort of ability-to-bear criterion,[44] "plug" them to be consistent with budgeted divisional profits,[45] assign arbitrary book profits to sales of by-products[46] or prorate global profits to divisions according to some formula,[47] such as calculating the ratio:

[39] See especially [pp. 434-37].

[40] Under Gordon's approach, the central office will always at least have the *power* to set outputs at whatever levels it will—see [Abdel-khalik, 1971, p. 786].

[41] Gordon construes fixed costs a bit more narrowly than some authors do—see [1970, p. 433].

[42] See also [Abdel-khalik and Lusk, 1974, pp. 21-22].

[43] See [Dearden, 1962a, p. 86].

[44] See [Horngren, 1977, pp. 503-05]. This approach can parallel the NRV approach to joint-cost allocation.

[45] See [Larson, 1974, p. 29].

[46] See [National Association of Accountants, 1957a, p. 20].

[47] See [Horngren, 1977, p. 688].

(Global profit) ÷ (Total standard variable costs of all divisions) then allocating book profits to each division by applying this ratio to its variable costs.[48] By now, the problem with such proposals should be familiar, and we need only apply Dearden's [1962a, p. 86] comment on the first of these to all: "In some cases, the impression is given to the divisional manager that he is playing a bookkeeping game."

Two-Part Market Prices for Transfer Goods

Until now, this chapter's discussions have assumed that there are no external markets for transfer goods. When such markets exist, the usual transfer-pricing rule is Chapter Eight's one of charging the going market price.[49] However, possible dysfunctional consequences of doing so have led authors to propose two-part market-price approaches that resemble the last section's lump-sum approaches.

Baughman [1970, p. 41] is one of several who have pointed out that use of market prices as transfer prices results in the variable costs of transfer goods on books of transferees exceeding their variable (or marginal) costs to the company as a whole.[50] For example, let's imagine a situation where it costs a manufacturing division (Mfg) £7 per unit (variable costs) to manufacture additional units of a transfer good, and a finishing and distribution division (Dst) £3 per unit of additional variable costs to sell them, a total of £10. The transfer good sells for £15 per unit in an intermediate market. Its usual selling price in the finished goods market is £20, but Dst encounters a one-time opportunity to sell 10,000 finished units for £16 without affecting its ordinary markets.

If there are restrictions on Mfg's sales in the intermediate market but no restrictions on either division's capacity, it's clearly to the company's global advantage that Dst accept this opportunity. But if the transfer price is the £15 market price, Dst can do so only at a book loss of £15 + £3 - £16 = £2 per unit—and may, therefore, dysfunctionally decide to ignore this opportunity. Baughman's remedy is a two-part transfer price, under which Dst's decision will

---

[48] See [Schwab, 1975, p. 47].

[49] Proposals of charging nothing for service-department services, mentioned in the last section, are an exception—see [Schaller, 1974] and [Cushing, 1976]; this practice seems rare. Of course, where *no* external market exists for such services companies often run service departments as cost centres, include their costs in general overheads and don't engage in explicit transfer pricing at all.

[50] Contrast [Hughes, 1971].

be influenced only by its and Mfg's variable costs. Similarly, Solomons' two-part transfer prices are explicitly designed for situations where divisions can deal either internally or externally and the goal is to have them do what's best for the company as a whole.[51]

Emmanuel [1977b, pp. 9-10] identifies another reason for using two-part market prices:

> There is some evidence in the U.K. context which indicates that volatile prices characterise the markets of intermediate goods and services . . . . The net effect for the internal selling and buying unit managers facing the external market is that not one but a range of market prices is available. In addition, there is no necessity that the range facing the seller will overlap, except in part, with the range facing the buyer.
>
> The presence of price competition in the external market for the intermediate commodity renders the relevance of all the forms of market-oriented transfer price open to doubt. If the transfer price is to be set by negotiation, each of the unit managers may be able to quote widely diverging prices at which they have recently dealt in the market. A compromise price may be regarded with dissatisfaction by both the unit managers, and it is unlikely to result in the internal trade taking place unless restrictions are placed on their use of external suppliers and buyers.[52]

Briefly, his proposed remedy is:

> At the time of transfer, a product cost equal to the standard variable cost of the selling division will be charged to the buying division. In addition, a period cost will be charged. This period cost will equal the net contribution which the selling division obtains from external sales of the same commodity in the same time period as the transfer took place . . . the period cost is calculated *ex post* and is not known at the budget-planning stage . . . [53]

Subject to the limitations that Emmanuel [1977a, p. 198; 1977b, pp. 21-22] mentions,[54] his modification of Solomons' two-part system seems well founded. Once again, though, readers are reminded that it's designed only for situations where there are external markets for transfer goods—i.e., for the least troublesome of all transfer-pricing situations.

---

[51] For instance, [Solomons, 1977, pp. 44·10-11] makes this clear.

[52] For more details on possible dysfunctions, see [Emmanuel, 1977b, pp. 1-13].

[53] [Emmanuel, 1977a, p. 197]. For details, see [Emmanuel, 1977b, pp. 15-21]; see also [Emmanuel, 1977c]. Please note that this *is* a market-price approach: variable cost plus contribution equals market price.

[54] And the traditional, implicit assumptions that he makes—compare [Butterworth, Hayes and Matsumara, 1977].

Conclusions

It remains to mention a few other transfer-pricing approaches that don't fit conveniently into our previous categories. As mentioned in Chapter Seven, in practice companies often select transfer prices strictly for tax or legal reasons. Readers are left to verify that transfer-pricing approaches designed to serve a company's tax or legal advantage will be behaviour-congruent on other dimensions only by coincidence—though, as [Thomas, 1971a] emphasized, companies often make a *pretense* of more general applicability.

Other transfer-pricing approaches are designed to encourage transferees to schedule their demands to coincide with transferors' slack (rather than peak) activity periods, and otherwise to smooth workloads and control bottlenecks[55] or to accomplish other, equally narrow, purposes.[56] None of these are apt to be behaviour-congruent elsewhere.

Summary

We have now surveyed all transfer-pricing possibilities that are discussed in the literature. All founder on the same problem. Here, in a nutshell, is that problem:

1. Allocated transfer prices require one-to-many allocations, as defined in Chapter One.

2. Such allocations are incorrigible (chaotically arbitrary).

3. An allocation method that is behaviour-congruent with respect to one decision and set of circumstances need not be with respect to others.

4. A possible remedy (or, at least, pallitive) for incorrigibility is for the company to choose allocation methods that are behaviour-congruent with respect to the decisions that the central office and division managers (in their particular circumstances) base on allocated data.

5. With transfer-price allocations, this remedy fails, for two reasons:

---

[55] See [Staubus, 1971, pp. 85-87], [Schaller, 1974, p. 46] and [Cushing, 1976, pp. 48, 50].

[56] See, for instance, [National Association of Accountants, 1957a, p. 20] and [Lemke, 1970, pp. 187-88]. Staubus [1971, p. 122] is aware of this narrowness.

a. Too many different kinds of decisions are apt to be based on them, and in too many different circumstances—no allocation method is anywhere near universally behaviour-congruent.[57]

b. Transfer-price allocations happen to be universally *perverse* with respect to decisions involving evaluations of division managers' performances.

Thus it follows that no reliable *overall* solution to the dilemmas of transfer pricing is apt to exist. One can't eliminate dysfunctions, only minimize them. The least troublesome case here is use of current market prices as transfer prices. But, as we have seen, even this doesn't escape substantial difficulties—and where such use of current market prices is appropriate the company is using allocation-*free* data, whereas whenever it must significantly modify such prices by allocation, the problems summarized immediately above inevitably emerge.

Up to a point, Part One's suggestion that companies that believe they must allocate should simultaneously use different allocation methods for different decisions[58] seems pertinent here, too. Both to facilitate this and because, as we've seen, complex, globally optimizing transfer prices are perverse along especially many dimensions, companies would do well to (a) keep their transfer prices just as simple as possible and (b) aim at satisficing rather than optimizing.[59] In practice, many companies do just that;[60] they should feel no intellectual embarrassment for doing so.[61]

But the similarity of different transfer-pricing methods' perversities (which makes it difficult to escape these by judicious combinations of approaches) and, in particular, their uniform perver-

---

[57]There is nothing unique about this conclusion:

Is there an all-pervasive rule for transfer pricing that will lead toward optimal economic decisions? The answer is negative, because the three problems of goal congruence, incentive, and autonomy must all be considered simultaneously. —[Horngren, 1977, p. 683].

This book's only contribution is its attempt to prove this conclusion by exhaustion (including, one fears, that of the reader).

[58]As in [Bierman, 1959, p. 431].

[59]Again, there is nothing unique to this conclusion; compare [March and Simon, 1958, pp. 205, 209].

[60]See [National Association of Accountants, 1957a, pp. 28-36], [Livesey, 1967, p. 99], [McCulloch, 1967, pp. 1-9], [Rook, 1971, p. 9], [Centre for Business Research, 1972, pp. 15-18, 30-31] and [Okpechi, 1976, pp. 101-02].

[61]Finally, we might echo [Cook, 1957, p. 78] by suggesting that whatever transfer-pricing system a company uses, it should base as many decisions as possible on special studies that don't use allocated transfer-price data.

sity in evaluating division managers' performances render things significantly worse than they were in Part One. This is especially true where these latter perversities threaten the very motivations upon which these approaches depend. One is left wondering whether companies shouldn't try to avoid transfer pricing altogether (save perhaps where use of current-market prices is possible and appropriate). The next chapter considers this possibility.

Meanwhile, if at the individual-company level of aggregation decentralization into profit centres runs into the difficulties described in the last four chapters, how much more so at the level of national economies! The same things that prevent universal behaviour-congruence of corporate transfer-price allocations rule out a government's central planning optimizing more than a few dimensions of social welfare without major dysfunctional consequences on other dimensions. In particular, the familiar question arises: Can central planning ever be compatible with autonomy—freedom?[62] The answer appears to be: Only if applied with a light hand and real willingness to accept extensive dysfunctions. This answer applies as strongly to Western economies as to those of the Russian and Chinese blocks.

---

[62] I hypothesize that the impossibility of attaining universal behaviour congruence contributes to the quasi-religious emphases that some totalitarian socialist regimes place on individuals subordinating their own needs and desires to those of the collective. Without such subordination, centrally planned economies are apt to experience major dysfunctions—witness much anecdotal evidence from Russia.

Although I suspect that this point may be quite important (and one reader of an earlier draft of this chapter was distressed to see it relegated to a footnote), its implications obviously extend far beyond this book's limited scope. Here is another arena for additional research.

CHAPTER TWELVE

WHAT TO DO?

...where the activities of two or more divisions of a company are in fact highly interdependent, it is very difficult to allocate total company profits among the divisions in a rational, precise manner. Under these circumstances, it becomes questionable as to how much weight can be placed upon these divisional "profits" in determining the effectiveness of the divisional executives. However convenient it would be for top management to have a single profit figure to summarize divisional performance to serve as a divisional incentive, it may turn out that such a simple but unrealistic criterion is less helpful than the more subjective but realistic bases which are commonly used for judging divisional management. —[Simon, et al., 1954, p. 41]

Although some techniques receive only scant attention now, I am not aware of a single cost-accounting technique which has been dropped from the text-books or professional examination requirements. Progress is interpreted solely as adding new developments or as grafting ideas from other disciplines to the existing stock of accounting techniques. To criticize is to be destructive. But surely selective destruction is essential to real progress. We just cannot go on adding and adding without going back over the existing stock of techniques to see if any have been superseded or have out-lived their usefulness. —[Wells, 1970, p. 486]

In this final chapter we shall be concerned only with situations where either there is no external market for a transfer good or reference to such a market is inappropriate. Here, several authors propose ceasing calculation and use of transfer prices.[1] Others propose such cessation whenever the transferor and transferee aren't independent of each other[2] —something that, as is evident from Hirshleifer [1956, p. 176], boils down to the same thing. Still others would impose more elaborate conditions upon use of transfer prices.[3] Though some favour centralization,[4] most authors per-

[1] For instance, [National Association of Accountants, 1957a, p. 9], [Bierman, 1963, p. 91], [Livesey, 1967, p. 102] and [Abdel-khalik and Lusk, 1974, p. 23].

[2] See, for instance, [Solomons, 1965, p. 164], [Henderson and Dearden, 1966, p. 145] and [Wells, 1968, pp. 174, 178-80]. Regarding the last, see also the debate between Lemke [1970] and Wells [1971].

[3] See [Dean, 1955, pp. 67-68], [National Association of Accountants, 1957a, pp. 8, 10] and [Dearden, 1962b, pp. 147, 149-51]. For *general* arguments that internal cost allocations are unnecessary for business purposes, see [Baxter, 1952, pp. 268-74], [Wells, 1970] and, the inspiration of both, [Edwards, 1952a]. For *non*-transfer-price difficulties with profit centres, see [Dearden, 1968, pp. 82-85].

Be it recognized, though, that merely abandoning allocations and profit centres doesn't solve all problems caused by divisions interacting—see [Cook, 1955, pp. 90-91].

[4] For instance, Dearden [1962b, pp. 140-47, 153] and Wells [1968].

ceive the problem as being one of eliminating arbitrary or dysfunctional transfer prices whilst somehow maintaining decentralization.

Traceable Costs and Divisional Contributions

Chapter One points out that, in contrast to the drastic arbitrariness of one-to-many allocations, one-to-one and many-to-one allocations can be satisfactorily legitimate. A common example of many-to-one allocations is assignment of traceable costs (such as direct costs) to work in process. Accordingly, on first blush it might seem appropriate to make transfer prices equal to the sum of whatever costs of the related transfer goods happened to be traceable to transferee divisions.

However, difficulties with this proposal become evident the moment we recognize that it boils down to Chapter Eleven's setting transfer prices equal to transfer goods' marginal (or incremental, or corresponding opportunity) costs. Indeed, this is the form that this proposal takes in the literature.[5] We need not repeat Chapter Eleven's discussion of this approach's perversities, but we should survey the ways in which the literature suggests dealing with them. There are three of these:

1. Chapter Eleven's analysis indicated that the marginal-cost approach credits the entire global profit on transfer goods (more or less) to whatever divisions (such as distribution divisions) are the final transferees prior to sale to outsiders. Companies might treat such divisions (and any other divisions that had significant revenues from *non*-transfer goods) as contribution centres.[6] The central office would then control such divisions via comparisons between expected and actual contributions.[7] Wells [1970, p. 485] points out one major difficulty with this proposal: divisional interactions would make tracing of many costs (and determination of independent divisional contributions) very difficult.

2. Another difficulty is that this approach isn't appropriate for divisions (such as Hirshleifer's manufacturing division) that produce only transfer goods—for, lacking outside revenues, their

---

[5]For instance, see [Henderson and Dearden, 1966, pp. 150, 156], which mentions some of the difficulties that this proposal could generate.

[6]I make the conventional distinction here between a division's book profits and its contributions to global profits and untraceable costs; the latter, of course, would include untraceable costs of transfer goods.

[7]See [Henderson and Dearden, 1966, pp. 144, 150-151], [Lemke, 1970, p. 187] and [Solomons, 1977, pp. 44·24-25]. Please note that any comparison of *absolute* divisional contributions would be meaningless because of the arbitrariness of each divisions' revenues on transfer goods.

"contributions" must be negative.[8] Companies would be reduced to treating such divisions as cost centres, exercising control over them by comparing standard with actual traceable costs. This isn't necessarily bad: such cost-centre treatment is common in practice and, as we saw at the outset of this chapter, is recommended by certain theorists.[9] It does, of course, involve substantial centralization—I argued earlier that it is hard to imagine such divisions as meaningfully autonomous. But, as we've also seen, some authors accept such centralization gladly.

3. Okpechi [1976, pp. 115-16] has suggested abandoning efforts to allocate joint global profits to individual divisions and, instead, has proposed attributing them to the entire *groups* of divisions that generate them:

> If the basic tenet of responsibility accounting suggests that divisional managers be held accountable for those aspects of their operations over which they have greater control, it seems a logical extension that divisional managers be evaluated jointly where there is interdependency. Joint evaluation and reward systems would compensate for the disruptive effects of interdependency. —[p. 116, corrected for a minor typographical error]

He mentions one possibly dysfunctional consequence of this approach [1976, p. 118]:

> But if divisional managers are truly rewarded based on the joint projects that they undertake with other divisions, in what kind of projects would divisional managers be engaged? Probably divisional managers would retain low risk projects in their various divisions but would go into high risk projects jointly.

There are at least two other problems: (a) if companies were to extend this proposal to service departments it would become terribly complex and (b) somehow, some supplementary way of distinguishing individual performances of group members must be found. When most of a division's projects are joint ones finding it could be quite difficult—at least if the company tries to evaluate individual *profit* performances. (Anyone who has served on a tenure and promotion committee and has had to cope with candidates whose publications are mostly co-authored will appreciate both the need to evaluate individual performances and the difficulty here.) The next subsection considers *non*-profit measures of managerial performance.

---

[8]Contrast [Shillinglaw, 1977b, p. 864].

[9][Simon, et al., 1945, pp. 4-5, 41-43] affords an additional, early, instance.

Non-Profit Measures

Various authors have suggested various non-profit measures of division-manager performance. These are appropriate both for the previous subsection's supplementary evaluations and for use in their own rights. The most comprehensive list will be found in [American Accounting Association, 1971, pp. 178-81],[10] which organizes things as follows:

Measures of physical productivity. These might include a variety of measures of the company's effectiveness in producing its products and providing its services. Besides reports on defective production, the Committee [p. 179] suggested measures of:

–yield in physical terms, per unit of scarce resource (footage, machine capacity, tonnage capacity, man hours, machine hours...)
–yield, in numbers and significance of ideas, product ideas, production method ideas, market penetration, absolute vs. potential
–quality control: measures of product reliability, process reliability, timeliness of product, and index of apparent serendipity
–performance data (on-time deliveries, for example)

Measures of marketing effectiveness. These might include reports on units of product sold per salesman or per advertising insertion, "...share of market measures, based either on actual product sales relative to actual sales of other firm[s] serving the market, or actual sales penetration relative to the potential market for the product..." [p. 179], quantitative data on product quality (derived from such things as consumer attitude surveys, committee appraisals of products, and information about the number of product innovations introduced by divisions) as well as data on product returns, amounts of warranty and guaranty services performed, and the timeliness of their performances.

Measures of personnel and organizational effectiveness. These might include figures on proportions of promotions filled within divisions or within the company, numbers of hours devoted to internal training programs, numbers of persons provided with specified skills by such programs, results of employee attitude surveys, measures of employee turnover, numbers of grievances

---

[10]But see also [March and Simon, 1958, p. 208], [Goetz, 1967, pp. 437-38], [Wells, 1968, p. 179; 1971, pp. 56-57; 1973a; 1976], [Manes, 1970, p. 572], [Murray, 1973, p. 28], [Abdel-khalik and Lusk, 1974, p. 23], [Buckley and McKenna, 1974, pp. 45-47] and, especially [Solomons, 1965, pp. 277-86].

and absenteeism, measures of effectiveness of employee participation in the formulation and implementation of budgets,
"...measures of...incidence of crises, of non-services, of lost opportunities...measures of acceptance of change...[and] tests of
adequacy of employee skills (cataloged) to meet intended future firm plans and programs." [p. 180]

Measures of the division's social responsibility. These might
include reports on various dimensions of divisions' efforts to
fulfil the company's public responsibilities—especially their generation of beneficent, and reduction of malign, social externalities (such as training and advancement of minority-group employees and women, and abatement of pollution).

Need for Book Profits and Transfer Prices

> Where top management believe that profit budgets are its tool for
> evaluating profit performance...it rarely tries to employ other, better
> means of evaluation. In short, the existence of a profit budget system
> obscures the fact that adequate evaluation is not being made. —[Dear-
> den, 1968, p. 84]

> Ultimately, the success of a division and of its management must be
> measured in terms of profitability. Even though in the short run there
> may be many other indices of success, sooner or later these must ex-
> press themselves in terms of profit or, what is really the same thing, in
> terms of an increase in the net worth of the enterprise. —[Solomons,
> 1965, p. 234]

> Again and again, organizations have found flexible budgets and cost
> centers insufficient. —[Horngren, 1972, p. 745]

Few if any would deny that some of the foregoing non-profit
measures mentioned by the Committee were potentially useful for
supplementary evaluation of division managers. But, despite that
Dearden makes a good point (above), the preponderate view is
that non-profit measures can't possibly *substitute* for calculations
of divisional book profits. As we saw in Chapter Seven, there is
reason for this: Ultimately, divisions must be evaluated in terms of
the contributions that they make to the company as a whole.
Since the real world, disregarding whatever theory might say, per-
sists in evaluating the company in terms of its profitability, it
seems inevitable that, in turn, the company will evaluate its divisions on the same basis, translating any other indices of success in-

to book-profit terms.[11] Unless a company is profitable, it is unlikely to survive for very long, and if it doesn't survive, nothing else much matters.[12] As Solomons [1977, p. 44·3] observes:

> ...profitability, better than any other single index of performance, reflects a great many other ingredients of performance, such as growth, market penetration, product leadership or productivity, all of which are bound to have an impact on a company's profit sooner or later.[13]

Yet, when there are no external markets for transfer goods, calculation of divisional book profits requires use of allocated transfer prices.

(Chapter Six's reluctance to conclude that joint-cost allocations should simply cease, irritating though that reluctance has been to some of my friends, was based in part on similar grounds: If companies are to calculate divisional book profits, often they must allocate joint costs, too. For brevity, I'll confine the remaining discussion to transfer-price allocations. But readers who are following the argument closely should keep in mind that parallel arguments usually apply to joint-cost allocations, too.)

There are additional reasons for calculating transfer prices. Sterling [1976, p. 85n] observes, "Of course, we can *legislate* the relevance of unexpired cost." Similarly, we've legislated the necessity of calculating transfer prices. In the U.S., the Cost Accounting Standards Board, the Defense Department, the Federal Trade Commission, the Internal Revenue Service, various State and local taxing bodies, specialized regulatory bodies and, often, the courts all impose rules that require such calculations. So do certain financial accounting practices.[14] Companies in Canada, the U.K. and

---

[11] Although I regard this explanation as true and important, clearly it's only an approximate, general one. It cannot be the whole story—for instance, 59% of Reece and Cool's [1978, p. 36] *Fortune* "1000" companies that used profit or investment centres defined "profits" somewhat differently from the ways they defined these for financial-accounting purposes. (The differences tended to be ones consistent with a concern for responsibility accounting). See also [Reece and Cool, 1978, pp. 41-42].

[12] [Solomons, 1977, p. 44·3].

[13] On these points, see also [Dean, 1955, p. 65] and [Okpechi, 1976, p. 118]. The latter [1976, p. 74] contends that division managers themselves prefer to be evaluated in terms of their book profits—rather than by non-profit measures. Horngren [1975, p. 23; 1977, p. 690] gives further support to such calculation of book profits—arguing, for instance, that use of profit centres furthers attainment of goal-congruence.

[14] For matters mentioned in the last two sentences, see [Dean, 1955, p. 66], [March and Simon, 1958, pp. 204-05], [Solomons, 1965, pp. 209-11], [McNally, 1973, pp. 20-21], [Dopuch, Birnberg and Demski, 1974, p. 581], [Financial Accounting Standards Board, 1974, pp. 7, 12, 27-30, 94-96; 1976, pp. 6, 13, 18, 30-31, 35], [Anthony, 1975], [Hedges, 1975], [Culpepper, 1976] and [Williams, 1976].

Australia experience similar pressures. Once again, whatever theorists may say, the world we live in dictates use of transfer prices.

Allocation-Free External Reporting

One might hope to attain relief by *changing* the world we live in. Elsewhere, I've argued that financial accounting should cease reporting one-to-many allocations.[15] Financial accountants could substitute at least three potentially allocation-free reporting systems for our contemporary, allocated ones: current-entry-value reporting,[16] current-exit-value reporting[17] and cash-flow (or net-quick-asset-flow) reporting.[18] Indeed, the last could be combined with either of the first two.

Use of such allocation-free approaches as substitutes for canonical external reporting practices would eliminate the previous subsection's main reason for calculating allocated book profits. Ultimately, then, one would expect regulatory and taxation authorities to cease demanding allocated data, too. But would such a change to allocation-free external reporting eliminate our transfer-pricing difficulties?

I used to hope so, but now don't see how it could. Consider cash-flow external reports. The corresponding divisional cash-flow reports would have to decide how much global cash receipts from sales of transfer goods to outsiders should be attributed to each division,[19] and this immediately leads to all the problems that plagued Chapters Eight through Eleven. Parallel problems would arise under the two current-value approaches. Therefore, although reform of external financial reporting practices might somewhat reduce pressures to calculate arbitrary transfer prices, it won't eliminate these pressures or the arbitrariness. *For the foreseeable future, we're going to be stuck with this problem.*

---

[15] [Thomas, 1969; 1974; 1975; 1978; 1979]; see [Meyers, 1976] as a first step in this direction.

[16] See [Edwards and Bell, 1961], [Johnson and Bell, 1976], [Anderson, 1979], [Bell and Johnson, 1979], [Kay and Johnson, 1979] and [Stamp, 1979].

[17] See [Chambers, 1966; 1970; 1974; 1979], [Sterling, 1970; 1975] and [Wells, 1973a; 1976]. For mixed current-entry- and current-exit-value approaches, see [Boatsman and Hite, 1979], [Carsberg, 1979] and [Mosich and Vasarhelyi, 1979].

[18] See [Lawson, 1956; 1957; 1969; 1970; 1971a; 1971b; 1975a; 1975b; 1976a; 1976b], [Solomons, 1961, esp. p. 383], [Lee, 1972a; 1972b; 1974; 1976; 1979], [Lawson and Stark, 1975; 1977], [Ashton, 1976], [Ijiri, 1977, 1979] and [Lawson and Bean, 1979]. The last is especially comprehensive. I have cited extensively here, since North American readers seem largely unfamiliar with this literature.

[19] See [Milburn, 1977, p. 41*n*].

Living With It

If so, the question is how best to live with it. Dearden [1973, p. 377] offers an answer that will work *some* of the time:

> The existence of serious transfer pricing problems is often a symptom of an illogical organization structure. Serious problems tend to occur when: (a) significant amounts of goods are transferred between two divisions; and (b) there is no reliable market price available. This often means that the manufacturing division really has no marketing responsibility and is a profit center in name only. Consequently, one solution to some chronic transfer pricing problems is to reorganize the divisions involved.

(More generally, of course, as Chapter Seven pointed out we can *always* eliminate the problems of transfer pricing *per se* by turning profit centres into cost centres.) Somewhat similarly, Butterworth, Hayes and Matsumura [1977, esp. p. 26] don't try to obtain central-office-optimal outputs and resource distributions by manipulating transfer prices. Instead, they say that these can be attained only by proper design of the company's internal organization.

Where this isn't possible, and where the central office believes it needs divisional profit data, management (both at the central-office and divisional levels) should be urged to ignore allocated transfer prices whenever they can. I fear though, that (as Chapter One's footnote 18 pointed out), they often won't be able to do so. The question here is whether or not appropriate allocation-free alternatives to decision methods that use transfer prices exist and are feasible. Where they don't or aren't, companies may feel forced to continue using transfer prices, if only in the traditional spirit of "I know the game is crooked, but it's the only game in town."

Certainly, if one thing is clear from this book's investigations it's that transfer prices possess only one other merit—their possible behaviour-congruence with respect to particular decisions and circumstances—and we've repeatedly seen how unreliable this virtue is. McNally [1973, p. 18] reflects the right attitude here:[20]

> Historically the evolution of transfer prices has been associated firstly with the need to obtain an inventory valuation for partly and fully completed production and secondly with a desire to determine the profit results for semi-independent sections of a business firm...When considered in this way transfer prices have a "passive" role, one which

---

[20]Even if his belief that transfer prices are little used internally seems contradicted by the empirical (and other) evidence in Chapter One.

they still have in the substantial majority of present day [management control systems]. That is they are considered an essential part of preparing a divisional profit statement, but have a minor role in assisting decision making, other than perhaps to assist in establishing prices and in decisions about the source of purchase for inputs.

What to do when decisions *must* be based on allocated transfer prices or, at least, management believe they must? If this book's analysis is to be trusted, our first rule should be to shun counsels of perfection—to be extremely skeptical of any transfer-pricing proposal that claims to offer a clear-cut solution. For any genuine answer must involve tradeoffs.

These are also circumstances in which theorists would be well advised to respect what practical men have learned by cut-and-try. In real life, we find many companies using negotiated transfer prices, and companies often treating some divisions as profits centres and others as cost centres.[21] I'd urge companies to so design their internal organizations that, whenever possible, divisions that deal with each other have approximately equal bargaining strengths, then encourage transfer-price negotiation. I don't recommend this out of any faith in the results, but merely because our analysis suggests that it's the least objectionable alternative.[22]

Where divisions are unequal and transfer goods are the main ones in which weaker divisions deal, such divisions should be treated as cost centres. Other divisions should be treated as profit centres only with a lively awareness that the absolute levels of their profits are misleading; in effect this should result in treating them as contributions centres.[23] In any event, companies should seek to make supplementary use of non-profit measures of divisional performance, and avoid the error identified in the earlier quotation from [Dearden, 1968].

Finally, one's orientation in transfer pricing should always be behavioural. The relevant question is never "What's the correct approach?" There *is* no correct approach, for "correct" implies exactly the sort of theory that is unobtainable here. Instead, the ap-

---

[21] See, for instance, [National Association of Accountants, 1957a], [Livesey, 1967], [McCulloch, 1967], [Mautz and Skousen, 1968], [Rook, 1971], [Centre for Business Research, 1972], and [Emmanuel, 1977c].

[22] Particularly if we're entitled to make appropriate assumptions about the shape of the core—see [Hamlen, Hamlen and Tschirhart, 1977].

[23] That's to say, revenue-minus-traceable-costs centres.

propriate question is the opportunistic (even slightly cynical) one: "What's apt to produce the sorts of dysfunctional behaviour that we best can live with?" Such questions:

> ...cannot be settled once and for all from a priori considerations, but must be decided in each case by reference to the empirical facts of the world. —[March and Simon, 1958, p. 204]

Certainly there's nothing very rigourous in these conclusions. But, as March and Simon imply, that's just the point: the situation thwarts rigour. And on that modest note, it's high time that we end this book.

APPENDIXES

APPENDIX A

THE KAPLAN AND THOMPSON/WELAM APPROACH

All the overhead charges that are allocated under a full or absorption cost system are also allocated to products under our method. However, under our method, the allocation is accomplished in such a manner that the relative profitability of products is not distorted; i.e., given product cost information both before and after the overhead allocation, the same optimal product mix decision would be made. The procedure [also recognizes] production and sales interdependencies that are not reflected in current direct cost systems. --[Kaplan and Thompson, 1971, p. 353][1]

Readers will note the almost explicit behavior-congruence of the foregoing. If we make the following substitutions for their notation on [pp. 354-55]:

$$j = i \qquad r_j = p_i$$
$$H = J \qquad c_j = f_i$$

it becomes evident that their "gross profit," p_j, is the same as our net realizable value, n_i, and that they allocate joint costs to individual products according to the formula $j_i = J \cdot n_i \div N$, where it's assumed that the company is at a profit-maximizing optimum.

Accordingly, their approach, both here and in [Kaplan and Welam, 1974], is simply an extension, in a programming format, of the NRV approach to joint overheads (which they call *common* overheads).[2] Be it noted that their procedure doesn't allocate joint costs of nonscarce resources (costs of goods present in excess capacity at optimal outputs). Nor does it allocate joint costs if their total is too great. But where it does allocate, it follows the NRV approach.[3]

This remains true of the more complicated versions of their approach described in the latter parts of their paper (for one thing, their allocations of traceable overheads raise no theoretical diffi-

---

[1] See also [Kaplan and Thompson, 1971, pp. 356, 359].

[2] This is correctly reflected by Dopuch, Birnberg and Demski's [1974, p. 574] citation of this work in connection with the NRV approach, and by [Bodnar and Lusk, 1977, p. 858].

[3] For a discussion, see [Kaplan and Welam, 1974, pp. 482-83].

culties insofar as these *are* traceable). However, once the author's analysis is modified to encompass sales and production inter-dependencies and managerial constraints [Kaplan and Thompson, 1971, pp. 359-61], what's meant by a product's *net realizable value* ("gross profit") becomes much more sophisticated than in textbook expositions of the NRV approach. The effect is to extend the NRV method's congruence properties to a much broader range of circumstances than those for which it's ordinarily behaviour-congruent.

The same can be said for extentions of their approach to non-linear programming situations and to linear models with non-linear objective functions [pp. 353, 354n, 362-64]. In particular, it applies to [Kaplan and Welam, 1974], *in toto*. (This work's behaviour-congruence dimension is particularly evident in the first full paragraph of its right-hand column on [p. 478]; see also [p. 481]'s Rule 1.

APPENDIX B

THE MARGINAL APPROACH WITH THREE OR MORE PRODUCTS

Chapter Three discusses the marginal approach for a joint process involving two products. A strictly algebraic discussion of situations involving three or more products will suffice for analytical purposes, as will continuing to assume horizontal cost functions and simple linear demand functions.

Presuppose a joint process yielding products c, d, e, . . ., m. For each product, i:

$$q_i = \alpha_i - \beta_i p_i$$
$$p_i = (\alpha_i - q_i) \div \beta_i = (\alpha_i \div \beta_i) - (1 \div \beta_i) \cdot q_i$$
$$TR_i = (\alpha_i \div \beta_i) \cdot q_i - (1 \div \beta_i) \cdot q_i^2$$
$$MR_i = (\alpha_i \div \beta_i) - (2 \div \beta_i) \cdot q_i$$

where α_i and β_i are constants. We may also define $MR_{cde...m}$ and $MC_{cde...m}$, as follows:

$$MR_{cde...m} = MR_c + MR_d + MR_e + ... + MR_m$$

$$MC_{cde...m} = f_c + f_d + f_e + ... + f_m + J.$$

Under the marginal approach, our first step is to set these total marginal revenues and costs equal to each other, then solve for a tentative output, $q_{cde...m}$:

$$MR_c + MR_d + MR_e + ... + MR_m = f_c + f_d + f_e + ... + f_m + J;$$
expanding the left-hand side:

$$(\alpha_c \div \beta_c) + (\alpha_d \div \beta_d) + (\alpha_e \div \beta_e) + ... + (\alpha_m \div \beta_m) - 2 \cdot (q_{cde...m} \div \beta_c$$
$$+ q_{cde...m} \div \beta_d + q_{cde...m} \div \beta_e + ... + q_{cde...m} \div \beta_m)$$
$$= f_c + f_d + f_e + ... f_m + J;$$

therefore,

$$2 \cdot [\beta_d \cdot \beta_e \cdot \ldots \cdot \beta_m + \beta_c \cdot \beta_e \cdot \ldots \cdot \beta_m + \beta_c \cdot \beta_d \cdot \ldots \cdot \beta_m$$
$$+ \ldots + \beta_c \cdot \beta_d \cdot \beta_e \cdot \ldots \cdot \beta_{(m-1)}] \div (\beta_c \cdot \beta_d \cdot \beta_e \cdot \ldots \cdot \beta_m)$$
$$\cdot q_{cde\ldots m} = (\alpha_c \div \beta_c) + (\alpha_d \div \beta_d) + (\alpha_e \div \beta_e) + \ldots + (\alpha_m \div \beta_m)$$
$$- (f_c + f_d + f_e + \ldots + f_m + J); \quad \text{therefore,}$$
$$q_{cde\ldots m} = [(\alpha_c \div \beta_c) + (\alpha_d \div \beta_d) + (\alpha_e \div \beta_e) + \ldots + (\alpha_m \div \beta_m)$$
$$- (f_c + f_d + f_e + \ldots + f_m + J)] \cdot (\beta_c \cdot \beta_d \cdot \beta_e \cdot \ldots \cdot \beta_m) \div 2$$
$$\div [\beta_d \cdot \beta_e \cdot \ldots \cdot \beta_m + \beta_c \cdot \beta_e \cdot \ldots \cdot \beta_m + \beta_c \cdot \beta_d \cdot \ldots \cdot \beta_m$$
$$+ \ldots + \beta_c \cdot \beta_d \cdot \beta_e \cdot \ldots \cdot \beta_{(m-1)}].$$

If, for each product, i, $[\alpha_i - 2 \cdot q_{cde\ldots m}) \div \beta_i] - f_i \geqslant 0$, then

$$j_i = [(\alpha_i - 2 \cdot q_{cde\ldots m}) \div \beta_i] - f_i \text{ and}$$
$$q_i = q_{cde\ldots m}.$$

Let's suppose, however, that one product fails this test. We can always label things so that this is product c. In that event, we set MR_c equal to f_c:

$$(\alpha_c \div \beta_c) - (2 \div \beta_c) \cdot q_c = f_c$$
$$(2 \div \beta_c) \cdot q_c = (\alpha_c \div \beta_c) - f_c$$
$$q_c = (\beta_c \div 2) \cdot [(\alpha_c \div \beta_c) - f_c] = (\alpha_c - f_c \cdot \beta_c) \div 2$$
$$j_c = 0.$$

We now set $MR_{de\ldots m}$ equal to $MC_{de\ldots m}$, and obtain:

$$q_{de\ldots m} = [(\alpha_d \div \beta_d) + (\alpha_e \div \beta_e) + \ldots + (\alpha_m \div \beta_m) - (f_d + f_e + \ldots + f_m + J)] \cdot$$
$$(\beta_d \cdot \beta_e \cdot \ldots \cdot \beta_m) \div 2 \div (\beta_e \cdot \ldots \cdot \beta_m + \beta_d \cdot \ldots \cdot \beta_m + \ldots +$$
$$\beta_d \cdot \beta_e \cdot \ldots \cdot \beta_{(m-1)}).$$

If, for each remaining product, i, $[(\alpha_i - 2q_{de...m}) \div \beta_i] - f_i \geqslant 0$, then:

$$j_i = [(\alpha_i - 2q_{de...m}) \div \beta_i] - f_i$$

$$q_i = q_{de...m} \cdot$$

If, however, product d fails this test, then:

$$q_d = (\alpha_d - f_d \cdot \beta_d) \div 2$$

$$j_d = 0.$$

and we now set $MR_{e...m}$ equal to $MC_{e...m}$ and proceed as before. Successive iterations, which are easily programmed (though not on the current generation of slide-rule calculators), will eventually yield q_i's and j_i's for all products, c, d, e, ..., m. Finally, each product's book profit will be:

$$b_i = q_i \cdot ([(\alpha_i - q_i) \div \beta_i] - f_i - j_i).$$

APPENDIX C

THE SHAPLEY FORMULA

The Shapley formula may be expressed in several ways, of which the following is one of the simplest:

$$b_i = [\sum_i (c-1)! \cdot (n-c)! \cdot \{v(C-i)\}] \div n!$$

$$\{v(C), v(C-i) \geqslant 0\}$$

where:

i = Any division, input, output or other decision locus.
b_i = The book profit allocated to locus i.
n = The total number of such loci deemed to be involved in the allocation situation.
C = Any coalition of locus i with zero or more other loci.
c = The total number of loci in any such coalition, $0 \leqslant c \leqslant n$.
$v(C)$ = The *value* of such a coalition, as reflected in the allocation situation's characteristic function. This will equal the maximum periodic profit (or other output) that would obtain either by operating this coalition (with all other loci inactive) or by dissolving it and accepting a zero profit.
$v(C-i)$ = Same as $v(C)$, except that the coalition has been bereaved of locus i (thus, the expression $v(C) - v(C-i)$ is an opportunity cost).
$\sum_i$ = Summation for all possible coalitions that include locus i.

The 3-locus example in Figure 4-4 had the following characteristic function:

C	v(C)	C	v(C)
θ	0	WX	82
W	20	WY	34
X	50	XY	64
Y	2	WXY	96

We may calculate product W's £28 batch book profit as follows, beginning with one-member, then two- and three-member coalitions, and recalling that ϕ is the null (no-member) coalition:

$$
\begin{aligned}
b_W &= [(1-1)! \cdot (3-1)! \cdot \{v(W) - v(\theta)\} + (2-1)! \cdot (3-2)! \cdot \\
&\quad \{v(WX) - v(X)\} + (2-1)! \cdot (3-2)! \cdot \{v(WY) - v(Y)\} + \\
&\quad (3-1)! \cdot (3-3)! \cdot \{v(WXY) - v(XY)\}] \div 3! \\
&= [0! \cdot 2! \cdot \{20-0\} + 1! \cdot 1! \cdot \{82-50\} + 1! \cdot 1! \cdot \\
&\quad \{34-2\} + 2! \cdot 0! \cdot \{96-64\}] \div 6 \\
&= [2 \cdot 20 + 1 \cdot 32 + 1 \cdot 32 + 2 \cdot 32] \div 6 \\
&= [40 + 32 + 32 + 64] \div 6 = 168 \div 6 = \underline{28}.
\end{aligned}
$$

Parallel calculations yield $b_X = 58$ and $b_Y = 10$.

Again, the 0-additive game decomposed and allocated in Figure 4-5 had the following characteristic function:

CO	v(CO)	CO	v(CO)
θ	0	KL	26
K	0	KM	8
L	0	LM	14
M	0	KLM	48

$$
\begin{aligned}
b_L &= [(1-1)! \cdot (3-1)! \cdot \{v(L) - v(\theta)\} + (2-1)! \cdot (3-2)! \cdot \\
&\quad \{v(KL) - v(K)\} + (2-1)! \cdot (3-2)! \cdot \{v(LM) - v(M)\} + \\
&\quad (3-1)! \cdot (3-3)! \cdot \{v(KLM) - v(KM)\}] \div 3! \\
&= [2 \cdot \{0-0\} + 1 \cdot \{26-0\} + 1 \cdot \{14-0\} + 2 \cdot \{48-8\}] \\
&\quad \div 6 \\
&= [0 + 26 + 14 + 80] \div 6 = 120 \div 6 = \underline{20}.
\end{aligned}
$$

Finally, here's how one may calculate b_X and b_Y for the two-locus game in Figure 4-14, whose characteristic function was:

C	v(C)
θ	0
X	33
Y	0
XY	36

$$
\begin{aligned}
b_X &= [(1-1)! \cdot (2-1)! \cdot \{v(X) - v(\theta)\} + (2-1)! \cdot (2-2)! \cdot \\
&\quad \{v(XY) - v(Y)\}] \div 2! \\
&= [0! \cdot 1! \cdot \{33-0\} + 1! \cdot 0! \cdot \{36-0\}] \div 2! \\
&= [1 \cdot 1 \cdot 33 + 1 \cdot 1 \cdot 36] \div 2 \\
&= [33 + 36] \div 2 = \underline{34.5}.
\end{aligned}
$$

$$
\begin{aligned}
b_Y &= [0! \cdot 1! \cdot \{v(Y) - v(\theta)\} + 1! \cdot 0! \cdot \{v(XY) - v(X)\}] \div 2! \\
&= [1 \cdot 1 \cdot \{0-0\} + 1 \cdot 1 \cdot \{36-33\}] \div 2 \\
&= [0 + 3] \div 2 = \underline{1.5}.
\end{aligned}
$$

APPENDIX D

THE SHAPLEY APPROACH
RELAXATION OF EXTERNALITIES ASSUMPTIONS

The generalization that the Shapley approach divides interaction effects evenly among joint products (or other loci) holds true over a much broader range of situations than the simplified ones that we've considered thus far — *if* we interpret externalities as additional positive and negative joint costs. It's best to show this by an example; to keep the exposition simple, I'll use one whose characteristic function has uniformly positive values save for $v(\theta)$, and will assume that it's impossible to buy joint products externally.

Let's suppose that a joint process that costs £78 per batch yields four joint products, A, B, C and D, whose net realizable values per batch are respectively £81, £93, £114 and £129. The company gives all four further processing. Figure D-1 depicts the characteristic function, profit allocation and joint-cost allocation for this process under the Shapley approach. As always happens

Figure D-1

Characteristic Function and Shapley
Allocations for a Four-Locus Joint Process

C	v(C)		C	v(C)
θ	0		BC	129
A	3		BD	144
B	15		CD	165
C	36		ABC	210
D	51		ABD	225
AB	96		ACD	246
AC	117		BCD	258
AD	132		ABCD	339

b_A	=	61.50	j_A	= 19.50	=	78÷4
b_B	=	73.50	j_B	= 19.50	=	78÷4
b_C	=	94.50	j_C	= 19.50	=	78÷4
b_D	=	109.50	j_D	= 19.50	=	78÷4
B	=	339.00	J	= 78.00		

when there's no need to adjust negative coalition values to zero, the Shapley approach divides the joint costs evenly among the products.

Now, let's introduce an externality: Products C and D interfere with each other — either by reducing each others' demands or by increasing each others' further-processing costs. In either event, this interference reduces the coalition value of any CD combination by £30 per batch, as shown in the starred characteristic values of Figure D-2. In particular, total profits have declined by £30 from £339 to £309.

It's evident from Figure D-2 that the Shapley approach interprets this £30 externality as an additional £30 cost, joint to products C and D (only), and divides it evenly between products C and D. To further elaborate this example, let's finally suppose that products C and D interfere with each other only in the absence of product B. Figure D-3 shows the results.

As you can see, the Shapley approach interprets product B's inhibition of the CD interference as a third joint cost (or interac-

Figure D-2

Same as Figure D-1
But With a C-D Externality

C'	$v(C')$	C'	$v(C')$
θ	0	BC	129
A	3	BD	144
B	15	CD	135*
C	36	ABC	210
D	51	ABD	225
AB	96	ACD	216*
AC	117	BCD	228*
AD	132	ABCD	309*

$$b_A = 61.50 \quad j_A = 19.50 = 19.50+0$$
$$b_B = 73.50 \quad j_B = 19.50 = 19.50+0$$
$$b_C = 79.50* \quad j_C = 34.50* = 19.50+30 \div 2$$
$$b_D = \underline{94.50*} \quad j_D = \underline{34.50*} = 19.50+30 \div 2$$
$$B = \underline{309.00*} \quad J = \underline{108.00*} = \underline{78 + 30}$$

*Changed from Figure D-1.

Figure D-3

Same as Figure D-1, But
With C-D and B-C-D Externalities

C''	$v(C'')$	C''	$v(C'')$
θ	0	BC	129
A	3	BD	144
B	15	CD	135
C	36	ABC	210
D	51	ABD	225
AB	96	ACD	216
AC	117	BCD	258*
AD	132	ABCD	339*

$$b_A = 61.50 \qquad j_A = \quad 19.50 = 19.50+ 0 \quad - 0$$

$$b_B = 83.50* \qquad j_B = \quad 9.50* = 19.50+ 0 \quad -30 \div 3$$

$$b_C = 89.50* \qquad j_C = \quad 24.50* = 19.50+30 \div 2 - 30 \div 3$$

$$b_D = 104.50* \qquad j_D = \quad 24.50* = 19.50+30 \div 2 - 30 \div 3$$

$$B = \underline{339.00*} \qquad J = \quad \underline{78.00*} = \underline{78 \quad + 30 \quad - 30}$$

*Changed from Figure D-2.

tion effect), this time a £30 *negative* one, which it divides evenly among the three interacting processes. In this sense, the Shapley approach *always* allocates joint costs evenly.

To the extent that, as here, one division generates positive externalities from which other divisions can't be excluded, companies may experience problems that parallel those characteristic of Samuelson's public goods: inabilities to develop joint-cost or transfer-pricing schemes that will guarantee optimal outputs of these externalities. See [Samuelson, 1954; 1955; 1958], [Margolis, 1955], [Strotz, 1958], [Ellickson, 1973] and [Hurwicz, Radner and Reiter,1975, p. 190] for starters.

Indeed, the relationship between the problems that we've explored and those of public goods may be even broader: interested readers might consult Buchanan's [1965] discussion of goods that are neither purely private nor purely public but, like those that generate joint costs, fall somewhere in between — and the subsequent [Pauly, 1967]. The underlying relationship between public-goods problems and the cooperative-games considerations out of which Shapley allocations arose is especially evident in these last two papers. Symptomatic is their suggesting identical allocations to all actors — see [Buchanan, 1965, p. 8] and [Pauly, 1967, pp. 317-18]. Shapley's work may be interpreted as a rigourous solution of the problem posed by Pauly in his first complete paragraph on page [319].

One must draw boundaries to any study, and I haven't pursued these matters further. But someone expert in welfare economics might find exploration of the imports of the public-goods literature for accounting's internal allocations an interesting research topic.

APPENDIX E

SHAPLEY ALLOCATIONS AS RESULTS OF AVERAGED EXPANSION PATHS; MARGINALITY CONSIDERATIONS

The Shapley approach allocates book profits as follows:

The players...agree to play the game v in a grand coalition, formed in the following way: 1. Starting with a single member, the coalition adds one player at a time until everyone has been admitted. 2. The order in which the players are to join is determined by chance, with all arrangements equally probable. 3. Each player, on his admission, demands and is promised the amount which his adherence contributes to the value of the coalition (as determined by the function v). The grand coalition then plays the game "efficiently" so as to obtain the amount v(N)—exactly enough to meet all the promises. —[Shapley, 1953, p. 316].

The allocator then iterates this procedure for all possible ways that coalitions might form; the profit eventually assigned to each player (factor, product, division or other locus) may thus be interpreted as either the average (mean) profit from all of these ways or as an equivalent, quasi-probabilistic, expectation.[1]

In the joint-cost case, the Shapley approach reduces to determining all possible expansion paths by which the company could start with one product then add successive products, basing allocations on each one's average contributions, as so calculated. [Thomas, 1974, pp. 20, 25, 141-44] showed that any allocation scheme based on such hypothetical expansion paths will be quite arbitrary, depending as it must on choices that are no more (nor less) defensible than any others.[2] Thus, I conclude that the Shap-

---

[1] Readers may verify these interpretations by studying the formula in Appendix C. In this sense (only) we can also say, with Mossin[1968, p. 466], that Shapley allocations depend only on the bargaining powers of the actors, as reflected in their averaged characteristic-function values. In turn, our Rule 2's even allocation of interaction effects among players, and Rule 1's tracing of separate effects to individual factors are both consequences of basing allocations on such bargaining powers.

[2] For a fundamental reason why this is so, see also [Ijiri, 1975, p. 184]. Either author's arguments apply quite as forcefully to averaged expansion paths as to individual ones. Much the same point is made by [Loehman and Whinston, 1971, p. 611]; see also [Roth and Verrecchia, 1977, pp. 2-3].

Here's a parallel example, using costs and contraction paths instead of profits and expansion paths. A service department serves three divisions, A, B and C. Here are the

ley approach is defensible here only in terms of its congruence properties, as revealed in Chapter Six.[3]

Marginality Considerations

This conclusion is reinforced by noting the sense in which the Shapley approach's incremental contributions *are* average ones. They will be so only if we assume that each locus must receive either all or none of its demands. For joint-cost allocations, this is equivalent to assuming that each product must either be entirely abandoned at split-off or entirely processed further. As we saw in our discussion of the marginal approach, this necessarily implies constant marginal costs and revenues.

I'll base my demonstration that, under the Shapley approach, each factor must receive either all or none of its demands on the example in [Loehman and Whinston, 1971, pp. 611-12], introducing two additional terms:

λ = The number of expansion (or contraction) paths assumed possible.

Δ = Some finite constant, $\Delta \geqslant 0$.

monthly costs of its serving each possible combination of these divisions:

Combination	Cost	Combination	Cost
ABC	20,000	A	14,000
AB	15,000	B	10,000
AC	16,000	C	12,000
BC	18,000	None	-0-

Let's suppose that the central office wanted to charge each division the amount of service-department costs that it "caused," and wished to calculate this as the cost that would be excaped by eliminating it from the coalition of divisions. In particular, let's focus on Division A.

The company could eliminate divisions in six different orders, resulting in four different amounts that could be saved by discontinuing Division A:

Order of Elimination	Amount Saved by Eliminating A	Explanation From	To
ABC	2,000	ABC	BC
ACB	2,000	ABC	BC
BAC	4,000	AC	C
BCA	14,000	A	None
CBA	14,000	A	None
CAB	5,000	AB	B
Total	41,000		

Averaging these, and charging Division A with the arithmetic mean ($£41,000 \div 6 \cong £6,833$), or, for that matter, with the *harmonic* mean ($\cong £3,767$), does not alleviate the basic ambiguity here. And readers will notice that the greater the number of divisions (or other cost loci), the greater this ambiguity.

[3] For parallel observations, see [Mossin, 1968, p. 469].

and slightly simplifying the authors' notation. Let's begin, as they implicitly do, by assuming that each user must receive all or none of its demands. Then:

$K_\theta = 0$ $FC = FC_{12} = 100$

$K_1 = 2$ $MC_\theta = \Delta$

$K_2 = 1,000$ $MC_1 = 1.0$

$K = K_{12} = 1,002$ $MC_2 = 0.5$

$FC_\theta = 0$ $MC = MC_{12} = 0.5$

$FC_1 = 4$ $\lambda = 2$

$FC_2 = 99$ $C(K) = 601$

$$@(1) = [\{(FC_1 - FC_\theta) + MC_1 \cdot K_1 - MC_\theta \cdot K_\theta\} + \{(FC - FC_2)$$
$$+ MC \cdot K - MC_2 \cdot K_2\}] \div \lambda$$
$$= [\{(4 - 0) + 1.0 \cdot 2 - \Delta \cdot 0\} + \{(100 - 99) + 0.5 \cdot 1,002$$
$$- 0.5 \cdot 1,000\}] \div 2$$
$$= [\{4 + 2 - 0\} + \{1 + 501 - 500\}] \div 2 = 8 \div 2 = 4.$$
$$@(2) = [\{99 + 500 - 0\} + \{96 + 501 - 2\}] \div 2 = 1,194 \div 2 = \overline{597}.$$
$$@(1) + @(2) = 4 + 597 = \underline{601} = C(K).$$

Now, let's slightly relax the author's implicit assumption, by assuming that user 2 might receive either 800 or 1,000 units. There will now be three possible expansion (or contraction) paths. Letting 2 signify the 800-unit case, these paths will be:

X: 1 2 2

Y: 2 1 2

Z: 2 2 1.

Assuming consistent new (starred) values where needed, this gives us the following:

$K_\theta = 0$ $FC_2 = 99$

$K_1 = 2$ $FC = 100$

$K_2 = 800$ $MC_\theta = \Delta$

$K_2 = 1,000$ $MC_1 = 1.0$

$FC_\theta = 0$ $MC_2 = MC_{12} = 0.55^*$

$FC_1 = 4$ $MC_2 = 0.5$

$FC_2 = 84^*$ $MC = 0.5$

$FC_{12} = 86^*$ $\lambda = 3$

                   $C(K) = 601.$

The new average incremental cost of user 1's demands will be:

X: $(4 - 0) + 1.0 \cdot 2 - \triangle \cdot 0$ = 6.0
Y: $(86 - 84) + 0.55 \cdot 802 - 0.55 \cdot 800$ = 3.1
Z: $(100 - 99) + 0.5 \cdot 1,002 - 0.5 \cdot 1,000$ = 2.0   11.1
λ   =   ÷ 3
@(1)   =   3.7

The new average incremental cost of user 2's demands will be the total of the average incremental costs of first supplying 800 units then of providing the additional 200 necessary to make up 1,000:

Incremental cost of the first 800:

X: $(86 - 4) + 0.55 \cdot 802 - 1.0 \cdot 2$ = 521.1
Y: $(84 - 0) + 0.55 \cdot 800 - \triangle \cdot 0$ = 524.0
Z: Same as Y   = 524.0

Incremental cost of the remaining 200:

X: $(100 - 86) + 0.5 \cdot 1,002 - 0.55 \cdot 802$ = 73.9
Y: Same as X   = 73.9
Z: $(99 - 84) + 0.5 \cdot 1,000 - 0.55 \cdot 800$ = 75.0   1,791.9
λ   =   ÷   3
@(2)   =   597.3
@(1) + @(2) = 3.7 + 597.3 = 601 = C(K).

This differs from the previous allocation and, therefore, from the Shapley allocation.

The upshot of this example is that (a) given a particular output, there are an infinite number of expansion paths by which the parties could have attained it[4] and (b) different paths generate different cost allocations. Since only one such allocation is consistent with the Shapley approach, it follows that the Shapley approach must assume that particular (all or none) path. This, in turn, implies that the Shapley approach suffers the same limitations as those of earlier-mentioned schemes that calculate inputs' individual contributions to productive processes in terms of their marginal contributions under assumed expansion or contraction paths.

---

[4] For brevity, I've illustrated only a minute subset of these.

In a later article, Loehman and Whinston [1976, esp. p. 88][5] generalize the Shapley approach to allow for the possibility that some subcoalitions of users are impossible, and that it's no longer true that all possible expansion paths in arriving at a coalition are equally likely. Readers are left to verify that this generalized approach experiences the same ambiguities as those described immediately above.

---

[5] See also [Hillman, 1976].

APPENDIX F

PROOFS THAT THE JIM AND JIL APPROACHES RELIABLY POSSESS THE ISROPM PROPERTIES

by Nancy L. Johnson[1] and Arthur L. Thomas

Chapter Six identified five situations in which it was not to a company's global profit advantage to produce a product, i, jointly:

A. $f_i \geqslant p_i$,

B. $f_i \geqslant x_i$,

C. $f_i < \min|p_i, x_i|$, but $F + J > P$,

D. $f_i < \min|p_i, x_i|$, but $F + J > X$, and

E. $f_i < \min|p_i, x_i|$, $F + J \leqslant \min|P, X|$, but $\Sigma(p_k - x_k) \geqslant P - F - J$.

Case A: $f_i \geqslant p_i$

Under either the JIM or JIL approach, if $f_i \geqslant p_i$ then $j_i = 0$ and, therefore $j_i + f_i = t_i \geqslant p_i$.

Case B: $f_i \geqslant x_i$

Under either the JIM or JIL approach, if $f_i \geqslant x_i$ then $j_i = 0$ and, therefore, $j_i + f_i = t_i \geqslant x_i$.[2]

Hereafter, we must consider the two approaches separately.

JIM

We will begin by proving that, in each of Cases C, D and E, $(F + J) \div Z > 1$. From this result, we will then prove that the JIM approach reliably possesses the ISROPM properties in each case.

Case C: $f_i < \min|p_i, x_i|$, $F + J > P$

Under the JIM approach:

$z_i = \min|(J + f_i), p_i, x_i|$.

Let's suppose that $z_i = J + f_i$. Then $J + f_i \leqslant \min|p_i, x_i|$. Therefore, $J + f_i \leqslant p_i$. But since $F + J > P$, this will be possible only if for some other product, ι, $f_\iota > p_\iota$. But that violates the stipulation that $f_i < \min|p_i, x_i|$. Therefore:

---

[1] Assistant Professor of Accounting, University of Houston.

[2] It will clarify the following proofs if hereafter we use $j_i + f_i$ instead of t_i.

$z_i = \min|p_i, x_i|$; therefore,

$Z \leqslant P$. But, since $P < F + J$,

$Z < F + J$, and $(F + J) \div Z > 1$.

Case D: $f_i < \min|p_i, x_i|, F + J > X$

Under the JIM approach:

$z_i = \min|(J + f_i), p_i, x_i|$.

Let's suppose that $z_i = J + f_i$. Then $J + f_i \leqslant \min|p_i, x_i|$. Therefore, $J + f_i \leqslant x_i$. But since $F + J > X$, this will be possible only if for some other product, $\iota, f_\iota > x_\iota$. But this violates the stipulation that $f_i < \min|p_i, x_i|$. Therefore:

$z_i = \min|p_i, x_i|$; therefore,

$Z \leqslant X$. But since $X < F + J$,

$Z < F + J$ and $(F + J) \div Z > 1$.

Case E: $f_i < \min|p_i, x_i|, F + J \leqslant \min|P, X|, \Sigma(p_k - x_k) \geqslant P - F - J$

$\Sigma(p_k - x_k) \geqslant P - F - J$; therefore,

$\Sigma p_k - \Sigma x_k \geqslant \Sigma p_k + \Sigma p_h - (F + J)$; therefore,

$F + J \geqslant \Sigma x_k + \Sigma p_h$; therefore, $\qquad\qquad$ (1)

$J + \Sigma f_k + \Sigma f_h \geqslant \Sigma x_k + \Sigma p_h$; therefore,

$J + \Sigma f_k \geqslant \Sigma x_k + (\Sigma p_h - \Sigma f_h)$.

Under the JIM approach:

$z_k = \min|(J + f_k), p_k, x_k|$,

which, by definition of k, implies that:

$z_k = \min|(J + f_k), x_k|$.

Since $f_i < \min|p_i, x_i|, (\Sigma p_h - \Sigma f_h) > 0$.

If $J + f_k < x_k$, then in order for $J + \Sigma f_k \geqslant \Sigma x_k + (\Sigma p_h - \Sigma f_h)$ there must be some other k-product, ι, such that $f_\iota > x_\iota$. But this violates the stipulation that $f_i < \min|p_i, x_i|$. Therefore, $z_k = x_k$.

Under the JIM approach:

$z_h = \min|(J + f_h), p_h, x_h|$,

which, by definition of h, implies that:

$z_h = \min|(J + f_h), p_h|$.

Let's suppose that $J + f_h < p_h$. Then $p_h - f_h > J$. Since for all products $f_i < \min|p_i, x_i|$, for all other h-products $p_h - f_h > 0$. Therefore, $\Sigma p_h - \Sigma f_h > J$. But since $f_i < \min|p_i, x_i|, \Sigma x_k - \Sigma f_k > 0$. Therefore:

$\Sigma p_h - \Sigma f_h + \Sigma x_k - \Sigma f_k > J$. Therefore,

$\Sigma p_h - \Sigma f_h + \Sigma p_k + \Sigma x_k - \Sigma f_k > J + \Sigma p_k$; therefore

$(\Sigma p_k + \Sigma p_h) - (\Sigma f_k + \Sigma f_h) - J > \Sigma p_k - \Sigma x_k$; therefore

$P - F - J > \Sigma(p_k - x_k)$.

But this violates the stipulation that $\Sigma(p_k - x_k) \geqslant P - F - J$. Therefore:

$z_h \quad = p_h$; therefore,

$Z \quad = \Sigma x_k + \Sigma p_h$; therefore, from (1),

$F + J > Z$; therefore, $(F + J) \div Z > 1$.

Having proved the foregoing, it is simple to prove that the JIM approach reliably possesses the ISROPM properties in these three cases. First, readers are invited to verify that we've shown that in all such situations $z_i = \min|p_i, x_i|$. Under the JIM approach:

$j_i + f_i \quad = (J + F) \cdot z_i \div Z$; therefore,

$j_i + f_i \quad = (J + F) \cdot \min|p_i, x_i| \div Z$. But since $(F + J) \div Z > 1$,

$j_i + f_i > \min|p_i, x_i|$ and, therefore,

$j_k + f_k > x_k$ and

$j_h + f_h > p_h$, which satisfies the ISROPM properties.

Desirable Joint Products: $f_i < \min|p_i, x_i|$, $F + J \leqslant \min|P, X|$, $\Sigma(p_k - x_k)$
$< P - F - J$

It only remains to prove that when none of Cases A through E hold, and it is to a company's overall profit advantage jointly to produce and sell a product, the JIM approach reliably yields $j_i + f_i < \min|p_i, x_i|$. Under the JIM approach:

$Z \quad = \Sigma \min| (J + f_k), p_k, x_k | + \Sigma \min|(J + f_h), p_h, x_h |$.

From the definitions of k and h, therefore,

$Z \quad = \Sigma \min|(J + f_k), x_k | + \Sigma \min|(J + f_h), p_h |$.

Let's consider the two extreme cases. If these minimums are always $J + f_k$ and $J + f_h$, then obviously $Z > F + J$. If these minimums are always x_k and p_h, then $Z = \Sigma x_k + \Sigma p_h$. But:

$\Sigma(p_k - x_k) < P - F - J$; therefore

$\Sigma p_k - \Sigma x_k < \Sigma p_k + \Sigma p_h - (F + J)$; therefore

$J + F < \Sigma x_k + \Sigma p_h$; therefore

$Z > F + J$.

It should be evident that in all intermediate cases $Z > F + J$ also. Therefore, $(F + J) \div Z < 1$. Under the JIM approach:

$j_i + f_i = (J + F) \cdot z_i \div Z$; therefore,

$j_i + f_i < z_i$. But,

$z_i = \min|(J + f_i), p_i, x_i|$; therefore,

$z_i \leqslant \min|p_i, x_i|$. Therefore,

$j_i + f_i < \min|p_i, x_i|$, which satisfies the ISROPM properties.

JIL

We will begin by proving that in each of Cases C, D and E, $J \div (MIN - F) \geqslant 1$. From this result, we will then prove that the JIL approach reliably possesses the ISROPM properties in each case.

Case C: $f_i < min|p_i, x_i|$, $F + J > P$
By definition, $MIN \leqslant P$. Since $P < F + J$, $MIN < J + F$. Therefore, $J \div (MIN - F) \geqslant 1$.

Case D: $f_i < min|p_i, x_i|$, $F + J > X$
By definition, $MIN \leqslant X$. Since $X < F + J$, $MIN < J + F$. Therefore, $J \div (MIN - F) \geqslant 1$.

Case E: $f_i < min|p_i, x_i|$, $F + J \leqslant min|P,X|$, $\Sigma(p_k - x_k) \geqslant P - F - J$
$\Sigma(p_k - x_k) \geqslant P - F - J$; therefore,

$\Sigma p_k - \Sigma x_k \geqslant \Sigma p_k + \Sigma p_h - (F + J)$; therefore

$-\Sigma x_k \geqslant \Sigma p_h - F - J$; therefore,

$J \geqslant \Sigma p_h + \Sigma x_k - F$. But,

$MIN = \Sigma \min|p_i, x_i|$, and by definition of h and k,

$MIN = \Sigma p_h + \Sigma x_k$; so,

$J \geqslant MIN - F$, and $J \div (MIN - F) \geqslant 1$.

The ISROPM properties will be satisfied if, whenever $J \div (MIN - F) \geqslant 1$, either $j_i + f_i \geqslant p_i$ or $j_i + f_i \geqslant x_i$. First, for any product, k, such that $x_k < p_k$, under the JIL approach:

$j_k = J \cdot (\min|p_k, x_k| - f_k) \div (MIN - F)$; by definition of k,

$j_k = J \cdot (x_k - f_k) \div (MIN - F)$. But since $J \div (MIN - F) \geqslant 1$,

$j_k \geqslant x_k - f_k$; therefore,

$j_k + f_k \geqslant x_k$.

Similarly, for any product, h, such that $x_h \geqslant p_h$:

j_h = $J \cdot (p_h - f_h) \div (MIN - F)$,

$j_h \geqslant p_h - f_h$,

$j_h + f_h \geqslant p_h$.

Desirable Joint Products: $f_i < min|p_i, x_i|$, $F + J \leqslant min|P, X|$, $\Sigma p_k - x_k) < P - F - J$

It only remains to prove that when none of Cases A through E hold, and it is to a company's overall profit advantage jointly to produce and sell a product, the JIL approach reliably yields $j_i + f_i < min|p_i, x_i|$. Since what follows parallels our earlier proofs, we have somewhat compressed its exposition. We know that:

$\Sigma(p_k - x_k) < P - F - J$; therefore,

$\Sigma p_h + \Sigma x_k < J + F$; therefore,

$MIN > J + F$, and $J \div (MIN - F) < 1$.

j_k = $J \cdot (x_k - f_k) \div (MIN - F)$; therefore,

$j_k < x_k - f_k$, and

$j_k + f_k < x_k$. But, by definition, $x_k < p_k$, so

$j_k + f_k < p_k$.

Next, we know that:

j_h = $J \cdot (p_h - f_h) \div (MIN - F)$; therefore,

$j_h < p_h - f_h$, and

$j_h + f_h < p_h$. But, by definition, $x_h \geqslant p_h$, so

$j_h + f_h < x_h$; therefore,

$j_i + f_i < min|p_i, x_i|$. *Q. E. D.*

APPENDIX G

HOW IMPORTANT IS DIVISIONAL AUTONOMY?

If Dobbs and Curtin had ever worked hard in their lives, they would have thought that what they were doing now was the hardest work anywhere in the world. For no employer would they have labored so grindingly as they did now for themselves. — [Traven, 1968, p. 89]

. . . the available empirical research from which one can build a theory is itself not mature, since many of the studies reported are admittedly exploratory. Not one area of inquiry presently being studied has been explored to the minimum limits required by scientific standards. —[Argyris, 1957, p. x]

Any reader of the mathematical programming literature on transfer pricing and internal resource allocation will soon recognize that preservation of divisional autonomy is a major, recurring concern. It's most tempting to take this concern as strong evidence that divisional autonomy *is* important to divisional-manager motivation, innovation and initiative and, thereby, to organizational efficiency. But other explanations are possible.[1]

For one, the *appearance,* but not reality, of autonomy might be valuable in decreasing resistance to central-office leadership. (This phenomenon is familiar in North American highschool student government.) Thus, Haire, Ghiselli and Porter [1966, p. 25] comment:

. . . a manager might advocate these participative practices not because of a belief that he would obtain more initiative, innovation, and the like, but because of a belief that his subordinates would then be more likely to go along with his ideas about the goals of the organization and the way in which jobs should be carried out.

We might call this *ceremonial autonomy.*

---

[1] As a perceptive reader of an earlier draft of this book noted, what follows disregards some structural, sociological features of organizations in which transfer pricing occurs—features that are discussed in such works as [Barnard, 1938], [Cyert and March, 1963], [Etzioni, 1964; 1975] and [Perrow, 1970]. This is deliberate. For doing so reflects the point of view from which most of the transfer-pricing literature that I review is written.

Thus, once again, as I repeatedly did in Chapter Seven, I shall make it as difficult as possible to prove my conclusions by accepting the assumptions of this literature then showing that, even so, its proposals are unsatisfactory.

For another, as Chapter Seven briefly noted, the mathematical programming literature descends from an economics literature of the 1920s and 1930s whose topic was national governments, not individual companies, and whose concern was to maintain traditional Western freedoms under systems of centralized state planning. This literature eventually bogged down, in part for lack of mathematical tools and data-processing equipment adequate to the complex calculations needed.

By the 1950s new tools were available. The literature was revived,[2] but, because of residual computational difficulties (and, perhaps, suggestive of that era's changed political atmosphere), mainly at the individual-company level. Concern over freedom was part of the traditional macro formulation of the planning problem under collectivism. The parallel micro concern for individual companies is divisional autonomy – and it would not be at all surprising had authors continued to worry about freedom even if doing so was no longer as necessary in the new context.

There are additional reasons for such suspicion. This mathematical-programming literature can be very entertaining, partly because many authors are obviously enjoying themselves in the way one might enjoy wrestling with elaborate chess problems. In any literature where there's a strong play element, one would *expect* authors to accept traditional constraints on a problem without questioning them (just as one accepts the received rules of any game). This is not to sneer at this mathematical programming literature: our accounting literature could be greatly improved by a similar delight in play. But it does suggest that we aren't entitled to rely on this widespread concern for divisional autonomy as being proof of its organizational importance.[3]

The remaining literature on transfer pricing doesn't help much, either – though, again, initially it *seems* to. As we saw in Chapter Seven, transfer pricing is requisite to decentralization of companies into profit centres, and although the main reasons for such decentralization probably lie in taxation, regulation and information economies, another common explanation is that decentraliza-

---

[2] See [Kornai, 1967b, pp. 377-79]; this work is a partial exception to what follows.

[3] Readers who are following the argument closely will note that I'm not claiming that this explanation is correct, but merely that I can't disprove it; that's why I cite no sources. Any who wish to pursue these matters might begin with the pre-1940 works indirectly cited in Chapter Seven's footnote 25. There is an embarrassment of intellectual riches here (and in more than one sense).

tion enhances the industry, innovative creativity and general élan of division managers who, given autonomy, supposedly will behave in ways traditional for entrepreneurs. For instance:

> Successful operation of a profit center under a miniature free-enterprise system within the corporate fold calls for talents and experience often summed up by the tag, "He is a good businessman." — [Dean, 1955, p. 72]

> ... a sufficient zone of discretion must be granted to the management of the division so that it will take an entrepreneurial, not a bureaucratic, view of its situation ... — [Heflebower, 1960, p. 12]

> While in the abstract an ideal set of instructions from corporate headquarters could achieve a profit optimum, in practice the incentives of sub-chiefs under a completely authoritarian system may be such as not to elicit their best efforts .... In short, the "profit center" institution attempts to capture the advantages for the corporation of having division heads acting as they would if they were in business for themselves. — [Hirshleifer, 1964, p. 28]

> ... concentration of decision-making responsibility in a small group of individuals at the center—or top—of an organization is inconsistent with research findings on the subject of motivation.—[Caplan, 1971, p. 97]

> The rationale for an internal pricing system is motivated by the *presumed* behavioral advantage of operating autonomous units in a decentralized firm in the absence of externally determined market prices for the internally exchanged commodities. — [Abdel-khalik and Lusk, 1974, p. 8 (italics supplied)] [4]

Abdel-khalik and Lusk's *presumed* is the key to the difficulty here. Save for Caplan, all four authors advance no empirical evidence of such purported behavioral effects of divisional autonomy. Unfortunately, when we scrutinize the research findings to which Caplan refers, the evidence isn't as conclusive as one would like.

---

[4] To varying degrees, these (and related) ideas may also be found in [Cook, 1955, pp. 93-94], [Dean, 1955, pp. 67-68, 70], [Murphy, 1956, pp. 84, 90, 91], [Kline and Martin, 1958, pp. 69-70, 74-75], [Burlingame, 1961, pp. 122, 124, 126], [Likert, 1961a, p. 85], [Dopuch and Drake, 1964, p. 10], [Tannenbaum, 1964, pp. 313-14], [Lemke, 1970, p. 185], [Ronen and McKinney, 1970, pp. 99-101], [Godfrey, 1971, p. 286], Freeland and Baker, 1972, p. 4], [Cushing, 1976, p. 48] and [Solomons, 1977, p. 44·2]. Finally, [Hofstede, 1968, pp. 8-14] offers background and additional bibliographical material.

Maslow's and Herzberg's Work

Once again, initially things look promising. Maslow and Herz-berg[5] provide widely accepted[6] models of human motivation under which one would expect division managers to desire autonomy and (by implication, at least) to satisfy the central office's wants more effectively if granted than if denied it. For instance, Maslow protrays humans as motivated by a hierarchy of basic needs:

1. Physiological (e.g., food and drink),
2. Safety,
3. Belongingness and love,
4. Esteem:
    a. Strength-independence,
    b. Reputation-prestige and
5. Self-actualization,[7]

where higher-level needs (5, 4a, 4b) have motivational impact only after lower-level needs (1, 2, 3) have been satisfied. For our purposes, it's especially important to recognize that the reverse purportedly holds true, too: satisfaction of lower-level needs immediately triggers need at the next-higher hierarchial level,[8] and the "organism is dominated and its behavior organized only by unsatisfied needs" [Maslow, 1970, p. 38]. This implies that if division managers have satisfied their needs through level 3 (as most will have), they will be motivated at either level 4 or 5. Maslow [1970, p. 45] describes the two kinds of level 4 needs as follows:

> These are, first, the desire for strength, for achievement, for adequacy, for mastery and competence, for confidence in the face of the world, and for independence and freedom . . . . Second, we have what we may call the desire for reputation or prestige (defining it as respect or esteem from other people), status, fame and glory, dominance, recognition, attention, importance, dignity or appreciation.

while level 5's self-actualization consists of being true to one's own nature, making one's potential actual, becoming everything one is

---

[5]See [Maslow, 1970], [Herzberg, Mausner and Snyderman, 1964] and [Herzberg, 1966]. Most commentators tend to attribute the entire [Herzberg, Mausner and Snyderman, 1964] accomplishment to Herzberg; for brevity, I shall follow suit. After all, that's a many-to-one allocation.

[6]See [Buckley and McKenna, 1974, pp. 51-52]. Authors influenced include McGregor [e.g., 1960; 1966; 1967], [Haire, Ghiselli and Porter, 1966] and Caplan [1971].

[7]See, for instance, [Maslow, 1970, pp. 35-47] and, for a summary, [Buckley and McKenna, 1974, pp. 50-51].

[8]Except for the need for self-actualization, which is deemed to be unsatiable.

capable of becoming [p. 46].[9] Finally, it's easy to develop from Maslow's work arguments that division managers will make greater contributions to global goals if the company doesn't frustrate their level 4 and 5 needs than if it does—for instance, see McGregor's [1960; 1966; 1967] writings (though, be it noted, McGregor's main concern is with workers and foremen, not managers).

It should be immediately evident[10] that managers are more apt to satisfy their level 4 or 5 needs if their divisions are autonomous than if they aren't. Therefore, on first blush Maslow's work seems to offer solid theoretical underpinning to the assumption that preservation of divisional autonomy is of considerable global benefit to companies.

Likewise Herzberg's work. Herzberg conducted a "study of the sources of job satisfaction and dissatisfaction among managerial and professional people" [McGregor, 1960, p. 55n].

> The factors that lead to positive job attitudes do so because they satisfy the individual's need for self-actualization in his work . . . to develop in one's occupation as a source of personal growth. — [Herzberg, Mausner and Snyderman, 1964, pp. 114-15]

These "satisfiers" offer individuals opportunities to use their training, skills and talents (rather than limiting individuals, forcing them to operate below their levels of competence), and are associated with high motivation and high performance [McGregor, 1966, p. 259].[11] Once again, the apparent implications for the importance of divisional autonomy are obvious and strong.

Empirical Research Results

What, then, is the trouble? Simply that neither Maslow's nor Herzberg's theories are as well supported by empirical research as one would like. Numerous studies have tried to verify or refute key aspects of both, and the evidence is mixed.[12] This isn't to say that either theory has been refuted, but neither has yet been solidly verified, either.

---

[9]What, stripped of its infantile and illegal aspects, the young mean by "doing your own thing."

[10]But if not, see [Caplan, 1971, pp. 48-49] and its context.

[11]See also [Caplan, 1971, p. 49], [Herzberg, Mausner and Snyderman, 1964, pp. 32, 80-82] and [McGregor, 1966, pp. 257-61].

[12]For surveys, see [Cofer and Appley, 1964, pp. 681-92], [Filley and House, 1969, pp. 365-67, 374-78, 382-86], [Filley, House and Kerr, 1976, pp. 183-210], [Buckley and McKenna, 1974, p. 51n], [House and Wigdor, 1975, pp. 106, 111-12], [King, 1975] and [Lawler and Suttle, 1975].

It's hard to tell just how cautious we should be here. Perusal of the surveys just cited reveals that Maslow's theory is enough better supported than Herzberg's that it may be unfair to couple the two. No critics question that Maslow's level 4 and 5 needs (or Herzberg's parallel needs) exist, or deny that they're important in explaining behaviour. But a lay reader is left with an uneasy suspicion that both theories may be oversimplified − and, more important, left unsure how the missing complexities might affect the importance of divisional autonomy.

Part of the trouble is that, except for Herzberg's work and the Vroom, Porter, and Haire, Ghiselli and Porter studies discussed below, little work on motivation has been done at the division-manager level, and even less that relates to the impact of autonomy (and its deprivation) on such managers.[13] The simple fact is that practical concerns over labour relations have dictated that most such research be done at the worker and foreman level.[14] And although it's all very well for McGregor [1966, p. 50] to say that:

> The fundamental characteristics of the subordinate-superior relationship are identical whether one talks of the worker and the supervisor, the assistant superintendent and the superintendent, or the vice president and the president. There are, to be sure, differences in the content of the relationship, and in the relative importance of its characteristics, at different levels of the industrial organization. The underlying aspects, however, are common to all levels.

the point remains that people who become division managers are probably almost as atypical as those who become professors.

Atypical *how*? Not surprisingly, Cummin [1975, pp. 65-66] finds that successful executives are highly motivated toward achievement and power; and Litwin and Stringer [1975, p. 53] observe that people with strong needs for achievement prefer situations in which they can take personal responsibility for finding solutions to problems. But all of this, though consistent with divisional autonomy's being important, is only thin support.[15]

---

[13] "...published findings that dealt with the motivations of executives specifically could not be found..." [Benston, 1963, p. 348*n*]. For a few examples of the kinds of studies—all quite useless in resolving our questions—that *are* common, see [Cofer and Appley, 1964, pp. 784-86].

[14] For instance, save for Vroom's own work, all of the studies summarized in [Vroom, 1964, pp. 115-19, 220-26] are at this level. So are virtually all studies summarized in [Filley and House, 1969, pp. 368-90].

[15] Indeed, one reason for citing these works is to suggest just how little help the typical motivation literature provides our problem.

Vroom's [1960] work is one of the rare instances where a re-searcher investigates motivations at the division-manager level [p. 20]. Unfortunately for our purposes his results were mixed:

> ... attitudes toward the job of low authoritarian persons and of per-sons with high independence needs are favorably affected by opportuni-ties to participate in making decisions in their jobs. On the other hand, the attitudes of highly authoritarian individuals and of individuals with low independence needs are relatively unaffected by this experience. − [p. 35]

Of course, participation isn't the same thing as autonomy, yet this clearly suggests that individual division managers will react dif-ferently to autonomy (or its deprivation), depending on their personalities.[16]

This implication is buttressed by McClelland's [1961, pp. 229-30] strong argument, based on a cross-cultural study of such individuals as Japanese and Russian executives, that autonomy is *not* necessary to produce good entrepreneurial behaviour − and perhaps further supported by Villers' [1954, esp. pp. 92-93, 95-96] evidence that *absolute* autonomy isn't necessary for positive moti-vation. Nor, as Arrow [1964a, pp. 326-27] points out, is there any clear-cut relationship between things that satisfy (or otherwise "favorably affect") people and their efficiencies:

> It is not surprising to one who has read the world's great literature that happiness in the sense of contentment is not apt to be associated with high productivity. − [p. 326]

−especially since we should remember that division managers (again like professors) aren't always fully rational and knowledge-able in their reactions.[17] As before, although none of this is con-clusive, it leaves one uneasy.

A few other authors cast fitful lights on these matters. Likert's [1961a, pp. 20-25] foremen and research scientists were more productive when free to do their own work than when not, but only in situations where there was high interaction and stimulation from their peers.[18] Bass and Leavitt's [1963] three-person teams of managers and supervisors were, on balance, more productive players of the authors' laboratory games if allowed to formulate their own strategies and tactics than if required to follow plans

---

[16] Vroom's conclusions are much richer and much more complex than this brief sum-mary can suggest−see, for instance, [pp. 37, 42, 45, 47-49, 61, 71].

[17] For nice examples of this, in a transfer-pricing context, see [Cushing, 1976].

[18] See also [Likert, 1961a, pp. 7, 77-78, 82-84, 98] for matters loosely connected to our concerns.

devised and administered by others. Argyris [1957, pp. 50-51, 66, 77-79, 81-82] discusses the dysfunctional consequences of frustrating employees' desires for self-actualization — saying, essentially, that if the company controls them too closely this is tantamount to treating them as infants and they're apt to respond by *acting* infantile.

Elsewhere, Argyris [1964, pp. 26, 33-34] traces connections between what correspond to autonomy and self-esteem, and [pp. 183-86] argues that organizations of the kind one would expect would grant little divisional autonomy are poor at developing innovative ideas, self-expression and self-actualization.[19] Finally, Tannenbaum [1964, pp. 302-03] concludes that:

> Individuals who are not able to exercise control [over their work] are, in general, less satisfied with their work situations than those who have some power. But their dissatisfaction often has the quality of apathy and disinvolvement. For the individual in control, added dimentions of personality come into play contributing to the energies which the individual puts into his work, and to the problems he may encounter. The man who exercises control gives more of himself to the organization. He is likely to be more identified, more loyal, more active on behalf of the organization.[20]

and that [pp. 306-312], with certain exceptions, organizations that allow more such control to their employees tend to be more productive than those that don't.[21] This conclusion seems fairly well supported by Rotter's and others' work on internal versus external control—for a survey, see [Rotter, 1966].

Still, once again all this is relatively thin gruel. And Bailey and Boe's [1976, p. 563] observation that "...empirical evidence suggests (divisions exist) that the costs of divisional autonomy are less than its benefits ..." is thin, too, despite the support that it receives from Reece and Cool's [1978] discovery of increasing tendencies to divisionalization. For many divisions aren't autonomous.

Perhaps the strongest empirical evidence of the importance of divisional autonomy comes from Haire, Ghiselli and Porter's

---

[19] See also [1957, p. 181] and [1964, p. 31].

[20] One doubts that as choice an example of rampantly male-chauvinistic language as this would be approved by Tannenbaum's publisher today. Our behaviour may not have changed all that much, but our manners have improved.

[21] Tannenbaum's research was primarily at the worker (rather than manager) level, but not exclusively so.

[1966] study of a large, international sample of managers.[22] This book, which used Maslow's need hierarchy as its conceptual framework, found Anglo-American managers scoring approximately 6 on a 7-point scale of autonomy and self-actualization needs [p. 102], with fairly little variation within countries (especially the U.S.) as to the importance of these to individual managers [pp. 106-07].[23] The authors comment [p. 75]:

> Our results point strongly to the relative salience of Self-Actualization and Autonomy needs for this international sample of managers. It appears obvious, from an organizational point of view, that business firms, no matter in what country, will have to be concerned with the satisfaction of these needs for their managers and executives.

Summary

My lay judgment is that the weight of the evidence surveyed above supports the assumption, traditional to discussions of decentralization and transfer pricing, that deprivations of divisional autonomy can have significantly dysfunctional impacts on satisfaction of central-office wants as a result of the ways that a substantial portion of division managers are apt to react to such deprivations. This is hardly an ironclad conclusion: for instance [Haire, Ghiselli and Porter, 1966]'s results are in uneasy harmony with the implications (discussed earlier) of the Vroom, McClelland and Villers studies. But *most* of the problems of supporting this assumption lie in lack of verification, rather than in confutation. What little we know usually is at least consistent with it. Would that we knew more.

Accordingly, in Chapters Eight through Ten I've taken the autonomy problem seriously. But readers should be aware that, given the problems faced by the behavioral sciences, it's very difficult to obtain clear-cut answers to *any* questions regarding managerial behavior.[24] Human behavior in organizations is just

---

[22] See also [Porter, 1964]. Such of the latter's conclusions (and those of the earlier studies that it cites on [p. 15]) as are important to us here are impounded in the Haire, Ghiselli and Porter book.

[23] There is, though, a joint variation between different countries and different levels of management:

> For example, in England there is a fairly strong trend for lower-level managers to attach more importance to the various needs across all five types of needs. In contrast, there is a trend in the United States (though neither as strong nor as consistent as in England) for higher-level managers to attach greater importance to the different needs. [p. 134]

[24] Skeptics should read [Hopwood, 1976].

too variable and affected by too many other considerations:

> Perhaps the major conclusion to be drawn . . . is that human motivation is so complex that it can only be discussed in simple propositions and dealt with in an abstract and general manner . . . — [Filley and House, 1969, p. 386] [25]

Certainly, here is a place where additional empirical research, directed explicitly at the managerial level, could be most helpful. Certainly, also, this appendix indicates that we should be very cautious of any suggestions that a particular transfer-pricing approach is optimal. For too much depends on how individual managers react. Instead, as was true of joint-cost allocations, we do best merely to list different approaches' congruence properties.

---

[25] See [Filley and House, 1969, pp. 368-90], generally, for background and empirical evidence on the complexity of factors affecting individual productivity—and for evidence that it's dangerous to talk glibly of what motivates people, and how.

ALGEBRAIC AND GRAPHIC ANALYSES OF SITUATIONS WHERE THERE IS NO INTERMEDIATE MARKET

What follows is analytical background on why the Hirshleifer approach cannot simultaneously provide central-office-optimal outputs and preserve divisional autonomies in situations where there is no intermediate market for a transfer good. For brevity, I shall assume linear functions and that there are only two divisions; as elsewhere, relaxation of these assumptions would strengthen my eventual conclusions. I'll begin with an algebraic analysis, then will follow it with a somewhat truncated graphic one, using the following notation throughout:

R = Unit revenue—the external selling price of one unit of output.

TR = Total revenue for a period.

MR = Marginal revenue for a period.

C = Unit cost—the internal cost, exclusive of any transfer prices, of manufacturing or distributing one unit of product.

TC = The total of a period's manufacturing and distributing costs.

MC = Marginal cost for a period.

Q = Periodic output—the number of units of output produced or sold during a period.

P = The unit transfer price that Dst pays to Mfg.

m,d = Subscripts signifying the manufacturing and distributing divisions; thus, C_m is Mfg's unit cost.

$*$ = Superscript signifying central-office optimality; thus, P^* is the central-office-optimal transfer price.

m = Also, superscript signifying that which is selfishly optimal for Mfg; thus P^m is the transfer price when Mfg acts as an internal monopolist.

d = Also, parallel superscript signifying that which is selfishly optimal for Dst; thus, Q^d is the output when Dst acts as an internal monopsonist.

Y = Periodic profit; thus, Y^m is the company's total profit if Mfg acts as an internal monopolist, and Y_m^d is Mfg's book profit if Dst acts as an internal monopsonist.

r,s,t,w,y,z = Constants.

Algebraic Analysis

Our no-inventories assumption implies that $Q_m = Q_d = Q$. We'll designate the company's cost and demand functions as:

$$R = r - w \cdot Q \tag{1}$$
$$C_m = s + y \cdot Q \tag{2}$$
$$C_d = t + z \cdot Q \tag{3}$$

From this, it follows that

$$TR = r \cdot Q - w \cdot Q^2 \tag{4}$$
$$MR = r - 2w \cdot Q \tag{5}$$
$$TC_m = s \cdot Q + y \cdot Q^2 \tag{6}$$
$$TC_d = t \cdot Q + z \cdot Q^2 \tag{7}$$
$$TC = \overline{(s+t) \cdot Q + (y+z) \cdot Q^2} \tag{8}$$

$$MC_m = s + 2y \cdot Q \tag{9}$$
$$MC_d = t + 2z \cdot Q \tag{10}$$
$$MC = \overline{(s+t) + 2(y+z) \cdot Q} \tag{11}$$

From equations (4), (6), (7) and (8) we know that, at any level of output, Q:

$$\begin{aligned} Y &= TR - TC \\ &= [r \cdot Q - w \cdot Q^2] - [(s+t) \cdot Q + (y+z) \cdot Q^2] \\ &= (r\text{-}s\text{-}t) \cdot Q - (w+y+z) \cdot Q^2 \end{aligned} \tag{12}$$

$$\begin{aligned} Y_m &= P \cdot Q - s \cdot Q - y \cdot Q^2 \\ &= (P\text{-}s) \cdot Q - y \cdot Q^2 \end{aligned} \tag{13}$$

$$\begin{aligned} Y_d &= r \cdot Q - w \cdot Q^2 - t \cdot Q - z \cdot Q^2 - P \cdot Q \\ &= (r\text{-}t\text{-}P) \cdot Q - (w+z) \cdot Q^2 \end{aligned} \tag{14}$$

Central-Office Optimum

Our task, therefore, is to specify P and Q. The central-office optimum will occur where marginal revenue equals marginal cost. From equations (5) and (11), this will be where:

$$r - 2w \cdot Q^* = (s+t) + 2(y+z) \cdot Q^*$$
$$2(w+y+z) \cdot Q^* = r\text{-}s\text{-}t$$
$$Q^* = (r\text{-}s\text{-}t) \div 2(w+y+z) \tag{15}$$

The transfer price must persuade Mfg. to produce exactly this output. In maximizing its book profits, Mfg will produce up to the point that its marginal costs equal its marginal revenue. But the transfer price *is* Mfg's marginal revenue. Therefore, from equation (9) we have:

$$P^* = s + 2y \cdot Q^* \tag{16}$$

Mfg an Internal Monopolist

If Mfg acts as an internal monopolist, it will allow Dst only net revenues $(R\text{-}P^m)$ equal to its marginal costs (MC_d) at the output level (Q^m) optimal to Mfg. Thus, the selfishly optimal transfer price, P^m, should be such that, at Q^m, $MR = MC_d + P^m$. From equations (5) and (10) we have:

$$r - 2w \cdot Q^m = t + 2z \cdot Q^m + P^m$$
$$P^m = r - t - 2(w+z) \cdot Q^m \tag{17}$$

As an internal monopolist, Mfg will maximize Y_m. First, we substitute equation (17)'s expression of P^m into equation (13):

$$\begin{aligned} Y_m &= [\, r - t - 2(w+z) \cdot Q^m - s\,] \cdot Q^m - y \cdot Q^{m\,2} \\ &= (r\text{-}s\text{-}t) \cdot Q^m - (2w+y+2z) \cdot Q^{m\,2} \end{aligned} \tag{18}$$

Taking the first derivative with respect to Q^m of equation (18), Y_m will be maximized when:

$$O = (r\text{-}s\text{-}t) - 2(2w+y+2z) \cdot Q^m$$
$$Q^m = (r\text{-}s\text{-}t) \div 2(2w+y+2z) \tag{19}$$

Dst an Internal Monopsonist

If Dst acts as an internal monopsonist, it will allow Mfg only revenues equal to Mfg's marginal costs (MC_m) at the output level (Q^d) optimal to Dst. But these revenues are also the transfer price. So, from equation (9) we have:

$$P^d = s + 2y \cdot Q^d \tag{20}$$

As an internal monopsonist, Dst will maximize Y_d. First, we substitute equation (20)'s expression for P^d into equation (14):

$$Y_d = (r - t - s - 2y \cdot Q^d) \cdot Q^d - (w+z) \cdot Q^{d\,2}$$
$$= (r\text{-}s\text{-}t) \cdot Q^d - (w+2y+z) \cdot Q^{d\,2} \tag{21}$$

Taking the first derivative with respect to Q^d of equation (21), Y_d will be maximized when:

$$O = r - s - t - 2(w+2y+z) \cdot Q^d$$
$$Q^d = (r\text{-}s\text{-}t) \div 2(w+2y+z) \tag{22}$$

Figure H-1 gives examples, calculated from equations (12-17), (19), (20) and (22), of all possible situations where the marginal costs of either division increase, are constant, or decrease. (Beyond assuring that outputs and transfer prices are uniformly positive, no attempt at economic plausibility has been made here.) These examples assume throughout that demand decreases with increasing price.

Both from these examples, and upon inspection of the formulas, it is evident that total profits at the two divisions' selfish optima usually will differ from those at the central-office optimum (the only exception occurs when a divisions' marginal costs are constant, and then only for the selfish optimum of the other division). Therefore, central-office-optimal profits are unattainable unless something prevents the two divisions from seeking to maximize their book profits. Chapter Eight argues that, barring a coincidence of bargaining, this can be accomplished only by central-office intervention.

Graphic Analysis

It's possible to reach the same conclusion by graphic analysis. To avoid visual clutter in Figures, what follows alters our previous assumptions in one, minor respect: demand for the company's final product will be assumed to be constant (horizontal), instead of decreasing with increasing output. Relaxation of this assumption merely pivots the various revenue curves clockwise (their fixed points lying on the Price axis), without changing any results.

Figure H-2 shows a central-office optimum in a situation where the marginal costs of both divisions increase with increasing output. The company maximizes its total profits by producing until its marginal revenues equal its total marginal costs (Point A) at the optimal output, Q*. The company sets the central-office-optimal transfer price, P*, equal to Mfg's marginal cost at output

Figure H-1
Examples of Central-Office and Selfish Optima
Where Divisional Marginal Costs are
Increasing (↑), Constant (→) and Decreasing (↓)

MCm↑ / MCd↑

		Global	Optima Mfg	Optima Dst
r	205			
s	19			
t	10			
w	0.5			
y	1			
z	0.7			
Q		40	25.88	27.50
P		99	132.88	74.00
Y		3,520	3,081.52	3,176.25
Ym		1,600	2,277.65	756.25
Yd		1,920	803.88	2,420.00

MCm→ / MCd↑

		Global	Optima Mfg	Optima Dst
r	205			
s	51			
t	10			
w	0.5			
y	-0-			
z	0.7			
Q		60	30	60
P		51	123	51
Y		4,320	3,240	4,320
Ym		-0-	2,160	-0-
Yd		4,320	1,080	4,320

MCm↓ / MCd↑

		Global	Optima Mfg	Optima Dst
r	205			
s	69			
t	10			
w	0.5			
y	(0.1)			
z	0.7			
Q		57.27	27.39	63.00
P		57.55	129.26	56.40
Y		3,608.18	2,625.99	3,572.10
Ym		(328.02)	1,725.65	(396.90)
Yd		3,936.20	900.34	3,969.00

MCm↑ / MCd→

		Global	Optima Mfg	Optima Dst
r	205			
s	19			
t	36			
w	0.5			
y	1			
z	-0-			
Q		50	37.50	30
P		119	131.50	79
Y		3,750	3,515.63	3,150
Ym		2,500	2,812.50	900
Yd		1,250	703.13	2,250

MCm→ / MCd→

		Global	Optima Mfg	Optima Dst
r	205			
s	51			
t	36			
w	0.5			
y	-0-			
z	-0-			
Q		118	59.00	118
P		51	110.00	51
Y		6,962	5,221.50	6,962
Ym		-0-	3,481.00	-0-
Yd		6,962	1,740.50	6,962

MCm↓ / MCd→

		Global	Optima Mfg	Optima Dst
r	205			
s	69			
t	36			
w	0.5			
y	(0.1)			
z	-0-			
Q		125.00	55.56	166.67
P		44.00	113.44	35.67
Y		6,250.00	4,320.99	5,555.56
Ym		(1,562.50)	2,777.78	(2,777.78)
Yd		7,812.50	1,543.21	8,333.33

MCm↑ / MCd↓

		Global	Optima Mfg	Optima Dst
r	205			
s	19			
t	43			
w	0.5			
y	1			
z	(0.05)			
Q		49.31	37.63	29.18
P		117.62	128.13	77.37
Y		3,525.69	3,327.92	2,938.32
Ym		2,431.51	2,690.66	851.69
Yd		1,094.18	637.26	2,806.63

MCm→ / MCd↓

		Global	Optima Mfg	Optima Dst
r	205			
s	51			
t	43			
w	0.5			
y	-0-			
z	(0.05)			
Q		123.33	61.67	123.33
P		51.00	106.50	51.00
Y		6,845.00	5,133.75	6,845.00
Ym		-0-	3,422.50	-0-
Yd		6,845.00	1,711.25	6,845.00

MCm↓ / MCd↓

		Global	Optima Mfg	Optima Dst
r	205			
s	69			
t	43			
w	0.5			
y	(0.1)			
z	(0.05)			
Q		132.86	58.13	186.00
P		42.43	109.69	31.80
Y		6,177.86	4,233.14	5,189.40
Ym		(1,765.10)	2,702.81	(3,459.60)
Yd		7,942.96	1,520.33	8,649.00

Q* (Point B); equivalently, this transfer price is set so that the per-unit revenue less the transfer price (Dst's net revenue) equals Dst's marginal costs at output Q* (Point C). This equivalence results in the internal-market-clearing intersections of the R-MC$_d$ and MC$_m$ curves at point B and the R-MC$_m$ and MC$_d$ curves at point C. Total company profit equals area DGA. Mfg's and Dst's book profits are areas EHB and FIC, respectively; their total equals area DGA, though that's not visually obvious.

Mfg An Internal Monopolist

However, both divisions can improve their book profits at the expenses of the other divisions and the company as a whole. In Figure H-3, Mfg acts as an internal monopolist. As such, it will

Figure H-2

A Central-Office Optimum
$(MC_m \uparrow, MC_d \uparrow)$

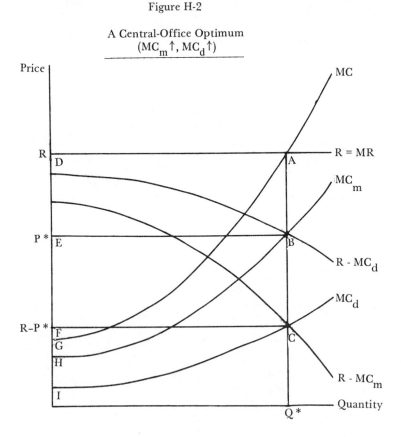

Figure H-3

Mfg an Internal Monopolist
$$(MC_m \uparrow, MC_d \uparrow)$$

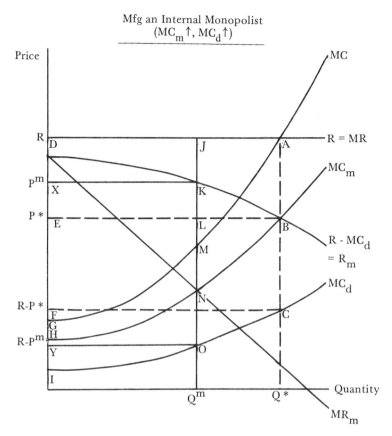

maximize its book profits by having Dst's net revenues $(R\text{-}P^m)$ exactly equal Dst's marginal costs at whatever output level, Q^m, is selfishly optimal for Mfg. Thus, Mfg's revenue curve effectively becomes the per-unit revenues less these marginal costs, or the $R\text{-}MC_d$ line. Line MR_m is the related *marginal* revenue curve; its intersection with Mfg's marginal cost curve (Point N) determines the selfishly optimal output, Q^m. *At* that output, Mfg's per-unit revenue is P^m, the selfishly optimal transfer price (see Point K). Total company profit is now area DGMJ — less than the central-office optimum by an amount equal to area JMA. Dst's book profit, area YIO, is also clearly smaller than its profit at the central-office optimum, FIC. But Mfg's new book profit, XHNK, exceeds its central-office-optimal book profit, EHB, by the amount that area XELK exceeds area LNB.

Dst An Internal Monopsonist

Figure H-4 shows what happens if, instead, Dst acts as an internal monopsonist. As such, it will maximize its book profits by setting a transfer price equal to Mfg's marginal costs at whatever output level, Q^d, is selfishly optimal for Dst. Thus, Dst's revenue curve effectively becomes the per-unit revenues less these marginal costs, the R-MC^m line.

Line MR_d is the related marginal revenue curve; its intersection with Dst's marginal cost curve (Point O) determines the selfishly optimal output, Q^d. The minimum transfer price necessary to get Mfg to produce that output, P^d, occurs at Point M, the intersection of output Q^d and Mfg's marginal cost curve. Total company profit is now area DGLJ, less than central-office-optimal profit DGA by area JLA. Mfg's book profit has fallen to area XHM, considerably less than its central-office-optimal profit of EHB. But

Figure H-4

Dst an Internal Monopsonist
$(MC_m\uparrow, MC_d\uparrow)$

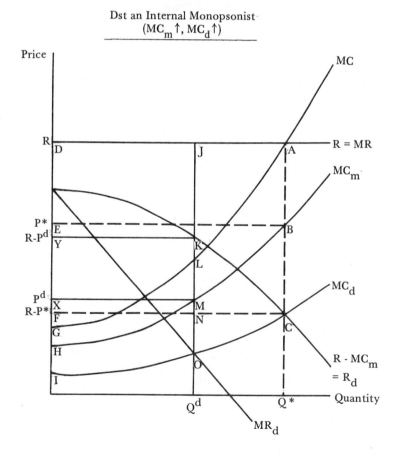

Dst's new book profit, area YIOK, exceeds its central-office-optimal book profit, FIC, by the amount that area YFNK exceeds area NOC.

Constant Marginal Costs

Figure H-5 reflects a situation in which Mfg's marginal costs are constant while Dst's increase with output. Once again, the central-office optimum (Point A) occurs at an output of Q*. Mfg will produce this output if the transfer price, P*, equals its marginal costs (Point B). Since the latter are horizontal, the transfer price and the MC_m line coincide, and Mfg's book profits are zero. This is characteristic of such situations. Accordingly, Dst's book profit, area GHC, equals the total profit, area DEA. If Dst were to act as an internal monopsonist, it couldn't improve on this book profit, so Dst's selfishly optimal output and transfer price are also Q* and P*.

Figure H-5

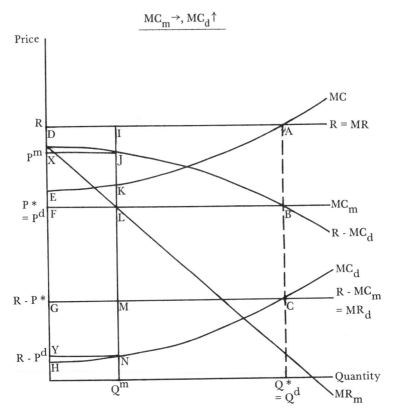

$$MC_m \rightarrow, MC_d \uparrow$$

However, Mfg can improve its book profits if it acts as an internal monopolist. Following the same logic as in Figure H-3, it would reduce output to Q^m and set a transfer price of P^m. Total profits would fall to area DEKI, and Dst's book profit to YHN. But Mfg's book profit would increase from zero to area XFLJ.

Figure H-6 gives the parallel analysis when Dst's marginal costs are constant. At the central-office optimum, total profit is area DFA, Mfg's book profit is the equal area EHB, and Dst's book profit is zero. Mfg's selfish optimum is the global one but, by the same logic as in Figure H-4, Dst can maximize its book profits (to YGLJ) by reducing output to Q^d. The new, reduced total profit and Mfg's book profit become areas DFKI and XHM, respectively.

Figure H-6

$$\underline{MC_m \uparrow, MC_d \rightarrow}$$

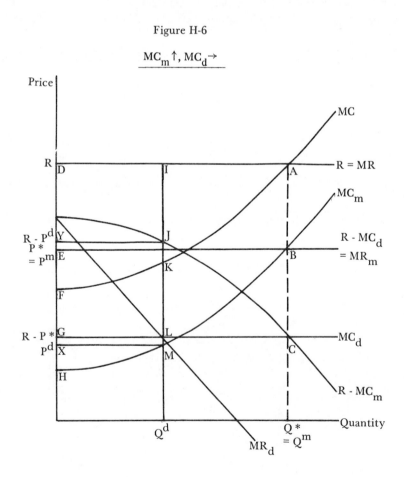

Declining Marginal Costs

Graphic analysis becomes a bit messy when marginal costs decline. However, Figure H-7 gives an instance, a case where Mfg's marginal costs decline while Dst's increase with increasing output. As before, the central-office-optimal output, Q*, occurs where MR = MC (Point A). By the same logic as in Figure H-2, this results in the central-office-optimal transfer price being such that, at this central-office-optimal output, Dst's net revenues equal its

Figure H-7

$$MC_m \downarrow, MC_d \uparrow$$

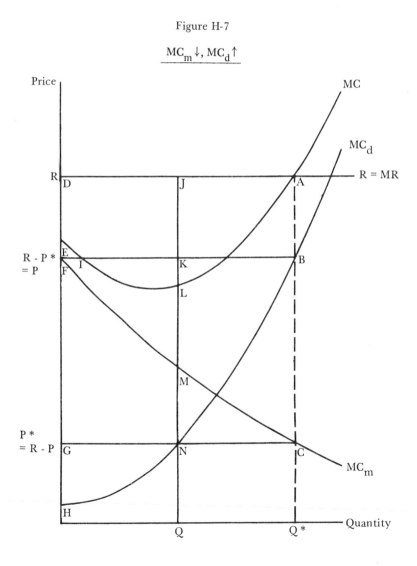

marginal costs (Point B); this gives the transfer price, P*, shown at Points C and G. Total profits are area DEILA. Mfg's book profits are *negative* (area FGC), whereas Dst's book profits, area FHB, exceed the total profits.

Figure H-7 makes no attempt to calculate selfishly optimal outputs, but Mfg can obviously make its book profits positive if it reduces output to, say, Q, and increases the transfer price to P. Mfg's book profit then becomes the positive area FMK. (I set Q at the intersection of P* and the MC_d curve merely to keep Figure H-7 as simple as possible; this coincidence has no other significance.

Readers may verify that Dst can also improve its book profits.

APPENDIX I

SHAPLEY ALLOCATIONS AS A GENERAL
SOLUTION TO THE ALLOCATION PROBLEM?

During the last decade, the accounting literature has often been enlivened by attempts to show that exogenous concepts or techniques are pertinent to our discipline. Even when these exotics have real merit for accounting, some researchers are apt to perceive them as offering broader solutions to our problems than, in sober hindsight, they eventually turn out to possess.

Such recent papers as [Hamlen, Hamlen and Tschirhart, 1977], [Hughes and Scheiner, 1977], [Jensen, 1977], [Roth and Verrecchia, 1977] and [Callen, 1978] could inspire like enthusiasm: Unwary readers could conclude from them that Shapley allocations offer a general solution to accounting's allocation problems. We've seen that they don't, and what follows is designed to drive this point home. But before beginning, I want to emphasize that nothing here is intended to disparage the papers just cited. They have revived important techniques and concepts that we were unwise to disregard when Shubik [1964] first raised them in an accounting context.[1]

Limitations of the Shapley Approach

I repeat: The danger is enthusiasm, not flaws in the Shapley approach. The latter is elegant, powerful, commodious and (as one discovers when experimenting with it) surprisingly subtle. It probably has valuable accounting applications. But, like all human inventions, it's also limited. Chapters Six, Ten and Eleven and Appendix E revealed some of these limitations. The Shapley approach:

 1. Is only one of a group of possible stable allocation procedures that fall within the core,

 2. Is based on assumptions that contradict important facts of real-world business life,

 3. Like all opportunity-cost (and -revenue) approaches:

  a. Is subject to gaming,

  b. Is transparently (or, at least, translucently) manipulative, thereby risking perverse élan effects,

---

[1] Personal correspondence reveals that at least three of these articles were initially written independently of each other. So was a precursor of my Chapters Four and Six. Perhaps Shapley allocations are an idea whose accounting time has come.

    c. Suffers from what I've called the expansion-path problem,

    d. Confuses evaluations of products, divisions and their managers (doing so in both its joint-cost and transfer-price applications), and thereby

    e. Suffers (in its transfer-price application, anyway) from what I've called the evaluation paradox,

    4. To generalize, like all one-to-many allocation approaches, is behaviour-congruent only with respect to some decisions, circumstances and central-office goals, its impact elsewhere being perverse,

and has various other, specific limitations in its joint-cost and transfer-price applications.

We saw point 4 illustrated in detail only for joint-cost allocations. But the brief discussions of Shapley transfer-price allocations at the end of Chapter Ten and the middle of Chapter Eleven suggest that an equally detailed analysis would reach the same conclusions for transfer pricing. Similarly, detailed analysis of the sort that [Thomas, 1974, Ch. 6] gave a behavior-congruent financial-accounting allocation approach (estimation theory), coupled with the results of Chapter Six and Appendix E, would reveal like limits to the Shapley approach's utility in financial accounting.[2] Since this book has placed the burden of proof squarely on those who would assert otherwise, I'll not go through the arguments here.[3]

---

[2] Callen [1978, *passim*] explicitly proposes such utility. Suggestions of it may also be found in [Mossin, 1968, pp. 464-66] and [Loehman and Whinston, 1971]. Callen accurately summarizes some of my main concerns about financial accounting's allocations with an efficiency that I've never been able to attain. I'm also in broad agreement with his exposition of the Shapley approach's implications. But, just as he [p. 307] finds my pessimism premature, I find his optimism a result of framing his inquiry too narrowly.

[3] Suffice for the nonce to observe two things besides the points raised in Chapters Six and Ten and Appendix E. First, Callen's [1978, p. 307] criterion for the acceptability of an allocation method is:

> Does the procedure satisfy a "reasonable" set of cost allocation axioms with respect to which it alone is optimal? Provided these axioms are perceived to be "reasonable" to those concerned, statement users and accountants, the allocation technique can be defended against rival approaches.

One trouble with this is that users will naturally judge the reasonableness of axioms (in Callen's sense) by their *results* – that's to say, by their congruence properties (or failures thereof). Real managers just don't accept plausible-sounding axioms then bravely live with their purported consequences, good or ill (especially when, as here, the calculations that determine these consequences are opaque to the laity).

Second, many financial-accounting allocations (such as depreciation) are of costs that can't, or can't entirely, be escaped by shutdown. As we saw in Chapter Four, the Shapley approach is unable to cope with such costs. Therefore, there is an important set of financial accounting allocations to which the Shapley approach is just irrelevent.

Figure I-1

A Joint Process and Its Earlier
Characteristic Function and Shapley Allocations

J	n_i	f_i	p_i		x_i
	32	38	70	W	∞
40	62	24	86	X	∞
	14	30	44	Y	∞

C	$v(C)$	C	$v(C)$
θ	0	WX	54
W	0	WY	6
X	22	XY	36
Y	0	WXY	68

Locus	j_i	t_i	b_i
W	15	53	17
X	19	43	43
Y	6	36	8
Total	40	132	68

A Final Example

However, we might conclude with a final instance of the Shapley approach's extreme sensitivity to things that seemingly are irrelevant to most decisions that are based (or are purported to be based) on one-to-many allocations.[4] Figure I-1 repeats the example of a joint process given in Figures 4-6, 4-7 and 4-10. In order to make discussions of Shapley joint-cost allocations compatible with those of other joint-cost allocation techniques, I've heretofore implicitly assumed that this example reflects a game with only three players, Divisions W, X and Y. But, of course, the central office may want to treat the joint producer (the division that incurs the £40 joint cost) as a profit centre, too. Let's denote it as Division J. Then, since the joint process is essential to the other divisions' activities yet can earn nothing by itself, we may calculate the revised characteristic function, consistent with this new situation, that is shown in the top part of Figure I-2.

[4] This analysis is based on [Butterworth, 1977].

Figure I-2

Same As Figure I-1, Except That
The Joint Producer is a Player

C	v(C)	C	v(C)
θ	0	WX	0
J	0	WY	0
W	0	XY	0
X	0	JWX	54
Y	0	JWY	6
JW	0	JXY	36
JX	22	WXY	0
JY	0	JWXY	68

Locus	j_i	t_i	b_i
J	(26.83)	(26.83)	26.83
W	20.83	58.83	11.17
X	37.17	61.17	24.83
Y	8.83	38.83	5.17
Total	40.00	132.00	68.00

Figure I-3

Same As Figure I-1, Except That the Central
Office Is a Player, and Is Essential for
Coordination of Coalitions of Two or More Divisions

C	v(C)	C	v(C)
θ	0	WX	22*
C	0	WY	0
W	0	XY	22*
X	22	CWX	54
Y	0	CWY	6
CW	0	CXY	36
CX	22	WXY	22*
CY	0	CWXY	68

*See Chapter Four's Rule 7; this two-member coalition can earn £22 by de-
volving into a single-member, X coalition.

Locus	j_i	t_i	b_i
C	(15.83)	(15.83)	15.83
W	20.83	58.83	11.17
X	26.17	50.17	35.83
Y	8.83	38.83	5.17
Total	40.00	132.00	68.00

The bottom part of Figure I-2 shows the revised Shapley alloca- tions;[5] the differences from those at the bottom of Figure I-1 are substantial. Exactly the same numerical results (though with different labels) may be obtained by following Baumes [1963, pp. 34, 39], Shubik [1964, e.g. p. 211] and Hass [1968, p. B·329] and treating the central office (instead of the joint producer) as an additional player, C, whose coordination of Divisions W, X and Y is essential. Alternatively, it might happen that (a) if need be, Divisions W, X and Y could each set up and exploit their own joint process without central-office coordination, (b) the central office is essential for coordination of coalitions of two or more further- processing divisions and (c) the central office doesn't want to treat the joint producer as a cost centre. Figure I-3 shows the resulting characteristic function and Shapley allocations.

Readers are invited to verify that the ratios of lowest to highest book profits in these three Figures are respectively 66%, 58% and 65% for products W, X and Y. Yet, this mutability depends far less on the public facts of the company's situation than on the central office's private choice of which loci shall be profit centres.

---

[5] It was with some reluctance that I included the j_i and t_i columns in Figure I-2, for the negativity of j_J and t_J is troublesome. All joint products have zero split-off values, so p_J *per se* is zero. Yet, since J is an essential process, the Shapley approach must assign a positive book profit to it. $t_J = p_J - b_J$ and b_J is positive, so t_J must be negative. Since there is no f_J as such, j_J must be negative, too.

I confess to being unable to give an economic interpretation to these negativities. Yet the logic of the related Shapley *profit* allocation seems unassailable. Am I just being dense?

APPENDIX J

NOTES ON VARIOUS INDIVIDUAL MATHEMATICAL PROGRAMMING APPROACHES

What follows is not so much a survey of the mathematical programming approaches discussed in Chapter Ten as a series of notes on a small sample drawn from their vast literature. Readers are warned that this appendix's individual sections are loosely integrated with Chapter Ten, but not with each other. Thus, read front-to-back, its organization is choppy. Moreover, with each work considered I've done no more than to raise points that might be of interest to a *novice* who wishes to read further in what, despite its seeming lack of practical utility, remains a most interesting literature.

Were I starting afresh in this literature, I'd begin with the relevant parts of [Hayek, 1944] and [Koopmans, 1957], then turn to [Baumol and Fabian, 1964], [Kornai and Lipták, 1965], [Hass, 1968], [Charnes, Clower and Kortanek, 1967] and [Freeland, 1973], in that order. The last though relatively uncited in the literature to date, belongs in any good accounting research library (as does the equally uncited [Wells, 1973b]).

[Arrow, 1959], [Arrow and Hurwicz, 1960]

These offer a globally optimizing, mathematical programming approach to decentralization that predates Dantzig and Wolfe's [1960; 1961] seminal decomposition procedure and is closely related to certain proposals made by economists during the 1930s.[1] Instead of a central office and divisions, the authors [1960, pp. 76, 80-81] have a "custodian" setting prices for an internal buyer and internal sellers, respectively called a "helmsman" and "process managers."[2] The custodian controls internal externalities by manipulating transfer (shadow) prices to clear the internal market. Readers may verify that these manipulations will be destructive of both what correspond to divisional autonomies and the significance of divisional book profits for evaluating managers' performances.

---

[1] For background, see [Malinvaud, 1967, pp. 180-86] and the first approach proposed in [Whinston, 1964].

[2] See also [Arrow, 1959, pp. 13-15].

274

[Dantzig and Wolfe, 1960; 1961], *[Baumol and Fabian, 1964]*

The two articles by Dantzig and Wolfe introduced the decomposition procedure, whereby a large mathematical programming (in this case, *linear* programming) problem could be divided into a set of smaller subproblems. Iterative solution of these yields the same end results as direct solution of the original large program would, while making much less demands on computer capacity. Baumol and Fabian recognized both the economic interpretation that could be given the decomposition algorithm by perceiving the subproblems as being solved by a company's central office and individual divisions, and the great information economies that this would yield for decentralization: the central office need have none of the detailed knowledge that the divisions use to solve their subproblems.[3] I'll denote the procedure common to all three articles by the authors' intials: DWBF; the DWBF approach has been immensely influential.

Technically, unlike subsequent price- and resource-directive algorithms the DWBF approach is book-profit-directive. That's to say, it motivates division-manager decisions by starting with the central office's specifying initial (unit) book profit figures then, in the successive iterations, modifying these by tariffs and subsidies similar to Hirshleifer's and reflective of the divisions' internal externalities:

> ... the decomposition procedure provides each division with net profit figures which are designed to compensate for the extenal economies and diseconomies caused by its activities. This is the secret of the procedure, the means whereby it achieves results that are optimal for the operation as a whole, though decision making remains decentralized, at least in form. − [Baumol and Fabian, 1964, p. 12]

The final clause, "at least in form," is significant. Besides the threats to divisional autonomies inherent in all such iterative algorithms[4] (discussed generally in Chapter Ten), the DWBF approach requires an exceptionally vigourous terminal intervention by the central office. In effect, the central office uses the mathematical programming iterations to discover what globally optimal outputs would be, then imposes these, directly and

---

[3] It also happens that Baumol and Fabian give what a non-mathematician will still find to be one of the clearest intuitive explanations of how such decomposition procedures work.

[4] For the iterative nature of the DWBF approach, see [Dantzig and Wolfe, 1960, pp. 101-02] and [Baumol and Fabian, 1964, pp. 3-5].

dictatorially, on the divisions.[5] Finally, under the DWBF approach divisional book profits are administered with equal vigour – and, as artifacts of the algorithm, are of scant significance for evaluation of division managers' performances.

[Kornai and Lipták, 1965], [Kornai, 1967a; 1967b; 1973]

Kornai and Lipták [1965] introduced resource-directive mathematical programming algorithms to the West, using a polyhedral game that, like Dantzig and Wolfe's [1960; 1961] decomposition procedure, was designed to make numerical solution of the mathematical program computer feasible.[6] Though designed for socialist central planning of industries (and, potentially, of entire national economies), Kornai and Lipták's approach is easily adapted to the micro level of an individual company and its divisions,[7] and has stimulated much subsequent research at this level.

[Kornai, 1967b, pp. 345-46, 355-65] gives a good picture of the iterative nature of this approach, while [Freeland and Baker, 1972, p. 26] brings out clearly how this iterative process threatens divisional autonomy. Chapter Ten's comments on the difficulties that such processes encounter were written with Kornai's and Lipták's work explicitly in mind.

[Whinston, 1964]

This work, which is fairly heavily cited in the literature, offers two approaches to decentralization. In one, similar to that of [Arrow, 1959] and [Arrow and Hurwicz, 1960], the central office manipulates transfer (and other) prices, raising them if particular resources are in excess internal demand and lowering them if they are in excess internal supply. Divisions are directed to maintain activities having zero profitabilities at a constant level, not engage in those with negative profitability and expand those with positive profitability. Therefore, at the central-office optimum all divisions report zero book profits on all activites.

Whinston's other approach is, in effect, the DWBF one.[8] My comments elsewhere on this approach apply here, too. Whinston's first approach inspired Chapter Ten's comment that mathematical

---

[5] See [Baumol and Fabian, 1964, pp. 2, 14-18], [Littlechild, 1970b, p. 325n], [Godfrey, 1971, pp. 292-93], [Abdel-khalik and Lusk, 1974, pp. 17-18], [Kydland, 1975, pp. 1029-30] and [Bailey and Boe, 1976, p. 561].

[6] See [Kornai and Lipták, 1965, pp. 141-43, 153-55] and [Ruefli, 1969, p. 63].

[7] As in [Burton, Damon and Loughridge, 1974].

[8] See [Whinston, 1964, pp. 421-23, 432-35, 438] for the matters summarized here, and [Whinston, 1962] for background.

programming algorithms yield book profits that are useless for evaluating any dimension of division managers' performances beyond their abilities to follow orders.

[*Samuels, 1965; 1969*]

The first of these works offers a linear programming approach to charging production departments for the services of service departments, these being very broadly interpreted to include such things as charges for floor space, supervision and machinery. As such, it is an excellent example of the overlap between transfer-pricing and joint-cost-allocation algorithms. Samuels' procedure here is an opportunity-cost analogue of Hirshleifer's procedures, and is subject to the same strictures. Besides, this approach leaves divisions with zero book profits at its final iteration, requiring terminal intervention by the central office to ensure central-office optimization.[9]

[Samuels, 1969] is similar: a linear programming approach whereby tariffs and subsidies similar to Hirshleifer's are used to motivate divisions to (central-office) optimize such things as their outputs and sales to outsiders. The subsidies reach maxima at the central-office optimum, but are otherwise arbitrary — chosen solely to motivate the desired managerial behavior. Finally, this is an everyone-first approach.[10]

As an alternative, Samuels [1969, p. 34] suggests attaining central-office optima by such devices as having the central office present demand schedules to the divisions. But the familar problems of autonomy and evaluation persist.

[*Balas, 1966*]

Balas' approach resembles Dantzig and Wolfe's [1960; 1961] in being one where the central office massively intervenes at the end of an iterative process, to dictate divisional decisions.[11] Kydland [1975, p. 1030] comments apropos both approaches:

> ... the solution with the final revised prices is usually not unique, and the divisions cannot find the correct one among the infinitely many alternative solutions without further information. The final step will generally involve delegating not only the final prices, but also weights for the divisions to use on solutions from previous iterations, which means that the central unit essentially tells the divisions what action to take, and the prices may have little importance at the end.

---

[9] All of the foregoing points are implicit in [Samuels, 1965, pp. 186-7]; see also [Kaplan, 1977, p. 14]. For additional comments, see [Bernhard, 1968] and [Manes, 1970, pp. 565*n*, 568-69].

[10] For the foregoing, see especially [Samuels, 1969, pp. 36-37].

[11] For instance, see [Balas, 1966, pp. 848, 851-53, 858-60].

Differences between the Balas and DWBF approaches[1][2] aren't significant for our purposes.

[Charnes, Clower and Kortanek, 1967], [Charnes and Kortanek, 1968]

These impound another attempt to deal with the stock problem of making divisions aim for maximization of global profits rather than maximization of their own book profits. Here, the central office tries to accomplish this by imposing a set of preemptive goals[13] on the divisions, enforcing these with heavy penalties for deviations.

Just as Hirshleifer's transfer prices indirectly dictated divisional outputs, so these preemptive goals indirectly dictate divisions' behavior and, despite the authors' claims to the contrary,[14] the upshot for divisional autonomies is much the same as with Hirshleifer's approach.[15] Finally, to the extent that this approach does get divisions to maximize global profits contrary to what otherwise would be their selfish interests, it renders their individual book profits ambiguous for evaluation purposes.[16]

[Hass, 1968]

Hass [1968] developed his quadratic programming algorithm out of concern (a) to avoid terminal interventions by the central office[17] and (b) that the linearity assumptions made by Dantzig and Wolfe [1960; 1961] and Baumol and Fabian [1964] are unrealistic:

> ... it is the general consensus that most industries are oligopolistic in nature; consequently, the flat demand and supply curves required by linear programming are not truly representative. The linear decomposition model also fails to take into account any type of demand or supply dependence, which involve, at a minimum, the product of the interacting variables in their mathematical formulation. — [Hass, 1968, p. B·312][18]

[12] See [Balas, 1966, pp. 859-60].

[13] Preemptive goals are merely goals placed in a priority order–see [Charnes, Clower and Kortanek, 1967, pp. 309-310] and [Abdel-khalik and Lusk, 1974, p. 18].

[14] For instance, [Charnes, Clower and Kortanek, 1967, p. 297].

[15] Contrast [Kydland, 1975, p. 1030]; but see [p. 1038].

[16] For matters discussed in this subsection, see [Charnes, Clower and Kortanek, 1967, pp. 296, 304-07, 310, 314-15]; for background, see [Charnes and Kortanek, 1968].

[17] See, for instance, [Hass, 1968, pp. B·329-30].

[18] See [pp. B·311-13], generally. For background, see [Charnes and Kortanek, 1968].

Nonetheless, the central office actively intervenes, manipulating division managers by presenting them with terminal demand and supply functions rigged to generate their central-office-optimal behaviour in the same way that Hirshleifer's demand and supply functions (discussed at the beginning of Chapter Nine) were designed to function. In effect, once again the central office specifies the transfer prices that will clear the internal market.[19] Moreover, the central office also intervenes decisively in determining just when iterations will terminate,[20] and in a few other, relatively minor, ways.[21]

The resulting central-office administration of divisional book profits would, by itself, suffice to confound evaluations of managers' individual performances. But this is aggravated by the approach's susceptability to gaming[22] and its penchant for allocating all interaction (synergistic) effects of divisional activities 100% to each division[23] (in what corresponds to an everyone-first way).

[Weitzman, 1970]

Under this iterative, resource-directive approach, the central office begins by stipulating input and output quantities. Divisions then argue with the central office that technological considerations make these unfeasible. The central office responds by changing its plans, and iterations continue until a feasible central-office optimum is attained.[24]

Like Chapter Ten's satisficing approaches, Weitzman's preserves substantial divisional autonomy – or, at least, its *appearance*. For division managers are likely to perceive themselves arguing with the central office, and "winning" often enough to preserve their self-images of running semi-independent operations. However (and also like the satisficing approaches), transfer prices and book

---

[19] See [Hass, 1968, pp. B·313-316, B·319, B·327, B·329-30]. Contrast [Bailey and Boe, 1976, p. 561].

[20] See [Godfrey, 1971, pp. 292-93].

[21] [Hass, 1968, pp. B·319, B·327]. See [Abdel-khalik and Lusk, 1974, p. 19] for additional problems here.

[22] [Hass, 1968, p. B·330].

[23] And to the central office itself, for that matter—see [Hass, 1968 pp. B·329-30].

[24] As the author points out [p. 62], this procedure is dual to the Dantzig-Wolfe [1960; 1961] price-directive one in several respects.

profits will still fluctuate drastically from iteration to iteration.[25] They are unstable, administered and, once again mere artifacts of the algorithm. Therefore, they don't really measure the managers' performances — something that sooner or later is bound to become apparent to them.[26]

[Onsi, 1970; 1974], [Talwar, 1974]

Onsi is especially concerned to make transfer prices behavior-congruent with respect to innovation decisions. His procedure resembles everyone-first ones in that total divisional book profits will exceed the global profit.[27] It's especially evident that the manufacturing division's book profits are administered here — they're whatever it pleases the central office to make them. But so are the distribution divisions' book profits, which impound most or all of the cost savings from the *manufacturing* division's innovation.[28] Finally, Onsi's approach is subject to gaming.[29]

[Godfrey, 1971], [Hayhurst, 1976]

Godfrey's approach differs considerably from other mathematical programming ones. His central office begins [p. 290] by obtaining complete knowledge of each division's situation, production function and the like. It then solves a large linear programming problem:

> . . . and from the solution calculates the amount of corporate resources to be allocated to each division. A report is sent to each division which includes:
>
> (a) Amount of corporate resources allocated,
> (b) Minimum expected profit contribution,
> (c) A *suggested* plan of operations.

---

[25] Weitzman [1970, p. 54] comments:
> The approach taken here views the planning procedure as a learning process whereby the center iteratively comes to understand more and more exactly the relevant parts of the production possibilities sets without ever requiring any firm to transmit the entire set.

It's this very designing of the algorithm to serve the central office's needs (for central-office optimization and for learning, but not learning so much as to sacrifice information economies) that would help eventually render the resulting transfer prices arbitrary-seeming from the vantage points of division managers.

[26] See [Weitzman, 1970, pp. 50-51, 61-63] for matters discussed in this subsection.

[27] See [Talwar, 1974, pp. 126-27] and [Onsi, 1974, pp. 130-31].

[28] See [Onsi, 1970, pp. 537-38].

[29] See [Talwar, 1974, p. 127]; that Talwar's approach is too ([Onsi, 1974, pp. 130-31]) is neither here nor there.

... the word "suggested" is stressed since there will be no control by central headquarters over the actual plan employed by a division .... the divisions are free to alter their operational strategies and to improve their book contribution potential above the minimum level specified by central headquarters. − [Godfrey, 1971, pp. 290-91]

Godfrey asserts that this procedure will preserve the desired consequences of divisional autonomy.[30] Hayhurst [1976, pp. 101-03] makes a similar proposal.

There are two main difficulties with Godfrey's approach. First, of course, it sacrifices any information economies and, with them, one of the main rationales for decentralization. More important to our analysis, the divisional book profits calculated under the centralized linear programming solution (upon which division managers are invited to improve) will have all the dysfunctional characteristics of Chapter Ten's mathematical programming book profits save those that arise from iteration. One is back in the situation of students encouraged to improve arbitrary grades.

[Jennergren, 1971; 1972; 1973]

Jennergren proposes a quadratic programming procedure whereby the central office responds to excessive demands for resources by raising their internal prices by non-constant amounts.[31] Save for this, his approach doesn't differ significantly (for our purposes) from Chapter Ten's generalized description of other price-directive methods: Divisions' book profits are to be determined by iterative exchanges with a manipulative central office, and are artifacts of the algorithm used.[32]

[Kydland, 1975]

This is a variation on [Dantzig and Wolfe, 1960; 1961] and [Balas, 1966], designed to escape their needs for terminal interventions by the central office. Besides the other limitations of these earlier approaches, it's evident [Kyland, 1975, pp. 1034-35]

---

[30] However, even Godfrey is prepared to have the central office charge divisions with a "penalty function" as a "deterrent to misuse of corporate resources," where "misuse" is determined by the dual values of such resources—see [pp. 291-92] (and [pp. 290-94] generally for the foregoing).

[31] See [Jennergren, 1972, pp. 1409-10] and [Abdel-khalik and Lusk, 1974, p. 17].

[32] One may reach similar conclusions from [Jennergren, 1973, pp. 975-77]. Jennergren [1971, p. 31] poses two questions that he deems to be decisive for the theoretical validity of mathematical programming procedures. Despite what he says on [1972, p. 1414], those questions clearly reveal, by what they *omit*, his approach's essential unconcern with divisional autonomy and meaningful evaluation of division managers.

that the hierarchical ordering that Kydland uses to avoid terminal interventions (and that determines final divisional book profits) can easily change from period to period. This provides yet another way in which divisions' book profits are mere artifacts of a procedure whose first and foremost intent is central-office optimization.[33]

[Hurwicz, Radner and Reiter, 1975]

The authors propose a very general, probabilistic, resource-directive procedure whereby divisions bid for commodities through a referee (the central office) that intervenes if bids are incompatible, requiring divisions to make new bids. When bids *are* compatible they are apt to achieve only a partial allocation of resources, thereby necessitating further iterations.

As usual, the central office's manipulations should be apparent to division managers and the Pareto optimum to which this procedure converges yields artifactual divisional book profits that aren't meaningful for evaluation of division managers' performances. Indeed, judging by the authors' descriptions, such book profits will be substantially matters of luck.[34]

Capsule Comments

I conclude this appendix with a series of very brief comments on other mathematical programming works sometimes cited in the transfer pricing literature.

[Dopuch and Drake, 1964]

This was a pioneering effort to acquaint accountants with the decomposition procedure. However, it's substance is adequately reflected in Chapter Ten's generalized characterization of such procedures.[35]

[Malinvaud, 1967]

In part a survey of early iterative procedures, the one proposed by the author [pp. 197-200] involves repeated central-office manipulation of transfer prices. His practical caveats [pp. 205-06] make an underlying central-office dictatorship all the more evident.[36]

---

[33] For background, see also [Kydland, 1975, pp. 1029-31, 1038].

[34] See [Hurwicz, Radner and Reiter, 1975, pp. 187-89, 191-96] for background.

[35] The casual reader might be especially interested in [pp. 18-19].

[36] See also [Malinvaud, 1967, pp. 175, 180, 186].

[*Kriebel and Lave, 1969*]

> A *transfer pricing system* is a procedure for control of resources in a decentralized organization in which input (factor) and output (product) prices for divisions are established by a central corporate authority (say, "company headquarters"). − [p. 185]

Thus, under their system, the central office specifies internal resource prices. For how this is done, and the manipulative, iternative nature of the authors' approach, see [pp. 191-94].

[*Bensoussan, 1972*]

This is an iterative approach to decentralized decision making that falls outside of usual mathematical-programming frameworks, but is subject to similar strictures.[37]

[*Geoffrion and Hogan, 1972*]

> This paper addresses the problem of coordinating an organization composed of several semi-autonomous operating divisions or departments, each of which may be pursuing different goals within the charter of the parent organization. We are particularly interested in non-market organizations such as are found in government and education. Since not all of the goals pursued in such organizations are commensurate with one another, the allocation of scarce resouces and other coordinating decisions must strive for the most preferred balance or trade-off possible between the performances of the various divisions. − [pp. 455-56]

Unlike procedures discussed in Chapter Ten, the central office's preference function here can be only implicit (if certain "fairly restrictive" assumptions are satisfied).[38] However, it's evident from [pp. 457-58] that although the authors' approach is a sophisticated extension of ordinary decomposition procedures it doesn't escape such procedures' all too familar problems.

[*Krouse, 1972*]

This is a sophisticated, resource-directive procedure designed to cope with (a) complex company objectives (a multivariate company utility function), (b) a company that keeps changing its satisficing targets heuristically and (c) interdivisional externalities[39] I must leave it to readers to verify, though, that despite the

---

[37] See especially [pp. 391-92, 398-99].

[38] See [p. 462].

[39] In addition, [pp. 545-46] offer background on the *general* need for decomposition of business decisions, and the author's bibliography is a good introduction to cognate literatures that, for brevity, I've felt obliged to disregard.

author's observations that immediately precede his example on [p. 550], Chapter Ten's conclusions apply to this paper, too.

[*ten Kate, 1972b*]

This is an interesting resource-directive (the author calls it *direct*) decomposition procedure. "The technique is essentially a dual formulation of the Dantzig-Wolfe method." — [p. 883]. Readers will notice on [p. 884] how a small change in one division's efficiency (as reflected in its ability to pay for resources) can affect other divisions.

[*Kornbluth, 1974*]

This is an instance of the use of goal programming. Transfer prices set by the central office effectively dictate divisional behaviour, though these prices must be supplemented by the central office's also specifying such things as preemptive goals and corporate preferences.[40]

[*Haneveld, 1976*]

The author [p. 9] claims that his decomposition algorithm converges to an optimum in one or two iterations. This is desirable: a multiplicity of iterations is apt to inflame division managers' suspicions of transfer prices and book profits. Unfortunately, as readers may verify, this paper suffers from Chapter Ten's remaining strictures.

[*Ismail, 1977*]

The author proposes another instance of the central office's using transfer prices to manipulate divisions into central-office-optimal behavior. Again, Chapter Ten's conclusions apply.

> Science est trop lente. — Rimbaud
>
> LIVRE. Quel qu'il soit, toujours trop long. — Flaubert, *Le dictionnaire des idées reçues*

---

[40] See especially [p. 295].

REFERENCES

Abdel-khalik, A. Rashad, "On Gordon's Model of Transfer-Pricing System," *The Accounting Review* (October 1971), pp. 783-87.
—, and Edward J. Lusk, "Transfer Pricing—A Synthesis," *The Accounting Review* (January 1974), pp. 8-23.
—, "Transfer Pricing—A Synthesis: A Reply," *The Accounting Review* (April 1975), pp. 355-58.
Albrecht, William Steve, ed., *Management Accounting and Control* (Wisconsin, 1975).
Alchian, Armen A., and William R. Allen, *University Economics*, 2nd ed. (Wadsworth, 1967).
American Accounting Association, 1951 Committee on Cost Concepts and Standards, "Report of the Committee on Cost Concepts and Standards," *The Accounting Review* (April 1952), pp. 174-88.
American Accounting Association, Committee on Non-Financial Measures of Effectiveness, "Report of the Committee on Non-Financial Measures of Effectiveness," *The Accounting Review* (1971 Supplement), pp. 164-211.
American Accounting Association, "Report of the Committee on the Social Consequences of Accounting Information" (August 1977).
Anderson, James A., "The Taxi Case: A Shift in Target Audience and the Selection of a Reporting Base," in [Sterling and Thomas, 1979].
Amey, Lloyd R., and Don A. Egginton, *Management Accounting: A Conceptual Approach* (Longman, 1973).
Anthony, Robert N., "Cost Concepts for Control," *The Accounting Review* (April 1957), pp. 229-34.
—, *Management Accounting Principles*, rev. ed. (Irwin, 1970).
—, "The Rebirth of Cost Accounting," *Management Accounting* (October 1975), pp. 13-16.
Anton, Hector R., "The Budgetary Process and Management Control, in [Bonini et al., 1964], pp. 227-36.
Argyris, Chris, *Personality and Organization* (Harper & Row, 1957).
—, *Integrating the Individual and the Organization* (Wiley, 1964).
Arrow, Kenneth J., "A Difficulty in the Concept of Social Welfare," *Journal of Political Economy* (August 1950), pp. 328-46.
—, "Optimization, Decentralization, and Internal Pricing in Business Firms," in *Contributions to Scientific Research in Management* (California 1959), pp. 9-18.

—, "Social Choice and Individual Values, " *Cowles Foundation Monograph 12,* 2nd ed. (Yale/Wiley, 1963).

—, "Research in Management Controls: A Critical Synthesis," in [Bonini et al., 1964a], pp. 317-27.

—, "Control in Large Organizations," *Management Science* (April 1964b), pp. 397-408.

—, and Leonid Hurwicz, "Decentralization and Computation in Resource Allocation," in Ralph W. Pfouts, ed., *Essays in Economics and Econometrics* (North Carolina, 1960), pp. 34-104.

Arvidsson, Göran, *Internal Transfer Negotiations—Eight Experiments* (The Economic Research Institute, Stockholm, 1973).

Ashton, Raymond, "Cash Flow Accounting: A Review and Critique," *Journal of Business Finance & Accounting,* 3, 4 (1976), pp. 63-81.

Avery, Harold G., "Accounting for Joint Costs," *The Accounting Review* (April 1951), pp. 232-38.

Bailey, Andrew D., Jr., and Warren J. Boe, "Goal and Resource Transfers in the Multigoal Organization," *The Accounting Review* (July 1976), pp. 559-73.

Balakrishnan, A. V., ed., *Techniques of Optimization* (Academic Press, 1972).

Balas, Egon, "An Infeasibility-Pricing Decomposition Method for Linear Programs," *Operations Research* (September-October 1966), pp. 847-73.

Barnard, Chester I., *The Functions of the Executive* (Harvard, 1938).

Barone, E., "The Ministry of Production in the Collectivist State," in Friedrich A. von Hayek, ed., *Collectivist Economic Planning* (Routledge, 1935), pp. 245-90 (originally published, in Italian, in 1908).

Barron, Michael J., "The Application of Linear Programming Dual Prices in Management Accounting—Some Cautionary Observations," *Journal of Business Finance* (1972), pp. 51-69.

Bass, Bernard M., and Harold J. Leavitt, "Some Experiments in Planning and Operating," *Management Science* (July 1963), pp. 574-85.

Baughman, Raymond H., "Accounting for Inter-Plant Sales," *Management Accounting* (September 1970), pp. 41-43.

Baumes, Carl G., "Allocating Corporate Expenses," *Business Policy Study No. 108* (The Conference Board, 1963).

Baumol, William J., and Tibor Fabian, "Decomposition, Pricing for Decentralization and External Economies," *Management Science* (September 1964), pp. 1-32.

Baumol, William J., et al., "The Role of Cost in the Minimum Pricing of Railroad Services," *The Journal of Business* (October 1962), pp. 357-66.

Baxter, W. T., "A Note on the Allocation of Oncosts Between Departments," in [Solomons, 1952], pp. 267-76 (originally published in *The Accountant,* November 5, 1938, pp. 633-36).

Beaver, William H., and Joel S. Demski, "The Nature of Financial Accounting Objectives: A Summary and Synthesis, "*Journal of Accounting Research* (1974 Supplement), pp. 170-87.

Bell, Philip W., and L. Todd Johnson, "Current Value Accounting and the Simple Production Case: Edbejo and Other Companies in the Taxi Business," in [Sterling and Thomas, 1979].

Bensoussan, Alain, "Price Decentralization in the Case of Interrelated Payoffs," in [Balakrishnan, 1972], pp. 391-406.

Benston, George J., "The Role of the Firm's Accounting System for Motivation," *The Accounting Review* (April 1963), pp. 347-54.

Bernhard, Richard H., "Some Problems in Applying Mathematical Programming to Opportunity Costing," *Journal of Accounting Research* (Spring 1968), pp. 143-48.

Bierman, Harold, Jr., "Pricing Intracompany Transfers." *The Accounting Review* (July 1959), pp. 429-32.

——, *Topics in Cost Accounting and Decisions* (McGraw-Hill, 1963).

——, "Inventory Valuation: The Use of Market Prices," *The Accounting Review* (October 1967), pp. 731-37.

——, and Thomas R. Dyckman, *Managerial Cost Accounting* (Macmillan, 1971).

Boatsman, James R., and Galien L. Hite, "On the Relevance of Entry and Exit Valuation for a Class of Firm Decisions Under Specified Market Regimes," in [Sterling and Thomas, 1979].

Bodnar, George, and Edward J. Lusk, "Motivational Considerations in Cost Allocation Systems: A Conditioning Theory Approach," *The Accounting Review* (October 1977), pp. 857-68.

Boer, Germain, et al., *Management Accounting Literature Abstracts* (American Accounting Association, 1976).

Boiteaux, Marcel, "Electrical Energy: Facts, Problems and Prospects," in [Nelson, 1964], pp. 3-28.

Bonini, Charles P., Robert K. Jaedicke and Harvey M. Wagner, eds., *Management Controls: New Directions in Basic Research* (McGraw-Hill, 1964).

Boulding, Kenneth E., *Economic Analysis,* 3rd ed. (Harper, 1955).

Brack, George E., "Allocating Personnel Department Costs," *Management Accounting* (May 1975), pp. 48-50.

Brief, Richard P., and Joel Owen, "A Least Squares Allocation Model," *Journal of Accounting Research* (Autumn 1968), pp. 193-99.

Buchanan, James M., "An Economic Theory of Clubs," *Economica* (February 1965), pp. 1-14.

Buckley, Adrian, and Eugene McKenna, "Budgetary Control and Business Behavior," in [Rosen, 1974], pp. 43-67 (originally in *Accounting and Business Research* (Spring 1972), pp. 137-50.

Buckley, Wm. F., Jr., "Puerto Rico's Choices," *On the Right* (September 22, 1978).

Burlingame, John F., "Information Technology & Decentralization," *Harvard Business Review* (November-December 1961), pp. 121-26.

Burton, R. M., W. W. Damon and D. W. Loughridge, "The Economics of Decomposition: Resource Allocation vs Transfer Pricing," *Decision Sciences* (June 1974), pp. 297-310.

Butler, John J., "Joint Product Analysis," *Management Accounting* (December 1971), pp. 12-14, 38.

Butterworth, John E., "Comparative Sterilization Properties of NRV and Shapley Joint-Cost Allocations—Discussion," in *Accounting Workshop* (Clarkson, Gordon Foundation, 1977).

——, David C. Hayes and Ella Mae Matsumura, "Negotiated Transfer Prices in an Uncertain Competitive World," presented at the 1977 Meeting of the Canadian Regional Group of The American Accounting Association.

——, Revision, *Working Paper No. 575* (British Columbia, 1978).

Callen, Jeffrey L., "Financial Cost Allocations: A Game Theoretic Approach," *The Accounting Review* (April 1978), pp. 303-08.

Caplan, Edwin H., *Management Accounting and Behavioral Science* (Addison-Wesley, 1971).

Carsberg, Bryan, "The Predictive Value Approach," in [Sterling and Thomas, 1979].

Centre for Business Research (in association with Manchester Business School), "Transfer Pricing," *Management Control Project Report No. 3* (Manchester, 1972).

Chamberlain, John, "Foreword," in [Hayek, 1944], pp. v-vii.

Chambers, Raymond J., *Accounting, Evaluation and Economic Behavior* (Prentice-Hall, 1966).

——, "Second Thoughts on Continuously Contemporary Accounting," *Abacus* (September 1970), pp. 39-55.

——, "Third Thoughts," *Abacus* (December 1974), pp. 129-37.

——, " 'The Taxi Company' Under COCOA," in [Sterling and Thomas, 1979].

Charnes, A., R. W. Clower and K. O. Kortanek, "Effective Control Through Coherent Decentralization With Preemptive Goals," *Econometrica* (April 1967), pp. 294-320.

Charnes, A., and K. O. Kortanek, "On the Status of Separability and Non-Separability in Decentralization Theory," *Management Science* (October 1968), pp. B·12-14.

Cherrington, J. Owen, and David J. Cherrington, "Budget Games for Fun and Frustration," *Management Accounting* (January 1976), pp. 28-32.

Clark, J. Maurice, *Studies in the Economics of Overhead Costs* (Chicago, 1923).

Coase, R. H., "The Nature of the Firm," *Economica* (November 1937), pp. 386-405.

——, "The Marginal Cost Controversy," *Economica* (August 1946), pp. 169-82.

Cofer, C. N., and M. H. Appley, *Motivation: Theory and Research* (Wiley, 1964).

Colberg, Marshall R., "Monopoly Prices Under Joint Costs: Fixed Proportions," *Journal of Political Economy* (February 1941), pp. 103-10.

Cook, Paul W., Jr., "Decentralization and the Transfer-Price Problem," *The Journal of Business* (April 1955), pp. 87-94.

——, "New Technique for Intracompany Pricing," *Harvard Business Review* (July-August 1957), pp. 74-80.

Cooper, William W., "Research Directions in Management Control," in [Bonini, et al., 1964], pp. 328-41.

Cost Accounting Standards Board, "Progress Report to the Congress 1975" (CASB, 1975a).

——, *Standards, Rules and Regulations* (CASB, 1975b).

——, "Part 410–Allocation of Business Unit General and Administrative Expenses to Final Cost Objectives," *Federal Register* (April 16, 1976a), pp. 16135-16145. [See minor corrections in *Federal Register* (June 2, 1976), p. 22241.]

——, "Allocation of Home Office Expenses to Segments," Proposed Amendment, *Federal Register* (November 30, 1976b), p. 52473.

——, *Progress Report to the Congress* (CASB, January 6, 1978a).

——, "Standards, Rules & Regulations, Supplement # 4," *Federal Register* (March 10, 1978b).

Crompton, Walter H., "Transfer Pricing: A Proposal," *Management Accounting* (April 1972), pp. 46-48.

Culpepper, James G., "Playing the Game," letter, *Management Accounting* (April 1976), p. 8.

Cummin, Pearson C., "TAT Correlates of Executive Performance," in [Steers and Porter, 1975], pp. 62-67.

Cupples, Richard A., "The Only Equitable Method for Pricing Funds," letter, *Management Accounting* (April 1972), pp. 8, 58.

Cushing, Barry E., "Pricing Internal Computer Services: The Basic Issues," *Management Accounting* (April 1976), pp. 47-50.

——, "On the Possibility of Optimal Accounting Principles," *The Accounting Review* (April 1977), pp. 308-21.

Cyert, Richard M., and James G. March, *A Behavioral Theory of the Firm* (Prentice-Hall, 1963).

Dantzig, George B., and Philip Wolfe, "Decomposition Principle for Linear Programs," *Operations Research* (January-February 1960), pp. 101-11.

——, "The Decomposition Algorithm for Linear Programs," *Econometrica* (October 1961), pp. 767-78.

Davidson, Sydney, "Discussion: The Budgetary Process and Management Control," in [Bonini, et al., 1964], pp. 237-39.

——, and Roman L. Weil, *Handbook of Modern Accounting*, 2nd ed. (McGraw-Hill, 1977).

Dean, Joel, "Decentralization and Intracompany Pricing," *Harvard Business Review* (July-August 1955), pp. 65-74.

Dearden, John, "Interdivisional Pricing," *Harvard Business Review* (January-February 1960), pp. 117-25.

——, "Problem in Decentralized Profit Responsibility," *Harvard Business Review* (May-June 1960), pp. 79-86.

——, "Problem in Decentralized Financial Control," *Harvard Business Review* (May-June 1961), pp. 72-80.

——, "Limits on Decentralized Profit Responsibility, *Harvard Business Review* (July-August 1962a), pp. 81-89.

——, "Mirage of Profit Decentralization," *Harvard Business Review* (November-December 1962b), pp. 140-43, 147,149-50, 153-54.

——, "Computers: No Impact on Divisional Control, " *Harvard Business Review* (January-February 1967), pp. 99-104.

——, "Appraising Profit Center Managers," *Harvard Business Review* (May-June 1968), pp. 80-87.

——, *Cost Accounting and Financial Control Systems* (Addison-Wesley, 1973).

Demski, Joel, "Optimal Performance Measurement," *Journal of Accounting Research* (Autumn 1972), pp. 243-58.

——, "The General Impossibility of Normative Accounting Standards," *The Accounting Review* (October 1973), pp. 718-23.

——, "Choice Among Financial Reporting Alternatives," *The Accounting Review* (April 1974), pp. 221-32.

——, "Uncertainty and Evaluation Based on Controllable Performance," *Journal of Accounting Research* (Autumn 1976a), pp. 230-45.

—, "Transfer Pricing Under Uncertainty," working paper (Stanford University, 1976b).

—, and Gerald A. Feltham, *Cost Determination: A Conceptual Approach* (Iowa State, 1976).

Dessus, Gabriel, "The General Principles of Rate-Fixing in Public Utilities," in [Nelson, 1964], pp. 31-49.

Devine, Carl Thomas, *Cost Accounting and Analysis* (Macmillan, 1950a).

—, "Cost Accounting and Pricing Policies," *The Accounting Review* (October 1950b), pp. 384-89.

Dopuch, Nicholas, Jacob G. Birnberg and Joel Demski, *Cost Accounting: Accounting Data for Management's Decisions,* 2nd ed. (Harcourt Brace Jovanovich, 1974).

Dopuch, Nicholas, and David F. Drake, "Accounting Implications of a Mathematical Programming Approach To the Transfer Price Problem," *Journal of Accounting Research* (Spring 1964), pp. 10-24.

Dyckman, Thomas R., "Management Accounting: Where Are We? A Critique," in [Albrecht, 1975], pp. 33-45.

Edwards, Edgar O., and Philip W. Bell, *The Theory and Measurement of Business Income* (California, 1961).

Edwards, J. Don, and Roger A. Roemmich, "Transfer Pricing: The Wrong Tool for Performance Evaluation," *Cost and Management* (January-February 1976), pp. 35-37.

Edwards, Ronald S., "The Rationale of Cost Accounting," in [Solomons, 1952a], pp. 87-104.

——, "Cost Accounting and Joint Production," in [Solomons, 1952b], pp. 310-20.

Ellickson, Brian, "A Generalization of the Pure Theory of Public Goods," *The American Economic Review* (June 1973), pp. 417-32.

Emmanuel, C. R., "The Birch Paper Company: A Possible Solution to the Interdivisional Pricing Problem," *The Accountant's Magazine* (May 1977a), pp. 196-98.

—, "Transfer Pricing: A Diagnosis and Possible Solution to Dysfunctional Decision-Making in the Divisionalized Company," forthcoming, *Management International Review* (1977b).

—, "Transfer Pricing in the Corporate Environment," unpublished working paper (The University of Lancaster, 1977c).

Etzioni, Amitai, *Modern Organizations* (Prentice-Hall, 1964).

—, *A Comparative Analysis of Complex Organizations,* Rev. ed. (The Free Press/Macmillan, 1975).

Feller, Robert E., "Accounting for Joint Products in the Petroleum Industry," *Management Accounting* (September 1977), pp. 41-44, 48.

Feltham, Gerald A., "Some Quantitative Approaches to Planning for Multiproduct Production Systems," *The Accounting Review* (January 1970), pp. 11-26.

Ferrara, William L., "Accounting for Performance Evaluation and Decision-Making," *Management Accounting* (December 1976), pp. 13-19.

——, "Production Costs," in [Davidson and Weil, 1977], Ch. 41.

Filley, Alan C., and Robert J. House, *Managerial Process and Organizational Behavior* (Scott, Foresman, 1969).

——, and S. Kerr, 2nd ed. (Scott, Foresman, 1976).

Financial Accounting Standards Board, "An Analysis of Issues Related to Financial Reporting for Segments of a Business Enterprise," *FASB Discussion Memorandum* (May 22, 1974).

——, "Financial Reporting for Segments of a Business Enterprise," *Statement of Financial Accounting Standards No. 14* (December 1976).

Fischer, David Hackett, *Historians' Fallacies* (Harper & Row, 1970).

Freeland, James Ross, *Conceptual Models of the Resource Allocation Decision Process in Hierarchical Decentralized Organizations,* unpublished doctoral dissertation (Georgia Institute of Technology, 1973).

——, "A Note on Goal Decomposition In A Decentralized Organization," *Management Science* (September 1976), pp. 100-02.

——, and Norman R. Baker, "Mathematical Models of Resource Allocation Decision Making in Hierarchical Organizations," working paper (Georgia Institute of Technology, 1972).

——, and Norman R. Baker, "A Framework for Analysis of Coordination Mechanisms in Decentralized Organizations," *Research Paper No. 197* (Stanford, March 1974).

——, and Norman R. Baker, "Goal Partitioning in a Hierarchical Organization," *Omega* (1975), pp. 673-88.

——, and Jeffrey H. Moore, "Some Organizational Properties of Resource Directive Allocation Mechanisms," *Research Paper No. 289* (Graduate School of Business, Stanford University, 1975).

Fremgen, James M., "Transfer Pricing and Management Goals." *Management Accounting* (December 1970), pp. 25-31; see also *errata* (March 1971), p. 16.

Geoffrion, Arthur M., "Primal Resource-Directive Approaches for Optimizing Non-linear Decomposable Systems," *Operations Research* (May-June 1970a), pp. 375-403.

——, "Elements of Large-Scale Mathematical Programming," *Management Science* (July 1970b), pp. 652-91.

——, and W. W. Hogan, "Coordination of Two-Level Organizations With Mulitple Objectives," in [Balakrishnan, 1972], pp. 455-66.

Godfrey, James T., "Short-Run Planning in a Decentralized Firm," *The Accounting Review* (April 1971), pp. 286-97.

Goetz, Billy E., "Transfer Prices: An Exercise in Relevancy and Goal Congruence," *The Accounting Review* (July 1967), pp. 435-40.

——, "The Effect of a Cost-Plus Contract on Transfer Prices," *The Accounting Review* (April 1969), pp. 398-400.

Golembiewski, Robert T., "Accountancy as a Function of Organization Theory," *The Accounting Review* (April 1964), pp. 333-41.

Gordon, Myron J., "The Use of Administered Price Systems to Control Large Organizations," in [Bonini et al., 1964], pp. 1-26.

——, "A Method of Pricing for a Socialist Economy," *The Accounting Review* (July 1970), pp. 427-43.

——, "A Method of Pricing for a Socialist Economy, A Reply," *The Accounting Review* (October 1971), pp. 788-90.

Gould, J. R., "The Pricing of Transactions Between Members of a Group of Companies," *Accountancy* (June 1960), pp. 345-48.

——, "Internal Pricing in Firms When There Are Costs of Using an Outside Market," *The Journal of Business* (January 1964), pp. 61-67.

Granot, Daniel, "Cooperative Games in Stochastic Characteristic Function Form," *Management Science* (February 1977), pp. 621-30.

Haire, Mason, Edwin E. Ghiselli and Lyman W. Porter, *Managerial Thinking: An International Study* (Wiley, 1966).

Hamlen, Susan S., William A. Hamlen, Jr., and John T. Tschirhart, "The Use of Core Theory in Evaluating Joint Cost Allocation Schemes," *The Accounting Review* (July 1977), pp. 616-27.

Haneveld, A. Klein, "The Role of Balanced Transfer Values in Decentralized Organizations," *Proceedings, Operations Research Society Annual Conference at Swansea, Wales, 21st to 24th September 1976*.

Harris, William T., Jr., and Wayne R. Chapin, "Joint Product Costing," *Management Accounting* (April 1973), pp. 43-47.

Hartley, Ronald V., "Decision Making When Joint Products are Involved," *The Accounting Review* (October 1971), pp. 746-55.

Hass, Jerome E., "Transfer Pricing in a Decentralized Firm," *Management Science* (February 1968), pp. B·310-31.

Hayek, Friedrich A., von, "Socialist Calculation: The Competitive 'Solution'," *Economica* (May 1940), pp. 125-49.

—, *The Road to Serfdom* (Chicago, 1944).

—, *The Constitution of Liberty* (Chicago, 1960).

Hayhurst, George, "A Proposal for a Corporate Control System," *Management International Review* (1976/2), pp. 93-103.

Head, J. G., "Public Goods and Public Policy," *Public Finance,* v. 17, no. 3 (1962), pp. 197-221.

Hedges, Thomas V., "The Feasibility of Eliminating Incorrigible Allocations in Managerial Accounting and Substituting Allocation-Free Procedures," unpublished working paper (Southern Methodist University, 1975).

Heflebower, Richard B., "Observations on Decentralization in Large Enterprises," *Journal of Industrial Economics* (November 1960), pp.7-22.

Heins, Robert H., "Steam Power as a Production Cost," *Management Accounting* (April 1972), pp. 25-26.

Heller, Walter P., and David A. Starrett, "On the Nature of Externalities," in [Lin, 1976], pp. 9-22.

Henderson, Bruce D., and John Dearden, "New System for Divisional Control," *Harvard Business Review* (September-October 1966), pp. 144-46, 149-52, 155-56, 159-60.

Henderson, James M., and Richard E. Quandt, *Microeconomic Theory: A Mathematical Approach* (McGraw-Hill, 1958).

Herzberg, Frederick, *Work and the Nature of Man* (World, 1966).

—, Bernard Mausner and Barbara Bloch Snyderman, *The Motivation to Work* (Wiley, 1964).

Hicks, J. R., *Values and Capital,* 2nd ed. (Oxford, 1946).

Hill, T. M., "A Criticism of 'Joint Cost Analysis as an Aid to Management'," *The Accounting Review* (April 1956), pp. 204-05.

Hillman, Arye Leo, "Discussion," in [Lin, 1976], pp. 103-06.

Hirshleifer, Jack, "On the Economics of Transfer Pricing," *Journal of Business* (July 1956), pp. 172-84.

—, "Economics of the Divisionalized Firm," *Journal of Business* (April 1957), pp. 96-108.

—, "Internal Pricing and Decentralized Decisions," in [Bonini et al., 1964], pp. 27-37.

Hofstede, G. H., *The Game of Budget Control* (Tavistock, 1968).

Holstrum, Gary L., and Eugene H. Sauls, "The Opportunity Cost Transfer Price," *Management Accounting* (May 1973), pp. 29-33.

Hopwood, Anthony, *Accounting and Human Behavior* (Prentice-Hall, 1976); first published in 1974 by Haymarket Publishing Limited.

Horngren, Charles T., *Cost Accounting: A Managerial Emphasis,* 3rd ed. (Prentice-Hall, 1972).

——, 4th ed. (Prentice-Hall, 1977).

——, "Management Accounting: Where Are We?" in [Albrecht, 1975], pp. 9-26.

Horwitz, Bertrand, "Accounting Controls and the Soviet Economic Reforms of 1966," *Studies in Accounting Research No. 4* (American Accounting Association, 1970).

House, Robert J., and Lawrence A. Wigdor, "Herzberg's Dual-Factor Theory of Job Satisfaction and Motivation: A Review of the Evidence and a Criticism," in [Steers and Porter, 1975], pp. 104-14.

Hughes, Jeffery L., "Inter-Plant Sales," (letter), *Management Accounting* (February 1971), p. 9.

Hughes, John S., and James H. Scheiner, "An Incremental Costing Approach to Allocating Common Costs," paper presented at the 1977 Southeastern Regional Meetings of the American Accounting Association.

Hurwicz, Leonid, Roy Radner and Stanley Reiter, "A Stochastic Decentalized Resource Allocation Process," *Econometrica* (March 1975), pp. 187-221, and (May 1975), pp. 363-93.

Ijiri, Yuji, "Theory of Accounting Measurement," *Studies in Accounting Research No. 10* (American Accounting Association, 1975).

——, "Cash Flow Accounting and Its Structure," *Graduate School of Industrial Administration Working Paper* (Carnegie-Mellon, 1977).

——, "A Simple System of Cash Flow Accounting," in [Sterling and Thomas, 1979].

Ismail, Badr E., "Transfer Pricing Under Demand Uncertainty: A Mathematical Programming Approach," working paper (State University of New York at Albany, 1977).

Jennergen, Lars Peter, *Studies in the Mathematical Theory of Decentralized Resource-Allocation,* unpublished doctoral dissertation (Stanford, 1971).

——, "Decentralization on the Basis of Price Schedules in Linear Decomposable Resource-Allocation Problems," *Journal of Financial and Quantitative Analysis* (January 1972), pp. 1407-17.

——, "A Price Schedules Decomposition Algorithm for Linear Programming Problems," *Econometrica* (September 1973), pp. 965-80.

Jensen, Daniel L., "The Role of Cost in Pricing Joint Products: A Case of Production in Fixed Proportions," *The Accounting Review* (July 1974), pp.465-76.

—,"Demand-Based Cost Allocations," working paper (Purdue, 1975).

—, "A Class of Mutually Satisfactory Allocations," *The Accounting Review* (October 1977), pp. 842-56.

Johnson, L. Todd, and Philip W. Bell, "Current Replacement Costs: A Qualified Opinion," *The Journal of Accountancy* (November 1976), pp. 63-70.

Johnson, Nancy L., and Arthur L. Thomas, "Joint-Cost Allocation: Extensions of the Moriarity and Louderback Approaches," unpublished working paper (1979).

Kaplan, Robert S., "Variable and Self-Service Costs in Reciprocal Allocation Models," *The Accounting Review* (October 1973), pp. 738-48.

—, "Application of Quantitative Models in Managerial Accounting: A State of the Art Survey," unpublished working paper (Carnegie-Mellon, 1977).

—, and Gerald L. Thompson, "Overhead Allocation via Mathematical Programming Models," *The Accounting Review* (April 1971), pp. 352-64.

—, and Ulf Peter Welam, "Overhead Allocation with Imperfect Markets and Non-linear Technology," *The Accounting Review* (July 1974), pp. 477-84.

Kay, Robert S., and James A. Johnson, "Can A Core Theory of Accounting Be Found Through Simplification of Accounting Problems?" in [Sterling and Thomas, 1979].

King, Nathan, "Clarification and Evaluation of the Two-Factor Theory of Job Satisfaction," in [Steers and Porter, 1975], pp. 115-34.

Kline, Bennett E., and Norman H. Martin, "Freedom, Authority, and Decentralization," *Harvard Business Review* (May-June 1958), pp. 69-75.

Koopmans, Tjalling C., "Allocation of Resources and the Price System," in *Three Essays on the State of Economic Science* (McGraw-Hill, 1957), pp. 1-126.

Kornai, János, "Mathematical Programming of Long-Term Plans in Hungary," in [Malinvaud and Bacharach, 1967a], pp. 211-31.

—, *Mathematical Planning of Structural Decisions* (North-Holland, 1967b).

—, "Thoughts on Multi-Level Planning Systems," in Louis M. Goreux and Alan S. Manne, eds., *Multi-Level Planning: Case Studies in Mexico* (North-Holland, 1973), pp. 521-51.

—, and Th. Lipták, "Two-Level Planning," *Econometrica* (January 1965), pp. 141-69.

Kornbluth, J. S. H., "Accounting in Multiple Objective Linear Programming," *The Accounting Review* (April 1974), pp. 284-95.

Krasney, Melvin, "Accounting Controls for Corporate EDP Costs," *Management Accounting* (March 1971), pp. 17-18, 26.

Kreps, T. J., "Joint Costs in the Chemical Industry," *Quarterly Journal of Economics* (May 1930), pp. 416-61.

Kriebel, Charles H., and Lester B. Lave, "Conflict Resolution Within Economic Organizations," *Behavioral Science* (May 1969), pp. 183-96.

Krouse, Clement G., "Complex Objectives, Decentralization, and the Decision Process of the Organization," *Administrative Science Quarterly* (December 1972), pp. 544-54.

Kuhn, H. W., and A. Tucker, "Nonlinear Programming," in J. Neyman, ed., *Proceedings of the Second Berkeley Symposium on Mathematical Statistics and Probability* (California 1951), pp. 481-92.

Kuhn, Thomas S., "The Structure of Scientific Revolutions," *International Encyclopedia of Unified Science*, 2nd ed. (Chicago, 1970).

Kydland, Finn, "Hierarchical Decomposition in Linear Economic Models," *Management Science* (May 1975), pp. 1029-39.

Larson, Raymond L., "Transfer Pricing in a Commercial Bank—A Differing Viewpoint," *Management Accounting* (December 1971), pp. 19-22.

——, "Decentralization in Real Life," *Management Accounting* (March 1974), pp. 28-32.

Lawler, Edward E., III, and J. Lloyd Suttle, "A Causal Correlation Test of the Need Hierarchy Concept," in [Steers and Porter, 1975],pp. 39-46.

Lawson, Gerald H., "Joint Cost Analysis as an Aid to Management—A Rejoinder," *The Accounting Review* (July 1956), pp. 439-43.

——, "Joint Cost Analysis as an Aid to Management—A Further Note," *The Accounting Review* (July 1957), pp. 431-33.

——, "Profit Maximization via Financial Management," *Management Decision* (Winter, 1969); reprinted in [Lawson, 1975b].

——, "Radical Changes in Financial Reports," *The Financial Times* (15th July 1970); reprinted in [Lawson, 1975b].

——, "Accounting for Financial Management—Some Tentative Proposals for a New Blueprint," in Sir Robert Stone and Basil Blackwell, eds. *Problems of Investment* (Oxford, 1971a), Ch. 3; reprinted in [Lawson, 1975b].

——, "Cash-Flow Accounting," *The Accountant* (October 28th, 1971b), pp.586-89; (November 4th, 1971b), pp. 620-22; reprinted in [Lawson, 1975b].

——, "Memorandum Submitted to the Inflation Accounting Committee—July 1974," *Working Paper Series 12* (Manchester, 1975a).

——, "Cash Flow Accounting," *Working Paper Series 16* (Manchester, 1975b).

——, "The Rationale of Cash Flow Accounting," text of an address to the 9th Congress of the European Federation of Financial Analysts Societies, Brighton, May 1976a.

——, "Initial Reactions to E. D. 18," *Certified Accountant* (December 1976b), pp. 357-58, 361-65, 422.

——, and A. W. Stark, "The Concept of Profit for Fund Raising," *Accounting and Business Research* (Winter 1975), pp. 21-41.

——, "Does Ford Cash Really Flow?" *Accountancy Age* (12th August 1977), pp. 8-9.

——, and G. H. Bean, *Enterprise Valuation: A Cash Flow Approach* (Prentice-Hall International, 1979).

Lee, T. A., "The Relevance of Accounting Information Including Cash Flows, " *The Accountant's Magazine* (January 1972a), pp. 30-34.

——, 'A Case for Cash Flow Reporting," *Journal of Business Finance* (Summer 1972b), pp. 27-36.

——, "Enterprise Income: Survival or Decline and Fall?" *Accounting and Business Research* (Summer 1974), pp. 178-92.

——, "Cash Flow Accounting," *Exposure Draft* (Edinburgh, 31st May 1976).

——, "The Simplicity and Complexity of Accounting," in [Sterling and Thomas, 1979].

Lemke, Kenneth W., "In Defense of the 'Profit Centre' Concept," *Abacus* (December 1970), pp. 182-88.

Lewis, W. Arthur, "Fixed Costs," *Economica* (November 1946), pp. 231-58.

Likert, Rensis, *New Patterns of Management* (McGraw-Hill, 1961a).

——, "Patterns in Management," in E. A. Frishman, ed., *Studies in Personnel and Industrial Psychology* (Dorsey, 1961b), pp. 376-92; originally published in "Developing Patterns in Management," *General Management Series No. 178* (American Management Association, 1955).

Lin, Steven A. Y., ed., *Theory and Measurement of Economic Externalities* (Academic Press, 1976).

Littlechild, S. C., "A Game-Theoretic Approach to Public Utility Pricing," *Western Economic Journal* (June 1970a), pp. 162-66.

——, "Marginal-Cost Pricing With Joint Costs," *The Economic Journal* (June 1970b), pp. 323-35.

—, "Common Costs, Fixed Charges, Clubs and Games," *Review of Economic Studies* (1975), pp. 117-24.

—, and G. Owen, "A Simple Expression for the Shapley Value in a Special Case," *Management Science* (November 1973), pp. 370-72.

Litwin, George H. and Robert A. Stringer, Jr., "Motivation and Behavior," in [Steers and Porter, 1975], pp. 51-62.

Livesey, F., "The Pricing of Internal Transfers," *The Accountant* (July 22nd, 1967), pp. 99-104.

Loehman, Edna, and Andrew B. Whinston, "A New Theory of Pricing and Decision-Making for Public Investment," *The Bell Journal of Economics and Management Science* (Autumn 1971), pp. 606-25.

—, "An Axiomatic Approach to Cost Allocation for Public Investment," *Public Finance Quarterly* (April 1974), pp. 236-51.

—, "A Generalized Cost Allocation Scheme," in [Lin, 1976, pp. 87-101].

Lorig, Arthur N., "Joint Cost Analysis as an Aid to Management," *The Accounting Review* (October 1955), pp. 634-37.

—, "A Reply," *The Accounting Review* (October 1956), pp. 593-95.

—, "Replying to 'A Further Note' On Joint Cost Analysis," *The Accounting Review* (January 1958), pp. 35-36.

Louderback, Joseph G., "Another Approach to Allocating Joint Costs: A Comment," *The Accounting Review* (July 1976), pp. 683-85.

—, and Geraldine F. Dominiak, *Managerial Accounting,* 2nd ed., (Wadsworth, 1978).

Lucas, William F., "An Overview of the Mathematical Theory of Games," *Management Science* (January 1972), pp. P-3-19.

Luce, R. Duncan, and Howard Raiffa, *Games and Decisions* (Wiley, 1957).

Malinvaud, E., "Decentralized Procedures for Planning," in [Malinvaud and Bacharach, 1967], pp. 170-208.

—, and M. O. L. Bacharach, eds., *Activity Analysis in the Theory of Growth and Planning* (MacMillan/St. Martin's Press, 1967).

Manes, Rene P., "Birch Paper Company Revisited: An Exercise in Transfer Pricing," *The Accounting Review* (July 1970), pp. 565-72.

—, and Vernon L. Smith, "Economic Joint Cost Theory and Accounting Practice," *The Accounting Review* (January 1965), pp. 31-35.

March, James G., and Herbert A. Simon, *Organizations* (Wiley, 1958).

Margolis, Julius, "A Comment on the Pure Theory of Public Expenditure," *Review of Economics and Statistics* (November 1955), pp. 347-49.

Marschak, Thomas A., "Centralization and Decentralization in Economic Organizations," *Econometrica* (July 1959), pp. 399-430.

——, "Discussion: Economic Theory and Management Control," in [Bonini et al. 1964], pp. 81-87.

Marshall, Ronald M., "Determining an Optimal Accounting Information System for an Unidentified User," *Journal of Accounting Research* (Autumn, 1972), pp. 286-307.

Maschler, M., B. Peleg and L. S. Shapley, "The Kernel and Bargaining Set for Convex Games," *International Journal of Game Theory* (1972), pp. 73-93.

Maslow, Abraham H., *Motivation and Personality,* 2nd ed. (Harper & Row, 1970).

Mattessich, Richard, "Budgeting Models and System Simulation," *The Accounting Review* (July 1961), pp. 384-97.

Mautz, Robert K., and K. Fred Skousen, "Common Cost Allocation in Diversified Companies," *Financial Executive* (June 1968), pp. 15-17, 19-25.

McClelland, David C., *The Achieving Society* (Van Nostrand, 1961).

McCulloch, John T., "Interdivisional Transfer Pricing," *Business Policy Study No. 122* (The Conference Board, 1967).

McGregor, Douglas, *The Human Side of Enterprise* (McGraw-Hill, 1960).

——, *Leadership and Motivation* (M. I. T., 1966).

——, *The Professional Manager* (McGraw-Hill, 1967).

McIntyre, Edward V., "Present Value Depreciation and the Disaggregation Problem," *The Accounting Review* (January 1977), pp. 162-71.

McNally, G.M., "Profit Centres and Transfer Prices—Are They Necessary?" *Accounting and Business Research* (Winter 1973), pp. 13-22.

Menge, John A., "The Backward Art of Interdivisional Transfer Pricing," *The Journal of Industrial Economics* (July 1961), pp. 215-32.

Meyers, Stephen L., "A Proposal for Coping With the Allocation Problem," *The Journal of Accountancy* (April 1976), pp. 52-56.

Milburn, J. Alex, "International Transfer Transactions: What Price?" *CA magazine* (December 1976), pp. 22-27.

——, "International Transfer Pricing in a Financial Accounting Context," unpublished doctoral dissertation (Illinois, 1977).

Milne, A. A., *Winnie-the-Pooh* (Dutton, 1926).

Moriarity, Shane, "Another Approach to Allocating Joint Costs," *The Accounting Review* (October 1975), pp. 791-95.

——, "Another Approach to Allocating Joint Costs: A Reply," *The Accounting Review* (July 1976), pp. 686-87.

Mosich, A. N., and M. A. Vasarhelyi, "The Valuation of Economic Activity: An Intuitive Approach," in [Sterling and Thomas, 1979].

Mossin, Jan, "Merger Agreements: Some Game-Theoretic Considerations," *The Journal of Business* (October 1968), pp. 460-71.

Most, Kenneth S., "Gordon's Transfer Price Model for a Socialist Economy: A Comment," *The Accounting Review* (October 1971), pp. 779-82.

Murphy, Robert W., "Corporate Divisions vs. Subsidiaries," *Harvard Business Review* (November-December 1956), pp. 83-92.

Murray, Lawrence M., "Management Audit of Divisional Performance," *Management Accounting* (March 1973), pp. 26-28.

Naert, Philippe A., "Measuring Performance in a Decentralized Firm with Interrelated Divisions: Profit Center Versus Cost Center," *The Engineering Economist* (Winter 1973), pp. 99-114.

National Association of Accountants, "Accounting for Intracompany Transfers," *Research Report No. 30* (N.A.A., 1957a).

——, "Costing Joint Products," *Research Report No. 31* (N.A.A., 1957b).

Nelson, James R., ed., *Marginal Cost Pricing in Practice* (Prentice-Hall, 1964).

Neumann, John von, and Oskar Morgenstern, *Theory of Games and Economic Behavior,* 3rd ed. (Princeton, 1953).

Niemi, Richard G., and William H. Riker, "The Choice of Voting Systems," *Scientific American* (June 1976), pp. 21-27.

Nove, A., "The Problem of 'Success Indicators' in Soviet Industry," *Economica* (February 1958), pp. 1-13.

Okpechi, Simeon Ogbulafor, "Interdivisional Transfer-Pricing: A Conflict Resolution Approach," unpublished doctoral dissertation (Ohio State, 1976).

Onsi, Mohamed, "A Transfer Pricing System Based on Opportunity Cost," *The Accounting Review* (July 1970), pp. 535-43.

——, " 'Transfer Pricing System Based on Opportunity Costs':
A Reply," *The Accounting Review* (January 1974), pp. 129-31.

Paik, Chei M., "A Conceptual Framework for Managerial Accoun-
ting: An Analysis of Its Failure," *Proceedings, 1975 Annual
Meeting, Mid-Atlantic Regional Group, American Accounting
Association* (A.A.A., 1975), pp. 77-88.

Parker, Lee D., "Goal Congruence: A Misguided Accounting Concept?" *Abacus* (June 1976), pp. 3-13.

Pauly, Mark V., "Clubs, Commonality, and the Core: An Integration of Game Theory and the Theory of Public Goods," *Economica* (August 1967), pp. 314-24.

Perrow, Charles, *Organizational Analysis: A Sociological View*
(Brooks/Cole, 1970).

Pfouts, Ralph W., "The Theory of Cost and Production in the
Multi-Product Firm," *Econometrica* (October 1961), pp.
650-58.

Piper, A. G., "Internal Trading," *Accountancy* (October 1969),
pp. 733-36.

Porter, Lyman W., *Organizational Patterns of Managerial Job
Attitudes* (American Foundation for Management Research,
1964).

Prakash, Prem, and Alfred Rappaport, "Information Inductance
and Its Significance for Accounting," *Accounting, Organizations
and Society* (1977), pp. 29-38.

Reece, James S., and William R. Cool, "Measuring Investment
Center Performance," *Harvard Business Review* (May-June
1978), pp. 28-30, 34, 36, 40, 42, 46, 174, 176.

Ridgway, V. F., "Dysfunctional Consequences of Performance
Measurements," *Administrative Science Quarterly* (September
1956), pp. 240-47; reprinted in [Rosen, 1974], pp. 284-90.

Ronen, Joshua, "Social Costs and Benefits and the Transfer
Pricing Problem," *Journal of Public Economics* (March 1974),
pp. 71-82.

——, "Transfer Pricing—A Synthesis: A Comment," *The Accounting
Review* (April 1975), pp. 351-54.

——, and George McKinney, III, "Transfer Pricing for Divisional
Autonomy," *Journal of Accounting Research* (Spring 1970),
pp. 99-112.

Rook, A., "Transfer Pricing: A Measure of Management Performance in Multi-Divisional Companies," *Management Survey
Report No. 8* (British Institute of Management, 1971).

Rosen, L. S., ed., *Topics in Managerial Accounting*, 2nd ed.
(McGraw-Hill Ryerson, 1974).

Roth, Alvin E., and Robert E. Verrecchia, "The Shapley Value as Applied to Cost Allocation: A Re-Interpretation," unpublished working paper (Illinois, 1977).

Rotter, Julian B., "Generalized Expectancies for Internal versus External Control of Reinforcement," *Psychological Monographs: General and Applied, No. 609* (American Psychological Association, 1966).

Ruefli, Timothy Walter, "Planning in Decentralized Organizations," unpublished doctoral dissertation (Carnegie-Mellon, 1969).

——, "A Generalized Goal Decomposition Model, " *Management Science* (April 1971a), pp. B·505-18.

——, "Behavioral Externalities in Decentralized Organizations," *Management Science* (June 1971b), pp. B·649-57.

——, "Analytic Models of Resource Allocation in Hierarchical Multi-Level Systems," *Socio-Economic Planning Sciences* (1974), pp. 353-63.

Samuels, J. M., "Opportunity Costing: An Application of Mathematical Programming," *Journal of Accounting Research* (Autumn 1965), pp. 182-91.

——, "Penalties and Subsidies in Internal Pricing Policies," *Journal of Business Finance* (Winter 1969), pp. 31-38.

Samuelson, Paul A., "The Pure Theory of Public Expenditure," *Review of Economics and Statistics* (November 1954), pp. 387-89.

——, "Diagrammatic Exposition of a Theory of Public Expenditure," *Review of Economics and Statistics* (November 1955), pp. 350-56.

——, "Aspects of Public Expenditure Theories," *Review of Economics and Statistics* (November 1958), pp. 332-38.

Sartoris, William, "Transfer Pricing in a Commercial Bank," *Management Accounting* (February 1971), pp. 33-34, 39.

Scarf, Herbert E., "The Core of an n Person Game," *Econometrica* (January 1967), pp. 50-69.

Schaller, Carol, "Survey of Computer Cost Allocation Techniques," *The Journal of Accountancy* (June 1974), pp. 41-42, 44,46.

Schlenker, Barry R., review of Leonard Berkowitz and Elaine Walster, eds., *Equity Theory,* in *Science* (25 June 1976), pp. 1325-26.

Schmeidler, David, "The Nucleolus of a Characteristic Function Game," *SIAM Journal of Applied Mathematics* (November 1969), pp. 1163-70.

Schwab, Richard J., "A Contribution Approach to Transfer Pricing," *Management Accounting* (February 1975), pp. 46-48.

Seed, Allen H., III, "The Rational Abuse of Accounting Information," *Management Accounting* (January 1970), pp. 9-11.

Shapley, L. S., "A Value for n-Person Games," in H. W. Kuhn and A. W. Tucker, eds., *Contributions to the Theory of Games* (Princeton, 1953), pp. 307-17.

——, "Cores of Convex Games," *International Journal of Game Theory* (1971), pp. 11-26.

——, and Martin Shubik, "On Market Games," *Journal of Economic Theory* (June 1969a), pp. 9-25.

——, "On the Core of an Economic System With Externalities," *American Economic Review* (September 1969b), pp. 678-84.

Shillinglaw, Gordon, "Guides to Internal Profit Measurement," *Harvard Business Review* (March-April 1957), pp. 82-94.

——, "Divisional Performance Review: An Extension of Budgetary Control," in [Bonini et al., 1964], pp. 149-63.

——, "Cost Analysis," in [Davidson and Weil, 1977a], Ch. 39.

——, *Managerial Cost Accounting,* 4th ed. (Irwin, 1977b).

Shubik, Martin, "Incentives, Decentralized Control, the Assignment of Joint Costs and Internal Pricing," *Management Science* (April 1962), pp. 325-43.

——, "Incentives, Decentralized Control, the Assignment of Joint Costs and Internal Pricing," in [Bonini et al., 1964], pp. 205-26.

Shulman, James S., "Transfer Pricing in Multinational Business," unpublished doctoral dissertation (Harvard, 1966).

Silverman, Gary L., "Primal Decomposition of Mathematical Programs by Resource Allocation," *Operations Research* (1972), pp. 58-93.

Simon, Herbert A., *Administrative Behavior,* 2nd ed. (Macmillan, 1957).

——, "On the Concept of Organizational Goal," *Administrative Science Quarterly* (June 1964), pp. 1-22.

——, Harold Guetzhow, George Kozmetsky and Gordon Tyndall, *Centralization vs Decentralization in Organizing the Controller's Department* (Controllership Foundation, 1954).

Singer, Isaac Bashevis, "The Destruction of Kreshev," tr. by Elaine Gottlieb and June Ruth Flaum, in *The Spinoza of Market Street* (Farrar, Straus and Cudahy, 1961).

Skinner, R. M., "Accounting for a Simplified Firm—The Search for Common Ground," in [Sterling and Thomas, 1979].

Smith, Adam, *An Inquiry Into the Nature and Causes of the Wealth of Nations* (Various publishers; first printed in 1776).

Smith, Dean C., "Profit Maximization and Joint Costs," *Purdue Institute of Quantitative Research in Economics Series No. 22* (Purdue, 1962).

Solomons, David, ed., *Studies in Costing* (Sweet and Maxwell, 1952).

——, "Economic and Accounting Concepts of Income," *The Accounting Review* (July 1961), pp. 374-83.

——, *Divisional Performance: Measurement and Control* (Irwin, 1965).

——, "Divisional Reports," in [Davidson and Weil, 1977], Ch. 44.

Sorenson, John R., John T. Tschirhart and Andrew B. Whinston, "A Game Theoretic Approach to Peak Load Pricing," *The Bell Journal of Economics* (Autumn 1976), pp. 497-520.

Stamp, Edward, "Financial Reports On An Entity: Ex Uno Plures," in [Sterling and Thomas, 1979].

Staubus, George J., *Activity Costing and Input-Output Accounting* (Irwin, 1971).

Steers, R. M., and L. W. Porter, eds., *Motivation and Work Behavior* (McGraw-Hill, 1975).

Sterling, Robert R., *Theory of the Measurement of Enterprise Income* (Kansas, 1970).

——, "Relevant Financial Reporting in an Age of Price Changes," *The Journal of Accountancy* (February 1975), pp. 42-51.

——, "Accounting at the Crossroads," *The Journal of Accountancy* (August 1976), pp. 82-87; originally published in *World* (Peat, Marwick, Mitchell & Co., Spring 1976).

——, and Arthur L. Thomas, eds., *Accounting for a Simplified Firm Owning Depreciable Assets: Seventeen Essays and a Synthesis Based on a Common Case* (Scholars Book Co., 1979).

Stigler, George J., *The Theory of Price,* Rev. ed. (Macmillan, 1952).

——, 3rd ed. (Macmillan, 1966).

Stone, Williard E., "Intracompany Pricing," *The Accounting Review* (October 1956), pp. 625-27.

——, "Tax Considerations in Intra-Company Pricing," *The Accounting Review* (January 1960), pp. 45-50.

——, "Legal Implications of Intracompany Pricing," *The Accounting Review* (January 1964), pp. 38-42.

Strotz, Robert H., "Two Propositions Related to Public Goods," *Review of Economics and Statistics* (November 1958), pp. 329-31.

Taggart, Herbert, F., "Distribution Costs," in [Davidson and Weil, 1977], Ch. 43.

Talwar, Akshay K., " 'Transfer Pricing System Based on Opportunity Costs': A Comment," *The Accounting Review* (January 1974), pp. 126-28.

Tannenbaum, Arnold S., "Control in Organizations: Individual Adjustment and Organizational Performance," in [Bonini et al., 1964], pp. 297-316.

Tannenbaum, Robert, and Fred Massarik, "Participation by Subordinates In the Managerial Decision-Making Process," *The Canadian Journal of Economics and Political Science* (August 1950), pp. 408-18.

Tastor, R. R., "Feed Back A Portion of the Loss," letter, *Management Accounting* (December 1972), p. 52.

ten Kate, A., "A Comparison Between Two Kinds of Decentralized Optimality Conditions in Nonconvex Programming," *Management Science* (August 1972a), pp. B·734-43.

—, "Decomposition of Linear Programs by Direct Distribution," *Econometrica* (September 1972b), pp. 883-98.

Thomas, Arthur L., "The Allocation Problem in Financial Accounting Theory," *Studies in Accounting Research No. 3* (American Accounting Association, 1969).

—, "Transfer Prices of the Multinational Firm: When Will They Be Arbitrary?" *Abacus* (June 1971a), pp. 40-53.

—, "Useful Arbitrary Allocations (With A Comment on the Neutrality of Financial Accounting Reports)," *The Accounting Review* (July 1971b), pp. 472-79.

—, "The Allocation Problem: Part Two," *Studies in Accounting Research No. 9* (American Accounting Association, 1974).

—, "The FASB and the Allocation Fallacy," *The Journal of Accountancy* (November 1975), pp. 65-68.

—, "Traceability, Corrigibility, and Sterilization of Managerial-Accounting Allocations," *The Emanuel Saxe Distinguished Lectures in Accounting 1975-76* (City University of New York, 1977), pp. 7-27.

—, "Arbitrary and Incorrigible Allocations: A Comment," *The Accounting Review* (January 1978), pp. 263-69.

—, "Matching: Up From Our Black Hole," in [Sterling and Thomas, 1979].

Thompson, Gerald L., "Discussion: The Budgetary Process and Management Control," in [Bonini et al., 1964], pp. 240-52.

Tomkins, Cyril, *Financial Planning in Divisionalized Companies* (Accountancy Age Books, 1973).

Traven, B., *The Treasure of the Sierra Madre* (New American Library, 1968); first published (Knopf, 1935).

Vatter, William J., "Limitations of Overhead Allocation," *The Accounting Review* (April 1945), pp. 163-76.

—, "Tailor-Making Cost Data for Specific Uses," in [Rosen, 1974], pp. 194-210; originally published in *N. A. A. Bulletin* (1954 Conference Proceedings).

Vendig, Richard D., "A Three-Part Transfer Price," *Management Accounting* (September 1973), pp. 33-36.

Vickrey, William, "Utility, Strategy, and Social Decision Rules," *The Quarterly Journal of Economics* (November 1960), pp. 507-35.

Villers, Raymond, "Control and Freedom In a Decentralized Company," *Harvard Business Review* (March-April 1954), pp. 89-96.

Vroom, Victor H., *Some Personality Determinants of the Effects of Participation* (Prentice-Hall, 1960).

—, *Work and Motivation* (Wiley, 1964).

Walters, A. A., "The Allocation of Joint Costs With Demands As Probability Distributions," *The American Economic Review* (June 1960), pp. 419-32.

Waterhouse, D. F., "The Biological Control of Dung," *Scientific American* (April 1974), pp. 100-09.

Watson, David J. H., and John V. Baumler, "Transfer Pricing: A Behavioral Context," *The Accounting Review* (July 1975), pp. 466-74.

Weil, Roman L., Jr., "The Decomposition of Economic Production Systems," *Econometrica* (April 1968a), pp. 260-78.

—. "Allocating Joint Costs," *The American Economic Review* (December 1968b), pp. 1342-45.

Weitzman, Martin, "Iterative Multilevel Planning With Production Targets," *Econometrica* (January 1970), pp. 50-65.

Wells, M. C., "Profit Centres, Transfer Prices and Mysticism," *Abacus* (December 1968), pp. 174-81; reprinted in [Rosen, 1974], pp. 229-36.

—, "Is the Allocation of Overhead Costs Necessary?" *The Australian Accountant* (November 1970), pp. 479-86.

—, "Transfer Prices and Profit Centres? No," *Abacus* (June 1971), pp.54-57.

—, "Costing for Activities or Products—Which Should It Be?" *Management Accounting in a Changing Environment* (Victoria University of Wellington, 1973a); individually paginated, pp. 1-28 + 6 pp. notes.

—, *The Monetary Quantification of Inventory Stocks and Flows in Multi-Product Firms: An Historical Perspective,* unpublished doctoral dissertation (Sydney 1973b); a revised edition appears (in two volumes) as *Accounting for Common Costs* (Center for International Education and Research in Accounting, University of Illinois, 1978).

——, "Costing for Activities," *Management Accounting* (May 1976), pp. 31-37.

Whinston, Andrew B., "Control and Coordination of Complex Economic and Managerial Systems," doctoral dissertation (Carnegie, 1962); also appears as "Price Coordination in Decentralized Systems," *O. N. R. Research Memorandum No. 99* (Office of Naval Research, 1962).

——, "Price Guides in Decentralized Organizations," in W. W. Cooper, H. J. Leavitt and M. W. Shelly, eds., *New Perspectives in Organizational Research* (Wiley, 1964), pp. 405-48.

Wiles, P. J. D., *Price, Cost and Output,* rev. ed. (Praeger, 1963).

Williams, Bruce R., "Measuring Costs: Full Absorption Cost or Direct Cost," *Management Accounting* (January 1976), pp. 23-24, 36.

Williamson, Oliver E., "A Model of Rational Managerial Behavior," in [Cyert and March, 1963], pp. 237-52.

——, "The Vertical Integration of Production: Market Failure Considerations," *American Economic Review* (May 1971), pp. 112-23.

Williamson, Robert W., "No Simple Solution," letter, *Management Accounting* (April 1973), pp. 7, 27.

Wingfield-Stratford, Esme, *The Victorian Aftermath* (Morrow, 1934).

Wiseman, J., "The Theory of Public Utility Price—An Empty Box," *Oxford Economic Papers* (February 1957), pp. 56-74.

Wright, Howard W., "Allocation of General and Administrative Expenses," *The Accounting Review* (October 1966), pp. 626-33.

INDEX

Abdel-khalik, A. Rashad, xv, 43n, 130n, 138n, 145n, 150n, 152, 154n, 168n, 173n, 179n, 180, 182n, 183n, 190n, 200n, 207n, 208, 214n, 217n, 249, 276n, 278n, 279n, 281n

Additivity, of games, 45

Administered transfer prices, defined, 195-96; for service departments, 203-05; gaming under, 204n; evaluation decisions under, 204-05, 208; lump sum, 205-07, 209-10; output decisions under, 205-07, 209-10; Solomons' approach, 205-07, 210; two-part, 206-07, 209-10; divisional autonomy under, 206-08; élan decisions under, 206, 210; Gordon's approach, 207-08; Baughman's approach, 209-10, Emmanuel's approach, 210

Alchian, Armen A., 4n

Alcott, Louisa M., 43

Algebraic notation. See Notation

Alienation, defined, 19

Allen, Carl, xv

Allen William R., 4n

Allocation-free, decision methods, 5, 6n, 15-16; analysis, behaviour-congruence of, 111n; transfer prices, 128, 134-36, 160; external reporting, 220

Allocations, defined 1; resource vs. notional, 1-2, 166n-167n; one-to-many vs. other kinds, 2-3; theoretical difficulties of, 3; may be unavoidable, 5n-6n, 15-16, 218-20; examples of perverse, 9-10; valid theoretical arguments for, 116; problems of originate in use of profit centres, 140; relationship between joint costs and transfer prices, 164; defined for purposes of Chapter Ten, 171

American Accounting Association committees, 4n, 22-23, 127n, 217-18

Amey, Lloyd R., 43n, 200n, 206n, 207n

Anderson, James A., 135, 220n

Anthony, Robert N., 11, 14, 16n, 71n, 117, 130, 219n

Anton, Hector R., 44n

Appley, M. H., 251n, 252n

Arbitrariness, of Hirshleifer approach, 147-48, 151-52; of Gould-Naert approach, 159-60; of profits, under mathematical-programming approaches, 179-83, 187-90

Argyris, Chris, 1, 145, 146n, 247, 254

Arrow, Kenneth J., 11n, 12n, 122n, 123-4, 126n, 127n, 131n, 135n, 142n, 158n, 169n, 172n, 178n, 184n, 253, 274, 276

Arrow's Possibility Theorems, 127n

Arvidsson, Göran, 129n

Ashton, Raymond, 220n

Assumptions, of joint-cost analysis, 25-27; of marginal approach, 37, 40; of Part Two, 130-32; relaxation thereof, 156-63, 168-70; of expansion and contraction paths in mathematical programming, 188-90; of externalities under Shapley approach, 233-36; of averaged expansion paths under Shapley approach, 237-41

Autonomy, effects of threats to, 19-20; need for, 124, 247-56; ceremonial, 145, 247; under Hirshleifer approach, 144-48, 151-52, 154, 160-63, 260; under Gould-Naert approach, 159-60; under linear programming, 169; under mathematical-programming approaches, 173-80, 185-88, 193, 274-82;